When Democracy Died

The Treaty of Lausanne, signed in Switzerland in July 1923, officially settled the conflict between the Ottoman Empire and the Allied forces. Not only did the Treaty establish the borders of the modern Turkish republic, but it also defined boundaries, political systems, and understandings of citizenship in the newly formed post-Ottoman nation-states. Here, Hans-Lukas Kieser recounts how the eight dramatic months of the Lausanne Conference concluded more than ten years of war and genocide in the late-Ottoman Empire. Crucially, the Treaty was in favor of a homogeneous Turkish state in Asia Minor and became the basis for the compulsory "unmixing of people" that facilitated the persecution of minority groups, including Armenians, Kurds, and Arabs. Not only did this significant yet oft-overlooked treaty mark the end of the League of Nations' project of self-determination and security for small peoples, but it was crucial in shaping the modern Middle East and dictatorships in Turkey and Europe.

Hans-Lukas Kieser is Associate Professor at the University of Newcastle, Australia, Adjunct Professor at the University of Zurich. His books include *Talât Pasha* (2018), *Nearest East* (2010), and the edited volume *Remembering the Great War in the Middle East* (2022).

When Democracy Died
The Middle East's Enduring Peace of Lausanne

Hans-Lukas Kieser
University of Newcastle, Australia

CAMBRIDGE
UNIVERSITY PRESS

Shaftesbury Road, Cambridge CB2 8EA, United Kingdom

One Liberty Plaza, 20th Floor, New York, NY 10006, USA

477 Williamstown Road, Port Melbourne, VIC 3207, Australia

314–321, 3rd Floor, Plot 3, Splendor Forum, Jasola District Centre, New Delhi – 110025, India

103 Penang Road, #05–06/07, Visioncrest Commercial, Singapore 238467

Cambridge University Press is part of Cambridge University Press & Assessment, a department of the University of Cambridge.

We share the University's mission to contribute to society through the pursuit of education, learning and research at the highest international levels of excellence.

www.cambridge.org
Information on this title: www.cambridge.org/9781009014267

DOI: 10.1017/9781009029957

© Hans-Lukas Kieser 2023

This publication is in copyright. Subject to statutory exception and to the provisions of relevant collective licensing agreements, no reproduction of any part may take place without the written permission of Cambridge University Press & Assessment.

First published 2023
First paperback edition 2025

A catalogue record for this publication is available from the British Library

ISBN 978-1-316-51642-3 Hardback
ISBN 978-1-009-01426-7 Paperback

Cambridge University Press & Assessment has no responsibility for the persistence or accuracy of URLs for external or third-party internet websites referred to in this publication and does not guarantee that any content on such websites is, or will remain, accurate or appropriate.

Contents

List of Figures   *page* vii
List of Maps   ix
Acknowledgments   x

Introduction: The Historic Near East Peace of Lausanne   1
"Unjust Peace Is Better than the Justest War"   2
Might Made Right   5
A Favored Model Dictatorship   11
The Book's Structure and Sources   15

Part I   A Century's Pivotal "Peace"   20
1. A Peace of Dominant Interests on the Back of "Others"   21
2. A Peace without Peace: Unaddressed Violence, Coercion, and Racism   24
3. Ultranationalism Appeased? The Paris–Geneva–Lausanne Constellation   36
4. Armenia: When Violence Won and Democracy Died   41
5. A Pivotal "Peace" to Be Reassessed   46

Part II   Against the Paris-Geneva Peace: Bolsheviks, Turkists, Islamists   50
6. Projecting Aftermaths during a Decade of War   51
7. A Vice-Plenipotentiary's World of Thoughts and Sentiments: Dr. Rıza Nur   55
8. "We Turanians": A Pervasive Ideology and Argument   65
9. At an Empire's Long End: CUP Rule Defeated, Nationalist Struggle Continued   71
10. Defying the Paris-Geneva Peace Project, Forcing the Road to Lausanne   79
11. Aborting the Sèvres Treaty: A Plural Anatolia and Western Justice   92
12. The Military and Diplomatic Road to the Lausanne Conference   102
13. Lausanne's Ottoman Diaspora: Preparing National Futures   111

Part III   A Protracted Conference: Redefining Turkey, Western Realpolitik   120
14. The Conference's Eve, Premises, and Grand Lines   121
15. Fascism's Historic Hour   127

16	Inauguration, Personalities, Early Imprints	137
17	Pivotal First Weeks	143
18	"Population Exchange" and Minorities	147
19	Lausanne's Armenian Catastrophe: No "Armenian Home," No Assyrian Independence	158
20	Mehmed Cavid, Ankara's Mindful but Sidelined Expert in Lausanne	170
21	Mosul	179
22	Diplomatically Framing History, "Civilization," Rule of Law	184
23	Conference Break – Interval – Continuation	194
24	After a Long Last Mile, the Treaty	201
25	The US Lausanne Treaty: A Paradigm Shift in the Middle East	214

Part IV Post-Lausanne Turkey: Most Favored Dictatorship? 222

26	Establishing "Peace" and Dictatorship in Republican Turkey	224
27	Cavid's End	232
28	"Revolution" in a Restive and Coercive, but Courted Country	237
29	Reassessing Lausanne-Based Kemalism: Lofty Claims, Clashes with Reality	245
30	Lausanne and Atatürk's History Doctrine	250
31	Dersim Genocide: Apex of Ultranationalism	259
32	Lozan Myth: Turkey's Betrayed, to Be Restored, Sultanate-Caliphate	264

In Lieu of a Conclusion: Time for Democratic Social Contracts   272

Dismantling Antidemocracy 273
Lausanne's Open Door for Fascisms 275
"Overcoming Lausanne" by Democratic Social Contracts 280
Violence, Peace, and Democracy: Dialectical Progress or Aporetic Spiral? 285

Annexes 289
Select Biographical Notes: Ankara's Lausanne Team 289
Select Chronology 297
Select Bibliography 309
Index 316

Figures

1 "Second [half of the] Lausanne Conference. [Madame] Peace: 'Who will look after me when there are so many beautiful women?'" *page* 4
2 "If the [war] machine, which made its way to Izmir, moves this time again, it will probably make all the bumps [problems] flat." 9
3 "Monument of Victory" (Zafer âbidesi). 10
4 Negotiation table in a subcommission meeting. 48
5 Rıza Nur side by side with Ismet Pasha (Inönü, on his left side) and the British plenipotentiary Horace Rumbold (on his right side). 56
6 Monument of the Republic on Istanbul's Taksim Square. 83
7 Alexandre Khatissian, foreign minister and prime minister ad interim of the Republic of Armenia, during a military parade in Yerevan, ca. 1919. 105
8 Mussolini arriving in Lausanne on 20 November 1922. 128
9 Mussolini in Lausanne, November 1920. 131
10 Curzon, satisfied, after the first Conference meeting. 138
11 Drawn by the artist Derso, this late 1922 postcard puts the interaction of an oversized Lord Curzon and a tiny Ismet Pasha who reluctantly shake hands with each other in its center. 139
12 Alexandre Khatissian in front of the Armenian Church in Paris in 1927. 166
13 "A box match out of season. Sirs Rıza Nur and Hüseyin Cahid." 177
14 Lord Curzon going to the Château d'Ouchy, the main meeting place of the Conference. 180
15 "Lausanne turns to a carnival. The British: Do not be embarrassed, gentlemen, our return [to London] coincides with the carnival." 197
16 "The question of interests. Would you allow me to put this gold bracelet on your arms as a souvenir of the conference?" 203

17 "In the Lausanne concert, Greece plays 'harp.'" 205
18 Signing the Treaty, 24 July 1923, as seen from where (in the foreground, from right to left) Ismet (İnönü), Rıza Nur, and, probably, Reşit Saffet (Atabinen) sat. 208
19 Karl Scheurer, president of the Swiss Confederation, speaking at the conclusion of the Lausanne Treaty, 24 July 1923. 209
20 Reşit Saffet (Atabinen), Ismet (İnönü), Joseph Grew, and Rıza Nur in a photo taken in Lausanne in early August 1923. 219
21 Cavid Bey after arrest, during the Independence Tribunal, summer 1926. 235
22 Photo taken in the entrance hall of the Palais de Rumine. 290

Maps

1 From the late-Ottoman Empire to the early-republican
  Turkey. *page* 73
2 Europe and the Ottoman Empire after the First World War. 88

Acknowledgments

I am happy to start this book with thanks and acknowledgments. This monograph has a long history of its own. First ideas about it emerged more than twenty years ago, when I was working at the University of Zurich on two separate research projects, one on the late-Ottoman diaspora in Switzerland, the other – working with colleagues – on the concept of a common "historical space" of the Armenian genocide and the Holocaust. For both topics, the Near East Peace Conference of Lausanne in 1922–3 popped up as pivotal. Some related insight, then acquired, appeared in published results of those researches, but was not elaborated on in depth.[1]

It took two decades more until a specific, Lausanne Conference–focused research project matured at my current University of Newcastle in Australia. Here, Philip Dwyer, Director of the Centre for Study of Violence, Catherine Oddie, Research Development Manager, and Tim Haydon, research consultant, helped me to prepare a specific submission. I was so fortunate to get the project funded by the Australian Research Council in 2020.[2] For sure, material support is of little value without a great deal of good will and wit, patient, collaboration, and open communication.

Scholarly competition on issues of significance transcends individual ambitions and corporatist interests. Sharing a constructive ethos of

---

[1] See H. Kieser, "Macro et micro histoire autour de la Conférence sur le Proche-Orient tenue à Lausanne en 1922–23," *Mémoire vive. Pages d'histoire lausannoise* 13 (2004), 42–48; Kieser, *Vorkämpfer der "Neuen Türkei": Revolutionäre Bildungseliten am Genfersee, 1870–1939* (Zurich: Chronos, 2005); Kieser and Dominik J. Schaller, "Völkermord im historischen Raum 1895–1945," in H. Kieser, ed., *Der Völkermord an den Armeniern und die Shoah/The Armenian Genocide and the Shoah* (Zurich: Chronos, 2014, first ed. 2002), 11–80. These researches had been made possible by the Swiss National Science Foundation and the Fonds zur Förderung des akademischen Nachwuchses (FAN) of the University of Zurich.

[2] ARC DP210100426, "The 'Peace' of Lausanne (1923): Genesis, Legacies, Paradoxes." Helpful synergies also with another, University of Melbourne-based ARC project, to be acknowledged here: DP200101777, "Aftermaths of War: Violence, Trauma, Displacement, 1815–1950."

Acknowledgments

scholarship with peers, research assistants, students, and library staff has greatly helped me in completing this study. Serhat Bozkurt, my research assistant in Istanbul, deserves a particular mention. I am happy to name also Khatchig Mouradian (New York), Ümit Kurt (Newcastle), Timothy Stanley (Newcastle), Guillaume Beausire (Lausanne), and Jan Bethsawoce and David Gaunt (Sweden). Other helping hands are mentioned at the related passages in the book. I acknowledge also my learning by teaching and supervising topics at the University of Newcastle related to the First World War and its aftermath. I like to mention Sacha Davis and Elizabeth Roberts-Pedersen, co-supervisors, Pearl Nunn and Caroline Schneider, tutors, as well as PhD student Wei Wang and my former PhD student Markos Carelos.

The wisdom that knowledge is a good that increases and progresses if shared, strongly applies to the making of this monograph. I am thankful for the rich correspondence and instructive meetings with colleagues who worked like me, partly on common projects, on the historical reassessment of the Lausanne Conference – in particular Jonathan Conlin and Ozan Ozavci of The Lausanne Project,[3] as well as Jay Winter and Michelle Tusan, both authors of forthcoming monographs. This book owes its title to Jay's suggestion.

I enjoyed the rare opportunity of a special roundtable to give me critical feedback on an early, uncomplete version of my book manuscript at the Ecole des Hautes Etude en Sciences Social in Paris. My thanks go to the organizers Ahmet Insel and Hamit Bozarslan, as well as the other participants: Boris Adjemian, Dzovinar Kévonian, Raymond Kévorkian, Rey Matthieu, Emmanuel Szurek, and Alexandre Toumarkine. I'd like also to mention the good collaboration I enjoyed with those leading the 2023 commemoration events in Lausanne itself, notably Gaby Fierz, the curator of a special exhibition, and Laurent Golay, the director of the Musée Historique de Lausanne.

Other beneficial opportunities for exchange in view of this study on the Lausanne Conference included a guest professorship at the University of Vienna in 2021, where I enjoyed the collegial hospitality of the professors Oliver Jens Schmitt and Yavuz Köse, giving two semestrial courses, one on the post–Great War peace attempts as a whole, the other mainly on the Lausanne Conference. I also benefited from presenting preliminary findings and thoughts in talks or seminars at the University of Lausanne, Columbia University in New York, Flinders University in Adelaide, the American College in Thessaloniki, University of Macedonia in Thessaloniki, and the Ecole des Hautes Etudes en Sciences Sociales in

---

[3] https://thelausanneproject.com

Paris. My thank goes to the hosts. Last but not least, I am grateful for the excellent collaboration with editor Maria Marsh and her editorial assistant Rachel Imrie from Cambridge University Press, and for the helpful and encouraging feedback by the anonymous reviewers; and particularly for the invaluable work of my copy editor Ursula Acton.

This book is dedicated to the political prisoners in Turkey.

Introduction
The Historic Near East Peace of Lausanne

The Middle East is a global hotspot. Peace in the Middle East is among the most significant challenges of the twenty-first century and the topic of this book. Of particular concern is the former Ottoman imperial core region that had remained part of the sultanate-caliphate until the 1910s: Anatolia (today's Turkey), Iraq, and "Greater Syria," including Lebanon, Palestine, and Jordan. The negotiators at the Near East Peace Conference in Lausanne in Switzerland, 1922–3, rightly insisted that they faced the challenge of "world peace," that is, of working for the world's most precious common good. This Conference and its outcome, the Treaty of Lausanne, mark the end of a world war that proved particularly long and devastating in the Middle East.

Recent wars have made us aware that neighboring regions in the North, from the South Caucasus to Crimea and the Ukraine, belong to a connected historical geography where the First World War "failed to end" in 1918, especially for those vanquished.[1] There, including countries like Turkey and Hungary, the "Great War," the end of empires, and related revolutions, agreements, and imperial legacies and losses still heavily impact politics. On 24 July 1923, the Treaty of Lausanne liquidated the Ottoman Empire. It concluded peace between the victors of the First World War and Turkey, a loser of this war, but winner of the subsequent wars in Anatolia under a Bolshevik-supported counter-government in Ankara. The Lausanne Treaty recognized the Ankara government that henceforth officially replaced and succeeded the Istanbul-based Ottoman sultanate-caliphate, an empire allied to Germany and Austria-Hungary during the Great War. It thus reintegrated Turkey into Western diplomacy after a decade of ruptures and wars. These constitute the real, decade-long "Ottoman Great War" that Lausanne ended.

---

[1] Robert Gerwarth, *The Vanquished: Why the First World War Failed to End* (New York: Farrar, Straus and Giroux, 2016).

"Unjust Peace Is Better than the Justest War"

Lausanne opened up a new era of post-Ottoman international relations, and it laid new legal and political foundations for Turkey and her Middle Eastern and Southeastern European neighborhood. It was widely considered the solution of modern Europe's notorious "Eastern Question": the future of the Ottoman realm and the sultanate-caliphate. The Eastern Question was the longest lasting and most intractable issue of modern European diplomacy. The Lausanne Treaty was the last of a series of post-Great War treaties of which all others were concluded in or around Paris.

In *When Democracy Died*, the Lausanne Conference and Treaty emerges as the pivotal endpoint of the Paris peace system – and as a basis and focus for dictatorial party-states afterward. The punitive Treaties of Paris–Versailles and Paris–Trianon, as well as related settlements that frustrated World War victors like Italy and Japan, undeniably contributed to the rise of resentful fascisms in Europe and Asia, as has been argued in many places. Also, it is well known that what the Chinese felt to be the betrayal of a deprived ally by the Paris Peace Conference radicalized Chinese nationalism and boosted the rise of communism.[2]

A Treaty like Lausanne, which rewarded revisionist violence, thus cancelling the Paris-Sèvres Treaty for the Ottoman Empire, had however a much more direct and assertive impact. It endorsed and certified an emerging radically nationalist and authoritarian republic, thus setting a shining example that fascinated "revolutionists" from the right. From early 1924, Gazi Kemal (Atatürk) spread his image on stamps: the very first ones of this sort commemorated the Lausanne Treaty while highlighting the great leader Gazi Kemal. Subsequently, the supreme leader pushed the cult of his personality by erecting heroic statues throughout the country.[3] Other upcoming actors of antidemocracy and coercive social transformation believed that they were entitled to emulate this model, after high diplomacy in Lausanne offered legitimacy to Ankara, fascist Rome, and Bolshevik Moscow.[4]

Europe's "era of tyranny" had begun with the imperial dictatorship of the warring Young Turks in 1913. From August 1914, state-centered

---

[2] Rogers R. Anthony and Nur R. Daut, "China in the First World War: A Forgotten Army in Search of International Recognition," *Contemporary Chinese Political Economy and Strategic Relations* 3.3 (2017), 1237–1269.

[3] M. Şükrü Hanioğlu, *Atatürk: An Intellectual Biography* (Princeton, NJ: Princeton University Press, 2011), 185–187. See also "Philately in Turkey," https://travelatelier.com/blog/philately-turkey.

[4] The term "antidemocracy" is broadly used in recent political studies. Although related to them, it transcends traditional studies of fascism, ultranationalism, and totalitarianism. See notably Hamit Bozarslan, *L'anti-démocratie au XXIe siècle: Iran, Russie, Turquie* (Paris: CNRS éditions, 2021).

authoritarianism started spreading to other countries affected by the First World War. In Paris of the Belle Epoque, democratic-minded intellectuals, first among them the philosopher and historian Elie Halévy, had "wondered whether the world would see a kind of federal democracy, Swiss-style, or a universalized Caesarism. The war chose: the Caesars won."[5] After Europe's seminal catastrophe, the political philosophy of the League of Nations briefly gave hope for a revision of this choice induced by total war. The Lausanne Conference, however, as *When Democracy Died* will argue, hammered the last nail in the coffin of the League's project of global peace through law and democratic self-determination. Real peace was lost from sight (Figure 1).

Nevertheless, this book also appreciates the complexity of the Lausanne Conference and gives room to positive diplomatic achievements. The Conference gathered Turkish, European, US-American, and Japanese representatives as – more or less – equal partners after a decade of protracted wars, united in the will to make peace in the particularly challenging Near East (as it then was called, looking from Europe). This book appreciates this fundamentally positive fact. It appreciates the mutual readiness to integrate the successor state of the Ottoman Empire into an intended global peace architecture, based on what it calls the Paris–Geneva (i.e. Western) post–Great War peace project. It also appreciates the desire, promise, and at least partial readiness on the Turkish side to depart to new social, cultural, and political horizons based on universal references. It has pondered the words of Erasmus on peace: "Even if the arbitrators [of a peace] are unjust ... the disagreeing parties come off with less injury than if they seek the outcome by war. Even a very unjust peace is generally better and preferable to the justest war."[6]

However, the truth of Erasmus' words does not preclude questioning settlements that, in the long term, enabled further violence, persecution, and grave injustice. *When Democracy Died*, therefore, looks carefully at the way the Near East Peace of Lausanne was made. It considers the dark sides and unfulfilled or deliberately broken promises of this settlement. Its critique has nothing to do with any nationalism and irredenta or any nostalgia of empire and caliphate. It is about democracy, human rights, and historical truths, versus amnesia, euphemism, and a pact of interests on the back of others. The Lausanne Treaty normalized mass violence

---

[5] C. Bouglé, "Préface," in Elie Halévy, *L'ère des tyrannies: Etudes sur le socialism et la guerre* (Paris: Gallimard, 1938), 12. Halévy suggested we understand the beginning of the Great War in 1914 as the opening of Europe's "era of tyrannies" (ibid., 214). One must consider that Turkey had remained outside Halévy's historical horizon.

[6] Desiderius Erasmus (of Rotterdam), *Querela pacis* (Basel: Frobenius, 1518), 31–32; and *Ein Klag des Frydens* (Zurich: Froschauer, 1521), xix. Both versions www.e-rara.ch.

4 Introduction

Figure 1 "Second [half of the] Lausanne Conference. [Madame] Peace: 'Who will look after me when there are so many beautiful women?'" The unattractiveness of real peace as long as the party goes on. (*Akbaba*, no. 38, 16 April 1923, 1. Drawn by Ramiz)[7]

and dispossession of civilians in a dimension far beyond anything experienced in Europe in 1914–18. It endorsed both politics of Western interests in the post-Ottoman Middle East and what genocidal violence had achieved during the last Ottoman decade in Asia Minor (Anatolia). Thanks to Lausanne, a unitary, modernist, and dictatorial polity could be built up there upon these "achievements."

---

[7] I thank Ilkim B. Okyar, Istanbul, who has drawn my attention to the subtle *Akbaba* caricatures.

The Lausanne Treaty is the international founding deed of the Republic of Turkey, declared three months after it was signed; it is rightly considered the new state's "birth certificate."[8] However, as this study will detail, Turkey's rebirth as a republic is a Lausanne-based fiction insofar as, in reality, imperial cadres of late-Ottoman Turkey got their way. The reorganization of Muslim power in Anatolia under the former Young Turk general Gazi Kemal Pasha – the later Atatürk – in Ankara after 1918 would have remained little more than a pathetic attempt to restore the sultanate-caliphate, had military victory not opened the road to the high-profile Lausanne Conference.

Leaving its marks on all parties concerned, the mega-event at Lausanne plunged a willing delegation from Ankara into the universe of Western references and exigencies. It gave a new nationalist actor the opportunity to compromise with the Great War victors and to inscribe itself at least partly in the self-declared "civilized world" of nominally liberal Western powers. These powers, however, themselves national empires of questionable democratic quality, discredited their liberal credo by abandoning elementary requirements of the Paris–Geneva peace project. They opened the door for ascending antidemocracy.

Might Made Right

All delegations in Lausanne emphasized the sublime task of achieving world peace by turning the page of the late-Ottoman past. Relations with Ankara's "new Turkey" (as was emphasized not only by the Kemalists, but also abroad) had to be normalized after continuous war since 1914 and troubled diplomacy since 1911, when Italy invaded Ottoman Libya. After a decade of wars, including the Great War and the demise of the defeated Ottoman Empire, the Lausanne Treaty shaped new post-Ottoman states with regard to boundaries, political systems, notions of citizenship, family law, minority concepts, and visions of history. These, together with Ankara's integration into Western diplomacy, are the achievements, "the bright side," of the Lausanne Treaty – as stated in numerous works by diplomats and academics during the twentieth century.

The Lausanne settlement, however, carried an ultimate, unmistakable, and deeply ambivalent message to the world: might made

---

[8] René Albrecht-Carrié, *France, Europe and the Two World Wars* (Geneva: Droz, 1969; first ed., 1960), 135.

right – not the peaceable principles of a fresh League of Nations in Geneva on which many had set great hope.⁹ The Covenant of the League of Nations was a first serious, if failed or only "experimental," attempt to promote democratic, human-rights–based national constitutions and to domesticate them within one binding global supra-covenant.¹⁰ However, the insertion of the League's new internationalism into treaties concluded in traditional logics of victorious powers, as in Paris, was unfortunate.¹¹ Antidemocratic detractors took this as carte blanche for revolutionary violence against the Paris–Geneva peace. However, this circumstance does by no means derogate from the powerful and elaborate democratic thought that underpinned the League's genesis and intellectual history, and the pro-League movements in general.¹² The democratic argument of those engaged for the League was popular, and both idealistic and realistic. But it could not, and did not want to, arouse the same (short-sighted) emotions, ideological fervor, and violence-prone militancy as did contemporary Turkism, Fascism, and Nazism on the one hand, and Bolshevism on the other. Sure enough, it depended too much on Western Europe's national empires.

The League experiment coincides with the end of premodern empires in wider Europe, and the emerging global competition between a liberal US-American, a Russian-led communist and a fascist projection of the future. People from various strands of society, from Eastern Europe and "Yiddishland" to Armenia and Kurdistan, had set great hopes on the bourgeoning League that was rivalled in its universal claim by Moscow's contemporary Comintern

---

⁹ A number of fresh and appreciative in-depth studies of the League of Nations have been published in the early twenty-first century, notably Susan Pedersen, *The Guardians: The League of Nations and the Crisis of Empire* (Oxford: Oxford University Press, 2017). Much of this new literature approaches the League "from a perspective of networks and ideas," and "interprets the League from being 'a failure' to being a 'father' or 'teacher' to many of today's international organizations, norms and practices" (Karen Gram-Skjoldager and Haakon A. Ikonomou, "Making Sense of the League of Nations Secretariat: Historiographical and Conceptual Reflections on Early International Public Administration," *European History Quarterly*, 49 (2019), 426. Most of the League's rich archives are now accessible online; see https://archives.ungeneva.org/lontad.

¹⁰ For an insider's view of the League, see William E. Rappard, *The Geneva Experiment* (Oxford: Oxford University Press, 1931). For a recent reflection on the search for a social contract–based world peace, see Philippe M. Defarges, *Une histoire mondiale de la paix* (Paris: Odile Jacob, 2020), 99–132.

¹¹ The League Covenant figures at the beginning of all Paris treaties. See also Jean-Michel Guieu and Stanislas Jeannesson "L'expérience de Genève (1920–1946)," Monde(s) 19 (2021), special issue *La Société des nations. Une expérience de l'internationalisme*, 18.

¹² See notably John A. Hobson, *Democracy after the War* (London: Allen and Unwin, 2017). See also Sakiko Kaiga, *Britain and the Intellectual Origins of the League of Nations, 1914–1919* (Cambridge: Cambridge University Press, 2021).

(Communist International, or Third International).[13] Among the League's strongest proponents were the internationalist sons and daughters – teachers, doctors, professors – of American missionaries whose parents had set foot in the Ottoman Empire during the nineteenth century where they founded modern educational and medical institutions. In line with constitutional currents in various Ottoman circles, they had hoped to contribute to democratizing modern "Bible lands" where peoples would be empowered to coexist in peace. Levant-centered late-Ottoman American millenarism had aimed for a modern and global "republic of Jesus" to emerge from a Near East that would democratize at last.[14]

The ultimate failure of covenant-based peace coincides with the liquidation of the Ottoman Empire at the Conference of Lausanne. The failed "great peace" after the Great War is an essential antecedent of the Shoah, the Jewish catastrophe in Europe culminating in the Holocaust. Put pointedly, Lausanne made Europe and international diplomacy safe for fascist party-states, minority repression, and future genocides – Ankara serving in this process as *the* model dictatorship. After Lausanne, the League's political project of a law-based, democratizing global order was dead – killed by compromises of a new realpolitik established during months of negotiations from November 1922 to July 1923. Though still using "League speech," the new realpolitik did without justice and repair for genocide, and made millions of persons objects of imposed population transfer. A comprehensive and serene historical perspective cannot positively assess Lausanne's official "population exchange," because it joins the dots with previous genocidal policies implemented by the Young Turk party state, the real predecessor of the Ankara government.

The Lausanne settlement led its Western signatories to use the euphemism of "model dictatorship," "developmental dictatorship," or "educational dictatorship" for Ankara's regime for decades. It silenced the experience of victims – in particular Armenian genocide victims – and established disregard, condescendence, and even contempt for the weak. It was, on the one hand, the discrete triumph of an ageing British Empire that had however to give up former imperial ethics as these had definitively come to its limits. On the other hand, it represented the triumph of a new state born in mass violence and driven by common interests of Anatolia's Sunni-Muslim majority population. This was the core group

---

[13] Alain Brossat and Sylvie Klingberg : *Revolutionary Yiddishland: A History of Jewish Radicalism* (New York: Verso, Paperback, 2017; first French ed. 1983).

[14] See H. L. Kieser, *Nearest East: American Millennialism and Mission to the Middle East* (Philadelphia, PA: Temple University Press, 2010), 15–97.

and *ümmet* (Islamic community) of the defeated Ottoman Empire in whose name the Young Turks had fought until 1918 and continued their armed fight from Ankara until 1922. Most cadres of the war regime in the Ottoman capital Istanbul took positions in the new power center in Ankara.

Not democratic negotiation and consent, but war against the Great War victors and Anatolia's Christians was the common denominator of Ankara's new National Assembly from 1920 (see Figure 2). "Ankara believes that all things can be solved by arms. ... They have not made proof of any other skill than soldiering," noted Mehmed Cavid in his diary in 1921.[15] An Ottoman minister of finance multiple times, Cavid was a seasoned Turkish nationalist, but became a secluded dissenter during the Lausanne Conference where he served as a counselor. The Conference and its Treaty empowered Ankara's leadership under Kemal Atatürk, which built up a dictatorial party-state in its immediate aftermath. Hailed by most Westerners, the coercive experiment of Kemalist modernization and ultranationalist indoctrination lost its breath with Atatürk's death in 1938. New economic and military life came from the American Marshal Plan and a new NATO partnership after the Second World War.

The immediate lesson to draw from Lausanne was that one must do it like Ankara. Only victors could sit and have a say at the same table with those who claimed to represent Western civilization. Woe to those who could not timely produce military victories and (forcible) domestic transformations. Woe to victims and those who had believed in the self-determination of constitutional and liberal nation-states under the League's roof, and not in vigorous, but illiberal authoritarianism (see Figure 3). The upcoming German National Socialists were among Ankara's greatest admirers. Solidly in power by 1937, they sent poison gas to Ankara that served to kill Alevi Kurds during the Dersim genocide, while Turkish Nazi sympathizers proudly reported how Hitler honored Atatürk as his role-model (see Part IV).

Belatedly concluding post–Great War peace-making in the Middle East, the Conference of Lausanne defined a new era of realpolitik that left Western diplomacy open to fascism. Only two triumphal, self-serving, and self-centric narratives of the Lausanne Conference could be produced: one, the predominant one, by Kemalists; the other – more discreet, because no one could deny the inherent moral defeat compared to the earlier ambitions – on the British side. These are narratives by the main opposite

---

[15] Cavid Bey, *Meşrutiyet Ruznâmesi* (Ankara: TTK, 2015), vol. 4, 326, diary entry of 28 September 1921, and 373, entry of 29 June 1922.

Might Made Right 9

Figure 2 "If the [war] machine, which made its way to Izmir, moves this time again, it will probably make all the bumps [problems] flat." Referring to the devastating defeat inflicted on the Greek army in summer 1922, this caricature gives a martial answer to heated discussions in Lausanne about Ankara's demand for Greek reparation payments (*Journal Zümrüdüanka*, no. 40, 28 May 1923). Trust in military might emerges in many other contemporary publications, notably after the Conference break in early January 1923 that induced renewed calls for war. One example from the wide-spread satirical journal *Karagöz*: "Commanders: 'We will not give a hair of our independence.' 'At your command, our excellence general. Let's feel our strength to those who do not acknowledge our rights! ... our enemies will recognize our right even before they taste our bayonets.'" (*Karagöz*, no. 1560, 28 February 1923)

powers sitting at the negotiation table, the latter representing the then-foremost Western power.[16] In its core, the Lausanne Treaty is therefore a deal and compromise between a regional and a global power holder – not

---

[16] For a triumphalist British version of the Lausanne Conference, see, for example, chapter XI, "Lausanne: The Final Triumph," in Harold G. Nicolson, *Curzon: The Last Phase, 1919–1925: A Study in Post-War Diplomacy* (London: Constable, 1934), 314–350. Kemalist triumphalism will be dealt with in detail in Chapters 26–32.

Figure 3 "Monument of Victory" (Zafer âbidesi). (*Akbaba*, no. 13, 18 January 1923, 1. Artist: Ramiz)

a peace of peoples and democratizing polities. Since its inception in 1920, Ankara was in need, and knew time and again to play different sides of geostrategic crises: during the Russian Civil War, the "Interwar period" (as experienced from Western Europe), the Second World War, the Cold War (though to a lesser extent), and again during the recent wars in Iraq, Syria, Libya, and Ukraine.

The mutually satisfying outcome for the main signatories explains the longevity of the Lausanne Treaty and the protracted silence on the Treaty's victims and dark sides. Logically, in the longer term, the rewarding outcome for the ruling class made socialism as well as political Islam universal languages of hope. For those excluded like the Kurds, the world became politically narrow and exclusionary after 1923, with conditions – as for Armenian genocide survivors – remaining highly precarious. The League's and US President Wilson's initial key term "democracy," including civil liberties and equality, nevertheless remained a supreme reference and goal for most of them. This is still true in the twenty-first century.

Cavid was one of the brightest minds among the early Turkish nationalists after the 1908 Young Turk Revolution. He put the fundamental challenge this way: "In order to ascertain its future, the country must exit its oligarchical state and subordinate itself to a democratic polity. If the Ankara government continues as an oligarchy, it will lead to the same negative and noxious consequences as did the Yıldız [Sultan Abdulhamid's Palace] and the Young Turk oligarchies."[17]

A Favored Model Dictatorship

Recognized by *Lozan* – Turkish for "Lausanne," shortcut for the Conference and Treaty of Lausanne – Ankara's government finalized the modernizing politics of its Young Turk predecessors during the 1920s. It did this within a single-party state, led by a supreme leader. Public discourse disdained those former Ottoman conationals who "did not make it," notably the Arabs, Kurds, and Armenians. Ankara's nationalists regarded those who had collaborated with the British enemy during and after the Great War as rebels, traitors, and losers who saw themselves finally abandoned by overstretched imperial Britain.

The Lausanne Conference meant the definitive end of promises and hopes nurtured among pro-Entente Ottomans who had turned to Britain, the League of Nations, and President Wilson's proclamation of a new world order. Liberal democracy indeed lost in Lausanne. By 1923, "the West" definitively let down previous friends. Its powers reached out to Wahhabi Islamists under Ibn Saud and to Bolshevik-supported Turkish nationalists, both ready to compromise if shielded from democratic critique. In the end, the post–Great War peace-makers thus enabled or appeased fundamentally illiberal post-Ottoman regimes.

Not only the Armenians and other non-Turkish native people from Anatolia but also neighboring Arabs (of Syria, Lebanon, Palestine,

---

[17] Cavid, *Meşrutiyet Ruznâmesi*, 262, diary entry, Switzerland, 9 April 1921.

Egypt) and Persia (neutral, but victimized, during the Great War) sent expectant representatives to Lausanne. They all left the city empty-handed in 1923, almost without any further faith in law-based liberal policy-making. As Ankara had rejected the Sèvres Treaty, the decisions on the Middle East and the mandates had remained in the balance until the conclusion of the Lausanne Treaty. Only the Conference of Lausanne legally and definitively liquidated the Ottoman Empire. Upcoming Western allies like Turkey and Saudi Arabia had used extreme unrepentant violence during their making and excelled in radical ideology: ultranationalism on the one side, the Wahhabi cause (*da'wah*) on the other. They emerged as winners in the new post-Ottoman order.

Ankara's reorientation in Lausanne entailed a sudden emancipation from the Muslim world and the past that it compensated by racial history. A critical "Turanian argument" therefore connected national claims and Turkey's grandeur with speculative Turanian prehistory, civilization, and Near Eastern indigenousness. Within a few years, this led to an entirely racialist national identity construction that crystallized in the so-called Turkish History Thesis. Personally promoted by Atatürk, this thesis insisted on the Aryan identity of (proto-)Turks. The Turanian argument among Ankara's nationalists at, and in the context of, the Lausanne Conference is worth a comparison to Germany's Aryan delusion a decade later.[18] Adaptive as it was to the era's prevailing vocabulary of a modern secular civilization with racial imprints, the Turkish delegation in Lausanne also set out on a promissory narrative of Westernizing reform. It did this in accordance with the civilizationist vocabulary of the post–Great War "Paris–Geneva peace" (i.e. in the parlance of this study, the Paris treaties underpinned by Geneva's League of Nations). In 1923, the initial Paris–Geneva peace turned into a Paris–Geneva–Lausanne peace settlement sui generis.

New Italian Prime Minister Benito Mussolini entered the world stage at the Lausanne Conference where he was positively welcomed. Western diplomats in Lausanne endorsed, albeit grudgingly, the results of genocidal politics by Ankara's Young Turk predecessors. Thus, the Lausanne

---

[18] Because there exist almost identical general notions of Turanism and pan-Turkism associated with expansive Islamic Turkism in the vein of Ziya Gökalp, the distinctive term "Turanianism" is used here for the idea by Rıza Nur, Kemal Atatürk, Ismet Inönü, and others, of an ancient (proto-)Turkish past in which autochthonous racial brothers, proto-Turkish "Turanians," built up civilizations from Central Asia to the Levant and beyond. They insisted on the Turanian argument in the context and aftermath of the Lausanne Conference.

Conference made fascism and ultranationalism diplomatically acceptable for the first time. Paradoxically or not, the Lausanne Treaty is the only post–Great War peace treaty to have survived the Second World War in its entirety, and is valid to this day. It escaped, so to say, the radar of critically revised international relations after the Second World War that remade Europe's political landscape (though still formally maintaining the Treaties of Trianon and St. Germain). Scholars may argue that the West's liberal–conservative embrace and domestication succeeded in the case of Interwar Turkey and Saudi Arabia, whereas conservative strategists in Italy and Germany entirely failed in taming future autocrats by domestically colluding with them. The hindsight of a century and the all-decisive criterion of long-term democratic development make this book argue differently.

A seemingly brand-new actor in the 1920s, the government in Ankara became the West's signature ally in the Middle East after the Second World War, and a highly valued member of the North Atlantic Alliance (NATO) since 1952. Even before the post-Lausanne Kemalist reforms, or "Turkish Revolution," the Lausanne Conference nurtured the promise of a new Turkey in Anatolia that would be a "factor of progress" (i.e. of modern secular civilization), for Asia and the Middle East. That orientalist portrait was a common trope and myth among Western diplomats during the twentieth century.[19] It went hand in hand with the myth of Atatürk as a benign dictator and of the Kemalist party-state as a progressive educational dictatorship – notwithstanding that his rule had continued a de-Christianizing Turkification of the country based on genocide, brutally repressed the Kurds, and committed a preplanned massacre of Alevi Kurds that amounted to genocide in the 1930s.

Mainstream diplomacy and academia almost entirely lost sight of the extreme violence – which had not entirely stopped afterward – of the decade before the Conference of Lausanne, and of violent key events which had enforced the Conference. Purposeful violence came along with violence-prone ideology. This fact requires careful attention. The present study is not a recipe of what should or could have been done better at Lausanne, but an analysis of what resulted from the given circumstances and ideas, including what mortgaged the future. Every period has its logics and contingencies that the wisdom of hindsight is invited to question and dismantle. Complexity, analytical grey zones, and the constant need for context

---

[19] This is well articulated, notably in the memoirs of Carlo Sforza, Italian foreign minister in 1920–1 and 1947–51. See Carlo Sforza, *L'Italia dal 1914 al 1944. Quale io la vidi* (Verona: Arnoldo Mondari, 1946), 71.

do not prevent us from perceiving the stamps, patterns, and, yes, historical amnesias left. It is more than an intellectual and moral exercise to question the power of facts established by war and violence, and not by conviction, consent-building, maturation, and democratic relations. Only the latter can underpin real peace that does not invite to further cycles of violence.

Along with its Levant-centric perspective and its focus on republican Turkey's emergence at the end of the Ottoman Empire, this study is about entangled, multi-perspectival history and therefore also looks closely at the situation in Europe. It delves into the remaking of international relations in the force field of the disputed post–Great War "Paris treaty system" (Treaties of Versailles, St. Germain, Neuilly, Trianon, Sèvres, 1919–20). It gives its due weight to this system's "Geneva pillar": the League of Nations. The treaties and related minority protection treaties with the new states in Eastern Europe and the Balkans depended on the League's principles, supervision, and mechanisms of revision and change. While coding collective rights, minority protection included individual human rights. The League of Nations, its evolving role, and its failed pacification of Europe and the world after the First World War is an important reference in this study.

The League's Covenant, principles, and new forms of international collaboration were thought to stand for a new era. Whereas all other treaties of the Paris treaty system included the League's Covenant, the Lausanne Treaty, the system's final pillar (i.e. last treaty), did without it. Lausanne's "Near East Peace" renounced the Covenant.[20] This indicated that all that the League had enshrined would henceforth play no more than subservient roles. There was now a new game of interwar realpolitik that, as far as the Middle East is concerned, survived the Second World War, when most other post–Great War treaties for Europe were gone (even though not all related conflicts and resentments had entirely disappeared, as in the case of Hungary and the Trianon Treaty). In this book, as Part I will explain in more detail, we are taking stock of what enduring Middle Eastern peace-making consisted of at the Conference of Lausanne. Endorsed violence, neglected traumata, denied rights, and missed moral benefits are substantial elements of a realistic historical assessment.

---

[20] In the early twentieth century, the traditional Euro-centric term "Near East" still generally designated the Ottoman Levant. After Lausanne, this came to be comprised in the henceforth prevailing broader – Atlantic-centric – notion of the "Middle East."

The Book's Structure and Sources

Looking forward to the Middle East's future, it is time to come back to Lausanne's open questions that shed light on a century of extremes and abysses. The modern democratic thought that implicitly underpins the exploration of *When Democracy Died* is detailed and referenced in Part I, and particularly again in the Conclusion.

The tour d'horizon in this book leads us from those more (the "victors" Turkey, Britain, France, Italy, Rumania, Japan, Greece) or less (Soviet Russia, SHS Yugoslavia, Bulgaria, USA) represented in Lausanne; to those almost or entirely excluded: Armenians, Assyrians, and Kurds, as well as Turkey's Arabic and Persian neighbors. It pays attention to seminal observers and commentators, notably internationalist humanitarians and lawyers, revisionist-minded Germans, as well as seasoned journalists and caricaturists.

Part I introduces the main topics, terminology, and historical approach applied in this book. It brings the League of Nations into a picture of the early interwar years when the League was a prominent actor and a shining reference. Elements of the Lausanne Treaty violated the beliefs of those working in Geneva who embraced the recognition of and support for ethno-religious diversity, democracy, civil liberties, rule of law, and public accountability. Part I seeks to clarify what "peace" meant, and would have meant, for an Ottoman world heavily affected by the Great War. Questioning the notion of peace in human polities, Part I briefly presents this book's understanding of successful peace as based on democratic social contracts – a topic to which the Conclusion returns.

Part II delves into the late-Ottoman prehistory of the Lausanne Conference that put an end to a formative decade of wars, single-party rule, demographic engineering, diplomatic ruptures, and imperial collapse. It starts with an analysis of visions of the aftermath of the Great War and a detailed exploration of the political and historical thought of Rıza Nur, the vice-chief of Ankara's delegation in Lausanne. In addition, it explores the cosmopolitan microcosm, including active diasporas from Turkey, at the Lake Léman (Geneva) in the years before the Conference. Diaspora organizations articulated new futures. In close relation with nationalist leaders in Anatolia and Europe, they played an influential role on the road to the Lausanne Conference. Parts I and II thus put up the mental and micro- and macro-historical framework of the 1923 Lausanne Near East Peace.

Part III, the book's central and longest part, offers a dense analysis of the course of the Conference, ranging from the stakes of the main players and their home-countries' expectations to influential micro-games in and around Lausanne in commissions, sub-commissions, plenary sessions, and informally. It analyzes Lausanne's discursive universe, including the diplomatically convenient framing of pasts and futures at the negotiation table. The theatre of the Conference itself comprised Lausanne, but also closely connected events, gatherings, and agencies in Switzerland, particularly in Geneva, the seat of the League of Nations, the associated International Labor Organization, and the International Committee of the Red Cross (ICRC). This Part takes stock of the lines that joined, and of the perspectives and interests that clashed, and that finally compromised or were sidelined in Lausanne. It elaborates on the central plot – the deal between Ankara and the neighboring mandatory powers Britain and France. It questions the seminal enabling of a unitary dictatorial nationalism by the Lausanne Conference under the thin guise of "world peace," "civilization," and related prospects of modernization.

"Imperially biased," the negotiations at Lausanne failed the test of democracy.[21] Only victors – of the First World War or the wars in Anatolia – sat at the negotiation table from late 1922 to mid-1923, deciding over the fate of millions in and from the post-Ottoman world not rightly represented by the delegates from Ankara or the mandatory powers. The Turkish delegation stood "under immense pressure from the rigid instructions from Ankara and a very strong national feeling at home."[22] Years of war, polarization, and anti-minoritarian violence had fueled ultranationalism. Lausanne – in contrast to the Conference of Sèvres – left this violence under an awkward veil of secrecy, while the Turkish delegation kept on stressing Greek destructiveness during the immediately preceding war in Western Anatolia. Against this background, democracy had little chance, and within two years after the Treaty, Turkey was a full-fledged dictatorship, and, notwithstanding laudatory international press, fascist and increasingly totalitarian by the end of the 1920s.

Part IV sheds light on how the Conference and Treaty framed the post-Ottoman century in Turkey and Turkey's neighborhood. It explores the defining roots of the Republic of Turkey in a Conference whose Treaty preceded the proclamation of the Republic by three months. It reveals direct lines from the terminology of "universal civilization" – so often invoked in peace efforts from 1919 to 1923 – to the radical Kemalist reforms that explicitly referred to a progressive West. These transformative

---

[21] The generic term "imperial bias" refers in this book to an understanding and projection of ruling power as top-down – imperial, subordinating, and (corporatist, capitalist, colonialist, or otherwise) exploitative – as opposed to egalitarian, (basic-) democratic, law-based, and well-institutionalized (i.e. not charismatic leader–centered).

[22] Demirci, *Lausanne Conference*, 97.

steps comprised the abolition of the caliphate and the sharia; the "revolutions" of law, alphabet, and calendar; and Atatürk's ethnocentric "Turkish History Thesis." With a few case studies, Part IV shows how, in Lausanne, an ambivalent and amnesiac Western walk on eggshells began with regard to the post-Ottoman world in general and Ankara in particular. The League of Nations facilitated the Treaty in various ways, notably for the implementation of the population exchange. But it was lastingly frustrated by Ankara's obstruction of effective minority protection. *When Democracy Died* argues consistently that the League lost its own political project in Lausanne. In macro-politics, the League became subordinate to the constraints of a new European realpolitik that appeased fascism and ultranationalism.

Under the title "Time for Democratic Social Contracts," the book's final section reflects main findings and asks how to go ahead "beyond Lausanne" without opening a new Pandora's box of Treaty revision. How to step toward a future that overcomes the Treaty's shortcomings? How to conceive this rethinking reasonably and radically, while basically keeping with the Lausanne boundaries of Turkey and its neighborhood? Despite several attempts and many promises – starting with proudly and unctuously proffered prospects at Lausanne's negotiation table – Turkey could hitherto not grow into a democracy with a well-performing justice system based on effective fundamental rights. A democracy of this quality is the all-decisive touchstone. It is sine qua non for the solution of problems shelved in Lausanne. A new understanding of realpolitik burgeoned from the Lausanne Conference in international diplomacy. Surviving the Second World War, it perpetuated forces inimical to democracy in the Middle East. As for post-Lausanne Turkey, its construction remains defined by the mantra of 1923. A ruling elite demanded "the same rights as every nation that was sovereign, independent and master of its destinies"[23] – but did not recognize the same rights for other Indigenous groups in the country. Former imperial cadres, they claimed all rights for themselves in the name of "the (Turkish-Muslim) nation" and failed to take responsibility for crimes against humanity. Recognition of the other is the crux and heart of any real democracy.

As shown in the footnotes, this study has benefitted from a multitude of multilingual sources and secondary literature. Besides the usual diplomatic documents, which are easily accessible in Western states and also in

---

[23] The chief delegate Ismet Pasha in a meeting of 2 December 1922. *Lausanne Conference on Near Eastern Affairs (1922–1923): Records of Proceedings and Draft Terms of Peace* (London: His Majesty's Stationery Office, 1923: hereafter LCP), 469.

the Ottoman State Archive in Istanbul,[24] it has made use of the contemporary press, in particular the Swiss and Turkish press, and Swiss police reports. Further critical sources used are diaries and other ego-documents of Lausanne Conference insiders. These shed light on mental maps and bigger contexts that matter in this study, but also on the Conference's unofficial meetings or private conversations that did not enter the Conference minutes. While the primary and secondary sources in *When Democracy Died* give the Turkish side its due weight, they also include hitherto underappreciated archives like those of the Armenian delegation whose cause and record remained sidelined after Lausanne.

Last but not least, the Conference's minutes, proceedings, and draft terms are primary sources for a study of the Lausanne Peace, together with the final Treaty itself.[25] Most research done hitherto rests on a widely used, but incomplete, British edition in one volume. Prints of the authorized and complete six-volume French edition are very rare.[26] This is perhaps characteristic for a questionable peace of which Western representatives felt embarrassed. Unsurprisingly, the situation is better on the Turkish side.[27] Though more comprehensive, the French edition

---

[24] Başbakanlık Osmanlı Arşivi. The case is different with the Republican Archives in Ankara (Başbakanlık Cumhuriyet Arşivi). Foreign ministry documents are still hardly accessible. Editions are: British Foreign Office, *Further Correspondence Respecting Turkey, October to December 1922*, Confidential Print 12330, FO 424/255 (London: FO, n.d.) and analogous following volumes; *Documents diplomatiques français 1922* (Bruxelles: Peter Lang, 2007) and analogous following volumes; Bilal Şimşir (ed.), *Lozan Telgrafları*, vols. 1–2 (Ankara: TTK 1990 and 1994), includes the telegrams between Mustafa Kemal and Ismet Pasha. Among the unofficial delegations, the united Armenian delegation has left particularly rich archives that are accessible in the Nubar Library in Paris (BNu), where the parts transferred to the National Archives in Erivan are also accessible on microfilm.

[25] For the full text of the Treaty and all related Conventions and Declarations in French and English, see *Recueil des Traites et des Engagements Internationaux enregistrés par le Secrétariat de la Société des Nations/ Treaty Series: Publication of Treaties and International Engagements registered with the Secretariat of the League of Nations*. vol. 28 (Geneva: League of Nations, 1924), 11–285.

[26] The British edition of minutes in one volume covers the first half of the Conference, up to early February 1923: *Lausanne Conference on Near Eastern Affairs (1922–1923): Records of Proceedings and Draft Terms of Peace* (London: His Majesty's Stationery Office, 1923). The official French edition is extremely rare and only available in very few libraries: *Conférence de Lausanne sur les affaires du Proche-Orient (1922–1923): Recueil des actes de la conférence* (Paris: Imprimerie Nationale, 1923; hereafter CLA). The tricky situation of the official minutes mirrors the complexity of an intricate and protracted diplomatic event where, though bound by their will to strike a deal, the delegations also followed disparate agendas with regard to what they wanted recorded. There was no supreme institution – and by 1922 no politically authoritative League of Nations – willing and in a position to independently impose a neutral and complete recording, including meetings and hearings in the sub-commissions. See also Andrew Ryan, *The Last of the Dragomans* (London: Geoffrey Bles, 1952), 190–191.

[27] Thanks to the efforts of Seha L. Meray, a professor of law at the Ankara University, there exists since 1969 a Turkish translation of the French version that fills a few gaps with

needs to be completed by other sources as far as the inauguration speeches, sub-commission discussions, and, of course, unofficial meetings are concerned. Diplomatic documents, diaries, and memoirs give insights into sub-commission discussions and private meetings;[28] press reports record public events, sideshows and interviews.[29] Secret police sources, finally, include otherwise unknown events.[30]

---

additional sources: *Lozan Barış Konferansı: Tutanaklar, Belgeler*, transl. and ed. Seha L. Meray (Istanbul: YKY, 2001; first ed., Ankara 1969).

[28] Among notable ego-documents are the following diaries and memoirs: Joseph C. Grew, *Diary*, Joseph Clark Grew papers, MS Am 1687, Houghton Library, Harvard University – a day-to-day source by a member of the observing US delegation on the whole Conference, including the immediate aftermath and the Turkish-American Treaty concluded in Switzerland; Cavid Bey, *Meşrutiyet Ruznâmesi*, diary by a Turkish nationalist dissenter that covers the first half of the Conference; Alexandre Khatissian, *Eclosion et développement de la République arménienne* (Athens: Editions Arméniennes, 1989, in Armenian 1930), a serene analytical memoir with particularly relevant annexes including minutes of private and sub-commission meetings; Rıza Nur, *Hayat ve Hatıratım*, ed. Abdurrahman Dilipak (Istanbul: İşaret, 1992), vol. 2: *Rıza Nur-İnönü kavgası, Lozan ve ötesi* – a subjective, at times unreliable, but highly instructive and detailed memoir by Ankara's vice-plenipotentiary in Lausanne who fell out with the Kemalists in 1926; Ismet İnönü, *İsmet İnönü'nün hatıraları: Büyük zaferden sonra Mudanya Mütarekesi ve Lozan Antlaşması* (Istanbul: Yenigün, 1998), the memoirs of Ankara's plenipotentiary in Lausanne, Atatürk's close collaborator and later president of Turkey; Semyon Aralov, *Bir Sovyet Diplomatının Anıları 1922–23* (Istanbul: Türkiye İş Bankası, 2010, first Russian publication 1960), Moscow's ambassador in Ankara before and during the Lausanne Conference is instructive for how the Conference impacted on the hitherto special Turkish–Soviet relations

[29] Several hundred international journalists in Lausanne produced daily news what makes the contemporary press a rich source. In addition to the press of involved nations focused on their delegations, Swiss papers are of particular interest; they reported abundantly from various angles, gave voice to unofficial delegations, and enjoyed privileged access to local sources; see notably the digitally accessible *Journal de Genève* (via www.letempsarchives.ch) and *Die Neue Zürcher Zeitung* (www.nzz.ch). Edited are the detailed reports by daily *Akşam* correspondant Necmeddin Sadık (Sadak), later a Turkish foreign minister, in *Necmeddin Sadık (Sadak) Bey'in Lozan Mektupları*, ed. Mustafa Özyürek (Ankara: Gece, 2019).

[30] The daily secret reports of the cantonal police (Canton de Vaud with its capital Lausanne) are in the file "Conférence de Lausanne 1922–23," S 112/95, Archives cantonales vaudoises, ACV, Lausanne.

Part I A Century's Pivotal "Peace"

Why title a book on the Near East Peace Conference in Lausanne with the phrase "When Democracy Died"? Why radically question the quality itself of the "Near East Peace of Lausanne"? This book's title is a statement. Although Lausanne's Near East Peace Conference was a highly complex event of global history and a diplomatically successful resettlement, its strongest message proved unambiguous: violence, including genocide, politically paid.

When Democracy Died is an analytical assessment from historical distance. Certainly, many of the diplomats involved had reason to candidly emphasize their achievements after eight months of negotiations. Wisdom of hindsight, however, calls for radical critique of the peace vocabulary used in Lausanne – for example, in the following statement by Joseph Grew, the American observer-delegate at the Conference, shortly before the signature of the Treaty: "A long period of warfare and disturbance affecting the whole of the Near East has been brought to a close . . .; we can now look forward with confidence to the coming period of reconstruction when the ideals of peace and tolerance which have inspired the deliberations of the conference will receive a long and fruitful application."[1]

Ideals of peace and tolerance receiving a long and fruitful application? Grew was so frank a few weeks later as to add several ifs during a talk in Interlaken. He added the caveat that while "a fertile field for financial investment and economic development may well open out to us . . . for the humanitarian, religious and philanthropic considerations, we can have less optimism."[2]

After the Lausanne Conference, removal and extermination of populations appeared not only as acceptable politics, but as a precondition for

---

[1] "Statement before the Delegations," 17 July 1923, Grew papers, MS Am 1687, Houghton Library, Harvard University.

[2] Joseph Grew, US delegate at the Lausanne Conference and ambassador in Bern, "Informal Talk at the Consular Dinner at the Hotel Victoria," Interlaken, 2 September 1923, 40–41, Grew papers.

final success of a high-handed nationalism fit for fossil-dependent capitalist investment. The name of Armenia stands evocatively for this fatality built in the Conference outcome. The fact that "violence won" in Lausanne means that methodical violence was enshrined in the architecture of an enduring Middle East settlement. The Lausanne Treaty liquidated any accountability for even extreme violence against civilians – in contrast to what diplomacy had called for in the Conference of Paris-Sèvres, based on principles of the League of Nations. For prominent Western observers before the late 1930s, authoritarianism counted as fit and fashionable for Asian and European countries, including Japan, Italy, Germany, Spain, and Turkey. This entirely changed during the 1940s – but not for Turkey. It is time to face – in a holistic scholarly picture – the darkness of ultranationalist rule and totalitarianism in a "new Turkey" based on the Lausanne Treaty – without denying other facets. Diplomacy too long used a cleansed political language that accommodated Europe and Ankara in 1923.

1   A Peace of Dominant Interests on the Back of "Others"

Why not highlight a thrilling saga, culminating in a showdown in Lausanne, of how Ankara succeeded in establishing a sovereign nation-state in entire Asia Minor? How did this counter-government of revolutionary nationalists arrive to foil claims by other groups and thus frustrate the will of imperialist Great War victors and Geneva's League of Nations? This would warrant a juicy combination of Kemalist and Bolshevik rhetoric of liberation that indeed was very effective on the eve of the Lausanne Conference.

Or why not foreground the achievements of compromise and realpolitik, not least the striking longevity of a Lausanne settlement that made Turkey lastingly – at least until the mid-2010s – look to the West? In other words, why not feature the complex narrative of a textbook compromise reached in Lausanne in 1923 and nonetheless concede Ankara's "great diplomatic victory at Lausanne?"[3] While the new Ankara government imposed itself in the Ottoman core land of Anatolia, Western Europe's victorious, but exhausted national empires definitively established their temporary dominance in most Arabic parts of the former Ottoman Empire via colony-like mandates.

The Lausanne Conference neither signed off on sovereign democracies in Turkey and the Middle East, nor stole them from there because

---

[3] Grew, "Informal Talk at the Consular Dinner at the Hotel Victoria," Interlaken, 2 September 1923, 3.

democracy was by then no longer a real issue.⁴ Where there had been democratic seeds in the late-Ottoman world – rooted in the 1908 constitutional revolution – they were gone by late 1922. The deals struck at the Lausanne Conference made certain that this fundamental fact would not change. For a century since 1923, democracy has remained sought after.

Yes, there are many reasons to drily state, "Rational and pragmatic thinking as well as a realistic assessment of the circumstances determined the course of the negotiations and encouraged the two parties towards a gradual rapprochement," meaning Ankara's government and the European Powers.⁵ But this assessment of Lausanne, if it stands alone, misses the nature and corrosive impact of a settlement and political birth certificate based on methodical mass violence and the blank disregard for millions. The "losers" were made "others," that is, outsiders of the circles and identity constructions that benefited from the deal. The label of rational pragmatism for the Lausanne Treaty underestimates the lack of democratic foundation for Ankara as well as Britain's, and generally the West's, critical loss of an ethical stand internationally.

By 1923, "a moralizing British Empire" had become "a less than legitimate voice of international justice mired in its own imperial struggles."⁶ It could less than ever claim to be a morally sensitive and responsible actor. The Peace of Lausanne – as this study will argue, resuming what a few contemporary legal experts already felt and expressed – was an undemocratic pact of interests brokered on the back of the weakest parties concerned. It is true that in terms of imperial strategy, London did not lose much by abandoning the Sèvres Treaty for the Lausanne settlement. "[The] British suffered a political defeat," as Turkish historian Sevtap Demirci wrote, "but lost hardly anything of importance. On the whole they were able to protect their interests and retain control over much of the Middle East. In other words, the Turkish success at Lausanne did not defeat the underlying aims of British diplomacy."⁷ As already stated,

---

⁴ Compare Elizabeth F. Thompson, *How the West Stole Democracy from the Arabs: The Syrian Arab Congress of 1920 and the Destruction of Its Liberal-Islamic Alliance* (New York: Atlantic Monthly Press, 2020).

⁵ Sevtap Demirci, "The Lausanne Conference: The Evolution of Turkish and British Strategies, 1922–1923" (London School of Economics and Political Science: Ph.D. Thesis, 1997), 3.

⁶ Michelle Tusan, "'Crimes against Humanity': Human Rights, the British Empire, and the Origins of the Response to the Armenian Genocide," *American Historical Review*, 119 (February 2014), 69.

⁷ Demirci, "Lausanne Conference," 3. A strength of this systematic study of diplomatic strategy at the Conference is the thorough use of British and Turkish archival material, the

a narrative of British success hand in hand with Kemalist triumph was plausible after the Lausanne Conference.

Beside the terms "peace" and "violence," "democracy" looms large in this study that takes the foundation of the Geneva-based League of Nations very seriously. If democratic peace was and still is a decisive issue globally and for the modern Middle East, we cannot help coming critically back to those universal hopes and notions after the Great War, carefully reconsidering them. Lausanne's spirit of a new realpolitik, as stressed in this book, markedly contrasted with the basically democratic "spirit of Geneva." The new realpolitik made the Western powers strike deals with post-Ottoman strongmen in Ankara, Riyadh, and later Tehran, all of whom were able enough to play the then-international game. They had violently secured dominance in their national domain; adapted, in time, then-current weapons of diplomatic courtesy besides brute force; and they could offer crucial commodities and geostrategic advantages.

Was this peace? Unsafe futures loomed for Europe and the Middle East after Lausanne and – as humankind has only decades later become more generally aware – catastrophic ecological consequences globally from excessive dependence on fossil fuel. Lausanne definitively let down many existing democratic-minded forces who, though less strong and vocal, sought and believed in internationally supported constitutional rule. In the long term, the Lausanne sort of peace settlement manifestly did not, or only very limitedly, promote viable polities. Antidemocratic practices (destructive of democracy), politics of violence, and recurrent conflicts abounded, together with the art of manipulating, not solving, crises. As a consequence, bereft of functioning social contracts, parts of the population had to leave their post-Ottoman home countries for better futures. Millions voted with their feet, leaving Turkey and other post-Ottoman countries during the decades to come.

Predominantly based on geostrategy, oil, or corporate interests, Lausanne-spirited deals cemented the mutual interdependence of Western national-imperial states with strangers to, or even despisers of, democracy and human rights. The lack of democracy meant that even the good intentions of ruling individuals or professional groups (e.g. lawyers in Kemalist Turkey), were built on sand. In his optimistic outlook right after the Lausanne Treaty, even Grew had to proffer many

latter however only limitedly, due to the lack of decent scholarly access to the files of the Ministry of Foreign Affairs. The most recent version of Demirci's study is the Turkish translation *Belgelerle Lozan* (Istanbul: Alfa, 2011) that is based on the thesis's publication as *Strategies and Struggles – British Rhetoric and Turkish Response: The Lausanne Conference 1922–1923* (Istanbul: ISIS Press, 2005).

ifs: "if Turkey is able to live up to the obligation of her sovereignty," "provided that they [Ankara's present leaders] can cope with domestic difficulties and opposition," et cetera. He conjured up good intentions on the part of these leaders and, lacking a factual basis, conceded that "we must take Turkey on trust."[8] This uncertain language of hope vis-à-vis antidemocracy hardly veiled the knowledge that Ankara's liberationist affirmation of sovereignty in reality justified discrimination and spoliation, thus finalizing politics of extermination started in 1915. Systematic denaturalization and the prohibition of Armenian return constituted "one of the levers for perpetuating the economic and financial transfer," started by Ankara's predecessor regime.[9] In Anatolia, the Lausanne "peace" was concluded on the back of those dissenters, democrats, and Indigenous groups that triumphant Turkish nationalism had made disposable "others."

In all its vibrancy, drama, and lofty vocabulary, the Lausanne Conference therefore amounted to deal-making between Western Europe's national imperialists with post-Ottoman potentates, not with representatives of democracy. Lausanne's wishful thinking, language, and diplomatic convenience however endured, so that the "Kemalist Republic was always misrecognized in the West as 'democratic'" – as a 94-year-old American historian recently observed.[10] In reality, the window of opportunity for more democratic futures, which the League of Nations had recently opened up to include late-Ottoman core lands, definitively closed down in Lausanne. Western actors henceforth involved in the Middle East cared little or not at all about constitutionality. Democracy – including human rights – became a value that again counted, at best, only in their own country for their own voters.

2 A Peace without Peace: Unaddressed Violence, Coercion, and Racism

"They All Made Peace – What Is Peace?" American author Ernest Hemingway poignantly thus titled a poem written during the Lausanne Conference that he briefly attended as a journalist.[11] Forty years after the

---

[8] "Informal Talk at the Consular Dinner at the Hotel Victoria," Interlaken, 2 September 1923, 41.
[9] Dzovinar Kévonian, "Usages du droit et espaces de pouvoir transnationaux: la pratique pétitionnaire de la section des minorités de la Société des nations face aux rescapés d'un crime de masse, 1920–1939," *Monde(s)* 19 (2021), 79–80.
[10] Harry Harootunian, *The Unspoken as Heritage: The Armenian Genocide and Its Unaccounted Lives* (Durham: Duke University Press, 2019), 150.
[11] Published in *Little Review*, Spring 1923, republished in Ernest Hemingway, *Complete Poems* (Lincoln: University of Nebraska Press, 1992), 63–64.

Lausanne Treaty, historian Matthew S. Anderson wrote, "With the Lausanne settlement the Eastern Question was no more," in his classic study of the Eastern Question.[12] Was it really no more, and if so, were its underlying issues solved?

Nearly 100 years later, we know that the basic theme of the "Eastern Question" – how to achieve viable futures in the modern Levant? – subsists to this day. In the early twenty-first century, this is more striking than ever, albeit in updated forms, and it comes with massive violence in various places. Containing atavistic elements, violence often brings perpetuated cleavages to the surface, but depends no less on concrete historical situations and developments. The modern politics of violence, which this book addresses, exploited premodern cleavages. At its end, the Ottoman Empire comprised the area of today's Turkey, Iraq, Syria, Lebanon, Palestine, and the Arabic peninsula. In this area, in particular, post-Ottoman state-building and statehood has not ceased to be violent.

Where does this stem from? One central factor, according to this study, is unaddressed, thus internalized, political violence. The Lausanne settlement of the modern Middle East was preceded by more than a decade of extreme violence and coercion that reshaped the human landscape in the late-Ottoman space. The 1910s saw an ultranationalist *and* Islamist dictatorship of the Young Turks. Most Kemalists and many Arab politicians were former Young Turks; many of them had been more shaped by the lessons of authoritarianism than by those of democratic constitutionalism. A latecomer, the Peace of Lausanne not only failed to address, but even endorsed, the mass violence in the decade that preceded the Conference. It legalized the results of forcible demographic engineering. It whitewashed the responsible actors who – except top leaders who fled into foreign exile – left the Ottoman capital Istanbul for the new capital Ankara. It built "peace" upon, not critically against, the dark side of the precedent decade.

What the Lausanne Conference remarkably resettled, was Western diplomacy with Turkey: It was henceforth no longer the half exploitative, half supportive relationship with a moribund empire, but based on parity. From 1923, interactions with Ankara thus comprise often strained, but enduring politics of interests with a geostrategically cherished partner, arduously to be appeased time and again. While the Lausanne Peace pacified international relations with Turkey and overcame notorious aspects of the Eastern Question – like the issues of imperial future, legal

---

[12] Matthew S. Anderson, *The Eastern Question, 1774–1923* (New York: St. Martin's Press, 1966), 388.

privileges of Westerners (capitulations), and boundary disputes – it could by no means establish societal peace in the former late-Ottoman core lands. In the long term, these remained areas of civil wars, autocracies, protracted crises, and genocides. Most recent is the genocide of the Yezidis during civil war and the rise of the "Islamic State" in Iraq and Syria. Less than thirty year earlier, other Iraqi Kurds were targeted for extermination by Saddam Hussein's forces. The least known post-Ottoman genocide is that of Alevi Kurds in Dersim, a province in Turkey, in the 1930s. The Lausanne Treaty's pact with Ankara and its – compared to the other treaties of the Paris system – dismantled minority protection shielded Ankara from even the slightest Western reprimands.

Thus, in the perspective of this study, protracted peacelessness in the former Ottoman core lands is built into the Lausanne Treaty. The reason is the deliberate repression of an immediate past marked by trauma, crime, and mass violence. Organized, purposeful violence – "liberationist" in Turkish-nationalist terms – informed the road toward the Conference and enforced the revision of the precedent Treaty of Sèvres. A new, explicitly racial discourse abruptly replaced late-Ottoman Islamism by Ankara's delegation in Lausanne, creating a religious–secular rift in "new Turkey" right from the start. *When Democracy Died* tackles racial social Darwinism with particular regard to vice-plenipotentiary Dr. Rıza Nur and Nur's anti-Armenian "Turanian argument."

The Conference's legal formalization of a hitherto unseen compulsory population transfer targeted nearly two million people.[13] It amounted to the completion of a decade of previous demographic policies in Anatolia by removing a remainder of 1.5 million Indigenous Christians. Only a quarter of a million or so remained from more than four million before 1914. During the wars in Anatolia before the Conference, the Kemalists had fiercely defended the demographic achievements of their predecessors, in particular the results of the Armenian genocide, in terms of dispossession and disenfranchisement. In other words, the Western powers bowed in Lausanne to an ultranationalist design that successfully de-Christianized the region by dispossession and extermination. Manifestly, this went far beyond the era's conceptual trend toward homogenized ethno-national states that the Geneva-based League of Nations would peacefully organize. Without being declared and named as what it really was, Lausanne's "solution" for ethno-religious conflicts set a shining example for exterminatory nationalisms to come.

---

[13] See Umut Özsu, *Formalizing Displacement: International Law and Population Transfers* (Oxford: Oxford University Press, 2015).

2 A Peace without Peace

The exacerbated Anglo–French contest was among the factors that facilitated Western yielding and correlate politics of forgetting in Lausanne. It centered on Turkey and Germany and culminated during the Conference. The French–British disagreement on reparations and the French occupation of the Ruhr on January 11, 1923, absorbed attention, foregrounding continental European issues closest to Western, especially French, diplomacy that sought security against reemerging German might.[14] Post-1923 diplomats and historians of interwar Europe nevertheless were wrong in considering Turkey as "eccentric and relatively secondary"[15] – thus ignoring Turkey's authentic, proactive, and paradigmatic, by no means eccentric or exotic, trajectory. Moreover, by focusing on statesmen and national strongmen as agents of history, they paid more attention to states and international deal-making than to concerned peoples and these peoples' memories. Humans constitute the "real history" that includes suppressed plights, justice, and causes. These unavoidably reemerge in the historical long term, as do elementary principles of human ethics. All these elements inform the "other history of Lausanne" that *When Democracy Died* aspires to tell.

Realpolitik, in the original sense of German journalist A. L. von Rochau, meant politics that take into account facts of power and interest, but still strive for a constitutional polity in which might could not trump right. It was about a fortunate liaison between right and might. He coined the term *"Realpolitik"* after Europe's failed *Völkerfrühling*, a revolutionary Springtime of the Peoples in 1848. Rochau then evolved from a radical revolutionary to a supporter of the German Chancellor Bismarck.[16] Whereas Rochau's realpolitik, consequently, accepted the use of force in limited wars or domestically, fifty years later, after the Peace of Lausanne, realpolitik legalized mass coercion and, implicitly, mass violence. Thus, post-Lausanne realpolitik endorsed the results of authoritarian repression, ultranationalism, and genocide that had followed Ottoman Turkey's failed constitutional revolution. As interwar liberalism condoned the redefinition of realpolitik that the Conference of Lausanne operated, it led itself into an impasse that left room for genocidal fascisms.

In his world of political sciences and diplomacy after the mid-twentieth century, historian Matthew S. Anderson could not feel but right saying that the Lausanne settlement "was given permanence and solidity by one

---

[14] Albrecht-Carrié, *France, Europe*, 134–135.   [15] Ibid., 135.
[16] August Ludwig von Rochau, *Grundsätze der Realpolitik, angewendet auf die staatlichen Zustände Deutschlands* (Stuttgart: Karl Göpel, 1859; first ed., 1853). See also Natascha Doll, *Recht, Politik und 'Realpolitik' bei August Ludwig von Rochau (1810–1873): Ein wissenschaftsgeschichtlicher Beitrag zum Verhältnis von Politik und Recht im 19. Jahrhundert* (Frankfurt am Main: Vittorio Klostermann, 2005).

overmastering virtue: it faced facts." It was realistic in a post-1945 American understanding of political realism, as by Hans Morgenthau, Reinhold Niebuhr, Georges Kennan, and Henry Kissinger. As a circumspect scholar, Anderson mentioned the Lausanne Treaty's "serious defects" that had notably affected Armenian, Kurdish, and Greek "human beings." He underlined that the Armenian "fate remains the greatest tragedy in the history of the modern Near East."[17] Anderson and many of his contemporaries took, however, this outcome not only as a tragic fatality, but also as the price necessarily to be paid for international stability in terms of "realpolitik." For them, Lausanne's decisions were "brutal, but effective."[18] Still conceptually bound to Lausanne realpolitik, they did not holistically join the dots with the recent experience of Nazism. Thus, they recoiled from naming the signature scandal peculiar to their own era – what international lawyer André Mandelstam had called, in 1925, "the implicit recognition [by the Lausanne Conference] of a general right for all peoples to consolidate their existence through the destruction or violent assimilation of other nations."[19] In other words, they did not really face contemporary history and analyze a central precondition of their era's Holocaust.

Contemporaries do not enjoy the privilege of hindsight: They must do without a comprehensive, "dewarped" retrospect. Francis P. Walters, the deputy secretary-general of the League of Nations, rightly insisted in his 1952 retrospective, "The fifteen-month period from the Assembly of [October] 1922 to the end of the year 1923 was disastrous to the moral and material recovery of Europe." He particularly emphasized the victory of "essentially nationalist and militarist" Fascism and of Mussolini's "personal dictatorship" in Italy, where constitutional rule was destroyed. He did not, however, note how important the synchronous Lausanne Conference was for the zeitgeist's turn to dictatorial party rule, with Turkey becoming the Nazis' paragon. A fine diplomat, but Western post-Lausanne mainstream, Walters ignored the dark side of Turkey's refoundation as a nation-state, including the fact that Ankara rested on Young Turk policies in Anatolia. He praised Atatürk as the architect of Turkey's post-1918 "military rebirth" and – a common trope among post-Lausanne diplomats and academics – "unique amongst dictators."[20]

---

[17] Anderson, *Eastern Question*, 375 and 397.
[18] Bernard Lewis, *The Emergence of Modern Turkey* (London: Oxford University Press, 1961), 250.
[19] André N. Mandelstam, *La Société des Nations et les puissances devant le problème arménien* (Paris: A. Pedone, 1925), 340.
[20] F. P. Walters, *A History of the League of Nations* (London: Oxford University Press, 1952), 231–233 and 561–562.

2 A Peace without Peace

Alas, post-Lausanne Turkey was less promising, less "independent, orderly, and self-confident" than Walters presented it. It was not until well after the Conference of Lausanne that Atatürk began to be seen as a non-populist leader. For his rise to undisputed power in 1923, he toured the country and made use of populist rhetoric in Islamic and Turkist/Turanian terms.

Since the 2010s, the mainstream that praised Turkey's and the Lausanne Treaty's stability for the Middle East, has fallen silent. However, internally and externally, peace and stability hardly existed throughout the twentieth century. For a majority, Europe's crises, the Second World War, and the Cold War represented the measure for almost all things contemporary. Holistic assessments comprising the post-Ottoman space were rare. By considering the Republic of Turkey as "by far the most stable political unit in the Near East,"[21] or as "a rare and on the whole unusually successful example of a nationalism at once intransigent, enlightened, and reasonable,"[22] a formative generation of Western scholars and diplomats almost entirely overlooked hard facts of trauma, genocide, and forestalled democracy. Many of them well perceived Turkey as illiberal and "highly nationalistic." But they cared little about antidemocracy and continued internal repression there, including the Dersim genocide that the League of Nations entirely and deliberately ignored in the late 1930s.

In their post-1945 retrospect, many knowledgeable contemporaries clearly saw and warned of the rise of continental Europe's fascism. But they did not – or did not want to – recognize the lines and twisted roads leading from Turkish ultranationalism, via Lausanne, to European fascisms, and from the Armenian Genocide and further genocides to the Holocaust. Many of them, nevertheless, had well understood that "Turkish nationalism meant the savage suppression of other national groups."[23] Simply stating this and truly pondering it historically, were however two different things. Those willing to understand the long-term consequences in terms of peace, stability, and rule of law stood outside the mainstream – like decades-long-jailed Turkish sociologist Ismail Beşikçi, the pioneer of Dersim genocide studies.[24] Most political and academic opinion leaders in the West did not expect the rapid expiry date of Lausanne's Kemalists in the late twentieth century.

An up-to-date historical analysis can no longer do without joining the dots. The answer to the question at the beginning of this Part I is therefore

[21] Anderson, *Eastern Question*, 389.   [22] Albrecht-Carrié, *France, Europe*, 135.
[23] Ibid., 397.
[24] See İsmail Beşikçi, *Tunceli Kanunu (1935) ve Dersim Jenosidi* (Ankara: Yurt, 1992; first ed., 1990).

straightforward and far-reaching: Although it successfully remade international relations with the West, the Treaty of Lausanne could not lay the foundation for a balanced and lasting domestic peace in the core lands of the defunct late-Ottoman Empire. Not only do current developments in Iraq, Syria, Turkey, and the South Caucasus prompt this conclusion in retrospect of a century, but, even more, a sober historical inquiry into the genesis, making, and immediate aftermath of the Peace of Lausanne itself sheds light on the conditions of an international peace that right from the start remained domestically peaceless.

An analysis that goes back to the Lausanne Peace's main roots ("radices" in Latin; i.e. a "radical analysis") is in place and motivates this study. A retrospective per se is intriguing in scholarly terms, but the quest for radical insight and clarification of root causes while looking forward toward Middle Eastern futures is an even stronger motivation. This inquiry into history asks for clear-sightedness for alternative, more peaceful futures, and for critical appreciation of roads not taken – but without nostalgia or the illusion that one could turn back the clock. *When Democracy Died* is therefore, above all, about taking stock of what was the case in terms of peace-making. The Conference of Lausanne rightly attempted, in a spirit of realism, to face facts created by violent power, but it went too far by endorsing and historically whitewashing them. Due to the terms and decisions imposed by the Conference, the word "peace" itself was violated in the minds of millions of sidelined or badly coerced people. Those targeted by Lausanne's legally formalized compulsory population transfer were only the most visible tip of the iceberg. Lausanne is thus a case in point for the fact that a lofty term like "peace" can endure historic abuse at a price that later generations have to pay.

***

The Conference of Lausanne rubber-stamped wide-ranging political, societal, and genocidal violence in the late-Ottoman core area. It accomplished former ethno-religious cleansing by an official, compulsory, so-called population exchange. At the same time, it buried previous attempts to come to terms with a coercive, violent past and to build up constitutional, accountable polities.

The Conference thus rewarded and perpetuated an underlaying rationale of violence-prone policies in nascent post-Ottoman polities. This was disadvantageous to peaceful efforts based on democratic contracts, not primarily on revolutionist might and ultra-ideologemes.[25] Moreover, it

---

[25] In accord with the use in my book, *Talaat Pasha*, I tend to employ the term "revolutionist" for violent domestic transformations that include those promoted by self-declared

2 A Peace without Peace

made domestic politics of violence attractive for fascist admirers and emulators in contemporary Europe who vocally sought a revision of their respective Paris peace treaties. The Treaty of Lausanne belatedly concluded the Paris treaty system whose first cornerstone had been the 1919 Treaty of Paris–Versailles for Germany. Closely followed by international press and radio, the Conference of Lausanne revised the August 1920 Paris–Sèvres Treaty, the hitherto last treaty of the Paris system.

This treaty for the Ottoman world, which was the longest in the making in Paris, collapsed within two years under prompt and concerted reaction of Bolsheviks and Kemalists in Anatolia and the Caucasus. Beside this main blow, to which we will come back in greater detail in Part II, important flaws and fissures in this Paris–Geneva peace for the Middle East were already manifest in the year of its conclusion. In a breach of the Sèvres Treaty, Paris began to compromise with the nationalists in Ankara in 1921, and ceded Cilicia to them. It did this in favor of its Syrian mandate, which it could only implement if it concentrated its limited forces and early countered the attempts of the Syrian National Congress to establish a constitutional federal monarchy under King Faisal over Greater Syria (i.e. including Palestine and Lebanon).[26] Faisal was the son of Hussein bin Ali, the ally of the Entente during the Great War. As the sharif of Mecca, Hussein led the Mecca emirate.[27] Hussein's relations with the British soured when they realized the warrior qualities and diplomatic skills employed by Hussein's successfully raiding tribal rival, the Wahhabi leader Ibn Saud (alias Abdulaziz bin Abdul Rahman). Internal British positions conflicted, but, all in all, they sought to compromise with both leaders, not to clearly stand with their tarnished ally. This stood in contrast to what most Arabs outside the peninsula had expected at the end of the Great War: loyalty to the former ally.[28]

Part of the Paris negotiation process, the April 1920 San Remo Resolution provisionally attributed post-Ottoman mandates to France and Britain. Although depending on the final peace treaty and the endorsement by the League of Nations, this resolution smelled of the

---

(proto-)fascist "revolutionaries." H. L. Kieser, *Talaat Pasha* (Princeton, NJ: Princeton University Press, 2018).

[26] The most recent, detailed and sympathetic account of these attempts is Thompson, *Democracy*, that offers rich insights into the interactions and evolving ideas of multiple, in particular Arab, actors.

[27] Thus member of the dynasty of the Hashemites (descendants of Hashim ibn Abd Manaf of the Quraysh tribe).

[28] Joshua Teitelbaum, *The Rise and Fall of the Hashimite Kingdom of Arabia* (New York: New York University Press, 2001), 249–282.

spirit of the notorious secret 1916 Sykes–Picot Agreement; that is, decision-making over the heads of concerned peoples outside Europe. The League certainly made a difference. Still, for Syrians, there was limited consolation in the fact that ex-Ottoman territories were to be so-called A Mandates, for which the League Covenant applied a lofty developmentalist language:

> Certain communities formerly belonging to the Turkish Empire have reached a stage of development where their existence as independent nations can be provisionally recognised subject to the rendering of administrative advice and assistance by a Mandatory until such time as they are able to stand alone. The wishes of these communities must be a principal consideration in the selection of the Mandatory.[29]

The predominant wishes of Syrians for an American or otherwise a British (but not French) mandate were not considered in San Remo or ultimately in Lausanne.

Since Russian and Armenian socialists had cooperated for decades in the Second Socialist International, many contemporaries were surprised to see revolutionaries from the far left and from an ultranationalist right in Ankara start to ally in summer 1920. At the same time, these new allies began to decry the League of Nations, the internationalist pillar of the Paris treaty system.[30] Bolshevik leader Vladimir Lenin actually upgraded the Turkish nationalists as fighters in a common anti-Western struggle, although, until 1920, Russian socialists had rejected Young Turks as chauvinistic imperialists. Until then, they endorsed Armenian causes not only within the Socialist International, but also in the aftermath of the Bolshevik October Revolution and during the early phase of the Russian Civil War.[31]

In the month of August 1920, when the Treaty of Sèvres was signed, Poland defeated the Red Army before Warsaw. Lenin's revolutionary dogma since his exile in Switzerland (i.e. immediate violent world revolution spreading from Europe, supported by the advancing Red Army) suffered a heavy setback. In consequence, the Bolsheviks turned to the "peoples of the East" and convoked the Baku Congress. They judged anti-Western nationalism and jihadism of critical importance for their own survival, considering Ankara an ideal partner. In a first step of

---

[29] "The Covenant of the League of Nations," *League of Nations – Official Journal*, February 1920, 3–12 (French and English versions).

[30] See Lenin's public address on 15 October 1920, "Speech Delivered at a Conference of Chairmen of Uyezd, Volost and Village," www.marxists.org/archive/lenin/works/1920/oct/15b.htm.

[31] See, for example, J. V. Stalin, "Turkish Armenia," 31 December 1917, www.marxists.org/reference/archive/stalin/works/1917/12/31.htm.

their cooperation, Ankara and Moscow divided the South Caucasus among them, thus putting an end to the young independent republics there in 1920–1.[32]

In retrospect, we see a powerful anti-liberal road beginning at the end of the Great War. It started most forcefully with the Kemalists' and Bolshevists' denigration, rejection, and division of Armenia, while simultaneously showing up in early mandate-related deals and the rise of Ibn Saud. From the triumphalist revision of the Sèvres Treaty in Lausanne, where the Armenians were definitively sidelined by the West as well, this fatal road finally led to the revilement of Poland as an "ugly, grotesque bastard of the Versailles Treaty" (Russian Foreign Minister Molotov)[33] by National Socialists and Soviets during the interwar period – in particular after the common invasion in September 1939. Anti-imperialist revolutionist violence from the right and the left served as a social-Darwinist crushing of what they regarded as weak nations in the way of their more grandiose political designs. For them, Armenia was a weak and contemptible project engendered by the victors in Paris, backed only by the Geneva-based League of Nations, a militarily impotent internationalist institution.

Allied to the Bolsheviks during the war for Anatolia, Ankara pioneered a "third way" after the Great War. This third way was, like the Bolshevik "second way," tantamount to an illiberal dictatorship. But it resulted from a revolution from the right; that is, an ultranationalist fight in the name of Islam and Turkishness that had begun by the Young Turk regime in 1913. Heirs of the Young Turks, the Kemalists managed, in Lausanne, to compromise with the "first way" of a liberal-capitalist West, the main pillar of the Paris–Geneva settlement. Successfully obstructing minority rights and without domestic liberties, it could henceforth (in contrast to the Soviet Union) participate in the capitalist world, take loans, and cooperate in the internationalism led by the League of Nations. To the League itself, in breach of the promise given in Lausanne, Ankara adhered only belatedly (i.e. in 1932), after confirming that the Western powers and the League would by no means impede the dictatorial party-state established in the meanwhile.

Like the other treaties of the Paris system, the Sèvres Treaty displayed clear flaws of victors' justice and imperial bias. Nevertheless, it had earnestly sought the implementation of rights for minorities and small

---

[32] Vefa Kurban, *Russian-Turkish Relations from the First World War to the Present* (Newcastle upon Tyne: Cambridge Scholars, 2017), 18.

[33] Quoted in M. K. Dziewanowski, *The Communist Party of Poland: An Outline of History* (Boston: Harvard University Press, 1976), 96. See also Maria Szonert-Binienda, "Was Katyn a Genocide?" *Case Western Reserve Journal of International Law*, 44 (2012), 689.

nations, accountability for mass violence against civilians, and repair for crimes against humanity. As a pact among victors that now included the sharply anti-liberal victors of the war for Anatolia, the Lausanne Treaty made entire Indigenous groups in Anatolia victims and losers of unitary politics, given no or only very weak rights. For a century, these people restlessly sought denied truth and justice. Blessed in Lausanne, the regime in Ankara, in contrast, emerged by the mid-1920s as a leader-led single-party dictatorship.[34] In spite of its growingly totalitarian nature and its use of extremely violent repression against dissenters and non-Turkish groups considered non-assimilable, it continued to enjoy Western appeasement and to reap the fruits of its endorsement in Lausanne.

***

The previous paragraphs have made clear why this study of the Lausanne Conference emphasizes the issue of force, violence, and coercion. Despite the straightforward answer to the question asked at the beginning, the analysis and argument in this book prove complex and – a disclaimer right at the start – far from any easy-going blame game.

Successful violence paid off in Lausanne. It deployed precedential force and transformed the League of Nations. Other radical nationalists came to see "contemporary Turkey, with its radical expulsion of the Greeks and its reckless Turkish nationalization of the country" as a role model.[35] Ankara proved to other would-be revisionists in Europe and Asia how to triumphantly defy the Paris–Geneva settlement – and gain recognition. It demonstrated how to deal with Western parliamentary democracies. It gave an example of how to get one's own way with, and benefit from, liberal-capitalist leaders on an autocratic path into the future.

What caused a fundamentally appeasing Western attitude in Turkey's case, and enabled Ankara's third way by 1923, were the military success in Anatolia; the vulnerability of the mandates in Turkey's southern neighborhood; and the area's general geopolitical weight, notably in international conflicts with the Soviet Union, Nazi Germany, and the Tripartite Pact between Germany, Italy, and Japan. In short, international relations made the difference – not domestic key elements of fascism and ultranationalism. In this study, ultranationalism means an illiberal social-Darwinist current of essentialist nationalism that, if

---

[34] Hanioğlu, *Atatürk*, 192.
[35] Carl Schmitt in the preface to the 1926 edition of his *Die geistesgeschichtliche Lage des heutigen Parlamentarismus* (Berlin: Dunker und Humblot, 1926); translated in Anton Kaes et al. (eds.), *The Weimar Republic Sourcebook* (Berkeley: University of California Press, 1994), 335.

politically successful, leads to rightist autocracy and the risk of genocide against minorities.[36] Genocide in the twentieth century has proven the "nuclear option" of autocracies that saw themselves faced with what they believed to be otherwise superior domestic and foreign enemy power.

All negotiators had their points in Lausanne; but not all were equally valid. Understandably, the main powers wanted to achieve a war-ending compromise in 1922, after years of blood-shed, diplomatic collapse, protracted peace negotiations in Paris, and follow-ups that all failed to pacify Anatolia and Mesopotamia. There France and Britain were involved as mandatory powers. This situation badly obstructed early interwar reconstruction all around. Early and lasting integration into a Western international architecture in Lausanne in 1923, distinguish Turkey's pioneering way from that of later continental Europe's fascists. Compared to Europe's fascists, Turkey had perpetrated major genocides and crimes against humanity two decades earlier.

Egalitarian democracy has also preserved attractivity and futurity in the twenty-first century. Democracy with intact civil liberties has kept being a central benchmark for any good polity. On a global scale, people continue to vote with their feet, seeking safer and better lives in more democratic and often more prosperous polities. For devoted insiders of the League of Nations and active members of League associations in many countries – including Switzerland, the League's host – their project meant much more than the affix or fig leaf of a liberal-capitalist West.[37]

A thriving element in a proficient system of semi-direct democracy, Geneva itself, the League's geographical and institutional heart, stood for a centuries-old republic and center of asylum far from empire. It was part of a federal state composed by different populations with faith in an agreed common democratic social contract. Cadres in the League, Swiss and foreign, carried the legacy of Protestant internationalism of which Geneva had been a crucial hub since the sixteenth century. From the mid-1800s, Geneva's highly international university attracted

---

[36] The term "ultranationalism" has also been used appeasingly, to demarcate "Japanese fascism" – without naming it so after 1945 – from Europe's fascisms. See Reto Hofmann, *The Fascist Effect: Japan and Italy, 1915–1952* (Ithaca, NY: Cornell University Press, 2015), 4 and 141.

[37] Thomas R. Davies, "Internationalism in a Divided World: The Experience of the International Federation of League of Nations Societies, 1919–1939," *Peace & Change* 37.22 (2012), 227–252; Jean-Michel Guieu, "La SDN et ses organisations de soutien dans les années 1920: Entre promotion de l'esprit de Genève et volonté d'influence," *Relations internationales* 151 (2012), 11–23.

hundreds of students from autocratic empires, including Russia and Ottoman Turkey. Spreading a new global internationalism, the League was more than a product of its main pillar in terms of power (i.e. the British Empire in its final decades).[38]

3 Ultranationalism Appeased? The Paris–Geneva–Lausanne Constellation

As the last post–Great War treaty, the Near East Peace Treaty of Lausanne invalidated the 1920 Treaty of Paris–Sèvres that had included the Covenant of the League of Nations. Belated and radically revisionist, it redefined the Paris treaty system and its political principles. It early on contributed to undermining them.

This book's theoretical framework is therefore the "Paris–Geneva–Lausanne" peace construct, with its built-in Lausanne (new realpolitik) versus Geneva (League) tension. It underlines the interplay between political realities ultimately negotiated in Lausanne in 1922–3, on the one hand, and the principles that underpinned the Geneva-based League of Nations, a central pillar of the Paris treaty system, on the other. As we will see, the regulations of the Lausanne Treaty were in many ways intertwined with the offices and services of the League of Nations. Consequently, the Lausanne Treaty contributed to transform the League, and thus also the Paris treaty system. Thus, a new Paris–Geneva–Lausanne system of interwar realpolitik emerged in 1923.[39]

The Paris treaty system's principles had initially rested on the League of Nations. This new internationalist cornerstone had to check, balance, develop, and, where necessary, revise the victor-dominated decisions in Paris, including the treaties themselves. For its mentors, founders, and most committed insiders, the League rested on a democratic credo – in President Wilson's famous words: "No peace can last, or ought to last, which does not recognize and accept the principle that governments derive all their just powers from the consent of the governed."[40] As this study will detail, the Conference of Lausanne endorsed the definitive sacrifice of the League's initial legal and democratic credo. Certainly,

---

[38] Compare Mark Mazower, *No Enchanted Palace: The End of Empire and the Ideological Origins of the United Nations* (Princeton, NJ: Princeton University Press, 2009).

[39] A new critical study on Turkey, the League of Nations, and internationalism in general is Carolin Liebisch-Gümüş, *Verflochtene Nationsbildung: Die Neue Türkei und der Völkerbund 1918–38* (München: De Gruyter Oldenbourg, 2020).

[40] "A World League for Peace" Speech, 22 January 1917, https://history.state.gov/historicaldocuments/frus1917Supp01v01/d22.

3 Ultranationalism Appeased?

this credo had previously already heavily suffered with the imposition, notably, of France's mandate in Syria and with the abandonment of Armenia.

Against its declared will, in 1920, the first year of its existence, the League proved incapable of protecting Armenians in Anatolia and the Caucasus or of implementing justice, as it could not find a mandatory power for the projected Armenia. In Lausanne, Armenians, Assyrians, and Syrians had to give up their last hope of any form of League-supported democratic self-determination in their native land. Despite a similar disappointment in Lausanne, for the Arabs in Iraq and Syria, there was at least hope of a foreseeable end of the mandates. The disillusionment over a temporary quasi-colonial mandate cannot be equated with the ultimate abandonment of victims of genocide not only in political terms (i.e. democratic self-determination), but also in terms of basic justice and historical truth. The latter amounted to a symbolic annihilation in public history.

Concluded in or next to Paris in 1919–20, the Paris system comprised the 1919–20 Treaties of Versailles, St.-Germain, Neuilly-sur-Seine, Trianon and Sèvres. These treaties were to integrate the new postimperial, republican states of Germany, Austria, and Hungary – imperial senior allies of Ottoman Turkey during the First World War – as well as a strongly curtailed, but still imperial-dynastic Ottoman Turkey into the new order, to be based on the new League of which the losers of the First World War were considering becoming members. Victory of Ankara's armed forces in its wars in Asia Minor was the main reason in 1922 for the revision of the Sèvres Treaty and with this the redefinition of the Paris-Geneva peace architecture that the Lausanne Conference carried out. Moreover, in contrast to Paris, a Soviet delegation participated in Lausanne, although only for specific meetings.

The Lausanne Treaty was of a markedly different character than the other treaties of the Paris system. Let us recall that, in contrast to treaties concluded in Paris in 1919 and 1920, the Covenant of the League of Nations does not figure on the first pages of the Lausanne Treaty. This means that by then, in high diplomacy, the League was no longer considered or believed to be the central pillar for peace, but rather an international institution adjoint, and largely subordinate, to the makers of realpolitik. The Ankara government would not have accepted insertion into a superordinate system, as it insisted on unrestricted national sovereignty and feared foreign control. Principled forces within, and associated to, the League showed continued, but ultimately failing, resistance to such downgrading of the

League. In the end, they realized that their commitment was an exemplary historic "experiment" at best, not a fulfilment.[41]

From late 1922, the League of Nations had to serve and supervise a new constellation under a revised political philosophy, including the compulsory transfer of populations between Turkey and Greece and an eroding minority regime in the newly founded Republic of Turkey. In line with the League's lack of power regarding Armenia in 1920, the new perspectives, roles, and tasks imposed to, and endorsed by, the League at the Conference of Lausanne vis-à-vis authoritarian Ankara amounted to a definitive game change by 1923. Further events and factors indicated a disenchanted League by late 1922, notably fascism's victory in Italy and the contempt of Benito Mussolini – a photogenic new leader of Italy at the Conference – for Geneva during the Italian occupation of Corfu in fall 1923. The latter crisis was solved by a conference of ambassadors in the style of traditional Great Powers politics, not the League, in ways that were unfair for Greece, the weaker part.[42]

In other words, the League's principles, philosophy, and hope of a nascent constitutional global federation of democratizing states – with its telling headquarters in the centuries-old republic of Geneva, the internationalist "Protestant Rome" – lost its initial central role and credibility most clearly with the Lausanne Conference. From then, a new type of interwar realpolitik openly prevailed. In the text of the Lausanne Treaty itself, rule of law, human and minority rights, accountability, and democracy, if they were not simply erased, became secondary to the constraints of realpolitik. What prevailed, was the post-Ottoman pact between Europe's ageing national empires and Ankara's young nationalists on their way to a unitary party state. In 1913, their immediate predecessors, the committee of the Young Turks, had pioneered a dictatorial single-party rule inspired by a new imperial nationalism, namely (pan-)Turkism.[43]

All delegates at Lausanne's main negotiation table in 1922–3 desired to forget the former decade of late-Ottoman wars, extermination, and ethnic cleansing, although they did so for different reasons. Extreme internal, state-orchestrated or state-condoned violence had concerned Anatolia and Mesopotamia from 1914. There, the party-state of the Young Turks – an elite almost identical with their Kemalist successor except for the top leaders – had committed genocide: dispossession, removal, and killing of Armenians had stood at the center of the

---

[41] Rappard, *Geneva Experiment;* William E. Rappard, *The Crisis of Democracy* (Chicago, IL: University of Chicago Press, 1938).
[42] Walters, *History of the League of Nations*, 244–255.
[43] On this topic, see Part II and Kieser, *Talaat Pasha.*

3 Ultranationalism Appeased? 39

Young Turks' comprehensive policy of Islamizing and Turkifying that great area during the First World War. The main driver toward an attitude of active forgetting in Lausanne was, for the allies, to leave behind a dark and disputed chapter of wars, mass violence, and endangered post-war reconstruction in the Levant (an older name for almost the same area designated by the twentieth-century term Middle East). Domestic and intra-European challenges commanded full attention in the early 1920s.

As for the government in Ankara, foremost it feared the Armenian question, that is, that the Conference would come back to demands of justice for crimes against humanity, as detailed in the Sèvres Treaty. In its successful attempt to prevent the Conference from rediscussing extermination and expropriation of Ottoman Christians, Ankara's delegation exclusively stressed destructive acts by defeated Greece during the war for Anatolia. This and similar blame games have gone on in diplomacy until the present.[44] Immediately preceding the Conference, the Turkish counteroffensive had ended in the carnage and arson of Izmir in September 1922. There are strong arguments to put the issue of violence in all its aspects – including its successes, denial, internalization, memory, trauma, and frustrated justice – at the center of a study on the war-ending, deal-striking Conference of Lausanne.

A second disclaimer: This focus and the related fundamental critique of the Lausanne Treaty in this monograph do not per se involve the call for a revision of the Treaty, in particular not of then-determined state borders. In this regard, I maintain an old position: Steps notably toward a solution of the Kurdish question have to start from "partial autonomies within existing state borders in order to avoid border disputes with unforeseeable consequences."[45] This wisdom, however, from the ending twentieth century may lose its validity, if, disregarding the Lausanne Treaty, state actors violate borders by acts of aggression and expansion. Tellingly, figures around Turkish President Erdogan – or even Erdogan himself, a partisan of expansive Islamist "neo-Ottomanism"[46] – are the most prominent recent proponents of revised Lausanne borders.[47]

---

[44] See, for example, "Greek president stands firm on genocide remarks sparking Turkish ire," *Ahval*, 16 January 2022, https://ahvalnews.com/greek-turkey/greek-president-stands-firm-genocide-remarks-sparking-turkish-ire.

[45] H. L. Kieser, *Kurdistan und Europa* (Zürich: Chronos, 1997), 8.

[46] Neo-Ottomanism is a broadly used term for the ideology of Erdogan and his circle. It, however, sounds wrong in the ears of traditional Ottomanists, that is, scholars of the Ottoman Empire who use the term Ottomanism particularly for a common late-Ottoman constitutional patriotism.

[47] "Miçotakis'ten Devlet Bahçeli'ye harita tepkisi," *Cumhuriyet*, 11 July 2022. See also Nick Danforth, "Notes on a Turkish Conspiracy: How the Looming End of a 100-Year-Old

Notorious since the second half of the twentieth century, the dissatisfaction of Turkey's Islamists with what they decry as a measly outcome at Lausanne stands in stark contrast with how *Gazi* – meaning a leading Islamic war hero – Kemal Atatürk, Turkey's interwar leader, interpreted the Treaty. In his seminal 1927 speech, *Nutuk* – which in its printed version became the Kemalist bible of contemporary history – this former Young Turk general called the Lausanne Treaty "a political victory unprecedented in the history of the Ottoman era!" For him, "The questions brought forward at Lausanne's peace table did not exclusively concern the new regime [in Ankara], which was only three years old, but centuries-old [Ottoman] accounts were settled."[48] These and similar statements prove the centrality of the Lausanne Treaty for Ankara's political elite. This went hand in hand with what has later been called a "Sèvres Syndrome," namely, conspiracist allegations of a centuries-old Western complot against Turkey.[49] In this political mindset, claiming both unique victimhood and triumph, *Nutuk* states that the Lausanne Treaty ensured "the collapse of a great murderous plot prepared against the Turkish nation for centuries and thought to have been completed by the Treaty of Sèvres."[50]

For Kemal Atatürk, an immigrant to Ankara from late-Ottoman Saloniki (Greek Thessaloniki since 1912), the Turkish nation-state in Anatolia had to be the exclusive land of Muslim Turks after the Empire's loss of the Balkans. His contemporary "Turkish History Thesis" comprehended Turkishness in racial terms. Main claims of this – at last craniology-based and state-sponsored, but widely speculative – Thesis already played a defining role at the time of the Lausanne Conference. In a public speech in Adana during the Conference break in March 1923, the Turkish president pretended, "The Armenians do not have any right in this prosperous country. This country is yours, it belongs to the Turks. This country is historically Turkish, which means that it is Turkish and will remain Turkish forever." In this vein, for Atatürk, the Conference of Lausanne not only settled

---

Treaty Exposes the Existential Paranoia at the Heart of Erdogan's Foreign Policy," *Foreign Policy*, 2 October 2014, https://foreignpolicy.com/2014/10/02/notes-on-a-turk ish-conspiracy; Shatha Khalil, "Can Turkey Renovate Its Empire by the End of the Treaty of Lausanne 2023 ... " (Ammann: Rawabat Center, online publication 2017), http://rawabetcenter.com/en/?p=2571.

[48] Gazi Mustafa Kemal (Atatürk), *Nutuk* (Istanbul: Kaynak, 2015), 510.
[49] Baskın Oran, *Türkiye'de azınlıklar. kavramlar, teori. Lozan, iç mevzuat, içtihat, uygulama* (Istanbul: Iletisim, 2004), 160–162. See also Fatma M. Göçek, *The Transformation of Turkey: Redefining State and Society from the Ottoman Empire to the Modern Era* (London: I. B. Tauris, 2011), 98–184.
[50] Kemal (Atatürk), *Nutuk*, 534.

centuries-old Ottoman accounts, as underlined in the *Nutuk*, but also issues of several millennia. His Adana speech continued:

> This beautiful country has suffered foreign invasion many times since time immemorial. The Iranians, who in reality are Turks and Turanians, had annexed these lands. Afterwards, Alexander [the Great] defeated them ... and finally, pouring out from the middle of Asia, brothers from the Turkish race came here and restored life to its true origins. Finally [in 1923], the country has been confirmed in the hands of its original owners.[51]

What foreign academics and diplomats have read at times, in certain party programs or individual declarations, as signs of a voluntarist Turkish nation based on common culture and political consensus, clearly diverged from actual policy and the ingrained beliefs of the leading decision-makers at the historic hour of Lausanne.[52]

4 Armenia: When Violence Won and Democracy Died

For decades, scholars contented themselves by saying, "In the end the Allied Powers completely abandoned Armenia and the Armenians" (at the Lausanne Conference)[53] – without further comment and analysis. There was an "unresolved question" in the Conference's parlance, but after some poignant moments during the negotiation, it seemed no longer to belong to this world. *When Democracy Died*, however, takes it as a core element of Lausanne, thus paying attention to the abandonment of the weak on which after diplomacy, post-Lausanne academia too turned its back. This book includes and emphasizes this "other history of Lausanne."

The Armenia and related abandonments shaped macro-history on many levels. It is hardly a coincidence that during the rest of the twentieth century in socialist countries and beyond, fictive Armenian "Radio Yerevan" was in charge of all matters that could be addressed only by jokes, not frankly and directly. In the world after Lausanne, the Armenian question as a whole appeared as a sad, anachronistic joke. The Holocaust took place in a Europe and West amnesic of the Armenians, except for the Yiddish victims themselves. Only after the Holocaust did public political ethics change. However, things only changed for Europe where open

---

[51] Mustafa Kemal Atatürk, *Atatürk'ün Söylev ve Demeçleri* (Ankara: Atatürk Kültür Dil ve Tarih Yüksek Kurumu, 1997), vol. 2, 130–132 (hereafter Atatürk'ün Söylev ve Demeçleri).
[52] See Sections 12–13. See also Erik-Jan Zürcher, "The Core Terminology of Kemalism: Mefkûre, Millî, Muasır, Medenî," in H. L. Kieser (ed.), *Aspects of the Political Language in Turkey*" (Istanbul: ISIS, 2002), 105–116; Kieser, "Europe's Seminal Protofascist", 439–447.
[53] Nicolson, *Curzon: The Last Phase*, 316.

social-Darwinist contempt for the weak and defenseless was no longer acceptable publicly and in politics. The unconditional condemnation of a disparaged people's murder was made the doctrinal cornerstone of political ethics after 1945.

Outside Europe, in and for the post-Ottoman world, however, the spirit and politics of Lausanne lived on. When concluding the Lausanne Treaty, there had been many (disquieting) reasons for weak Western democrats to acquiesce in inacceptable ideologemes. No one embodied these more strikingly than Dr. Rıza Nur, the vice-chief of the Turkish delegation. He had acted as Ankara's first education minister and was one of its foremost representatives. "The Treaty of Lausanne has buried the Armenian question," he states in his derogatory *History of the Armenians*, a book manuscript he wrote mostly before and during the Conference. "The Armenian is weak and incapable. His impotence is established by his only 2,000 years-old [political] life and fate."[54] In contrast, so-called "Turanians" (thus Turks for the matter of Ankara and the delegation in Lausanne) were war heroes, state builders, pioneers of civilization as well as – an important argument – indigenous to Asia Minor and the Middle East for at least 4,000 years. "We Turanians, we are the pure, unmixed [indigenous] population."[55] In contrast, he categorized the Armenians as "foreign elements," that is, of foreign – non-Turanian – background.

There is not only an analogy with the Aryan obsession of Nazis a few years later and an overlapping of anti-Jewish and anti-Armenian racism, but from 1922, Nazis increasingly admired the successes of Turkish nationalism and looked for concrete recipes from the Turkish experience. With Lausanne, triumphant Ankara became the Nazis' number one paragon. By September 1922, it was Nazi belief that Turkish nationalism had shown "what we too" must do "to set ourselves free."[56] In November 1922, Adolf Hitler made explicit that he appreciated Atatürk and Mussolini as role models for Germany. In a Lausanne-induced amnesia, twentieth-century literature on Nazism ignored and omitted these early inceptions. Among a few exceptions are Theodor

---

[54] Rıza Nur, *Ermeni Tarihi*, Ottoman manuscript, 508 pages (Staatsbibliothek zu Berlin, Ms. Orient Quart 1394), 473. Cordial thanks to Yavuz Köse, Vienna, who has supplied me with a transcribed version of this text.

[55] Ibid., 459.

[56] Hitler's secretary Fritz Lauböck to Hans Tröbst, a German officer fighting for Ankara during the Anatolia wars; quoted in Thomas Weber, *Becoming Hitler: The Making of a Nazi* (Oxford: Oxford University Press, 2017), 275. The Turkish experience made Tröbst believe in the necessity of a reckless national savior and of eradicating "foreign elements." "For us Germans this heroic Turkish struggle is of utmost importance. We, too, must fight for our place in the sun again, whatever the cost. . . . Life issues are not solved by talk and majority decisions, but only by blood and iron": Tröbst, *Soldatenblut: Vom Baltikum zu Kemal Pascha* (Leipzig: Koehler, 1925), 329.

Adorno with his "Education after Auschwitz,"[57] and before him, of outstanding importance, Franz Werfel, the author of the documentary novel, *Forty Days of Musa Dagh*.[58]

In its Yiddish translations, Werfel's epic novel on the Armenian genocide accompanied hundreds of thousands of Jews during the Holocaust. The "most popular novel among the Adults in the ghetto" was for Turkish authorities and their press the reprehensible product of a greedy Jew.[59] They battled it more viciously and ferociously than the Nazis did. In the USA, Mehmet Ertegün – Ankara's leading legal advisor during the Lausanne Conference, before finally becoming a combative ambassador in Washington – succeeded in aborting the book becoming a Hollywood film and in censuring its American translation. Ertegün personifies the continuity from Young Turk leader and Grand Vizier Talaat Pasha to Atatürk, Talaat's successor, via Lausanne.[60]

During the Great War, Ertegün had been a collaborator of Talaat, the architect of Anatolia's genocidal Turkification. This is what German lawyer Carl Schmitt admired in the aftermath of the Lausanne Conference as the "reckless Turkish nationalization of the country," and what the German officer Hans Tröbst bluntly praised as the "Turkish proof" in the Nazi journal *Heimatland*: "The Turks have provided the proof that the purification of a nation of its foreign elements on a grand scale is possible." Concretely: "The bloodsuckers and parasites on the Turkish national body were Greeks and Armenians. They *had to be* [in bold print] eradicated and rendered harmless; otherwise the whole struggle for freedom would have been put in jeopardy." As a rule, "those of foreign background" in the combat area had to die.[61]

Werfel was a poet and novelist, but also a sensitive analyst of what he considered religion-like murderous totalitarian ideologies of his time, including Turkism, Nazism, and Bolshevism. He labeled Enver Pasha, the number two after Talaat, a "childish anti-Christ" who made the Armenians "plague bacilli" in a "world of nihilism with its ersatz

---

[57] In *Critical Models: Interventions and Catchwords*, trans. Henry W. Pickford (New York: Columbia University Press, 2005), 191–204.
[58] *Die vierzig Tage des Musa Dagh* (Berlin: Zsolnay, 1933).
[59] Arcadius Kahan, quoted in Roy Knocke and Werner Tress, eds., "Einleitung" to *Franz Werfel und der Genozid an den Armeniern* (Berlin: Walter de Gruyter, 2015), 1.
[60] Emmanuel Szurek, "Autodafé à Istanbul: La première crise négationniste de la Turquie nationaliste (1935)," forthcoming in *Cahiers de la Méditerranée* 2022. I thank the author for sending me this manuscript.
[61] Carl Schmitt in the preface to the 1926 edition of his *Die geistesgeschichtliche Lage des heutigen Parlamentarismus* (Berlin: Dunker und Humblot, 1926), 10–23. Hauptmann [Hans] Tröbst, "Mustafa Kemal Pascha und sein Werk (VI)," *Heimatland*, 15 October 1923, quoted in Stefan Ihrig, *Atatürk in the Nazi Imagination* (Cambridge, MA: Harvard University Press, 2014),85–86.

religions."⁶² Hitler, in contrast, exalted the same Enver as a pioneering hero who had introduced a "new spirit" of national rebirth in Istanbul, a city "contaminated by democratic-pacifistic, internationalized people." Hitler's defense during his trial in Munich in 1924 also praised "the insubordination of the Turkish general Kemal Pasha against the sovereignty of Constantinople" (i.e. the traditional Istanbul government), against which Kemal established the militant National Assembly in Ankara in 1920.⁶³

What most haunted the Nazis a decade before they publicly burnt the *Forty Days of Musa Dagh* in 1933, was the Armenian experience of victimhood and abandonment. Like Nur, they explained Armenian powerlessness by weakness and lack of combativeness. In Munich during the Lausanne Conference, early Nazis internalized the fear of "becoming like the Armenians," and concluded that adversaries of Germany must preventively be annihilated. The Conference's abandonment of the Armenians confirmed them in their stance. In an interview with a Munich newspaper at the end of December 1922, Hitler denounced the Jews as agents of Bolshevism and claimed, "A solution of the Jewish question must to be found." Otherwise, he warned, "the German people will become a [defeated and subservient] people like the Armenians or the Levantines" – what was a priori unacceptable and contemptible. Thus, it was clear for Hitler that "a bloody clash will follow" against Jews and Bolsheviks.⁶⁴

While Armenians and Jews belonged for Nazis and Turkish ultranationalist to the same category of inferior people, the Armenians, not the Jews, counted for Rıza Nur and his kind as the most despicable domestic enemies and foreign agents. The Armenians continued to haunt Hitler as the example of a "pitiful existence" that perpetration of violence had to prevent for Germany's future.⁶⁵ Nur was by no means alone with his social-Darwinist convictions and the Turanian tenets of his racial history. In varying degrees, he shared them with the nationalist press and most opinion and decision makers of his cohort, including delegation chief

---

⁶² Werfel, *Die vierzig Tage*, 191–192; " Können wir ohne Gottesglauben leben?" A speech given in 1932, quoted in Werfel, *Zwischen oben und unten* (Stockholm: Bermann-Fischer Verlag, 1946), 85 and 121.
⁶³ Quotations from Hitler's defense speeches in Ihrig, *Atatürk in the Nazi Imagination*, 97–98.
⁶⁴ Adolf Hitler, *Sämtliche Aufzeichnungen: 1905–1924*, in Eberhard Jäckel and Axel Kuhn (eds.) (Stuttgart: Deutsche Verlags-Anstalt, 1980), 775.
⁶⁵ Quoted in Max Domarus, *Hitler: Speeches and Proclamations 1932–1945* (Wauconda, IL.: Bolchazy-Carducci Publishers, 1990), 2779. Regarding the Armenians, Hitler was inspired by Erwin von Scheubner-Richter. Introduced to Adolf Hitler by Nazi ideologist Alfred Rosenberg, a native of the Baltics, Scheubner-Richter was one of the first National Socialists. During the Great War, he had been a vice-consul and witness of genocide in

4 Armenia

Ismet Pasha and supreme leader Kemal Atatürk. Racial claims also concerned, in particular, the Kurds. "They are not from Iranian roots, on the contrary, they are Turanians," the Lausanne correspondent of *Akşam*, a Turkish nationalist daily, wrote on 28 December 1922, in compliance with Ankara's delegation.[66]

In Nur's vision, all other – non-Turanian – peoples in Asia Minor and the neighboring Middle East, in particular the Armenians, "were only guests."[67] After 2,000 years of miserable existence, by 1915 "the Armenian" had "remained like a malign tumor in our [the Turk's] body and needed to be removed by a surgical operation," Nur – a surgeon by profession – concluded. For the likes of him, by 1923, the Armenians should finally have understood that "they lack any rightful claim in the presence of the Turk."[68] On the dark side of Turkish nationalism and the Lausanne Conference, the Armenians occupy a central place.

As we will see in more detail in Part II, Nur's historical-political thought is a mélange of Turan ideology, anti-Armenian racism, anti-Christian hate, anti-Semitism, genocidal violence, and denial of responsibility. All related to contemporary social Darwinism, these toxic ingredients had their seminal say in the making of the Lausanne Peace. A century after 1923, mindful scholars, diplomats, and public intellectuals have to face the facts, notwithstanding diplomatic convenience. There was a synergy of early Nazism with triumphant Turkism; and of contempt for the Armenians with that for the Jews. It is true that – starting at the eve of the Lausanne Conference as we will see – Ankara made use of Jewish and later also Israeli representatives for its politics of denial. Mutual opportunism on the back of the weak and the victims does not change basic truths, however.[69]

Erzurum. He there identified with the Armenian victims, but was therefore reprimanded by Turkish authorities and German superiors. After traumatic experiences in Bolshevik-attacked Riga, his home-town, this once upright young officer turned to exterminatory anti-Jewish and anti-Bolshevik radicalism and became Hitler's close collaborator. See also Weber, *Becoming Hitler*, 276–277.

[66] *Akşam Gazetesi Başyazarı Necmeddin Sadık (Sadak) Bey'in Lozan Mektupları*, ed. Mustafa Özyürek (Ankara: Gece, 2019), 187.
[67] Nur, *Ermeni Tarihi*, 456.   [68] Ibid., 473–474.
[69] For analogous opportunism during the 1910s, see Kieser, Talaat Pasha, 295–314. For new critical Jewish scholarship on this intricate theme, see Rıfat N. Bali, *Musa'nın evlatları, Cumhuriyet'in yurttaşları* (Istanbul: Iletisim, 2003), and Bali, *Devlet'in Yahudileri ve 'öteki' Yahudi* (Istanbul: Iletisim, 2004); Marc Baer, *Sultanic Saviors and Tolerant Turks: Writing Ottoman Jewish History, Denying the Armenian Genocide* (Bloomington: Indiana University Press, 2020).

5   A Pivotal "Peace" to Be Reassessed

With the wisdom of a century's hindsight, it is timely and worthwhile to radically rethink the aspects and consequences of the "enduring peace" brokered in Lausanne. It is time to include and tell "the other history" of Lausanne in a comprehensive historical approach hitherto lacking.

In a traditional Western reading of the Treaty, Lausanne's coordinates define Turkey's space of action and international behavior; they thus also underpin Turkish NATO membership that started twenty-nine years after the Treaty. In line with Ankara's new criticism of the Lausanne Treaty and its expansive Islamist neo-Ottomanism since the 2010s, this membership displays dysfunction to a degree never experienced before. This draws attention to the superficial character of long-held convictions. Conventional Western diplomacy and academia have considered the Treaty of Lausanne "the most successful and durable of all the post-war settlements," and the Republic of Turkey that rested on upon it, "the success story of the Near East," according to a British historian at the beginning of the twenty-first century.[70]

As for Lausanne's dealing with non-Turkish groups and with genocide, two political scholars at Princeton University worded the traditional approach half a century earlier, when "genocide" just had become an established legal and historical notion. A few years after the Holocaust, when Turkey was to join NATO, they wrote:

> With the definitive excision of the total Christian population from Anatolia and the Straits Area ... [the] processes of Turkification and Moslemization had been advanced in one surge by the use of force. ... Had Turkification and Moslemization not been accelerated there by the use of force, there certainly would not today exist a Turkish Republic, a Republic owing its strength and stability in no small measure to the homogeneity of its population, a state which is now a valued associate of the United States.[71]

Viewed through the prism of a beneficial geopolitical alliance, these US-American scholars in the aftermath of the Second World War considered extermination in the struggle for Anatolia, whose outcome had forced the revision in Lausanne, "a fight which could have only one winner. It was to be take all or lose all."[72] Lausanne informed a double speech of Western diplomats and applied scholars after 1945: on the one hand, post-Holocaust insights and ethics; on the other, bluntly continued

---

[70] Zara Steiner, *The Lights that Failed: European International History 1919–1933* (Oxford: Oxford University Press, 2007), 123–125. Same view in M. L. Dockrill and J. D. Goold, Peace Without Promise: Britain and the Peace Conferences,1919–23 (Hamden, Conn.: Archon, 1981).
[71] Lewis V. Thomas and Richard N. Frye, *The United States and Turkey and Iran* (Cambridge, MA: Harvard University Press, 1951), 61–62.
[72] Ibid.

5 A Pivotal "Peace" to Be Reassessed 47

post-Lausanne realpolitik and social Darwinism. It took many more decades until both the US Senate and House of Representatives remorsefully acknowledged, in late 2019, that they had left the Armenian Genocide unrecognized for reasons of diplomatic expediency.[73] Too long, there prevailed disinterest in, or ignorance of, what it really would have meant to lead Turkey, this fragile post-genocidal polity in the Middle East, to democracy.

In the vein of the quoted scholars, traditional diplomatic history also looked positively on the so-called Greek–Turkish population exchange that concluded (and implicitly endorsed) a decade of extremely violent demographic engineering in Anatolia. A model for the whole twentieth century, this compulsory transfer involving nearly two million people was considered a clear and clean solution for seemingly unending conflicts: After the end of Greater Europe's continental empires, different ethnic-religious populations should stop sharing territories. Though the recipe for official "unmixing" rested on a landmark decision taken in the first weeks of the Lausanne Conference, it was principally informed by Ankara's stance in line with demographic engineering during the Great War. Praise for the course set at Lausanne and for Ankara's diplomatic triumph in 1923 came also from very different quarters. Anti-colonialist and anti-imperialist narratives spread by Ankara's and Moscow's interwar propaganda were embraced by far-right nationalists to Muslim spokesmen, from Germany to Egypt, Iran, and India. Preconditioned by the outcome of the Conference itself, the positive judgment of the Treaty of Lausanne was reinforced in the Western world at the end of the Second World War, when Turkey took its place among the allies, and thus among the founders of the United Nations Organization. The victors applied the inauspicious recipe of unmixing populations in Eastern Europe.[74]

After democratization, Germany was integrated into a post-1945 Western world. In this case, democracy preconditioned stability, at least to a substantial extent. Lausanne's Near East Peace had worked differently. Tensions and contradictions during the Cold War, therefore, left a post-Ottoman space excluded from democratic reconstruction – because still based on the Lausanne settlement – particularly bereaved. Holocaust recognition and Armenian genocide denial; praise for democracy and embrace of autocracy; human rights talk and secret services' lessons in torturing; verbal support for rule of law in electoral democracies and involvement in putsches went all hand in hand during the Cold War

---

[73] www.congress.gov/congressional-record/volume-165/house-section/page/H8559-8568.
[74] Norman M. Naimark, *Fires of Hatred: Ethnic Cleansing in Twentieth-Century Europe* (Cambridge, MA: Harvard University Press, 2002).

in the Middle East. The post-1945, US-led alliances valued Turkey as their strongest partner there and treated the country – now a threatened neighbor of the Soviet Union, after having been the latter's close pre-1923 anti-Western ally – with care, concern, and an even more appeasing habitus.

This book takes stock of the preexisting interpretations. In addition, it exploits the benefits of hindsight, including the experience of an early twenty-first century that violently shook the Middle East, Turkey, the Caucasus, and Ukraine. Long-held assumptions about Turkey's post-Ottoman fundaments recently waned. Topics from a hundred years ago – like the caliphate, the Kurdish question, the Armenian genocide, the Straits, and border disputes from the Aegean to Mosul – have vigorously reemerged. Simultaneously, the Conference of Lausanne and its decisions have reentered debate from various sides. Among minoritarian

Figure 4 Negotiation table in a subcommission meeting. The American delegate Joseph Grew, standing, is reading a statement; at his right sits the British delegate Horace Rumbold. Vis-à-vis them, before the mirror, sit (from left to right): Rıza Nur, Ismet (Inönü) Pasha, Reşit Saffet (Atabinen), and (probably) Mehmet Münir (Ertegün) from the Turkish delegation. (Bibliothèque de Genève)

5 A Pivotal "Peace" to Be Reassessed

losers not sitting as Lausanne's table in 1922–3, debates had never ended. *When Democracy Died* is more than – or en passant only – an antithesis to a century of often diplomatically motivated praise in the political and academic establishment. Its analysis seeks to uncover the view of the historical node and milestone of the Lausanne Conference, in particular its "archeology" in the 1910s.

Criticism of the Lausanne settlement has existed since 1923 – voiced by legal scholars, minoritarian natives, and internationalist missionaries, on one side, and by Islamists who link Lausanne to the loss of the Ottoman sultanate-caliphate, on the other. In the interwar period, Islamic criticism was mostly raised outside Turkey,[75] but this changed markedly after the end of Kemalist single-party rule. Among the particularly victimized, though entirely disregarded in Lausanne, are the Ottoman Armenians of Anatolia. The Ottoman-Armenian population there had barely survived the genocide of 1915, and the Treaty virtually sacrificed the survivors, after the Conference excluded their delegation from sitting at the negotiation table. *When Democracy Died* takes seriously this and other sidelined groups' experience, and what we can learn from them. A century's retrospect provides an opportunity for a deepened and more circumspect history of the Lausanne Treaty.

Unaddressed trauma, denied justice, forceful exclusion, and the question of democracy are not consistently elaborated in traditional historiography. Since 1923, the Treaty of Lausanne is, on the contrary, as we have seen, generally appreciated as a solid and constructive diplomatic milestone; a compromise that made a clear break between before and after, war and peace, diplomatic collapse and repaired relations, old Ottoman and new Kemalist Turkey. Most presentations have put special emphasis on the fact that it was a "negotiated peace" and not, like the rest of the treaties in the Paris system, a peace imposed by the victors.[76] For many people on the ground, and for all survivors from Anatolia, it was, however, entirely a "peace" of victors, rulers, and perpetrators (see Figure 4).

---

[75] Notably by the prominent Lebanese writer Shakib Arslan, a former CUP collaborator; see Mehdi Sajid, *Muslime im Zwischenkriegseuropa und die Dekonstruktion der Faszination vom Westen: Eine kritische Auseinandersetzung mit Šakīb ʾArslāns Artikeln in der ägyptischen Zeitschrift al-Fatḥ (1926–1935)* (Berlin: EB-Verlag, 2015).

[76] For current works in this vein, see, for example, Roland Banken, *Die Verträge von Sèvres 1920 und Lausanne 1923: Eine völkerrechtliche Untersuchung zur Beendigung des Ersten Weltkrieges und zur Auflösung der sogenannten 'Orientalischen Frage'* (Berlin: LIT, 2014); William Hale, *Turkish Foreign Policy since 1774* (London: Routledge, 2013), 38–41; Steiner, *The Lights that Failed*, 123–125. For a diverging short piece, see Kieser, "Macro et micro histoire autour de la Conférence sur le Proche-Orient tenue à Lausanne en 1922-23," 42–48.

Part II Against the Paris-Geneva Peace: Bolsheviks, Turkists, Islamists

No study on post-Ottoman peace-making is complete without fully taking into account the last decade of the Ottoman Empire, its predominant radical ideologies, and its practices of rule. This last Ottoman-imperial phase was informed by the dictatorial party regime of the Committee of Union and Progress (CUP). A lot of solid research has been done in this formerly under-researched field during the last twenty years. Defining and seminal, the ideologemes and practices of the last Ottoman decade need to be carefully connected to the eventual negotiations and Conference outcome in Lausanne.

In terms of cadres and nationalist ideology, the CUP party-state – if curtailed – successfully transitioned into the new government in Ankara, its immediate successor, which, while it founded a new republic, rested on the achievements of its predecessor. Starting in 1913, a war-focused CUP implemented imperial single-party rule together with comprehensive demographic engineering. In terms of quantity (millions of citizens) and quality (genocide), this was a novelty in Greater Europe (i.e. in Europe including Russia and the Near East). The CUP's policy of centralization and Turkish–Muslim unification radicalized former Sultan Abdulhamid's politics of Islamic unity. It thus evolved into the genocide of unwanted Christian nationals. Although assassinated in Berlin in 1921, Talaat Pasha, the CUP's main leader, was present in Ankara through his former young cadres who took leading positions in the new government. Talaat's close political friend Ziya Gökalp, the party's chief ideologist, lived and worked in Ankara as a devoted servant of Mustafa Kemal Pasha (Atatürk) during the Lausanne Conference. He was, in the words of CUP finance expert Mehmed Cavid, "the incarnate representative of the CUP's spirit."[1]

At Western universities, comprehensive research free of blinkers into Turkey's history of violence and related ideology is relatively recent. The Ottoman Great War (1914–18), CUP rule, and the genocides committed

---

[1] Cavid, *Meşrutiyet Ruznâmesi*, vol. 4, 309, diary entry of 23 July 1921. See also Hans L. Kieser, "Europe's Seminal Proto-Fascist? Historically Approaching Ziya Gökalp, Mentor of Turkish Nationalism." *Die Welt des Islams*, 61 (2021), 411–447.

by this party-state largely remained a closed Pandora's box during the twentieth century. The Lausanne Conference indeed set effective limits in diplomacy and historiography, as its participants wanted to rebuild relationships and forget their dark recent past. While emphasizing the most contemporary events during the Graeco–Turkish War (1919–22), the delegates at the negotiation table underplayed the previous years, in line with Ankara's oversensitivity on this issue. Post–Great War peace-making, nevertheless, had been designed to be about the Eastern Question in general and about the wars and breaks since the early 1910s in particular. This was the initial challenge and one that remained unmet in many respects.

Part II summarizes the historical background of the Lausanne Conference, that is, the 1910s with the establishment of CUP wartime dictatorship and the Anatolia wars of the early 1920s. It leaves the Young Turk and Kemalist agencies the proactive center-stage in a holistic assessment of Lausanne and the genesis of the Conference. Predominantly composed of ex–Young Turks, the new organization of power in Ankara not only successfully enforced the revision of the Sèvres Treaty, but actually prevailed in the main aspects of peace-making in Lausanne. This Part describes the post–Great War conjuncture and coincidences that enabled these actors to impose, with Bolshevik support, a revisionist road from Paris-Sèvres to Lausanne. They battled the Paris peace treaty system in three arenas: militarily in Anatolia; by agitation in Europe; and, coordinating with Moscow, in the South Caucasus.

When Democracy Died takes the confrontation with the dark and extremist side of the Lausanne Treaty seriously. Before detailing the CUP legacy and the CUP-based struggle against the Paris-Geneva peace, Part II therefore looks at Ankara's vice-plenipotentiary, Dr. Rıza Nur. Minister Nur, Ankara's senior diplomat in Lausanne, signed the 1921 Moscow Treaty. His story and mind map show us, in medias res, an ultranationalism both religiously underpinned and profoundly racist. This and a pervasive Turanian imaginary – comparable to Aryanism in Germany ten years later – determined the sharply anti-Armenian politics of Turkish nationalism. Beforehand, Chapter 6 is a brief summary on how various aftermaths of war for the Ottoman world were imagined during war.

6 Projecting Aftermaths during a Decade of War

Before the Conference of Lausanne started, various visions of the aftermath of war were voiced, most of them finally frustrated. Few of them possessed the potential for democratic contracts in the Ottoman world, or at least in Anatolia. The constitutional patriotism of the 1908 revolution had run out of steam, followed, from 1911, by long years of war and internal violence. The "stimulus of war" always took precedence over political negotiation and consent finding. These were, however, prerequisites for constitutional futures. For Muslims in Anatolia after 1918, "nationalism meant primarily an armed struggle against Armenians, Greeks and Allies."[2]

From the First Balkan War, but with unique intensity from August 1914, the "new Turkey" (yeni Türkiye) was conjured up in visions produced in pamphlets, essays, novels, poems, discussions, and speeches. The authors were the mentors, writers, and leaders of a novel CUP party-state, established and centered in Istanbul from 1913. Because of Russia's imperial collapse in the Caucasus in 1917, the imagination of new and grandiose futures of national-imperial Turkey again proliferated toward the end of the Great War. Allied with Wilhelmine Germany, wartime Turkey's opinion leaders projected utopias that promised to restore and expand the Ottoman Empire and compensate for (supposed) Muslim victimhood since the eighteenth century.

Imagined by Ziya Gökalp and his circle of young adepts who met in the CUP headquarters in Istanbul, these visions were about a modern party-state cum Turkish-led bi- or tricontinental sultanate-caliphate.[3] While united by Islamic religion and Turkish culture, great Turkey had to be enlightened and empowered by Western science and civilization. During the First Balkan War, Gökalp had already linked his vision of progress with Lausanne at the Lake Léman where many Turks studied. In an influential poem, he imagined there a "Turkish village" to become the nucleus of education for Turkey. He called it "Kızılelma," Turkey's premodern symbol for the conquest of European metropoles. Although there is some self-critique, exalted pan-Turkism prevails in the poem:

> The science of the Turks, it is in free land/ That it wants to start to shine . . ./ Let us build a Turkish village, a city in Switzerland, from there/ A new stream, a river of enlightenment shall pour to Turan/ One day, indeed, this river will turn into an ocean/ Let the name of this city be Kızılelma/ . . . Next to Lausanne a Turkish city has flourished. A school for every science.[4]

In Kemalist interpretation, republican Ankara realized the utopian Kızılelma (i.e. the dreamed-of place of progress and civilization, engendered in Lausanne).[5]

---

[2] Joseph C. Grew, *Turbulent Era: A Diplomatic Record of Forty Years 1904–1945* (Boston: Houghton Mifflin, 1952), 885.
[3] For a synthesis, see Kieser, "Europe's Seminal Proto-Fascist?" 431–438.
[4] "Kızılelma," *Türk Yurdu*, 23 January 1913, transcribed ed. (Ankara: Tutibay, 1998), vol. 2, 118, and the chapter on Ziya Gökalp.
[5] Tekin Alp, *Le Kemalisme* (Paris: Librairie Félix Alcan, 1937), 24.

Opposite Turkism in power since 1913, indigenous Christian groups sought bare survival, while their representatives in exile lobbied for retributive justice and national renaissances. They spread the vision of Turkish misrule throughout history, imagining self-determined national futures in autonomous territories. In their hope of support by a liberal West, they were betrayed to inflated demands by the defeat of the Central Powers in 1918. "We had created a dense atmosphere of illusion in our minds," wrote Hovhannes Kajaznuni – a member of the Dashnaksutiun (Armenian Revolutionary Federation) and leading figure in the Republic of Armenia from 1918 to 1921 – during the Lausanne Conference.[6] Alexandre Khatissian, in contrast, underlined in his more serene retrospective, written in the late 1920s, the justice of the Armenians' main cause that was not lost but deferred to a far future. He agreed that there had been number of illusions, miscalculations, mistakes, and misplaced or inflated expectations. Khatissian had served in Kajaznuni's cabinet, but, in contrast to the latter, he was also a member of the united Armenian delegation in Lausanne. This delegation was composed of former representatives of the Republic of Armenia and of Paris-based diaspora leaders headed by Gabriel Noradounghian, a former Ottoman diplomat and liberal-conservative foreign minister, who took up the role of Boghos Noubar Pacha, the Armenian wartime leader in exile.[7]

After Turkey's official entrance into war in November 1914, the Entente powers (the Allies) nurtured conflicting designs. Britain, France, and Russia made up the secret Sykes–Picot–Sazonov agreements on how to divide the Ottoman Empire. These ranged from imperial realpolitik, including tricky promises in favor of their allies and associates, to the declared will to punish Turkish regime members for crimes against humanity. From late 1917, the Allies committed to Jewish and Armenian autonomies. Support for a Jewish "national home" in Palestine was declared in the same breath with support for Armenian "independence" including an eastern corner of Anatolia. The USA's entrance into, and Bolshevik retreat from, war was accompanied by anti-colonialist pledges on both sides. This induced a revision of openly imperialistic plans without annulling them. At the same time, numerous third parties – including the

---

[6] Hovhannes Katchznouni, *The Armenian Revolutionary Federation (Dashnagtzoutiun) Has Nothing to Do Anymore: The Manifesto* (New York: Armenian Information Service, 1955, written 1923), 6.

[7] Alexandre Khatissian, *Eclosion et développement de la République arménienne* (Athens: Editions Arméniennes, 1989, in Armenian 1930), 317–428.

pope, the Zimmerwald Socialist International, and representatives of neutral countries – tried to promote a general peace or separate peace treaties to bring a speedy end to the bloodshed. These actors were not able to achieve significant momentum, especially not in the Ottoman Empire where wartime leaders could not and would not bring into accord the expected outcomes of war and required compromises for peace.

As already alluded to, three main political world views emerged during the Great War. There was the Marxist-Bolshevik insistence on violent world revolution, most prominently preached by Lenin, a marginal member of the Swiss Socialist Party in Zurich, and – after his train travel from Zurich to St. Petersburg in April 1917 – in revolutionary Russia. There he enjoyed a great audience. A post-Tsarist constitutional-republican future had shortly shone up in the February Revolution in 1917, but was defeated by chaos and disciplined Bolsheviks.

The universal claim of Lenin's communism was contrasted by an equally universal, but liberal projection of the future – a global reordering to be led by democratic states and the latter's global constitution in a league. US President Woodrow Wilson was the most prominent promotor of this vision.

Less known in conventional Western history is the third way into the future that had forcefully emerged, but without global and pan-human appeal. At work in the imperial party-state that the CUP pioneered from 1913 to 1918 in the Ottoman realm, it may be called a proto-fascism and ultranationalism that preceded Europe's fascisms by a decade. Anti-Western and anti-minoritarian revanchism fueled an imperial Turkish-Islamic nationalism, embraced by the party and its press. Young imperial elites, self-declared modernizers, carried forward this late-Ottoman proto-fascism that "accepted the basic geopolitical tenets of nineteenth-century imperialism, while jettisoning its liberalism."[8]

Istanbul's wartime leaders could not and did not want to bring into accord expected outcomes of the Great War and the required compromises for peace before autumn 1918. They even preferred to take the risk of World War defeat, while anticipating a continued armed struggle. They prepared reorganizing power in the interior of Anatolia, far from the exposed capital, Istanbul. In continuity with the Great War, these élites and their provincial affiliates fought the war for Anatolia in the name of

---

[8] As Mark Mazower pointedly put it with regard to European fascists. Mark Mazower, *Dark Continent: Europe's Twentieth Century* (London: Penguin, 1999), 72.

the Turkish-Muslim nation and the Ottoman sultanate-caliphate. Their victory cancelled the territorial, political, and legal provisions of the Sèvres Treaty. It made the Kemalists negotiators on a par with the Western powers in Lausanne.

7 A Vice-Plenipotentiary's World of Thoughts and Sentiments: Dr. Rıza Nur

Dr. Rıza Nur (1879–1942), Ankara's senior diplomat in Lausanne, was a representative of pre-Lausanne ideology and also, in nucleo, of what, nearly a hundred years later, has (re-)emerged in Turkey as Eurasianism.[9] This section will show how representative the main lines of Nur's politico-historical thought were during Ankara's wars in Anatolia; for the Kemalist delegation in Lausanne; and more generally, for the elite that founded the Turkish nation-state.

In contrast to chief delegate Ismet Pasha, Nur was a founding member of the Ankara government and, by late 1922, already possessed considerable political experience. He was not as close to Gazi Mustafa Kemal Pasha (Atatürk) as General Ismet (İnönü), Atatürk's former subordinate, but he was one of Ankara's most influential figures in Lausanne (see Figure 5). Shortly before the Lausanne Conference, Ismet was appointed foreign minister. A year later, he was made prime minister of the newly declared Republic of Turkey, whereas Nur lost favor in Ankara by the mid 1920s.

A prolific writer, Nur publicly took a position against the Paris-Geneva peace from 1919.[10] He served as the first minister of education before taking other ministerial offices in Ankara's counter-government. Before, during, and after the Lausanne Conference, Nur authored books that lay bare his politically relevant historical imagination. He clearly explains why the immediate victory against Greece in Anatolia determined Ankara's stance in 1922–3 and how articulate racial and civilizationist arguments on the ancient past played a critical role at Lausanne's negotiation table. Both Turanian exaltation and victory over Greece (and thus for many in Ankara over "Christian Europe") were instrumental in suppressing or watering-down the near past of the Great War, its defeat, and its dark genocidal shadows.

Nur was central, not marginal, in 1922–3, although he disappeared from Ankara and Turkey in 1926, to return only after Atatürk's death.

---

[9] Suat Kınıklıoğlu, "Eurasianism in Turkey," *SWP Research Paper* 2022/RP 07, 22 March 2022, https://doi.org/10.18449/2022RP07.
[10] For biographical data on Nur, see George S. Harris, *Atatürk's Diplomats* (Istanbul: ISIS, 2010), 340–341; Ali Birinci, "Nur, Rıza," *Osmanlı Ansiklopedisi* (Istanbul: Yapı Kredi, 1999), 372–373. These brief biographies include further references.

Figure 5 Rıza Nur side by side with Ismet Pasha (İnönü, on his left side) and the British plenipotentiary Horace Rumbold (on his right side) in Ankara's hour of diplomatic triumph, 24 July 1923. Between Nur and Ismet Pasha is Hüseyin (Pektaş), the interpreter of Ankara's delegation, a graduate of the (American) Robert College in Istanbul. (Bibliothèque de Genève)

In a climate of growing autocracy, repression, and politically motivated persecution in the aftermath of the Lausanne Conference, Nur felt that he might happen to be on the receiving end of state violence. He therefore chose exile in Paris and afterwards in Cairo, while remaining in contact with ideologically like-minded writers like Reşit S. Atabinen. Although an early CUP member like so many other former students of the Military Medical School in Istanbul where he finished his studies in 1901, Nur had not been involved in the CUP party-state. After entering the Ottoman parliament as a CUP deputy of Sinop in 1909, he resigned from the party and moved between different currents, at times cooperating with Prince Sabahaddin's Liberal Party. When the CUP party-state was established and started to crack down on all potential political adversaries in 1913, he got a state scholarship and went abroad.[11]

---

[11] Rıza Nur, *Hayat ve Hatıratım*, ed. Abdurrahman Dilipak (Istanbul: İşaret, 1992), vol. 1, 402–403; hereafter Nur, *Hayat ve Hatıratım*. If not specified otherwise, references are to this 1992 edition.

7 Dr Riza Nur

The new center of power in Ankara rested mainly, but not exclusively, on CUP luminaries and affiliates. Nur returned at the end of the Great War and again became a deputy for Sinop, moving to Ankara at the beginning of 1920. He was of particular value there, as he shared radically nationalist positions, while serving as Ankara's fig leaf and show piece – not only for Western eyes, but also for people in Anatolia who had learnt to hate the CUP.[12] Almost all other high-ranking politicians and functionaries of the counter-government hailed from the CUP state. Moreover, the Bolsheviks had become familiar with Nur during his diplomatic work in Moscow in 1921.[13]

In contrast to Nur, Dr. Nihat Reşat (Belger), another member of the Turkish team in Lausanne, was of Kemalist use only in Western Europe until the Lausanne Conference, because he did not share hardline positions. Before daring to transition to Ankara's counter-government, everybody sought to appear as impeccably nationalist, anti-Entente, anti-liberal, and anti-minoritarian. Some published booklets to affirm loyalty and dissipate any doubts if, like Nur, they had had possibly dubious contacts or led questionable activities in the past.[14] Dr. Reşat was suspect for his closeness to the ostracized liberal leader Prince Sabahaddin, despite his commitment to Ankara's cause in Europe. More than other late-Ottoman Muslim leaders, Sabahaddin had enjoyed trusted relations with non-Turkish and non-Muslim groups, besides being pro-British.[15]

In Nur's case, xenophobic racism was less a means to accredit himself as a nationalist in Ankara, but rather came from deeper convictions. In many respects, he represented the dark side and, as it were, a significant political resource of the era's ruling group. This dark side comprised religious and racist hate or contempt and the embrace of violence. Nur's is certainly "a history of disease," both in the individual-mental and political sense. He blatantly lacked balance and wisdom, particularly the humble confidence to respect others. His obsession with racial grandeur and strength versus weakness and disease is, however, less an individual feature than a conscious embrace of social Darwinist biopolitics by

---

[12] Ibid., 557.
[13] Basri Bey (probably the Ankara deputy Hasan Basri Çantay), on visit in Geneva: "Many Turks regretted that he [Ismet] was accompanied by Riza-Nour, but the latter is persona gratissima in Moscow and, no doubt, it seemed to the Angora government that it was useful to secure the confidence of the government of the Federative Republic of Soviets by his choice. The foresight of the West must help the new Turkey to free itself from the onslaught of the Soviets. The signing of the peace agreement will help to defeat all extremists [in Ankara]." *Journal de Genève*, 179, 3 July 1923, 2.
[14] In this vein, Nur's *Hürriyet ve İtilaf nasıl doğdu nasıl öldü?* (Istanbul: Kitabevi Yayınları 1919).
[15] Cavid, *Meşrutiyet Ruznâmesi*, 205; Ahmed Bedevî Kuran, *İnkılap Tarihimiz ve Jön Türkler* (Istanbul: Kaynak, 2000; first ed., 1948), 449–450.

himself and his peers. Nur's testimony transcends the person himself and the nascent Republic of Turkey to which it is inscribed. Like many others, his pen whitewashes genocide and exalts perpetrators – notably Topal Osman, a sadist and one of the worst mass murderers of the period from 1915 to 1923.[16] Nur stands for a whole era and cohort. He labeled himself an "extreme Turkist nationalist" (şiddetli Türkçü nasyonalist) and anti-communist. Arguably a fascist, he became notorious as a vilifying enemy of Atatürk in the 1930s. Because offensive to the latter's memory, Nur's memoirs were legally banned in Turkey until the end of the twentieth century.

Dr. Rıza Nur hailed from a broad Gökalpian school of Turkish nationalism at the end of the Ottoman Empire. His basic thought was common to, and internalized by, Atatürk and the overwhelming majority of nationalists inspired by Turkism in the 1920s and early 1930s. Like others, but often more radically, Nur espoused an ultimate belief in Turkishness whose definition oscillated between Islamic, cultural, civilizational, and racial references. Like the others, he took an anti-minoritarian and – politically – anti-Western stance, believing in a splendid Turkish past. "After a brilliant civilization and unique conquests, Ottoman Turkey fell into a period of awful decline that lasted for two centuries."[17] Like Talaat Pasha and others in their memoirs, Nur insisted on the "true Turkish blood" (halis Türk kanı) without "intermingling of foreign blood" in his lineage, thus being himself a pure Muslim Turk.[18] Since the mid-twentieth century, ideologemes originating from the end of the Ottoman Empire have, via Nur and others, inspired currents that attempt at a reactionary refoundation of the Turkish state and the caliphate.

Most of Nur's related ideas have had a considerable political impact. His "party program" for a "total renewal of Turkey," dating from 1929, demanded Islam as the state's official religion; that women return to the hearth; the parallel use of both the Arab and the Latin alphabet; the restoration of the caliphate; the punishment of Kemalist leaders; the abolition of Kemalist (Atatürk-centric) national celebrations; the establishment

---

[16] Nur wrote a panegyric opera for Topal Osman. "With this work, I told an important episode of the national movement. One of my purposes is to keep alive the name of a Turk who has done service for the nation. This Turk is Topal Osman, a national hero. A nation should know those who serve it, love it and keep it alive in their memory.... This example is to teach Turkish generations heroism, effort and sacrifice for the sake of Turkishness." Quoted in the first edition of Nur's *Hayat ve Hatıratım* (Istanbul: Altındağ, 1967), 28. Because of a ban in Turkey, this first edition was reprinted in Frankfurt by K. G. Lohse.

[17] This is how the prologue of his 1929 party program starts. See 1967 edition Nur's *Hayat ve Hatıratım*, 10.

[18] Nur, *Hayat ve Hatıratım*, vol. 1, 73–74.

of a "race directorate"; the establishment of missionary lodges spreading Islamic pan-Turkism; and a confederation of "all Turks" (in line with Gökalp's Great War vision). A first more comprehensive public debate of Rıza Nur and his work emerged in the early 1960s, when his unpublished works were partly made known, although they still remained unedited.[19]

***

Nur's memoirs are a valuable source. Finished in the late 1920s, they were published in a censured version in the 1960s in three large volumes, one of them dealing with the Lausanne Conference. To be sure, as highly subjective retrospective texts, memoirs are not particularly reliable on facts, but they reveal an author's mental world.[20] Of particular interest for *When Democracy Died* is a contemporary 76,000-word manuscript in Ottoman Turkish, entitled *Armenian History* or *History of the Armenians* (Ermeni Tarihi). According to its prologue of May 1918, Nur wrote the text in Cairo during the Great War. But its last thirty-five or so pages were certainly written later, as were other passages on previous pages. During the second half of the Lausanne Conference, Nur found time to enhance the manuscript and tasked a secretary of the delegation to copy-edit it.[21]

The Prologue begins: "There are a number nations living among us in our country who are less numerous than we are. But time and again, they stand up against the Turks with their national claims and spirits. They want to exterminate the Turks and take the Turks' place."[22] Nur labels his work a "patriotic service of the first order," because it would inform "the Turk" about the emptiness of the minorities' claims enshrined in the Paris-Geneva peace. Enlightened by Nur's presentation, "the Turk can better defend his own right." The derogatory, even exterminatory, condescension and racism in Nur's *Armenian History* is almost unparalleled for a book that gives itself a scholarly outlook, quoting Western authors as much as he could. "All that I say are the words of European authors," he asserts, with a considerable degree of exaggeration.[23]

---

[19] See several related articles in the Turkish press in 1963–4, reproduced in Nur, *Hayat ve Hatıratım*, vol. 1, 31–68. See notably Cavit O. Tütengil, "Gizli kalmış önemli bir belge," *Cumhuriyet*, 9 March 1964, 2, reproduced in ibid., 36–40. The party program is partly reproduced in the 1967 edition of *Hayat ve Hatıratım*, 9–17, and in full extent in vol. 2, 463–532, of the 1992 edition.

[20] Nur, *Hayat ve Hatıratım*, vol. 2. See also Hülya Adak, "Who Is Afraid of Rıza Nur's Autobiography?" in Olcay Akyıldız, Halim Kara, and Börte Sagaster (eds.), *Autobiographical Themes in Turkish Literature: Theoretical and Comparative Perspectives* (Würzburg: Ergon, 2007), 125–141.

[21] Rıza Nur, *Ermeni Tarihi*, handwritten Ottoman manuscript, 508 pages (Staatsbibliothek zu Berlin, Ms. Orient Quart, 1394), 3–4. Added parts appear to start on page 473, but pages 422–428 are clearly added under the title "The Armistice and the Lausanne Treaty." See Nur, *Hayat ve Hatıratım*, vol. 2, 411.

[22] Nur, *Ermeni Tarihi*, 267.   [23] Ibid., 13, see also 424.

In its racial approach, this unpublished book manuscript overlaps with Nur's best-known historical work, his fourteen-volume *History of the Turks* (*Türk Tarihi*), published with Ankara's ministry of education after the Conference of Lausanne (except the two last volumes).[24] Whereas in the 1910s and early 1920s, he made do with emphasizing the Turks as racially belonging to the "Turanians," in line with Gökalp, in *Türk Tarihi* he started to insist on the Turks' racial whiteness. "The Turks are from the white race; beautiful, with healthy body, and perfect brain, they have talents equal to Europeans in terms of art and civilization and are even a higher race. They are the most outstanding nation in the world. Only, they need to be educated."[25]

Minister Nur brought to the Lausanne Conference a mindset and historical universe that was extremely racist and civilizationist even in the context of European discourse in the early 1920s. His thought requires careful analysis in any account of Turkish nationalism and the Lausanne Conference. Our first encounter with him in the Introduction of this book, made clear that he was a hardliner who frantically believed he had found an ultimate anchor in Turkishness. Nonetheless, he remained a vehement seeker and researcher. "My only ambition is to serve the Turks and science until I die," he wrote in the prologue to his memoirs in 1929.[26]

Although by no means "in every way a thorough, scientific mind,"[27] Nur exposed himself in his memoirs more disarmingly and in-depth than a multitude of other contemporary nationalists who also wrote their memoirs. This includes the frank and shameful confession of his failed attempt, as a student of medicine, to rape a niece in his parents' house in Sinop. Passages in his memoirs express existential aporia. "What ugly creatures are humans. ... What to do? I do not know."[28] Emotionally vulnerable, attached to his revered mother throughout his life, Nur believed himself to be outstandingly intelligent, trained, and educated. Complacency, conceit, and narcissism mark much of his writing. Emotional vulnerability cohabits with essentialist nationalism and merciless extremism.

His blunt frankness makes his often-resentful memoirs an interesting insider source, at times even a voice of truth. One example is a criminal act in Lausanne, hushed up by the local authorities. "I was awakened because

---

[24] Rıza Nur, *Türk Tarihi* (Istanbul: Toker Yayınları, 1994), vols. 1–12, 14 vols. originally published 1924–6 by the ministry of education.
[25] Nur, *Türk Tarihi*, vol. 11–12, 428.   [26] Nur, *Hayat ve Hatıratım*, vol. 1, 69.
[27] Philipp Wirtz, *Depicting the Late Ottoman Empire in Turkish Autobiographies* (London: Routledge, 2017), 26 and.
[28] Nur, *Hayat ve Hatıratım*, vol. 1, 145–146.

Zekai raped the maid in his hotel. The woman fought back, but Zekai forced her. The woman tore Zekai's face and bit his finger. When she got rid of him, she went right to the police. The chief of police didn't make it official," thus allowing for a settlement of money through delegation secretary Reşit Saffet, as ordered by Nur.[29] Delegation counselor Aziz Zekai (Apaydın), Nur's close colleague, was a founding member of the National Assembly and several times a minister in Ankara until his death in 1935.

In his early ministerial office in Ankara in 1920–1, Nur came to meet and admire Topal Osman Agha who knew only one creed: "I am a Turk and Muslim. . . . Yes, I work to save the Turk and the religion from the infidels." Topal was an uneducated man, but an efficient killer of Rûm (Greek-Orthodox Ottoman nationals) and Alevi Kurds. "How splendid" that Osman Agha was "both pious and Turkist." Minister Nur admonished him during the genocide of the Pontus Rûm, "Agha, cleanse thoroughly the Pontus. . . . Destroy also the churches and take their stones far away, so that, just in case, nobody can say that there were ever churches here."[30] A few years later, in exile, Nur reproached Atatürk for having for years benefitted from Osman Agha, who, besides his genocidal commitments, served as Atatürk's personal guard in Ankara. The commander-in-chief and leader of the national Assembly had Osman shot on 2 April 1923, after the latter had served as a useful, but finally inconvenient mass killer. Shortly before his death, Osman Agha had arranged the assassination of Ali Şükrü, Atatürk's gifted adversary in the National Assembly. This happened during the heated interval of the Lausanne Conference.[31]

By and large in line with Gökalp's verbose and convoluted, but thoroughly essentialist articulation of nationalism, Nur's salient trait is his self-declared anti-Christian Turco-centrism. "For some reason or other, I have an eternal and unquenchable love for the Turkish Nation and a great ambition to serve it," he declared in the prologue of his memoirs.[32] As if spoken from his own heart, Nur quoted passages from the French novelist Pierre Loti. In exoticizing, sweepingly idealizing sentences, Loti associated all humanly noble traits with the "really genuine Turks. They are right, righteous, spotlessly honest, committed to their parents with infinite esteem, clean, unfailingly hospitable," etc.

Who comes from Europe and mingles among Turks, immediately becomes aware that they quietly live in trust and peace. One has the impression that they live in

---

[29] Nur, *Hayat ve Hatıratım*, vol. 3, 265–266. [30] Ibid., 163–164.
[31] Ibid., 163; Andrew Mango, *Atatürk* (London: John Murray, 1999), 381–384.
[32] Nur, *Hayat ve Hatıratım*, vol. 1, 69.

the golden age. They have only one fault. When Muslims are in danger, they blindly and fanatically make war. Yet, what shall they do? ... The Armenians, these big spoilt children, do every minute evil against the Turks.[33]

The flipside of Nur's exalted love of Turks and Turkishness was a pronounced hate of the Armenians. "Look, the Armenians are since a thousand years the enemy of the Turk and the Turk's religion. The Armenians wanted to create metastases in the Turk's body, they aimed at poisoning the Turk and to reach a vicious plague-like power position."[34] "The Armenians live among us totally separated from Turkishness and Turkish currents of ideas."[35] "Between the Turks and them there is age-old hatred. It is absolutely impossible to overcome this ill will."[36] Contradictorily, Nur's nationalist hate also told a story of deceived, allegedly abused love. "We Turks knew the Armenians as closest to us among the non-Muslim peoples.... We had warmed up one to the other. They got along with the Turks like siblings. ... But we were duped. We Turks are unwary people."[37]

Nur's hate disguised envy and a multitude of fears. Armenian proximity to the American Protestants and the latter's educational institutions in Anatolia was one of them. "These American schools are all dens of mischief."[38] All their liberal-democratic reform demands were for him nothing other than a subterfuge for getting Armenian independence from the Turks. He suspected an American conspiracy promoting the alliance of Armenians, Alevis, and Kurds. Armenian centers of education from Istanbul, Merzifon, and Etchmiadzin to Venice, Geneva, Paris, Calcutta, and the USA were all "dens of mischief against the Turks."[39]

While he often compared them to Jews, Nur's hate and contempt targeted primarily the Armenians and other Christians. "Their oldest and most respected national historian is a Jewish ignoramus," he opined in his presentation of ancient Armenian history.[40] "They are like the Jews a wretched and dispersed people. ... Like the Jews, they had to live under the domination of other nations ... and could only commit themselves to commerce. ... Since ever, this people is infatuated with swaggering about pleasure and pomp."[41] All what Nur considered as bad, he related to the Armenians. He qualified them altogether repetitiously as "shrewd," "malicious," "seditious," "very egoistic," "uncivilized," "dirty," "immoral," "full of body hair," "imitators" (of other nations' cultural achievements), "hardworking but stupid," and "their language the most

---

[33] Nur, *Ermeni Tarihi*, 378–379. The passages are from Loti's *Les massacres d'Arménie* (Paris 1919).
[34] Ibid., 473.   [35] Ibid., 487.   [36] Ibid., 382.   [37] Ibid., 387.   [38] Ibid., 370, 415.
[39] Ibid., 311–317   [40] Ibid., 10.   [41] Ibid., 239 and 268.

7 Dr Riza Nur

crude of the world."⁴² They were admittedly "the world's most oppressed people" – however, by their own fault and lack of political talent. "Lacking any true patriotism" since ancient times, with some exceptions in the modern era, "they are restless like the Jews. Both peoples' obstreperousness and bad character invite disaster upon them. Thus, they were always crushed and ... massacred."⁴³ He insisted, without evidence, that most Armenians in their heartland at Lake Van had descended from "Jewish captives, abducted from Palestine" in the first century BC.⁴⁴

***

"It appears that being massacred is the Armenians' historical fate." For Nur, Jews and Armenians belonged to peoples that were dominated, suppressed, and massacred throughout millennia – and this was their fate and largely their own fault. "The reasons for the massacres of the Armenians are to be sought in the Armenians themselves." The reasons were the "Armenian national character traits of selfishness ... disloyalty, treason, boisterousness and readiness to be instrumentalized by foreigners."⁴⁵

Nur's rejection of any blame and scandal regarding the Armenian genocide thus consisted not only – as is usual in Turkish nationalist apologias – in emphasizing allegedly overwhelming Armenian wrongdoing and/or denying factual extermination and state responsibility. But it comprised also an almost voyeuristic, repetitious mentioning of innumerable humiliations and decimations that unavoidably must afflict an "unfit people" (in social Darwinist terms) throughout the ages. "In history, they were unable to display any strength as brave soldiers."⁴⁶ To Riza Nur, Armenian demography pointed to their political weakness. He labored to prove that Armenians formed almost everywhere in Asia Minor and beyond only comparatively small or even insignificant minorities.⁴⁷

His conclusion was entirely social Darwinist, far from any understanding of an egalitarian and democratic, law-based polity.

> It is against nature that a Christian people, which is a minority only, lives in Asia Asia Minor and the Caucasus. Such a people is like an alien body [cismi-i ecnebi] in Asia. For the Armenians, there is no solution except to bow to the unavoidable heavy consequences of this unnatural state; or to convert to Islam; or to disappear.⁴⁸

Besides lacking any rights of self-determination based on numerical and historical considerations, the Armenians had proved martially inferior, thus devoid of any right of the sword and conquest with which the

---

⁴² Ibid., 267, 270, 286–287, 290, 335, 444, 481.   ⁴³ Ibid., 153, 482.   ⁴⁴ Ibid., 226.
⁴⁵ Ibid., 426–428.   ⁴⁶ Ibid., 438.   ⁴⁷ Ibid., 226–235, 250–259.   ⁴⁸ Ibid., 490.

superior Turks were honored.[49] Readers must keep in mind that in Lausanne, Nur was to lead Ankara's delegation in the sub-commission on minorities, including the question of an Armenian home.

In Nur's account, anti-Armenian violence in late-Ottoman Turkey appears as an episode, although he concedes, "The Armenian were utterly routed during the World War. For the Armenian nation, which has been routed by Persians, Romans, Byzantines and Arabs since BC, this disaster ranks among the great disasters."[50] However, he argued, the CUP had long behaved too tolerantly toward the Armenians.[51] What they suffered happened within a given perpetual historical scheme of mass violence that they had to suffer as a weak people. They were a priori doomed and must always know their inferior place. "It is very regretful that the Armenians did such bad things against the Turkish fatherland and the Turks, thus provoking Turkish reaction. . . . Every people, including the Armenians, has the right to national sentiments and to revolutions toward achieving independence. . . . But if they fail, the consequences of such efforts are fatal. . . . One must bear them."[52]

"During the war starting in 1914, they the Armenians have totally perished. Their number has gone down to nearly zero." The "reason of their affliction was their imprudence."[53] As a result, "there were no longer Armenians in Turkey" in 1918, and the West "could no longer ask rights for the Armenians from the Turks."[54] Abandoned by the Europeans, the Armenians were given "the last lesson and last stroke" at the Lausanne Conference, as he wrote during the Conference.[55] Nur's manuscript delves into "the events of 1914–1915" on dozens of pages and reflects efforts to blame the victims.[56] These passages are largely based on the CUP's 1916 propaganda book *The Armenian Revolutionary Aspirations and Movements* whose plot he copied. Interior minister and architect of genocide Talaat Bey (the later Pasha) was the book's spiritus rector and provided tailored documentation that turned the historical narrative upside down.[57]

---

[49] Ibid., 454. [50] Ibid., 422. [51] Ibid., 331–333. [52] Ibid., 376. [53] Ibid., 437.
[54] Ibid., 377–378. [55] Ibid., 424. [56] Notably: Ibid., 339–403.
[57] *The Armenian Revolutionary Aspirations and Movements* is the translated title for *Ermeni amâl ve harekât-ı ihtilâliyyesi tesâvir ve vesaik* (Istanbul: Matbaa-ı Amire, 1332/1916). Esat Uras was involved in the making of this fundamental official apologia published in Ottoman, French, English, and German in 1916–17. On Uras' involvement, see German journalist von Tyszka to the Undersecretary of State in the Foreign Office, Zimmermann, Istanbul, 1 October 1915, German Foreign Office Archive, DE/PA-AA/R14088, and Talin Suciyan, "Can the Survivor Speak?" in H. Kieser, Pearl Nunn, and Thomas Schmutz (eds.), *Remembering the Great War in the Middle East* (London: I. B. Tauris, 2021), 276–279.

"As soon as the plan for the rebellion in Anatolia was completed, the Armenian civil population expected the day of their rebellion. ... Everywhere it became manifest among the Armenians that rebellion was now close. ... In the churches, they prayed for the victory of the Russian and the English."[58] Armenians committed atrocities, arson; they stabbed the army in the back and desecrated cemeteries and houses of worship, while "from our side no such things were done."[59] Finally, they all were deported. "As for the Armenian population outside the war zones, these too had collectively rebelled where they lived." As for desperate Armenian resistance against annihilation, "one must not forget that they had prepared the rebellion well before the war."[60] Like a dogma from which all depended, he repeated this tenet: "However, previous was the Armenian rebellion."[61] If this was not true, Nur's house of cards falls. His Turanian phantasmagorias were equally built on sand.

8   "We Turanians": A Pervasive Ideology and Argument

All aforementioned arguments and ideologemes were to influence in varying degrees the vice-chief and his team in Lausanne. The envisioning of the ancient past of Asia Minor and its neighborhood as Turanian was, however, particularly relevant at the negotiation table. It not only informed the outlook of the Turkish delegates sitting there, but also of Mustafa Kemal, the commander-in-chief during the wars in Anatolia, Turkey's upcoming supreme leader whose instructions directly defined the position of the delegation in Lausanne in critical situations.

The sweeping argument of Turanian indigenousness and descent was cognate to Gökalp's grandiloquent and vague, but seminal myth of Turan. He understood it as the Turk's "great and eternal homeland" between Europe and China. On the first pages of Nur's *Armenian History* – which was intended to address an educated post-1918 Turkish public – we read, "The history of the Armenians is not important, because the Armenian people is not important. Since that is the case, the Armenians have not produced important events in their history." A few lines later, follows that the name of Ararat – the Armenian's holy mountain, as it were – "descends from a Turanian [Turan cinsinden] nation that lived in that region before the Armenians." For Nur, the Armenians were thus immigrants "coming from Thessaly" (in Greece) to a place where Turanians had lived for millennia.[62] In contrast, "We Turanians, we are the pure, unmixed indigenous population."[63]

---

[58] Nur, *Ermeni Tarihi*, 342–343 and 350.   [59] Ibid., 372.   [60] Ibid., 374–375.
[61] Ibid., 389.   [62] Ibid., 7–9, 273.   [63] Ibid., 459.

In Nur's Turanian vision, only the Turks possessed "national and historical rights" in places historically called Armenia and diplomatically claimed as such in Paris-Geneva. "On the contrary, that land belongs to the Turanians. They are its legitimate owners. It is more correct to call those places Turan, Turkey and Turkistan."[64] He insisted in stressing the Turanian argument and referred to speculations of contemporary European authors.

This proves that since 4000 or at least since 2000 B.C., the true autochthonous population in Central and Eastern Anatolia, on the whole Black Sea Coast and in the Caucasus and on the territory which is now called Armenia are the Turanians. ... Look, on the land called Armenia, our forefathers the Turanians lived from a historically unknown time, but at least since 4000 years until 300 B.C., that is 3700 years, and 900 years later we Turks lived there again until today, that is for 3700 years. Well, our lineage lived in Armenia since 4700 years. ... The Armenians lived there only under the condition of being minoritarian. For two centuries only they possessed states, whereas the Turanians lived there always as state-builders and as a majority.[65]

The Sumerians, Hittites as well as Urartu – the name of "Ararat" might hail from the kingdom Urartu at the Lake of Van, established in the ninth century BC – were of particular interest to Nur's cohort of politician-historians. In the Turanian vision, the Armenians – not medieval Turkic people – were Anatolia's immigrants and invaders. Thus, the recent removal of Armenians from Anatolia did nothing more than restore the historical rights of the Turks. Notably, Armenians allegedly penetrated into the territory of a Turanian Urartu.[66] For serious scholars, there is a well-documented history of medieval Turkic immigration into Asia Minor, but not of Turkic settlements there before. Contemporary linguistics falsified the claim of Sumerians and Hittites as Turkic. But this knowledge had escaped the attention of, or was ignored by, those who amply proffered the argument of ancient Turanians or proto-Turks from the 1910s to the 1930s. During the debate on Mosul at the Lausanne Conference, plenipotentiary Ismet Pasha used the Turanian argument to claim the Kurds, including the Yazidis, as members of the Turkish nation (see Part III). Nur's cohort of Turkish nationalists generally claimed the newly discovered, or recently rediscovered, ancient oriental peoples as Turanian. Sure enough, this assumption was speculative, wrong, or fictive, both in narratives by a few European authors in question, and even more so in the statements of the interested Turkish historian-politicians who made use of them.

---

[64] Ibid., 454.   [65] Ibid., 463–465.   [66] Ibid., 19.

Meant seriously or used for the purpose, the Turanian vision of ancient history served as a critical political argument in the context of the Lausanne Conference. The striking contemporary faith in the Turanian vision is evident from Nur's memorandum to President Wilson and other Western statesmen, dating from 1919, in which he again ostentatiously emphasizes European sources.[67] While in this memorandum, Nur somewhat restrained his social Darwinist depreciation of the Armenians, he appears to fully believe in the racial, historical, civilizational, and demographic value of the Turanian argument. The memorandum's goal was to substantiate the nationalist claim: The Armenians had no right whatsoever of self-determination in parts of the eastern provinces or Cilicia. The memorandum gives an account of millennia of Anatolian history in which Armenians allegedly played only a very marginal role, and – with the short-lived exceptions of Tigranes the Great's kingdom and a Cilician kingdom backed by the Crusaders – only rarely enjoyed very limited self-rule in small regions. Their fate was to be dominated by greater nations. In a somewhat absurd turn – given the Armenians' alleged insignificance – he then stated that, with the invading Seljuks (i.e. from the eleventh century AD), "the Turks again took back the homeland that the Armenians had robbed from their ancestry" (i.e. the indigenous Turanians).[68]

Nur's historical-political thought demonstrates the entanglement of Turan ideology, Turkish nationalism, anti-Armenianism, social Darwinism, "naturalized" genocide, and the denial of responsibility for perpetrated evil. Within this entanglement, the Armenians take center stage. In his manuscript, Ankara's vice-chief delegate in Lausanne states with outright satisfaction that during the Great War, "combats with Turks, deportation, flight, migration, death by illness and massacre have terminated the Armenians in Turkey." In his additions to the manuscript, he underlined that Lausanne also finished them off in diplomacy.[69] For him, force and violence had to triumph, and they finally triumphed, also at the Conference. On this outcome, Nur therefore expressed perfect satisfaction in terms that overlap with those used by Atatürk in his fundamental 1927 speech, the so-called *Nutuk* (see Part IV). In Nur's words:

We signed the Treaty. Now, I think, we have given the nation the peace that we have sought throughout depressions, but that sometimes resembled a dream flying out of our hands. And this with great profit, with great honor. We reckoned with nine centuries of Turkey's Seljuk and Ottoman history and made the

---

[67] The memorandum is reproduced in Ottoman language in Nur, *Ermeni Tarihi*, 499–508.
[68] Ibid., 501–502.   [69] Ibid., 259.

necessary corrections. We dealt with all of Europe. Now we enjoyed satisfaction. ... This treaty is so important. It has eliminated the contaminations and mistakes, piled-up by Turkey's sultans and leaders during six or seven centuries. It threw them away, freed Turkey from every condition and made her a completely independent and European [Avrupâi] state.[70]

However, in his retrospective on Lausanne, Nur found also fault with compromises. This partial dissatisfaction of a main insider – combined with his radical Islamic Turkism, his supposedly scientific approach, and a peculiar personal frankness – is why Rıza Nur posthumously became a central reference for Lausanne Treaty revisionism in Turkey. Tellingly, Kadir Mısıroğlu, one of the editors of Nur's memoirs in the 1960s, later wrote Turkey's main revisionist interpretation on the Lausanne Conference and Treaty.[71] Nur's critique of Lausanne included these words:

However, this perfect treaty has a flaw. We gave freedom to the Bosporus instead of full Turkish control, we could not give autonomy to Western Thrace, we could not get reparations from the Greeks, we could not take the Turks of Iskenderun into our borders, and Mosul was left to be settled later.[72]

***

Nur's Turanian arguments were in tune with other contemporary Turkish authors. They prove the fundamental use of pseudo-history for the politics of Turkifying Asia Minor in the 1910s and early 1920s already, that is, more than a decade before Atatürk's "Turkish History Thesis." An example is a late-1922 book, very probably written by Ahmed Ağaoğlu. He insisted, the "Turkish race has been present in Anatolia since the oldest and most unknown times," "the first inhabitants of Anatolia were Turanians," many "dynasties have ruled these people under various governments," and "the Rûm and Armenians, however, arrived later in Anatolia."[73]

According to Ağaoğlu's lectures at the University of Istanbul and work published in June 1913, "proto-Turkish" Hittites, were the ancient rulers and true precursors of exclusive Turkish rule in Anatolia.[74] These were erroneous speculations and a false lineage fabricated by politicized historians

---

[70] Nur, *Hayat ve Hatıratım*, vol. 2, 445–447
[71] Kadir Mısıroğlu, *Lozan: Zafer mi, hezimet mi?* (Istanbul: Sebil, 1992; first eds., 1965–79), vols. 1–3.
[72] Nur, *Hayat ve Hatıratım*, vol. 2, 447.
[73] Ahmed Ağaoğlu, *"Mukaddime" to Pontus Meselesi* (Ankara: Matbuat ve Istihbarat Müdüriyet-i Umumiyyesi, 1922), quoted in Can Erimtan, "Ottomans and Turks: Ağaoğlu Ahmed Bey and the Kemalist construction of Turkish nationhood in Anatolia," *Anatolian Studies*, 58 (2008), 150–162.
[74] Ahmed Agayef (alias Ağaoğlu), "Türk medeniyeti tarihi," *Türk Yurdu*, 2.140 (new edition: Ankara, 1999), 303–307.

who started to serve power in Ankara after having frequented the CUP headquarters for years. By 1915, serious scholarship had already proven that Hittite was part of the Indo-European family of languages. The crucial point is that distorted history directly impacted on politics, as in the case of Ağaoğlu's book on Pontus. It assured nationalist leaders that they had acted rightly by exterminating the Pontus people. Immediately after the Lausanne Conference, Gazi Kemal boasted before the National Assembly in a long self-appraisal that under his leadership Armenia had been decimated. Turning to the issue of "the Pontic Government" he said: "It was to be established on the most beautiful and richest shores of the northern Black Sea, but has been completely eliminated together with its supporters."[75]

Nur and Ağaoğlu's cohort revolted against the fact that the others' historically proven presence went back millennia, while Turks entered Anatolia in medieval times. The Rûm in Pontus had claimed self-determination according to the League's initial gospel. Another young historian, Mehmet F. Köprülü, a protégé of Gökalp in the early 1910s, published a *History of Turkey* in 1923 that Gazi Kemal himself owned and praised. For Köprülü, as for Nur, "The Turks' deeds in world history are so lofty that they cannot be compared to those of any other nation." Alleged greatness and indigenousness underpinned the nationalists' exclusionary claims. Köprülü's and his cohort's narrative made Turks a heroic master race spreading from China and India to Europe, Arabia, and Africa. Everywhere, therefore, where "Turkish blood" flowed. Köprülü also insisted on rejecting any association of Turks with the "yellow race."[76]

In Kemal Atatürk's political view during the Lausanne Conference, and in his "History Thesis" afterwards, the argument of Turanian, or proto-Turkish, indigenousness and civilizational grandeur was a cornerstone. During the interval of the Lausanne Conference he went on a provincial tour in view of new elections, visiting several towns, emphasizing the salvation of the nation thanks to the recent victories, and suggesting links with millennia of local Turkish history. He was particularly explicit in formerly French-occupied Adana. In a speech on 16 March 1923, he made Turanian claims in full compliance with Nur:

> The Ottoman government has, finally, become a thing of the past, but had unfortunately promoted for centuries a wrong mentality: they did not like to see craft and business emerging from their Muslim peoples, even the majestic Sultan

---

[75] "İkinci dönemi açarken," 13 August 1923, in *Atatürk'ün Söylev ve Demeçleri*, vol. 1, 336.
[76] Köprülüzade (Mehmet Fuat Köprülü), *Türkiya Tarihi: Anadolu istilasina kadar Türkler* (Istanbul: Kanaat Kütüphanesi, 1923), 4–6. For Gökalp and Köprülü as reacting to other contemporary, notably Balkan historiographies, see also Dimitris Stamatopoulos, *Byzantium after the Nation: The Problem of Continuity in Balkan Historiographies* (Budapest: Central European University Press, 2022).

Suleiman the Magnificent.... Armenians have invaded our places of craftsmanship and behaved as if they were the owners of this country. No doubt, there is no bigger injustice and impertinence. The Armenians do not have any right in this prosperous country. This country is yours, it belongs to the Turks. This country is historically Turkish, what means that it is Turkish and will remain Turkish forever. It is true that this beautiful country has suffered foreign invasion many times since time immemorial. The Iranians, who in reality are Turks and Turanians, had annexed these lands. Afterwards, Alexander defeated them and took over the country.... Afterwards, the Romans invaded, then East Rom, that is the Byzantines, got them, until the Arabs came and chased out the Byzantines; and finally, pouring out from the middle of Asia, brothers from the Turkish race came here and restored life to its true origins. Ultimately, the country has been confirmed in the hands of its original owners. Neither the Armenians nor anyone else has any right here whatsoever. These blessed lands are a truly and thoroughly Turkish country.[77]

Mustafa Kemal's speech reacted against (by then obsolete) claims to self-determination by non-Turks. He thus justified the de-Christianization and de-Armenization of Cilicia, inspiring confidence in his Muslim audience. Muslims had to take up functions in craft and commerce that they first had to learn. In line with Nur's *History of the Armenians*, Kemal argued that making entire Anatolia a unitary Turkish state amounted to restoring an original prehistorical habitation by Turanians.

In the words that immediately follow the quoted passage, Kemal combined the historical argumentation of Turkism with Islamic rhetoric. His Turanian argument thus still went along with insistence on Muslim identity and solidarity, Ankara's real force of coherence during the war. He praised Adana's men for having made Friday a holiday, and thus fulfilled a duty of the sharia. He stressed common sense and warned against false religious teachers. He emphasized Muslim identity as distinguished from non-Muslim unbelievers such as Armenians and their foreign supporters, enemies of the Turkish-Muslim project in Anatolia. "Elhamdülillah praise God, we are all Muslims, we are all faithful," he exclaimed. Thus, he still stuck to Islam in provincial Adana in 1923, yet took his distance from the Ottoman Empire because of the place it had left to Armenians. His rhetoric had immediate serious consequences for the local Christians, who were boycotted by the Muslim majority, intimidated, and forced to close their shops on Fridays.[78]

---

[77] *Atatürk'ün Söylev ve Demeçleri*, vol. 2, 130–132. For Izmir, see ibid., 88; for Samsun, ibid., 204.

[78] Maurice Herbette, sous-directeur d'Asie-Océanie, to the Turkish legation, Paris, 30 March 1923, *Documents Diplomatiques Français 1923*, I, 370.

9 At an Empire's Long End: CUP Rule Defeated, Nationalist Struggle Continued

In late 1922, the press close to Ankara did all it could to win the trust of "every Turk and Muslim" for the Turkish delegation's effort in Lausanne, applying an anti-European rhetoric the public was used to since 1911.[79] This last long Ottoman decade, dominated by the ideas and cadres of the CUP, defines the contemporary background of the Lausanne Conference.

Virtually all cadres in Ankara hailed from the CUP, including a few who had fallen out with the CUP party-state. Those Muslims who identified with Ankara's wars in Anatolia – but also by and large with those previously waged by the CUP – were distrustful of any compromise. They tended to reject territorial concessions at peace talks with Western powers. Their pan-Islamic solidarity, stressed by all rulers since Sultan Abdulhamid II, comprised loyalty to the caliphate that had to be preserved. Their fear of the caliph's weakening or abolition was very tangible when the Lausanne Conference started. Though making him a representative – now no longer *ruling* – figure, the CUP had fought its wars in the name of the imperial sultan-caliph, as did the Kemalists, very explicitly, until fall 1922.

In the years before the Young Turk Revolution in 1908, the CUP had become the strongest underground organization within a broad Young Turk opposition that rejected Sultan Abdulhamid II and his "despotism." While modernizing the late-Ottoman Empire infrastructurally, this last *ruling* sultan had started to exploit the potentials of global pan-Islamism and domestic Muslim nationalism in his autocratic politics of Islamic unity. Side by side with the Armenian Revolutionary Federation, the CUP organized the constitutional Young Turk Revolution of 23 July 1908, which, as historian Hamit Bozarslan insists, did not hail from popular revolutionary awareness and organization, but from a threatening declaration (*pronunciamiento*) by the CUP central committee, supported by army officers. The sultan was thus compelled to reinstall the first (1876) Ottoman constitution and accept revisions. That resulted in a brief liberalizing and democratizing "Ottoman spring."[80]

---

[79] Necmeddin Sadık, "Lozan Mektupları: 27–28 Kanûn-i Evvel 1922," in Mustafa Özyürek (ed.), *Akşam Gazetesi Başyazarı Necmeddin Sadık (Sadak) Bey'in Lozan Mektupları* (Ankara: Gece, 2019), 197–198.

[80] Hamit Bozarslan, *Histoire de la Turquie: De l'Empire à nos jours* (Paris: Tallandier, 2013), 226. See also Kieser, *Talaat Pasha*, 65. For this whole chapter, see Kieser, *Talaat Pasha*, 61–180.

The CUP, however, was not serious about constitutional rule in a shrinking Empire that faced European imperialism, intra-Ottoman nationalisms, and political rivalries. It therefore soon evolved into a cartel of power that betrayed the true friends of constitutional patriotism. During the Balkan Wars (1912–13), the main CUP leaders embraced a Turkish-Islamic nationalism that combined the rallying power of Abdulhamid's Islamism with a new Turkism whose ethnonationalist appeal galvanized educated élites. This became an explosive and warmongering mix of imperial revanchism, (pan-)Islamism, and (pan-)Turkism. "As representatives of the ruling nationality [millet-i hâkime] who have the army behind them," these rightist Young Turks wanted "to be and remain nationalist centralists," as contemporary observers, liberal- or socialist-minded (among them the young journalist Leon Trotsky), noted. They rejected a state "on democratic-federal basis, Swiss- or American-style," while embracing a "pseudo-realistic skepticism" and "counter-revolution."[81]

The new authoritarian power cartel of the CUP excluded non-Muslims as such, not only the political rivals and former collaborators in the revolution (some exceptions prove the rule). It mustered the CUP members in the capital und provincial towns together with xenophobic urban notables and reactionary Sunni lords in the countryside. Most of these had rejected the 1908 constitution. Country-wide repression of dissent, and a press and mosques brought into line, helped mobilize malleable, opportunistic, docile, and fearful crowds. Based first on religion and, second, on race and ethnicity, it began to implement restrictive conditions of belonging to the state and the state's nation in 1913.[82]

From 1913, the CUP party-state sought to restore the Empire by external war, to regain lost territory (see Map 1), and internal "war" (boycotts, pogroms, expulsion, genocide) against Ottoman Christians. War- and violence-prone in this comprehensive way, the radicalized party rulers attempted to conduct an ultranationalist social revolution. In its social Darwinist language, the non-Muslims counted henceforth as foreign elements in the body of the Turkish-Muslim polity. Both extremist and corrupt, CUP rule allowed for individual enrichment of party members and the preservation or expansion of vested privileges by

---

[81] Leo Trotzki, *Die Balkankriege 1912–13* (Essen: Arbeiterpresse, 1996), 30 and 174.

[82] There is a line from the Crescent Committee in 1906 – the exclusively Muslim predecessor of what was redefined as the more inclusive Ottoman Liberty Committee – that prefigured the CUP central committee of the 1910s, to the early, exclusively Muslim reorganization of ex-CUP power under Mustafa Kemal in the congresses of Erzurum and Sivas in 1919.

9 At an Empire's Long End

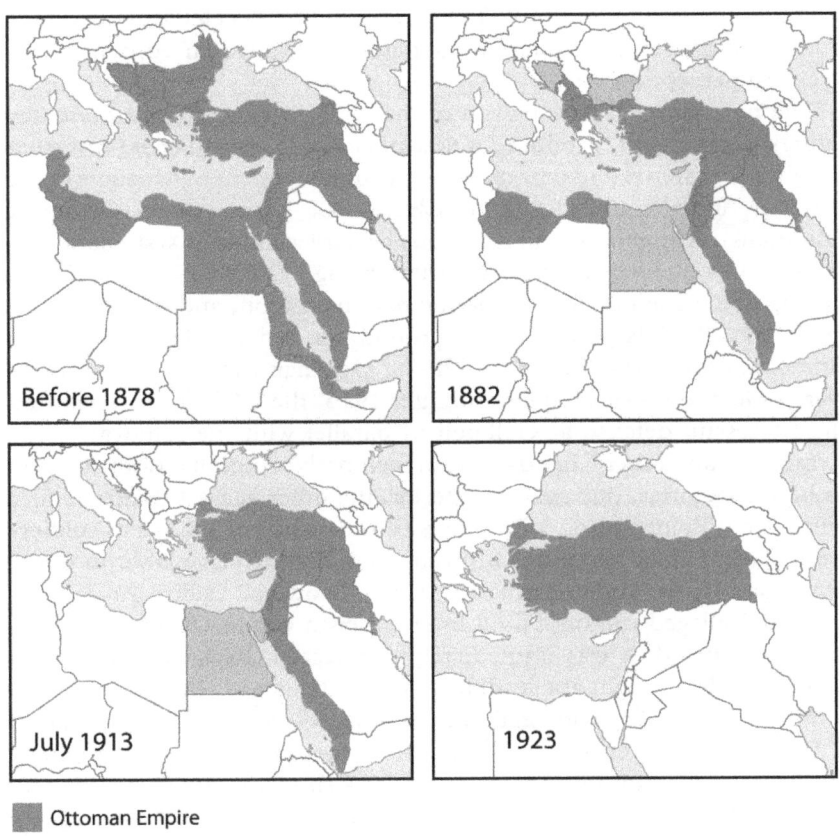

Map 1 From the late-Ottoman Empire to the early-republican Turkey: before 1878; after 1878; 1913–14 (Egypt was administered by Great Britain from 1878, but it was still Ottoman before November 1914, Libya was invaded by Italy in 1911); 1923 (the Lausanne borders of the Republic of Turkey). In 1939, Antakya and Alexandretta in Northwestern Syria were added to Turkey

conservative acolytes in the provinces. In an Ottoman Empire turned party-state, Interior Minister Mehmed Talaat predominated politically, his friend Ziya Gökalp ideologically. Both men were long-standing members of the CUP central committee. War Minister Enver Pasha can be counted the political number two in the central committee, Navy Minister Cemal Pasha number three. Enver had lived in Berlin and spoke German, and, because Wilhelmine Germany celebrated Enver as a political and military star, he generally prevailed in contemporary Western perception.

The new imperial nationalism of the CUP in general, and these key figures in particular, produced a new policy of "national economy" that sought the material and entrepreneurial empowerment of Muslims at the cost of indigenous Ottoman Christians. Rûm (Greek-Orthodox Ottomans), Armenians, and Assyrians became victims of systematic dispossession, removal, and genocide from spring 1914. By 1918, the CUP's demographic engineering, economic nationalization, and cultural monopolization had largely laid the ground for unitary Turkish rule in Anatolia, notwithstanding the CUP-led Ottoman Empire's defeat in its war at Germany's side. In late summer 1915, the CUP press celebrated the successful defense at Gallipoli in parallel with the removal of the Armenians and other Christians from their native Anatolia. Both counted as heroic victories, one against exterior, the other against domestic foes and aliens. Before being killed, tens of thousands of Christian soldiers were used in labor battalions for what amounted to slave labor in transport, road repair, and construction work. Bloodshed against *gavûr* (infidels) and alleged traitors raised little criticism within Ottoman society, and when it did, it was immediately suppressed. Berlin timidly raised objections, but sought above all not to alienate its war ally.[83]

When the CUP ship sank in autumn 1918, discussions around Turkey's future intensified. CUP activists, propagandists, and diplomats left Istanbul for Europe and chose the Turkish Home Associations there as a main vessel to remobilize the diaspora for the nationalist cause. They also reactivated the pan-Islamic networks of the Great War and played the card of Muslim solidarity. In 1919, after months of political depression, confusion, and fermentation in Istanbul and the European diaspora, a broad nationalist front began to crystallize. On the shores of Lake Geneva (Lake Léman), ex-CUP nationalists resided side by side with leaders and sympathizers of the liberal wing, most of them exiled CUP opponents.[84] In the decisive year of 1919, the liberals failed to promote their cause and to prevail against ex-CUP currents. In the eyes of the nationalists, liberals compromised themselves by agreeing to cooperate with the postwar Ottoman government in Istanbul, which depended on

---

[83] Kieser, *Talaat Pasha*, 258–94; Erik J. Zürcher, "Ottoman Labour Battalions in World War I," in H. Kieser and D. J. Schaller (eds.), *The Armenian Genocide and the Shoah* (Zurich: Chronos, 2000), 187–195.

[84] See Orhan Koloğlu, *Aydınlarımızın Bunalım Yılı* (İstanbul: Boyut Yayınları, 2000), and H. L. Kieser, *Vorkämpfer der "Neuen Türkei": Revolutionäre Bildungseliten am Genfersee* (Zürich: Chronos, 2005), 82–98.

the victorious Allies. Most liberals had opposed participation in the Great War, thus excluding themselves from the *ummah* or (Ottoman) *ümmet*, the Muslim community under the sultanate-caliphate. The *ümmet* formed the main basis in Anatolia for the continued struggle.

The key event that mobilized nationalism both domestically and in the diaspora was the Allied-approved Greek invasion of Izmir in May 1919. This coincided with a Turkish-nationalist congress in Lausanne that focused on the project of a Turkish state in the whole of Asia Minor. The program that resulted from this congress brought to the fore progressive ideas nurtured in the local *Foyer Turc* (Turkish Home Association, *Türk Yurdu Cemiyeti*) at the expense of the role that political and public Islam had still played in the CUP party-state.[85] Mahmut Esat (Bozkurt), the president of the Turkish Home Association in Lausanne, and his comrade Şükrü Saraçoglu, the president of the Turkish Home Association in Geneva, took the Greek campaign as a call to arms and departed back to Anatolia. Since armed resistance against the Greeks corresponded to Italian expansionist interests in the Eastern Mediterranean, their trip to Izmir was organized by an Italian agent. Their career in the resistance was short-lived however: Mustafa Kemal summoned both of them to Ankara where, barely thirty years old, they were made members of parliament before becoming ministers.

What most seriously threatened CUP achievements and thus unitary Turkish rule in Anatolia after Great War defeat, were the postulates of justice; the return of surviving Armenians to their homes in Anatolia; the restitution of properties; and the prosecution of perpetrators. These issues forcefully emerged at the peace conference in Paris. The Treaty of Sèvres (10 August 1920) included them, but without providing for the operational power to implement them. The moral guarantor of the Paris Treaties, the League of Nations, was left without the support and membership of the USA, the strongest and most promising Western power after Europe's catastrophe in the Great War. The US Senate rejected the Treaty of Versailles and its built-in Covenant of the League of Nations on 19 November 1919. Half a year later, it voted against an American mandate for Armenia.[86] Without appropriate means, the League was

---

[85] Friedrich Schrader, "Das Jungtürkische Lausanner Programm," *Die Neue Zeit* 38.2 (1920), 6–11, 31–35.
[86] On 1 June 1920. See "Senate Rejects the Treaty of Versailles," www.senate.gov/about/powers-procedures/treaties/senate-rejects-treaty-of-versailles.htm. See also Lloyd E. Ambrosius, "Wilsonian Diplomacy and Armenia: The Limits of Power and Ideology," in Jay Winter (ed.), *America and the Armenian Genocide of 1915* (Cambridge: Cambridge University Press, 2003), 141.

not in a position to investigate injustice and to engage in a democratic reconstruction of Anatolia, according to League principles.

Former cadres in and outside the country immediately scented the opportunities for action despite defeat in the World War. Under CUP ex-general Mustafa Kemal Pasha, later Atatürk, the former forces started to reorganize in the eastern provinces. There intact army units waited for orders, and regional notables feared Armenian claims. Kemal benefitted from timely CUP preparations and armed networks. He soon enjoyed overwhelming support in the army, the nationalist intelligentsia, and among all those in the provinces who had sided with, and profited from CUP rule. Moreover, his rhetoric of heroic defense of the sultanate-caliphate against Western-Christian intruders assured him the general backing of Sunni Muslims, including Kurds. In early 1920, the National Pact (*Misaki-i Millî*) enshrined the sacrosanct tenet, "the seat of the Caliphate must be sheltered from any attack."[87]

CUP agents and leaders in European exile built up centers for propaganda and agitation, supported by new or already existing nationalist and/or pan-Islamic diaspora associations. They demanded the whole of Anatolia as Turkish homeland in line with former CUP policy, thus failing to balance rights of other natives with their own national cause. Most Rûm, Armenians, and Assyrians, in turn, rejected Turkish overlords after the experience of war, deportation, and genocide. Ex-CUP propagandists and associated young activists countered the maximalist demands and the shrill voices of minoritarian victims. They used former war propaganda, depicting Turks and Muslims as the most victimized in modern history in general and, from 1919, by the Paris Peace Conference in particular. Their propaganda sidelined and disparaged the most vulnerable groups in Anatolia: Armenian genocide survivors, Kurdish Alevis close to them, and other victims or liberal dissenters of CUP rule. In 1919–20, threatened populations and dissenters had to endure the reestablishment of provincial forces in power under the CUP. The upcoming counter-government in Ankara enabled them to reorganize. The Allied Western victors did not occupy larger parts of Anatolia, while the postwar liberal-conservative governments in Istanbul remained weak in the country's interior. Civil war in Russia, political turmoil in continental Europe, and hunger crises in the defeated countries as well as in Russia absorbed

---

[87] Kemal's pre-1924 writing, religious rhetoric abounds, for example, in the documents collected in *Atatürk'ün Söylev ve Demeçleri*, vols. 1–3, and in Kemal Atatürk, *Nutuk: Vesikalar* (Ankara: TTK, 1991). For the transliterated Ottoman version of the National Pact, see Sefer Yazıcı (ed.), *Millî Egemenlik Belgeleri* (Ankara: TBMM Basımevi, 2015), https://tr.wikisource.org/wiki/Misak-ı_Millî_Beyannâmesi.

9 At an Empire's Long End

the West's and League's attention. Western actors lacked the means and the will to take action.

The best informed and most prominent agitator abroad, the former CUP party boss and grand-vizier Talaat Pasha in Berlin, corresponded with the nationalist forces and Mustafa Kemal. Though not very close, both men were long-standing acquaintances and respected one another. Until summer 1918, Talaat had fully bet on German World War victory. During his visit to Berlin in September 1918, he had belatedly understood the reality of German defeat and domestic crises. He was quick in reorienting himself and prepared to go underground again after the Armistice of Mudros. His subversive networking and agitation in the years before 1908 had given him considerable experience in this field. As the leader of the Ottoman delegation at the Conference of Brest-Litovsk in early 1918, he knew the Bolshevik leadership well, in particular Karl Radek, a member of the Russian delegation close to Lenin and Trotzki. A member of Talaat's delegation in Brest-Litovsk was the young lawyer Mehmet Münir (Ertegün). He proved a skillful expert in Ankara's delegation in Lausanne.

Talaat understood the need for anti-Western synergies in rebuilding Turkish power; he therefore sought contact and straightforward collaboration with the Bolsheviks. A good opportunity for him was the presence of Karl Radek in Berlin. Sent by Lenin in the hope of expanding the Bolshevik revolution to Germany, Radek had failed to do so during the Spartacus uprising and was arrested. Germany was far from ready for a Marxist revolution, though Lenin wrongly believed it to be. From August 1919, in view of his transfer back to Moscow, Radek remained under protective military arrest. Such a comparatively privileged situation continued until early January 1920 and allowed him to receive visitors at discretion, among them the industrial leader and later Chancellor and Foreign Minister Walther Rathenau. Radek thus contributed to both the German and the Turkish rapprochement with Bolshevik Moscow. His efforts resulted in the Treaty of Moscow between Kemalists and Bolsheviks (1921) and the German–Russian Treaty of Rapallo (1922). The fact that Berlin's authorities, instructed by the foreign office (Auswärtiges Amt), planned to fly Radek to Moscow in autumn 1919 together with Enver Pasha, sheds light on the origin of entangled developments. These resulted in effective anti-Western, anti-"Paris-Geneva" synergies.[88]

---

[88] Otto-Ernst Schüddekopf, "Karl Radek in Berlin: Ein Kapitel deutsch-russischer Beziehungen im Jahre 1919," *Archiv für Sozialgeschichte*, 2 (1962), 87–166. In parallel to the rapprochement in Berlin, Bolsheviks contacted Kemal's Pasha, the leader of the

From early August 1919, Talaat was among Radek's first visitors and paid several visits to him in Moabit prison. Radek writes, "Within a few days my cell had become a political salon.... Two of my first guests were the former Grand Vizier Talaat Pasha, the head of the Young Turk Government, and his War Minister Enver Pasha.... [T]hey were planning how to conduct the further defense of Turkey." Enver maintained his relationships with his German comrades in the army and, according to Radek, "was the first to bring home to the German militarists that Soviet Russia was a new and growing world force with which they would have to count, if they in fact meant to struggle against the Entente." Talaat "kept saying that the Moslem East could free itself from slavery only with the support of the popular masses and an alliance with Soviet Russia." Radek learnt from Enver and Talaat that Kemal Pasha "was leading the defense of Turkey after her defeat in the world war" and that he was "compelled to dissociate himself from the fallen Young Turk regime," but that "there were no earnest divergences between them, and they were organizing help for him abroad." Radek "tried to persuade them to go to Russia, which in fact Enver Pasha did later on."[89] Arriving from September 1920, and well established from late spring 1921, financial and military support by the Bolsheviks proved critical for the war waged by the Turkish nationalists.[90]

Radek continued to build bridges to militant nationalist groups who, in his view, "walked into the void," if left without the universal aspiration and horizon of Marxist-Leninist communism.[91] Nationalists who led armed struggles as well as groups then labeled "national Bolsheviks" in Germany[92] should be won over for the Moscow-based Communist International (Comintern), the League's ideological competitor, to expand the scope of action of internationally isolated Bolshevik Russia. As we have seen, the Bolsheviks' primary focus on Europe and Germany shifted, by 1920, to Middle and Far Eastern, notably Islamic peoples, all

---

nascent nationalist movement, as early as the June 1919 meeting in Amasya (resulting in the "Amasya Circular") of the upcoming nationalist leaders. See Stefanos Yerasimos, *Türk-Sovyet Ilişkileri: Ekim Devrimden Milli Mücadeleye* (Istanbul: Boyut, 2000), 105–106 and 123; see also Mehmet Perinçek, *Atatürk'ün Sovyetler'le Görüşmeleri: Sovyet Arşiv Belgeleriyle* (Istanbul: Kaynak Yayınları, 2005), 35–36.

[89] *Die Zukunft*, no. 19, 7 February 1920. Partial English translation in www.marxists.org/archive/radek/1926/november/ch08.html. Full text and further documents in Schüddekopf, "Karl Radek in Berlin," 152–153.

[90] Yerasimos, *Türk-Sovyet Ilişkileri*, 101–312. See also Ankara's foreign minister Bekir Sami, in a conversation with Cavid Bey, diary entry of 27 June 1921, Cavid, Meşrutiyet Ruznâmesi, vol. 4, 304.

[91] Karl Radek, "Leo Schlageter: The Wanderer into the Void," Speech at a plenum of the Executive Committee of the Communist International, June 1923, www.marxists.org/archive/radek/1923/06/schlageter.htm.

[92] Otto-Ernst Schüddekopf, *Nationalbolschewismus in Deutschland 1918–1933* (Frankfurt: Ullstein, 1972).

henceforth labeled "oppressed," and therefore supposedly predestined for revolutionary violence, even if they were antidemocratic oppressors themselves.

In his continued search of expanded opportunities for revolution in Germany – a revolution the Bolsheviks still desired – Radek welcomed acts of sabotage both by far-right Freikorps members and communists against the Versailles peace. He welcomed protest from both sides against the occupation of the Ruhr on 11 January 1923, that is, during the Lausanne Conference.[93] As we will see, the French occupation of the Ruhr in the long aftermath of the Versailles Treaty seriously troubled the ongoing Conference and deflected international attention from peace-making for the Near East in a critical phase. What united disparate camps and the leaders of the "peoples of the east" was primarily the rejection of the Paris-Geneva peace, not viable projects based on universal values. Included in the "peoples of the east" were the Indian Muslims of the Khilafat Movement who supported revolutionist Ankara. Like most other Muslims all over the world, they believed that the Turkish nationalists under Gazi Kemal Pasha struggled for a continued re-empowered sultanate-caliphate in Istanbul.[94]

10 Defying the Paris-Geneva Peace Project, Forcing the Road to Lausanne

Ex-CUP cadres and upcoming Kemalists drew little inspiration from Marxist authors – except claiming class struggle for attacks against, and dispossession of, Christian conationals.[95] But they shared with Bolshevists the desire for a powerful modern state, a sovereignty unchecked by the League and Western powers, and a unified society beyond classes. In both cases, in the name of a greater cause, the leader-led collectivity took precedence over individual rights.

Without seeking adherence to the Comintern, the struggle for sovereign Turkish rule in Asia Minor sought maximal benefit from a globally emerging polarization after 1917. Turkish leaders found scope of action in the tension between the West and Bolshevik Russia; between

---

[93] Schüddekopf, *Nationalbolschewismus*, 108–38.
[94] Gail Minault, *The Khilafat Movement: Religious Symbolism and Political Mobilization in India* (New York: Columbia University Press, 1982).
[95] On the subtle role, though, of Helphand Parvus in blending class and ethno-religious struggle in the minds of Turkish nationalists in 1910s Istanbul, see H. Kieser, "World War and World Revolution: Alexander Helphand-Parvus in Germany and Turkey," *Kritika: Explorations in Russian and Eurasian History*, 12.2 (Spring 2011), 387–410.

the Paris settlements and intended world revolution; between a free world centered on a liberal League of Nations and that to be prepared by the Comintern in favor of all "wretched of the Earth" (as reads the communist anthem). The Kemalists sought to make their own post–Great War way: an ultranationalist revolution in equidistance, or so, from Moscow's world revolution and the West's Paris-Geneva peace architecture.

Since the aftermath of 1908, the CUP had desired to be of the West, but not under the West – however without accepting the duties and risks for imperial power that went along with the exercise of the rule of law and freedom. In the 1910s, the CUP had proved its readiness to sacrifice these principles and whole peoples for what it called the primacy of imperial "national sovereignty." Proud sons of empire (*evlad-ı fatihan*) and (for many of them) a Turanian master race, they understood themselves as the appointed bearers of sovereignty. Defeat in the Great War had only briefly led to soul-searching, critical introspection, and attempts at honest history among disoriented élites. Very quickly, entrenched nationalist discourses of self-righteousness and victimhood, as practiced in the 1910s, returned in their revised (i.e. Kemalist) versions. This choked burgeoning empathy with the true victims of CUP rule in particular and of age-old imperial bias in general. What rightly irritated Turkish nationalists, however, was the drive for maximal imperial advantage by the victors in Paris. Still, they underestimated the related, though less visible, internationalist dynamics at work in Geneva, which sought to operate in the name of global justice and welfare.

Arab dissidents and victims of the CUP dictatorship cherished the League's principles and the constitutional legacy of 1908 more than Turkish nationalists hailing from the CUP party-state. Turkish nationalists stressed Wilson's Fourteen Points to secure their sovereignty in Anatolia. They rejected decentralized, plural rule on a multireligious basis – in contrast to the General Syrian Arab Congresses of 1919–20. The questions remain: how far would the democratic experiment of Greater Syria's Arabs have gone without discriminating against non-Arabs and non-Muslims; and where would their anti-Zionist stance have finally led them? It is however clear that democratic seeds among Syria's Arabs under a constitutional King Faisal fell victim to the ruthless implementation of France's mandate over Syria in 1920. Arab nationalists were by no means keen to wage war in the form of an anti-Western jihad, and thus of no use for the Bolsheviks, had they had the opportunity to cooperate. They failed in their attempted resistance against the neo-colonial character of

France's mandatory regime, which actively resisted Geneva's oversight.[96]

The developments in Anatolia in 1919–20, in contrast, closely interacted with the Bolsheviks' amplified anti-capitalist propaganda during Russia's civil war, and with a new openness for all those, Marxism-prone or not, who led anti-Western jihad or national struggles. The Bolsheviks welcomed anti-Western ultranationalism among "peoples of the East," while they generally fought similar nationalists and fascists in continental Europe. In China, Moscow's Comintern supported the nationalists of Kuomintang together with the nascent communist movement. It called Sun Yat-sen University – after the Chinese constitutional revolutionary and national leader Sun Yat-sen – a sister institution of the Comintern's Communist University of the Toilers of the East in Moscow. In this line of early interwar development, we see Radek finally presiding at the Sun Yat-Sen University for Chinese nationalists and communists in 1925. In contrast, the Bolshevik-Turkish cooperation was strategic and functional, without common doctrinal ground. Gökalp's organicist Turkism, which fueled Turkish-Muslim nationalism, was impermeable to the universalist messages of an atheistic communism, although both were prone to collectivist coercion. In contrast to Turkey, the Bolshevik investment in China proved remarkably enduring. It went along, however, with China's parallel integration as a founding member in the League of Nations.

Nobody defied the Paris-Geneva peace project, from its start, in harsher terms than Lenin. His rejection overlapped with the interests of the Turkish nationalists who, a little later, when they had established military victory, were eager to seek Western "accreditation" in Lausanne. For Lenin, in October 1920, it had become "plain that the League of Nations was non-existent, that the alliance of the capitalist powers is sheer fraud, and that in actual fact it is an alliance of robbers, each trying to snatch something from the others."[97] Lenin then still enthusiastically insisted "that the Russian revolution is but a single link in the chain of the world revolution, and that our cause is strong and invincible because the cause of revolution is developing throughout the world; economic

---

[96] For the democratic-spirited Resolutions of the General Syrian Congress of 2 July 1919, see J. C. Hurewitz, *Middle East and North Africa in World Politics A Documentary Record* (New Haven: Yale University Press, 1979), 180–182. For a detailed and dedicated treatment of this chapter of Syrian history, see Thompson, *How the West Stole Democracy*, 107–248.

[97] Public address on 15 October 1920, "Speech Delivered at a Conference of Chairmen of Uyezd."

conditions are evolving in a way that is making our enemies weaker and us stronger with every day."

With all its grains of truth, Lenin's speech was by no means a truthful analysis. While he denigrated the League of Nations, this same League and its associated agencies provided efficient support against epidemics and famine in Russia, including in Soviet-controlled areas, and for prisoners of war.[98] His exaggerations served his immediate Bolshevik cause during a fierce civil war against forces supported by Western Europe. The experience of this deadly polarization, together with the conviction that the world must burn in the apocalypse, or "volcano" – revolutionary class struggle – explain Lenin's denigratory stance.

> This is no peace, but terms dictated to a defenseless victim by armed robbers. Through the Treaty of Versailles, Germany's enemies have deprived her of all her colonies. Turkey, Persia and China have been enslaved. ... That is why this international system in its entirety, the order based on the Treaty of Versailles, stands on the brink of a volcano, for the enslaved seven-tenths of the world's population are waiting impatiently for someone to give them a lead in a struggle which will shake all these countries.[99]

What Lenin here called "order based on the Treaty of Versailles" was pars pro toto for the Paris-Geneva peace.

Where European empires fell in 1917–18 and Lenin's appeal remained weak, nationalist currents struggled for a unitary state in as large a part of the new post-imperial spaces as possible. In Eastern Europe, notably in Ukraine and Poland, this was accompanied by war with Bolsheviks. This left decisions on boundaries in the Paris treaties suspended. In Anatolia, the ex-CUP nationalists enjoyed Moscow's support and achieved their goal militarily, and, in Lausanne, diplomatically. The success of the ex-CUP forces in Anatolia rested on the cooperation of the main anti-liberal currents of the 1910s (i.e. on revolutionism from the left and the right, see also Figure 6). Talaat Pasha's agitation center in Berlin and his visit with Enver Pasha to Karl Radek in August 1919 had contrived an anti-Western synergy that became operational a year later and was recognized in the Treaty of Moscow on 16 March 1921.

***

---

[98] Walters, *History of the League of Nations*, 101–102; Bruno Cabanes, *The Great War and the Origins of Humanitarianism, 1918–1924* (Cambridge: Cambridge University Press, 2014), 189–247.

[99] Lenin, "Speech Delivered at a Conference of Chairmen of Uyezd."

10 Defying the Paris-Geneva Peace Project   83

Figure 6 Monument of the Republic on Istanbul's Taksim Square. Established in 1928, this first monument to commemorate the foundation of the Ankara-based Republic of Turkey was designed by the Italian artist Pietro Canonica. Forefront, left to right: General Ismail Inönü, the Turkish delegation chief in Lausanne; Kemal Atatürk; General Fevzi Çakmak. Between Inönü and Atatürk: Bolshevik friends General Mikhail Frunse and, probably, Aralov. (Clip, WikiCommons, A. Savin)

Committed pioneers, friends, and – as it were – missionaries of the League of Nations organized from late-1910s associations in many countries. They offered civil and popular support, at times almost religious devotion, to a project whose institutionalization, however, mostly involved educated political elites only.[100] Country associations joined in

---

[100] Walters, *History of the League of Nations*, 199–202. Together with the successful popular vote for adhesion to the League in 1920, in Switzerland, the League's host, strong groups existed in favor of the League. See Patrick Lehmann, *Die Schweizerische Vereinigung für den Völkerbund* (Zürich: Lic. phil. I Univ. Zürich, 1995). For a country-wide pro-League student organization, see *Feuille Centrale de Zofingue*, no. 10, July 1924, 12. Examples of almost life-long commitments to the League are the aforementioned Rappard as well as Ernest Bovet, a leading intellectual and prolific leader and spokesperson of the Swiss friends of the League of Nations (Schweizerische Vereinigung für

the International Union of Associations for the League of Nations. The International Union of Religious Socialists, presided by the charismatic Leonhard Ragaz, promoted and interpreted the League in light of the gospel, basic democracy, and pacifist socialism.[101] Minority questions stood particularly close to the heart of the League-related civil society organizations.[102]

For the League's friends, after the horror of the Great War, it was about establishing worldwide peace and free societies, underpinned by constitutional rule, individual rights and civil liberties. Nations would become well interconnected, but also would perfect their social contracts and code them in democratic constitutions. For committed friends, the League's Covenant, adopted in 1919, represented the start for an evolving, perfectioning League, based on growing institutions in Geneva and worldwide. The constructive development would allow to peacefully revise, if required and justified, the evidently imperfect Paris peace treaties. This faith did not pertain, though, to a few associations founded from above – as in Turkey, whose friendship association was established in 1921, eleven years before Turkey's accession to the League. In this case, the association served the international recognition of a national project that sought to avoid any serious League-related liability, notably in matters of minority protection.[103]

Optimism and idealism, but also much pragmatism after the dark experience of the Great War accompanied the emergent League of Nations. While enthusiasm proved short-lived, many promotors and supporters kept on being loyal to the League's idea of peace based on

den Völkerbund). The latter, at times, used religious vocabulary in his public conferences in favor of the League; see, for example, Ernest Bovet, *Les neutres et la Société des nations: Conférence* (Boulogne: Comité national d'études sociales et politiques, 1926). On Bovet and League idealism, in the critically appreciative perspective of a contemporary theology of revelation: Adolf Keller, "Wissen und Leben," in *Ernest Bovet: Festschrift*, ed. Association Suisse pour la Société des Nations (Bern: Paul Haupt, 1940), 24–39.

[101] See Markus Mattmüller, *Leonhard Ragaz und der religiöse Sozialismus. Eine Biographie*, 2 vols. (Zollikon: EVZ, 1957 and 1968). See also LONSEA: Searching the Globe through the Lenses of the League of Nations, www.lonsea.de/pub/person/3606.

[102] See the bi-monthly bulletin *Les Minorités Nationales*, published by the International Union of Associations for the League of Nations, 1926–32, and the *Rapport de la commission spéciale sur les minorités de race, de langue & de religion, présenté a la conférence plenière de l'Union Internationale des Associations pour la Société des Nations, Prague 5–8 Juin 1922* (Brussel: Bureau de l'Union, 1922). Unsurprisingly, any critique of Turkey's crimes against, and ongoing dispossession of, Armenians led to rapid concerted ripostes that sought to silence critics. For example, " Les bien des Arméniens en Turquie," *Les Minorités Nationales*, 1 (1930), 9–14, and "La Commission des minorités de l'Union internationale," in 2–3 (1930), 26–27. For reactions to the 1922 *Rapport*, see Liebisch-Gümüş, *Verflochtene Nationsbildung*, 358–359.

[103] Liebisch-Gümüş, *Verflochtene Nationsbildung*, 351–362.

democracy, freedom, disarmament and collective security; many, but not all of them belonged to the post–Great War strand of pacifism. Seekers of new horizons, they remained open to novel forms of human coexistence and cooperation. They believed in human capacities, common sense and maintained utopia – i.e. constructive vision howsoever far from current realities. The much-conjured "public opinion," "world opinion" or "global conscience" – part also of the Lausanne Conference vocabulary – were by far not yet a the level to be able to efficiently press governmental decision-makers. Governments obstructed, and prevailing Interwar realpolitik eroded, the League's idea and principles.

Loyal friends of the League considered reactionary "the faith in security based on armaments," although they knew about the weaknesses of a modest institution that depended on the goodwill of its members. They were well aware of the flaws of the Paris treaty system, but trusted that "the injustices of the peace treaties could be righted via the Covenant's Article 19."[104] They did not ignore lack of goodwill by member states, i.e. the deficit of commitment for the League's common good. Still, they kept hope that with time, matured members and made more perfect, the League – or a better successor organization – would be able to provide fair representation and democratic decision-making, worldwide. This is how destructive conflicts would be effectively prevented, and real peace secured.

Underpinned by liberal optimism, but also by post–Great War skepticism, the League was never thought to be a "world government." In contrast to the interwar party dictatorships from the left and the right, it focused on liberty and voluntary solidarity, not on centralized and personalized hard power. Because of President Woodrow Wilson's strong contribution to the making of the League and its Covenant, many friends of the League believed the USA, the Great Power least touched by the Great War, would become the strongest promotor and stand as a pillar for the League's beliefs. Among the most marked expectations in 1920 was a safe future for the surviving Armenian people, best via an American Mandate. This expectation underestimated, as we have seen, strong in-country tensions and counter-currents in the West, in particular the USA, where a majority did not share the League's philosophy or was not ready to engage at all.

---

[104] Ernest Bovet, *Die neue Ordnung* (Lausanne: Schweizerische Vereinigung für den Völkerbund, 1933), 40. Covenant Article 19 reads: "The Assembly may from time to time advise the reconsideration by Members of the League of treaties which have become inapplicable and the consideration of international conditions whose continuance might endanger the peace of the world."

The USA neither joined the League nor – and this was not automatically excluded – accepted a mandate over Armenia or the whole of Anatolia. As a consequence of the American rejection of the League, implementation of the League and implementation of the Sèvres Treaty depended on Britain and France, two powers bound by considerable interests in the Arab parts of the Ottoman Empire. Four months before concluding the Treaty of Sèvres, a conference of the World War victors made Britain a mandatory power for Iraq and Palestine including today's Jordan; and France the mandatory power for Syria including Lebanon (San Remo resolution on 25 April 1920). Added to local resistance, the mandate areas were vulnerable to Islamist and irredentist agitation steered from Ankara. Bolsheviks, Kemalists, and Islamists knew how to emphasize the League's flaws and divisiveness. The League notably lacked the univocal affirmation of the equality of races.[105]

In a major breach of universal principles, only defeated or new states, but not the founding World War victors or neutral states, were subject to the League's control of minority rights. Still, there was clear progress as compared to a world before the League.[106] Geneva centralized and implemented expert knowledge and institutionalized cooperation on issues of global importance, from health and finances to labor rights and humanitarian aid. The Mandates Section and Commission supervised the situation in the mandates, received petitions by natives and stood in touch with local representatives, as did the Minorities Section. Petition-induced interventions in other countries' affairs by decision of the League's Council depended on French and British realpolitik. Nevertheless, the open discussions in the League's Assembly influenced these and other decisions. Following a Council resolution shortly after the Lausanne Conference, the League however rejected not only petitions that questioned the Geneva system itself, but also those that did not "abstain from violent language."[107] While the minority protection

---

[105] Rejected by Washington. For the racial equality proposal by the Japanese delegation at the Paris Peace Conference, see Naoko Shimazu, *Japan, Race and Equality: The Racial Equality Proposal of 1919* (London: Routledge, 1998). Britain and the USA defeated the proposal as unsuitable to be part of the Covenant of the League of Nations.

[106] For an insightful contemporary assessment, in which pros clearly prevail, see League friend Albert Oeri, "Der Völkerbund um die Wende seines ersten Jahrzehnts: Ein Rückblick und ein Ausblick," in Oeri et al., *Zehn Jahre Völkerbund* (Glarus: Glarner Nachrichten, 1930), 3–45.

[107] Resolution of 5 September 1923, in League of Nations, *Protection of Linguistic, Racial or Religious Minorities by the League of Nations. Resolutions and Extracts* (Geneva: League of Nations, 1929). For discussion of a concrete case, see Scheuermann, *Minderheitenschutz*, 329–333. See also Roger Cussó, "The League of Nations and Minorities: The Non-receivability of 'Non-Treaty' Petitions," *International Journal of Minority and Group Rights*, 26.1 (2019), 67–91.

scheme certainly required some measures against abuse, this limitation meant sanitization in all-too-real cases of terror and extreme violence – when, for example, a Kurdish Alevi representative in exile described the mass murder of civilians during the Dersim genocide. His letter to the League was condemned to "no action."[108]

Despite all its flaws, the League contributed to global awareness and fostered informed exchange in and outside the organization on issues of global interest in light of the rule of law, far beyond the circles of diplomats and statesmen. Through petitions and informal letters, locals at many remote places were given a voice, if only for the historical record. Long before the age of the Internet and beyond its institutional channels and friendship associations, the League thus promoted global political communication, information, debate, and memory. The League's adversaries, and some of its nominal members, did all they could to cut their spheres of power off from Geneva's influence.

***

Initially, the Paris-Geneva peace project was defeated in the Caucasus. There, a new situation developed in spring 1920, when the Red Army entered, establishing Soviet rule in Azerbaijan, in April 1920; in (eastern) Armenia, in December 1920; and finally also in Georgia, in February 1921. Early talks for a friendship treaty with Ankara stalled because, until July 1920, Moscow insisted on Armenian rights and territorial claims that corresponded to those to be enshrined in the Sèvres Treaty (i.e. including a north-eastern corner of Anatolia, see Map 2).

What, therefore, had priority for Ankara's new government, founded on 23 April 1920, was a destructive blow against Armenia in the South Caucasus without delay. The CUP's Caucasus campaign two years earlier, after Tsarist Russia's collapse, had been motivated by the fear that Armenia would become "a kind of Bulgaria in the East," where the West had its say. The CUP's War Minister Enver Pasha, consequently, considered it "necessary to do all in order to weaken them [the Caucasian Armenians] completely and leave them in an entirely destitute state so that their deprived life conditions prevent them from organizing themselves."[109] Armenian resistance in extremis saved Erivan in May–June 1918. The Ottoman Great War defeat undid the Ottoman Islamic

---

[108] See "Political Situation in Turkey – Various correspondence," File R3640/1/12279/12279, LNA, https://archives.ungeneva.org/political-situation-in-turkey-various-correspondence. In this and in other similar cases, Ankara's non-recognition of the Kurds as a minority played a major role. As we will see, Ankara's stance rested on decisions in Lausanne.

[109] War Minister Enver Pasha to General Vehib Pasha, 9 June 1918, quoted in Kieser, *Talaat Pasha*, 366.

Map 2 Europe and the Ottoman Empire after the First World War. Asia Minor is the central part of the new belt of states or mandates from the Baltic Sea to the Gulf of Aden. Turkish territorial gains are meant in comparison to the Sèvres Treaty. This Treaty had attributed a part of northeastern Anatolia to independent Armenia. It had planned plebiscites to decide whether Izmir/Smyrna would ultimately belong to Greece or Turkey, and also whether parts of Mesopotamia adjoining to planned Armenia would belong to a future Kurdistan that could ultimately be unified with Iraqi Kurdistan.

10 Defying the Paris-Geneva Peace Project 89

Army's vast gains in the rest of the South Caucasus. Plans in the Sèvres Treaty to implement justice, restitution, and independence for the Armenians triggered the renewed Caucasus campaign by Ankara that had been planned months before. The goal was to decimate Armenia's forces and reduce its territory before any pro-Armenian Western intervention. In vain, the Armenian government asked for muscled support.[110]

Lacking support, the democratic experiments in the Caucasian republics of Azerbaijan, Armenia, and Georgia, all connected with the Paris-Geneva peace project, came to an end by 1921. In late September 1920, forces under the former CUP general Kâzım Karabekir rapidly conquered Sarıkamış, Kars, Ardahan, Artvin, and Alexandropol (Gümrü). Ankara's ultimatum demanded the re-implementation of the Treaty of Brest-Litovsk in the South Caucasus, in contravention to the Sèvres Treaty. Outgunned, the Armenian government was forced to cede territory promised in Sèvres and to sign the Treaty of Alexandropol.

The League hotly discussed Armenia's situation in fall 1920, but could not act. The Western powers were not ready to militarily intervene nor in a position to do so. In March 1921, the Treaty of Moscow endorsed the division of Armenia, and thus the main territorial regulations of the Alexandropol Treaty.[111] "They the Bolsheviks wanted to befriend us in order to use us as a trump card against the British and French. We too used the Russian as a trump card. We knew, when required, we would break the bond," Rıza Nur wrote in his recollection. He added, by then, "We still wanted to occupy Baku. The main reason was to open the way to Turan."[112] Nur had signed the Moscow Treaty.

The Moscow Treaty defined Turkey as encompassing the entirety of Anatolia plus a few additions, as according to the National Pact. This charter of the post-1918 nationalist movement was agreed on by the Ottoman Parliament in Istanbul in early 1920, in agreement with the Kemalists. It contended that all territories with a Muslim majority that were not occupied at the end of the Great War, belonged to the Turkish national home (Türk Yurdu), that is, the Turkish nation-state in the making. The Treaty of Kars of October 1921 confirmed the National

---

[110] Edita Gzoyan, "The Turkish-Armenian war of 1920 and the League of Nations," *Central and Eastern European Review* 5 (2011), 2–15; Richard G. Hovannisian, *From London to Sèvres, February–August 1920: The Republic of Armenia 3* (Berkeley: University of California Press, 1996) and Hovannisian, *Between Crescent and Sickle: Partition and Sovietization. The Republic of Armenia 4* (Berkeley: University of California Press, 1996).

[111] For the Treaty text in current Turkish, see İsmail Soysal (ed.), *Türkiye'nin Siyasal Antlaşmaları. Vol. 1: 1920–1945* (Ankara: TTK, 1983), 32–38, https://tr.wikisource.org/wiki/Moskova_Antla%C5%9Fmas%C4%B1.

[112] Nur, *Hayat ve Hatıratım*, vol. 3, 167.

Pact boundaries in the Caucasus, as fixed by the Treaty of Moscow, thus annulling the regulations of Paris-Sèvres. It was concluded in the presence of not only a Soviet Russian plenipotentiary, but also of Soviet Georgian, Armenian, and Azerbaijani ministers. All these treaties were, properly understood, agreements enforced by military might between revolutionary governments. Of these, Ankara lacked international recognition almost entirely, Bolshevik Moscow still largely.

From the late nineteenth century, Turkey's possible democratization and constitutionality had critically depended on configuring the Turkish-Armenian future. The erasure of the late-Ottoman Armenian Question with its international dimension stood at the heart of how Turkish nationalists grasped the implementation of their sovereignty and unitary rule in Asia Minor. As we will see, this also defined Ankara's instruction to its delegation before the Lausanne Conference. A Turkish nation-state, according to the borders and understanding of the National Pact, thus meant more than the rejection of an independent Armenia comprising a corner of Eastern Asia Minor as in the Sèvres Treaty. It also meant weakening any Armenian polity in the Caucasus and implementation of a state of isolation from the West. Armenia had to be incapacitated to the point it could not claim rights, or internationally assert its memory and understanding of history.

This outcome, and with it the erasure of fundamental justice, was by no means predetermined in the immediate aftermath of the Great War. The National Pact was initially to comprise a paragraph on the prosecution of Great War criminals who had brought "damage to the state and the nation."[113] This crucial regulation, however, fell victim to rapidly growing anti-Armenian and anti-Western momentum among Anatolia's Muslim opinion leaders. As far as anti-Armenianism (the denigration of Armenian identity and history, the rejection of Armenian rights) is concerned, there was no basic difference between Mustafa Kemal's circle (the "First Group") and his adversaries in the so-called Second Group who became particularly vocal in Ankara's National Assembly during the Lausanne Conference.

Instead of becoming a true foundation of a new democratic contract and constitutional rule, the National Pact thus united the Muslim interest groups in Anatolia and led them back under a new version of centralist rule by former CUP cadres. Brighter minds among hopeful young nationalists had sought a clear departure from the dark period of CUP dictatorship, but they all were to bow to the will of Ankara's strongmen within

---

[113] Baskın Oran, *Türk dış politikası. Vol. 1: Kurtuluş Savaşından Bugüne olgular, belgeler, yorumlar. 1919-1980* (Istanbul: Iletisim, 2019), 105–107.

a few years. Alternative visions of the national future had come to the fore during the aforementioned "Turkish Congress" that, from 1919, held its annual meeting in Turkish in Lausanne. There, the participants demanded democracy, gender equality, "the complete secularization" (which would also give room for a "national church" of Christians), and "the complete decentralization" in a "reconstituted Turkey." They thus envisioned Turkey in Anatolia as a modern and secular state that, though based on "racial Turkish bonds," would be decentralized and religiously tolerant.[114]

Before the Great War, the CUP had categorically rejected regionalizing and democratizing reforms in the eastern parts of Anatolia, as enshrined in the international Agreement of 8 February 1914. Aborted by the Great War, this hopeful Agreement, which foresaw effective international monitoring, had implemented Articles 60–61 of the 1878 Berlin Treaty by way of compromise with the Ottoman government. Although genocide put the postulate of Armenian independence in the foreground, the League maintained main principles of the 1914 Agreement on rule of law, political participation, inclusionary state employment, and minority protection. Before consorting with Ankara, the Bolsheviks, too, had still felt bound to these principles in favor of the Armenians. The CUP's (and their Kemalist successors') response, however, to Western-influenced proposals that promoted rights of non-Turkish natives was – in their own vocabulary – "the fist."[115]

In the historical approach of *When Democracy Died*, which connects CUP nation-building from 1913 with that after 1918, Turkish politics pioneered one of three main models emerging from the Great War, namely a proto-fascist unitary nationalism versus the bourgeoning liberal Paris-Geneva peace project. In contrast to the Bolsheviks, Kemalists wanted, and succeeded in Lausanne, to partly liaise with the Western project on their own terms, thus transforming it into a Paris–Geneva–Lausanne combination. In the early days of the Ankara counter-government, its leader – *Gazi* and commander-in-chief Mustafa Kemal Pasha – explicitly claimed a distinct form of government, without separation of powers. He called it "the people's government." In reality, it was the concentration of all power in the National Assembly that he

---

[114] Confidential report by the Cantonal Police, 24 May 1921, S112/88, ACV. See also Schrader, "Das Jungtürkische Lausanner Programm," 9–10, 32–33.

[115] H. L. Kieser, Mehmet Polatel, and Thomas Schmutz, "Reform or cataclysm? The agreement of 8 February 1914 regarding the Ottoman eastern provinces," *Journal of Genocide Research*, 17.3 (2015), 285–304. In this context, it is important to note that historian Yusuf Bayur starts his *History of the Turkish Revolution* with the 1878 Ayastefanos and Berlin Treaties: Bayur, *Türk inkılâbı tarihi*, vol. 1.

dominated. "Sirs, our government is not a democratic government and not a socialist government."[116]

For Mustafa Kemal, Ankara's was a form of government that "did not yet exist in the history books." Together with military victory, it should bring about progress and education for all, including women and people in the country side. For this purpose, however, the new national society needed Gökalpian unity, conformity, and military spirit. It had to eliminate non-compliant "elements." Talking about education in March 1922, the leader insisted on the following requirements before the National Assembly.

> Dear Sirs! Our children and young people, regardless of the level of education they will receive, must be taught first and foremost the necessity to fight against all elements that are enemies of Turkey's independence and her national personality and culture [applause]. According to the international situation, there is no life and independence for individuals, and for societies composed of individuals, who have not been equipped with the necessary mental qualities needed for such a struggle [voices shouting bravo].[117]

11 Aborting the Sèvres Treaty: A Plural Anatolia and Western Justice

Might and right quickly drifted apart after the Great War. They did not combine in a happy liaison for real peace so solely needed. This was most manifest with Europe's revolutionist outsiders, Russia and Turkey, one leftist-Bolshevik, the other rightist-ultranationalist. As we have seen, both joined forces against the Paris-Geneva project.

Moscow now took Talaat Pasha's growingly powerful successors in Ankara as "revolutionaries," in contrast to the Entente-supported "reactionary" government of the sultan in Istanbul. All of a sudden, the National Pact boundaries now read in Bolshevik vocabulary as those warranting "the unity of the Turkish nation in its ethnographic delimitations." Henceforth the Bolsheviks took pride in holding Ankara's back in the Black Sea and the Caucasus safe, and in supporting unitary Kemalist nationalism against the claims of others. These were labeled West-leaning reactionaries and a "compradore bourgeoisie" allied to capitalism and imperialism.[118]

---

[116] Atatürk, "Bakanlar kurulunun görev ve yetkisini belirten kanun teklifi münasebetiyle," 1 December 1921, *Atatürk'ün Söylev ve Demeçleri*, vol. 1, 211.
[117] Atatürk, "Üçüncü toplanma yılını açarken," 1 March 1922 *Atatürk'ün, Söylev ve Demeçleri*, vol. 1, 246.
[118] See discourse and vocabulary in the memoirs of Semyon Aralov, Moscow's ambassador in Ankara before the Lausanne Treaty: *Bir Sovyet Diplomatının Anıları 1922–23* (Istanbul: Türkiye İş Bankası, 2010, first Russian publication 1960), quotation p. 213.

The demand of exclusive Turkish rule implemented by force made any other "theory for the future of Asia Minor" (i.e. any form of egalitarian coexistence), moot by 1922. Georgios Streit, an international lawyer from Greece and later a judge of the League's Permanent Court of Arbitration, still proposed – quixotically – in late August 1922, "the Government and Administration of the larger part of Western Asia Minor should be taken over entirely by the League of Nations." In a meeting with League Secretary-General Eric Drummond, Streit stated "that it could not be held that any one race in Asia Minor was in the majority over the others; the country really was composed of a conglomeration of these nationalities, and that, therefore, ordinary Treaties for Minorities Protection were not adequate and some special arrangement must be made." This astute observation was bypassed by nearly ten years of demographic engineering. Speaking in the name of the Greeks, Streit added, "What they could not agree to would be to hand the populations from these areas back to the Turks to be administered according to ancient Turkish methods."[119] This was consistent with President Wilson's Fourteen Points, according to which non-Turkish groups "under Ottoman rule should be assured an undoubted security of life and an absolutely unmolested opportunity of autonomous development" (Point 12). Violence had overruled this requirement by 1922.

***

The Turkish nation-building project emerged from the ruins of the prewar order at the same time as the League of Nations, whose Covenant figures in the first 26 articles of the Paris-Sèvres Treaty. The Covenant enshrined international arbitration, various forms of supervision, and the principle of mandatory administration which concerned the former Ottoman empire in the first place. It went hand in hand with a generous protection of minorities. The Versailles Treaty – the first to include and spread the League's Covenant – identified war guilt entirely with the Central Powers' "war of aggression." The one-sided attribution of war guilt in the Paris treaties proved a crucial element of asymmetry, and thus instability, of the Paris-Geneva peace project in general. Attributing

---

[119] Greek foreign minister in 1914–15 in the cabinet of Eleftherios Venizelos, Streit espoused neutrality in the Great War, but resigned when Venizelos leaned toward the Entente. In Greece's "National Schism" from late 1916, he remained royalist. Quotation from "The Eastern Question – Secretary General – Records an interview with Dr. Streit during which the latter explained his theory for the definite settlement of the future of Asia Minor," 28 August 1922, Lontad, R603/11/22490/22901, https://lontad-project.unog.ch/idurl/1/7424. Thanks to Markos Carelos who drew my attention to this document. See also Streit's analogous interview in *Gazette de Lausanne*, 11 September 1922, 2.

territory or zones of influence to European allies discredited the Turkish-Ottoman component of this project in particular. Yet, in early 1919, nobody in London, the foremost power, was in a position to "foresee that France would evacuate Cilicia and make a separate peace with Turkey, that Italy would abandon Adalia [at the Anatolian Southcoast], that the United States would repudiate all further responsibility, that Russia would join with the Turks, and that the concert of the Powers would leave Greece isolated, unsupported and alone," Harold Nicolson, a member in the British delegation at Lausanne, stated in retrospect.[120]

The principles that guided the Paris-Geneva project – including the League's various actors, associates, and sub-organizations – in trying to shape the postwar order "were deeply ambivalent," Liebisch-Gümüş wrote in her recent exploration of Turkey and the League of Nations.

> On the one hand, they were based on the Wilsonian vision of a global community of nation-states. ... No less influential, on the other hand, were imperialist conceptions of world order from the 19th century. ... The League of Nations stood for a universal cooperation of independent states and yet was part of a highly asymmetric world order, in terms of power, to which it itself contributed.[121]

In other words, there was both universalism and Western imperial bias in the Paris-Geneva peace project. The imperial bias of the Great War victors opened an ideological gateway for those who wholesale opposed the Western peace project.

The Treaty signed in Paris-Sèvres on 10 August 1920 sought to establish post-Ottoman self-determination in accordance with Wilson's Point 12 and Anatolia's human geography before genocide, and thus curtailed the plan of an exclusive Turkish national home in Anatolia. The Treaty planned a plural Anatolia that, beside minority protection under the League, gave room for collective self-determination also by non-Turkish natives, while it punished the Ottoman Empire for the Young Turk party dictatorship, deliberate entrance into the World War, and mass crimes. By extension, it put age-old Sunni Muslim rule and social predominance in the Ottoman space in doubt. Given US refusal of a mandate and the League's lack of an army, it could not provide the required robust roof under which its vision of coexisting Turkish, Greek-Rûm, Armenian, and Kurdish communities in Anatolia would be realized and permit the people to live their ethno-religious diversity in peace.

The Treaty of Sèvres envisioned the northeastern corner of Anatolia as part of an expanded Republic of Armenia, but left the delicate question of future boundaries between Turkey and Armenia (Articles 88–93) in

---

[120] Nicolson, *Curzon: The Last Phase*, 93.
[121] Liebisch-Gümüş, *Verflochtene Nationsbildung*, 4.

suspense. "Turkey and Armenia as well as the other High Contracting Parties agree to submit to the arbitration of the President of the United States of America the question of the frontier to be fixed between Turkey and Armenia in the vilayets of Erzerum, Trebizond, Van and Bitlis" (Article 89). South of Armenia, the Sèvres Treaty planned Kurdish self-determination that might develop into an "independent Kurdish State" of Kurds both in southeastern Anatolia and in Northern Iraq (see Map 2).

If within one year from the coming into force of the present Treaty the Kurdish peoples... shall address themselves to the Council of the League of Nations in such a manner as to show that a majority of the population of these areas desires independence from Turkey, and if the Council then considers that these peoples are capable of such independence..., Turkey hereby agrees to execute such a recommendation, and to renounce all rights and title over these areas. (Article 64)

The Treaty made Turkish sovereignty provisional not only over Kurdish regions, but also over Izmir and its surroundings, possibly to become part of Greece (Articles 65–83). Many Rûm, as well as non-nationalist Levantines, had lived there in the late-Ottoman era. From Izmir and its neighborhood at the Aegean coast, CUP operations had ethnically cleansed nearly 200,000 Rûm in the first half of 1914. After five years of Greek rule from 1920, belonging would be determined by parliamentary vote or – if required by the League – by a plebiscite. "When a period of five years shall have elapsed after the coming into force of the present Treaty the local parliament... may, by a majority of votes, ask the Council of the League of Nations for the definitive incorporation in the Kingdom of Greece" (Article 83).

It is true that the Sèvres Treaty combined the postulate of self-determination for hitherto imperially subordinate groups in the Ottoman Empire with imperial designs of European states. Though not part of the Treaty itself, a "Tripartite Agreement Respecting Anatolia" of 10 August 1920 between Britain, France, and Italy attributed temporary zones of influence and control in Southern Anatolia to France and Italy.[122] Still, Sèvres was a far cry from a total dismemberment of Anatolian Turkey. Western textbooks after Lausanne often included maps of the Sèvres Treaty according to early Kemalist propaganda material, suggesting the Treaty meant the complete partition of Anatolia, leaving Turkey as a mini-state. These maps wrongly suggested that the zones of influence were no longer Turkish territory.[123] In reality, by far

---

[122] " Tripartite Agreement Between the British Empire, France and Italy Respecting Anatolia," *American Journal of International Law*, 15 (April 1921), 153–159.
[123] Such a Kemalist map is reproduced and critically commented in Liebisch-Gümüş, *Verflochtene Nationsbildung*, 154.

the major part of Anatolia remained attributed to the Turkish state even in the case that all non-Turkish indigenous groups would benefit from the Treaty's provisions for separation.

Quixotically, as it were, the Treaty of Sèvres decided on an Armenian state, including northeastern Anatolia, where all pro–Paris-Geneva forces, except those of weak Armenia, had already left when the Treaty was concluded, and a fortiori, when Wilson decided on the Turkish–Armenian frontier on 22 November 1920.[124] The Treaty envisaged Kurdish self-government in parts of northern Mesopotamia, where British intervention meant imperial overreach, even if troops from occupied but restive Iraq were comparatively close. Possible Greek sovereignty over Izmir depended almost entirely on forces from Greece, Turkey's western neighbor and principal foe after the Balkan Wars. The CUP cabinet had prepared a revanchist war against Greece from late 1913 that was only forestalled by the Great War. In sum, the Treaty of Sèvres clearly lacked a sound and viable concept of peace, based on the balance of right and might; nor did it have an honest Western commitment and a holistic project for the region's future.

***

While identifying critical anti-liberal agency in the might- and violence-prone Russian–Turkish synergy, it would be simplistic to put too much blame for the failure of the Paris-Geneva peace on it. Democratic core values like human dignity, equality, freedom, social security, and the rule of law well counted, to a relevant extent, in Europe's polities, but far less outside Europe or overseas in colonies or mandates. There was imperial and racial bias in the Paris-Geneva peace, although this project possessed better means and better workable answers than the others, and better instruments for self-correction.

Western consensus on how to promote, and how far to engage in peace in the Near East was the trickiest issue in Paris from January 1919 – and it remained far from achieved a year and a half later. Longer in the making than all other treaties in Paris, the Sèvres Treaty came latest on 10 August 1920, due not only to the inherent difficulties, but also the European priorities of the main negotiators. The "Turkish settlement was regarded in Paris, not as an integral problem requiring solution in its own terms, but as the area of least resistance in which compensations could be found wherewith to bribe several esurient Powers to relinquish their claims in Europe itself." These were "to be paid in Turkish territory for

---

[124] Ara Papian, "The Arbitral Award on Turkish-Armenian Boundary by Woodrow Wilson (Historical Background, Legal Aspects, and International Dimensions)," *Iran & the Caucasus*, 11.2 (2007), 255–294.

the sacrifices" demanded of them during the Great War, as Nicolson, a diplomatic insider member of the British delegation both in Paris and in Lausanne, astutely wrote.[125]

Thus, the Sèvres Treaty was the most fragile and inauspicious of all the Paris treaties, and the only one not to be ratified, but to be radically revised. When it was signed by the representatives of Istanbul in Paris, war raged in Anatolia, where the Istanbul government had already largely lost its influence. At that moment, as we have seen, the Bolsheviks made a turn toward Kemal's counter-government, siding with the strong and letting down the weak, the surviving Armenians in the Caucasus. A little earlier, in a letter to Lenin on 26 April 1920, Kemal had stigmatized the Armenian leadership as an "imperialist government" to be attacked. He asked for Moscow's help in the name of Ankara's new National Assembly.[126] Power politics thus combined with negative (i.e. rejectionist) ideology, consisting in the rejection of the Paris-Geneva peace terms and the division of West-leaning Armenia. This was social Darwinism and disregard for the unequivocal victim of oppression in the 1910s. It contradicted both the socialist human rights credo and Wilson's Point 12. Contempt for the weak, who claimed universal support and understanding, thus defined the bourgeoning Bolshevik and Kemalist state projects. Both discredited themselves by their rejection of a democratic contract and by unchecked affirmation of political violence.

Hatred and violence was called for and celebrated in a struggle against alleged agents of imperialists. "Every time you massacre a Greek you are pulling down one of the cornerstones of the British Empire. ... O sweating, naked, starving workmen, let there circulate in your arms the boiling blood of hatred against the British," Turks read in the daily *Peyam-Sabah* in January 1922.[127] Even an experienced general of the brutal Russian civil war like Mikhail V. Frunze, a faithful socialist, who passed through northeastern Anatolia in late 1921 was shocked by the violence that he witnessed against Rûm civilians, and by treatment of Greek hostages beneath contempt. According to careful allied statistics,

---

[125] Nicolson, *Curzon: The Last Phase*, 79. This is a rich narrative and astute analysis by an insider. Focusing on Curzon, Nicolson, who was Curzon's private secretary, is fascinated by and in sympathy with his chief's personality, intellectual capacity, and diplomatic skills.

[126] Letter to Lenin, 26 April 1920, quoted in Mete Tunçay, *Türkiye'de sol akımlar 1908–1925* (Istanbul: Iletisim, 2009), 263. See also Richard G. Hovannisian, "Armenia and the Caucasus in the Genesis of the Soviet-Turkish Entente," *International Journal of Middle East Studies*, 4.2 (April 1973), 129–147, and Aralov, *Bir Sovyet Diplomatının Anıları*, 7–8.

[127] *Peyam-Sabah*, 13 January 1922, quoted in Roderic H. Davison, "Middle East Nationalism: Lausanne Thirty Years after," *Middle East Journal*, 7.3 (1953), 328.

partly based on the knowledge of American academics living in Anatolia, the number of Greek prisoners in Turkish hands at the eve of the Lausanne Conference was about 30,000; to be added to these were 70,000 to 120,000 deported male Rûm.[128] All these were doomed men, according to refugee and war prisoner expert Fridtjof Nansen: "To judge from the previous experience of Turkish labour battalions, they might not live in Anatolia until the spring. The mortality during the war in Turkish labour battalions composed of non Muslims has been higher than at the front." US High Commissioner Bristol in Istanbul, a friend of Ankara, confirmed that these men "were fed badly and treated like animals."[129]

Frunze alluded to the "horrible disease" of Turks with "offended national feelings." Even far away from the Western fronts of the Greco-Turkish war, units and local forces allied to Ankara continued anti-Armenian patterns of killing and starvation against the Rûm population. High emissaries of Lenin in Ankara, like Frunze and Ambassador Semyon I. Aralov, brought their observations into line with doctrine, accusing "imperialists" as the ultimate culprit for misdeeds and evil on the ground. Sticking to the catechism of a true doctrine and a morally clean leadership, they excluded the main leaders in Ankara and Moscow from blame for atrocities – as in this statement of Frunze on his way back to the Caucasus, when he spoke to Aralov who went to Ankara. Howsoever explained, a saddened Frunze insisted on the outrages committed by Turkish forces against innocent people:

The Rûm in the region were displaced or killed. I was very concerned to see what was done. You will see it as you go along the way. It's a scary sight! I suggest you go on horseback, look to your right and left once in a while, you will see this terrible disgrace. Do not hide my great sadness from Mustafa Kemal Pasha. Mustafa Kemal has nothing to do with this business. On the contrary, I know that he gave strict orders for the humane treatment of the deportees and captives. These murders, these outrages, this indifference to the tortures of innocent people cannot be tolerated in a country that liberates itself from imperialist tyranny. The global public opinion will condemn it. There is no doubt that the main responsible for this is the British and French imperialists and the sultan's government. They created this mess here. They put forward the stupid idea of establishing a "Pontic State" and provoked the Rûm population to this revolt. However, it is necessary to speak very cautiously about these issues in order not to hurt national feelings. Recall Lenin's warning that offended national feelings are a horrible disease.[130]

---

[128] *CLA*, first series, vol. 1, 103.
[129] "Minutes of a Conference held at the British Embassy on Thursday, October 12, 1922, to Discuss the Refugee Problem in Greece and Asia Minor with Dr. Nansen," FO Confidential Print 12330, 207–208.
[130] Frunze, quoted in Aralov, *Bir Sovyet Diplomatının Anıları*, 35–36 and 49.

11 Aborting the Sèvres Treaty

For the makers of the Paris-Geneva peace project, a "terrorist regime" had "existed in Turkey since November 1, 1914," as stated in Article 142 of the Sèvres Treaty. The CUP regime was responsible for the massacre, deportation, and dispossession of "Turkish subjects of non-Turkish race ... forcibly driven from their homes." Istanbul's postwar government, therefore, must do all in order to "repair so far as possible the wrongs inflicted." Thus, it "recognises the injustice of the law of 1915 relating to Abandoned Properties (Emval-i-Metroukeh), and of the supplementary provisions thereof, and declares them to be null and void, in the past as in the future" (Article 144). Also, according to the same Article, it "solemnly undertakes to facilitate to the greatest possible extent the return to their homes and re-establishment in their businesses" of survivors. Though claiming lofty national liberation, Bolshevik-backed Ankara did all to obstruct such return and reparation. It thus gave ample room for continued violence against survivors and those seen as close to them.

The Sèvres Treaty not only sought return and material restoration for the victims of genocide, it tackled also the issue of forced conversions and of missing persons. Hence, it obliged the Turkish government to offer "all the assistance in its power or in that of the Turkish authorities in the search for and deliverance of all persons, of whatever race or religion, who have disappeared, been carried off, interned or placed in captivity since November 1, 1914." The Treaty sought to address the problem of conversion that had taken place under hardship or by coercion. Thus, "all persons who were non-Moslems before November 1, 1914, will be considered as still remaining such, unless, after regaining their liberty, they voluntarily perform the necessary formalities for embracing the Islamic faith" (Article 142). "Arbitral commissions," composed of one representative of the Turkish government and another from a victimized – notably the Ottoman-Armenian – community were to be appointed by the League of Nations to handle conflictual claims. In particular, they should have power to remove from office "any person who, after enquiry, shall be recognised as having taken an active part in massacres or deportations or as having provoked them" (Article 144).

The Sèvres Treaty took the need of an international court for crimes against humanity seriously. It sought prosecution of those "responsible for the massacres committed during the continuance of the state of war on territory which formed part of the Turkish Empire on 1 August 1914." It gave the victors "the right to designate the tribunal which shall try the persons so accused," hoping that the League of Nations would create an international criminal court "competent to deal with the said massacres" (Article 230). By summer 1920, the prosecution of war crimes by the

Ottoman postwar government in the so-called Istanbul trials (court-martials) had entirely lost steam; it had become a show of goodwill toward the West, instead of legal and historical soul-searching.[131] By summer 1920, the political momentum in Anatolia clearly favored Ankara's nationalist regrouping of ex-CUP cadres under Mustafa Kemal's leadership. Potential war criminals were welcomed and won influential posts in Ankara, in particular all those who had belonged to former interior minister and grand vizier Talaat Pasha's circle. Atatürk respected Talaat who, since late 1918, was leading nationalist agitation from his exile in Berlin. In a long letter to Talaat on 20 February 1920, Kemal identified himself as in consensus with Talaat, rejecting any prosecution for war guilt or war crimes.[132]

In the Article 231 of the Sèvres Treaty, Turkey recognized "that by joining in the war of aggression which Germany and Austria-Hungary waged against the Allied Powers she has caused to the latter losses and sacrifices of all kinds for which she ought to make complete reparation." Although the same article waived all claims, it, and several following Articles, established a "Financial Commission" to supervise Turkey's finances and to satisfy the Allies' claims, including those regarding pre-1914 Ottoman debts and the costs for Istanbul's occupation. Istanbul recognized "the transfer to the Allied Powers" of its debts to the Central Powers, in particular huge loans from Germany. The Allies, though, renounced on repayment (Article 238). Istanbul was heavily patronized in financial matters. "No other defeated power had to subject itself to such a compromise of its sovereignty," historian Leonhard Smith recently concluded.[133]

As these regulations demonstrate, the Sèvres Treaty approached Turkey in a punitive and paternalistic way, not primarily as a state soon to be constitutionally and democratically built up. The Treaty openly displayed Turkey as unfit to become an equal and legitimate member of the international system in the near future. In any case, successful implementation of the Treaty provisions would have required comprehensive military occupation of Anatolia, not only of Istanbul; and certainly not occupation by ex-Ottoman Greece, an irredentist proxy with half qualified, half excessive claims.

---

[131] Vahakn Dadrian and Taner Akçam, *Judgment at Istanbul: The Armenian Genocide Trials* (New York: Berghahn, 2011).

[132] İlhan Tekeli and Selim İlkin, "Kurtuluş Savaşı'nda Talât Paşa ile Mustafa Kemâl'in mektuplaşmaları," *Belleten* 44 (April 1980): 312–30. See also Kieser, *Talaat Pasha*, 401.

[133] Leonhard V. Smith, "Post-war Treaties (Ottoman Empire/ Middle East)," in *1914–1918 Online: International Encyclopedia of the First World War* (Berlin, 2014). https://doi.org/10.15463/ie1418.10357.

11 Aborting the Sèvres Treaty

Experienced members of the internationalist Protestant community in Anatolia, which had emerged from networks of American missionaries in the late-Ottoman Empire, immediately qualified this allied use of a proxy as "the worst possible solution."[134] They agonized over delays by the Western decision makers in the crucial year of 1919. Based on both the 1908 concept of a constitutional Turkey and the expectation of a powerful League of Nations including an American Mandate, they believed,

> The attention of the Paris Peace Conference should be centered upon giving the Turks a good government rather than upon delivering the Armenians and Greeks from Turkish government. Because it will be of little profit to establish an Armenia, more than half of whose people will be Turks, if alongside of this new State there remains a Turkey of the old type. ... To save the Armenians and Greeks you must save the Turks also.

These internationalists espoused "absolute religious liberty for all"; the future of Istanbul as "a free City" and possibly as a seat of the League of Nations; the internationalization of "the waters from the Black Sea to the Mediterranean"; and renewed coexistence in Eastern Anatolia after repatriation of Armenian survivors and Kurdish refugees.[135]

The Western victors in Paris-Sèvres were neither willing nor able to positively address – and, in a new international framework, lawfully "domesticate" after war and genocide – basic national wishes by leaders of Anatolia's Turkish-Muslim majority. It is true that most of these had stood behind the discredited CUP, and again stood behind the Ankara government, and that justice for mass crimes was a sine qua non for any future constitutionality. Except complete surrender and occupation, nationalist leaders could never stomach the Treaty. In comparison, after Germany's unconditional surrender in 1945, the victors proved capable of combining prosecution, construction, and territorial concessions in a way that, in the long-term, yielded political results of substantial quality. The context, at that time, was new and different, as Germany was entirely occupied. The extermination of minorities by ultranationalists received a strong name and a punitive convention (the 1948 UN Convention on the Prevention and Punishment of the Crime of Genocide). In the 1940s, the coalition of allies disintegrated only with the emerging Cold War, that is, after the relevant conferences on Germany's future – not already before, as was the case in Turkey on the eve of the Lausanne Conference.

---

[134] Alexander MacLachan, president of the International College in Smyrna, quoted in Joseph L. Grabill, *The Protestant Diplomacy and the Near East: Missionary Influence on American Policy, 1810–1927* (Minneapolis: University of Minnesota Press, 1971), 172.

[135] "Plan for the Peaceful Repatriation of the Armenians and Kurds," ABCM Ussher Personal Papers, quoted in H. Kieser, *Der verpasste Friede* (Zürich: Chronos, 2000), 365.

12 The Military and Diplomatic Road to the Lausanne Conference

Western divisiveness and self-righteousness, and the gap between right and might being built-in, the Sèvres settlement inauspiciously invited a decision by force (i.e. armed struggle). It thus led away from constitutional futures and lawful prosecution of crimes.

Whereas Britain stuck to the Sèvres settlement's principal lines, the diverging imperial interests of Italy and France in the Levant rapidly undermined common support from late 1920. Rome, in particular, resented Greece's preponderant role as promoted by Britain's prime minister Lloyd George. There was some support for the Armenian cause in Rome, but not as a priority. For Carlo Sforza – Rome's High Commissioner in Istanbul in 1919 (who early on grasped Ankara's rise), before becoming Italian foreign minister in mid 1920 – economic cooperation was paramount and well worth a revision of Sèvres. With French backing, the Italian government organized the January 1921 "Rome Conference," a series of meetings with Turkish nationalists and representatives of Ankara, as well as leaders in European exile. French diplomacy in Paris had approached Ahmed Rıza, a former intellectual leader and deputy of the CUP who had fallen out with the main party leaders, to make contact with Ankara and to preside over the Rome meetings.[136]

Abdülkadir Câmi (Baykut), Ankara's man in Rome in January 1921, alleged "extreme nationalism" among the Muslims in the eastern provinces to argue, in his conversation with Mehmed Cavid Bey, against any territorial concessions to the Armenians. Cavid – a former CUP finance minister and comparatively moderate nationalist as readers know already – advocated a "viable Armenia" side by side with "a viable Turkey," and possible compromises on Kars and Van. His diaries, however, often lament warmongering and extreme nationalism in his political entourage, that made his conciliatory prospects quixotic. Cavid participated with Câmi at several sessions of the Rome Conference.[137] In a personal meeting, Sforza welcomed Cavid with "exquisite courtesy" and opined, "Anatolia must entirely be brought back under Ottoman sovereignty." Sforza still insisted, however, on the need of some international monitoring, notably in Izmir. This, all Turkish nationalists categorically rejected.[138]

---

[136] Erdal Kaynar. *Ahmed Rıza (1858–1930): Histoire d'un vieux Jeune Turc* (Paris: Doctoral thesis EHESS, 2011), 820–822.
[137] Cavid, *Meşrutiyet Ruznâmesi*, vol. 4, 186–188, entries of 4 and 7 December 1920. Cf. Cavid's meeting with Calouste S. Gulbenkian in Paris in March 1921; see Cavid, *Meşrutiyet Ruznâmesi*, vol. 4, 253, and Avedis Aharonian, *From Sardarabad to Sèvres and Lausanne (political diary)* (Boston: Hairenik Press, 1943, in Armenian), 116–117.
[138] Cavid, *Meşrutiyet Ruznâmesi*, vol. 4, 198, diary entry of 30 December 1920.

12 The Military and Diplomatic Road to Lausanne   103

Seeking a rapprochement with Turkey, Sforza asked for Talaat's help via the Italian embassy in Berlin, as he assumed the former leader's ongoing influence on the nationalists. He did not shrink from hosting this former minister in Rome, though Talaat was put on an international wanted list, after being sentenced to death by the Istanbul trial.[139] Sforza believed that accommodating Ankara by revising the Sèvres Treaty would promote Italy's economic influence. In March 1921, he signed an agreement with Ankara's foreign minister Bekir Sami Bey (Kunduh) that, like the simultaneous Moscow Treaty, amounted to the recognition of the National Pact and a betrayal toward the Armenians. In his memoirs, written in the early 1940s, Sforza complacently praised "my Turcophile policy," that led to "a never-seen economic expansion of Italian business in the Levant." An otherwise judicious adversary of Mussolini, Sforza admired the "unique dictator," Atatürk.[140]

Paris, for its part, resigned to the aggressive pressure of Kemalist forces, rallied to armed and well-organized gangs in Urfa, Aintab, and Marash. British troops had conquered most of the Ottoman territory during the Great War, but Paris insisted on assuming control over Cilicia in late 1919. The small local French forces soon proved incapable to hold the terrain. A volte-face by Paris in early 1920 made the outnumbered French rapidly retire to the south. This left the genocide survivors who had returned under the supposed guardianship of a great power unprotected. A ferocious massacre of Christian civilians – all-too-notorious in the region – killed about ten thousand defenseless Armenians in Marash in February 1920. A thousand or so of those who had managed to flee from Marash died of severe cold and exhaustion.[141]

Withdrawing the troops to Syria and precociously compromising with Ankara permitted France to concentrate her forces on the Syrian mandate. Paris had prioritized this mandate and obtained it in San Remo, against strong Syrian and some League resistance.[142] Negotiations with Ankara therefore progressed on the back of both Anatolian Christians, let down by France, and Syrians seeking independence, but left alone by Ankara. On 20 October 1921, French emissary Henry Franklin-Bouillon concluded the Ankara Accord, which definitively ended the French–Turkish war by ceding a large territorial belt from Adana to Aintab,

---

[139] Fabio L. Grassi, *İtalya ve Türk sorunu 1919–1923: Kamuoyu ve dış politika* (Istanbul: YKY, 2003), 138–40.
[140] Sforza, *Italia*, 71 and 118–119; Khatission, *Eclosion*, 307.
[141] The most complete Western eye-witness account is Stanley E. Kerr, *The Lions of Marash: Personal Experiences with American Near East Relief, 1919–1922* (New York: SUNY, 1973).
[142] Thompson, *Democracy*, 124–133.

Urfa, and Mardin.¹⁴³ More than a year before the Lausanne Conference began, this Accord factually revised Sèvres and anticipated a frontier that the Lausanne Treaty was to recognize. Most Christians living in the ceded zone were abandoned to massacre or hasty flight (in any case to dispossession), while France was free to enforce its rule in Syria.¹⁴⁴ French opportunism at the back of its British ally went even further. Quasi rivalling Bolshevik influence in Ankara, France secretly started to send weapons to the Turkish nationalists, as did the Italians.¹⁴⁵ With their overstretched ambitions, exhausted representatives of imperial France stood with their back to the wall and therefore sought the favor of ultranationalists.¹⁴⁶

Having met Franklin-Bouillon before the he left Paris, Khatissian (see Figure 7) could not but look back scoffingly at that encounter.

> [He] promised me to keep Armenian interests in mind during his negotiations. ... At the same time he asked me to recommend him to the Armenian population of Cilicia and to give him a letter of introduction to the Armenian Catholicos of Sis. I did not accede to either of these requests ... it was quite clear: he was leaving to conclude an agreement with the Turks at any price.¹⁴⁷

After the Accord and the resultant catastrophe for the Christian population, Franklin-Bouillon went so far as to call those skeptical of his efforts and machinations "enemies of Peace." He and his French colleagues accused "Anglo-Greek-Armenian agents" of having provoked the exode of the Christians and cried conspiracy – thus proving themselves ignoramuses of contemporary regional history.¹⁴⁸ On the eve of the Lausanne Conference, Khatissian met Franklin-Bouillon again in Paris. Quixotically and ironically, this new friend of the Kemalists recommended to the

---

¹⁴³ " Accord en vue de réaliser la paix, avec protocole y relatif, protocole relatif à sa mise en vigueur et échange de notes, signés à Angora, le 20 octobre 1921," in *Publication of Treaties and International Engagement registered with the Secretariat of the League of Nations* (Geneva: SdN, 1926–7), Vol. 65, 177–193.
¹⁴⁴ Ümit Kurt, *The Armenians of Aintab: The Economics of Genocide in an Ottoman Province* (Cambridge, MA: Harvard University Press, 2021), 165–167.
¹⁴⁵ Keith Jeffery and Alan Sharp, "Lord Curzon and Secret Intelligence," in Christopher Andrew and Jeremy Noakes (eds.), *Intelligence and International Relations* (Exeter: Exeter University Press), 113–114.
¹⁴⁶ In retrospect, one can hardly help noting that, twenty years later, politicians of this quality proved no match for Nazis – actually, even supported the latter in herding up Jewish citizens of France for transport from Paris to Auschwitz, while many Jews and Armenians joined forces in the armed French *Résistance*.
¹⁴⁷ Khatissian, *Eclosion*, 312.
¹⁴⁸ Dzovinar Kévonian, *Réfugiés et diplomatie humanitaire: Les acteurs européens et la scène proche-orientale pendant l'entre-deux-guerres* (Paris: Publications de la Sorbonne, 2004), 90–91.

12 The Military and Diplomatic Road to Lausanne

Figure 7 Alexandre Khatissian, foreign minister and prime minister ad interim of the Republic of Armenia, during a military parade in Yerevan, ca. 1919. (Courtesy ARF Archives, Boston)

Armenian survivors "to make peace with the Turks without any further delay, and then, having secured their friendship in this way, to present them with requests in favor of Armenia." In his more serene (rather than bitter) reassessment of those years, Khatissian comments, "This is the kind of advice we were given, often in an ironic tone!"[149]

Franklin-Bouillon again met Mustafa Kemal in Izmir in September 1922. He served as a self-declared mediator between Kemalists and the Allies. "No doubt, he motivated them the Kemalists to even more extreme demands," Cavid noted in his diary, calling Franklin-Bouillon an ignoramus of Turkey.[150] The French–Turkish Ankara Accord recognized France's authority in mandatory Syria; in return, it amounted to the factual recognition of the Ankara government by a Great Power. A first step toward recognition had already been the invitation of a delegation from Ankara to the London Conference in February–March 1921 – a kind of official follow-up to the Rome meetings. This time, Bekir Sami led the delegation that included Câmi. Ankara's men sat together with Grand Vizier Tevfik Pash, the representative of the Istanbul government at the negotiation table. The London

---

[149] Khatissian, *Eclosion*, 312. After meeting with Franklin-Bouillon, on 12 February 1922, Avedis Aharonian commented bitterly and ironically in his diary; see Aharonian, *From Sardarabad to Sèvres and Lausanne*, 187–190.

[150] Cavid, *Meşrutiyet Ruznâmesi*, vol. 4, 392, entry of 5 October 1922.

Conference was an attempt by the allies to come to terms with Ankara by softly revising the Sèvres Treaty without giving up the Treaty's principles. This effort failed. Ankara rejected ratification even for minor agreements signed in London, including on prisoner exchanges. In contrast to Ankara's bold and demanding stance, London however made a substantial concession. It released a number of suspected war criminals, the so-called Malta exiles (Malta sürgünleri), while Ankara set free a few British officers taken hostage. From then, the Sèvres Treaty's provisions on the prosecution of war criminals, *génocidaires*, were dead.[151]

At the same time as Ankara won international visibility for, and respect by, many Westerners in London, it secured its Friendship Treaty with Moscow that wholeheartedly supported Ankara's categorial rejection of the Sèvres Treaty. Moreover, the March 1921 treaty with Afghanistan was an official recognition by a Muslim state that added weight to "the tremendous support Ankara and Gazi Kemal Pasha enjoyed from the Muslims of India." A congratulatory telegram by the newly established Afghan embassy in Ankara, which the press published, caused uneasiness with the putative jihad hero Gazi Kemal and Ankara's young diplomacy however, as it carried Islamist phrases such as "In the name of all Muslim peoples" and "Final war against the Christian infidels."[152]

As a result of the tectonic changes in 1921, the future of the Sèvres Treaty looked bleak: It now depended almost entirely on a Greek army whose home country was in turmoil after Prime Minister Venizelos had resigned and King Constantine returned. Since the outbreak of the Great War, Greece was divided by a National Schism that heavily impacted on the country for decades. In its first years before the Lausanne Treaty, the Schism opposed Venizelists and Royalists. The latter had advocated neutrality during the Great War, whereas the Venizelists saw a brilliant future for Greece at the side of the Entente and had therefore promoted Greece's entry into war that finally took place in 1917.[153]

Though weakened and disgusted by the unilateral initiative of Italy and particularly of its French ally, Prime Minister Lloyd George and his liberal government still wanted to stand by the Sèvres Treaty. But

---

[151] Hasan Kayalı, "The struggle for independence," in Reşat Kasaba (ed.), *The Cambridge History of Turkey. Vol. 4: Turkey in the Modern World* (Cambridge: Cambridge University Press, 2009), 135–136; Andrew Mango, *Atatürk* (London: John Murray, 1999), 306–310.

[152] Quoted in Aralov, 92-93. See also Demirci, *Lausanne Conference*, 24.

[153] Thomas W. Gallant, *Modern Greece: From the War of Independence to the Present* (London: Bloomsbury, 2016), 193–198.

12 The Military and Diplomatic Road to Lausanne

Britain found itself thrown back on its own resources alone. It continued to modestly back the Greek army that had been allowed to occupy Izmir in May 1919, according to lines that the Sèvres Treaty was to enshrine in August 1920. The Greeks, including soldiers recruited among the Rûm, advanced further to the east in late 1920, and were encouraged to do so by Lloyd George in order to coerce Ankara into accepting Sèvres. The battles at Inönü in January and March, followed by the battle at Sakarya in August 1921, brought the Greek advance to a decisive halt however. British-leaning non-Turkish people in Anatolia were now more than ever targeted as treacherous agents of foreign powers. Woe to those who did not side with Ankara and its local allies in those struggles before the Lausanne Conference. For a century, "traitor" was to become a knockout argument against any strand of liberalism or "deviating minoritarians" in Turkey. A dangerous demagoguery against any consideration of indigenous minority groups took root, even more deeply as it had already entrenched itself in the late-Ottoman era. Such and similar language also penetrated the Turkish argumentation in Lausanne, as we will see in Part III.

Many members of the Ottoman war *ümmet*, well beyond CUP cadres – notably in the Ottoman eastern provinces and in Mesopotamia – had connived at the dispossession, killing, or enslavement of Christian fellow citizens during the Great War. Local perpetrators and profiteers had participated in a genocide they believed was a jihad against *gâvur* (infidels) and traitors. For them, the post-1918 war in Anatolia was the natural continuation of former violence and served to preserve the former gains.[154] Repressing these facts and the direct line of CUP succession, post-1918 Turkish nationalists propagated the compensating myth of the nation's innocence in order to shape their war in Anatolia in a new and positive light. Domestic Kemalist rhetoric from 1919 to 1923 was bellicose, monotonous, and hyperbolical, as in these lines by Gazi Kemal: "It is impossible to imagine any Muslim who would be willing to see the Khalifate and Sultanate crumble, the Armenians trample on our homeland, and our nation become their slave. All the attempts of our enemies are aimed at dismembering the homeland and enslaving the nation."[155] Half true at best, the myth of the Turkish nation's innocence attacked anti-Turkish prejudices and self-righteous Western victors. Above all, however, it deflected attention from

---

[154] Kurt, *The Armenians of Aintab*. Ugur Üngör, "Disastrous Decade: Armenians and Kurds in the Young Turk Era, 1915–25," in Joost Jongerden and Jelle Verheij (eds.), *Social Relations in Ottoman Diyarbekir, 1870–1915* (Leiden: Brill, 2012), 273–274.

[155] Mustafa Kemal in his letter to Sheykh Mahmud Efendi, 13 August 1919, in: *Nutuk: Vesikalar*, 651.

Turkey's own crimes, playing down continuity with the CUP. It mobilized Ankara's popular base of power with religious catchwords.

Within less than two years, the Greek campaign resulted in a military catastrophe. It was triumphally concluded by the arson of non-Muslim quarters, and the carnage of Rûm and Armenian Christians in Izmir in September 1922. Trustworthy observers on the spot, including the Kemalist journalist Fatih Rıfkı Altay and other Turks, were univocal on the perpetration by forces under commanding general Nureddin Pasha, a "severe fanatic and demagogue," in Altay's words.[156] Turkish propaganda, however, spread "alternative facts" on the authorship of these signature-crimes against humanity. This massacre, too, remained unaddressed in Lausanne, perhaps not least because the allies – present with their warships before Izmir – had decided to keep strict "neutrality." They concentrated on their own nationals and failed to offer resolute assistance to the main victims.[157] Whereas Gazi Kemal and Ankara's National Assembly had hitherto endeavored to disguise their direct rooting in the CUP, they now no longer showed restraint. After having let the notoriously brutal CUP general Nurettin Pasha violate Pontus, Kocgiri, and Smyrna, they appointed arch-perpetrators from Talaat's ministry of the interior to high positions in reconquered Izmir: Mustafa Abdülhalik (Renda) as governor of the province and Mehmet Şükrü (Kaya) as mayor of the town. The latter was elected while he was an advisor in Rıza Nur's team at the Conference of Lausanne. They all represented the exterminatory, proto-fascist current of Turkism.[158]

The British War Office referred to French schadenfreude over the Greek defeat and reported

"a widespread conviction that this will lead to a collapse of British policy in the Near East, which, with the triumph of M. Poincaré in the matter of Reparations, will

---

[156] Falih R. Atay, *Çankaya* (Istanbul: Pozitif, n.d.), 375–76. Kemal Atatürk's *Nutuk* settles account with Nurettin Pasha whom it portrays as a vain commander with a weak character: *Nutuk*, 484–498.

[157] Hervé Georgelin, *La fin de Smyrne, du cosmopolitisme aux nationalismes* (Paris: CNRS, 2005); Michelle Tusan, *Smyrna's Ashes: Humanitarianism, Genocide, and the Birth of the Middle East* (Berkeley: University of California Press, 2012), 144–174; Leyla Neyzi, "Remembering Smyrna/Izmir: Shared History, Shared Trauma," *History and Memory*, 20 (2008): 106–27; Garabed Hatcherian, *An Armenian Doctor in Turkey: Garabed Hatcherian: My Smyrna Ordeal of 1922*, ed. Dora Sakayan (Montreal: Arod Books, 1997). See also "Qui a mis le feu à Smyrne?" *Journal de Genève*, 23 September 1922, 3.

[158] On Mustafa Abdülhalik and Mehmet Şükrü see Kieser, *Talaat Pasha*, 266–267 and Erik Jan Zurcher's unpublished paper "Smyrna, September 1922: the Return of the Unionists" (my thanks to the author). Shortly after the Lausanne Conference, Nurettin Pasha published the booklet *Muzaffer Ordumuzun Kumandanı Muhteremi Ferik Nurettin Pasha Hazretlerinin İzmir Müftüsü Rahmetullah Efendi Hazretlerine Yazdıkları Mektubun Suretidir* (Istanbul: Matbaa-i Osmaniye, no date). In the vein of Rıza Nur, he used exterminatory anti-Christian, especially anti-Rûm language.

12 The Military and Diplomatic Road to Lausanne 109

eventually lead to the fall of Lloyd George, and the general triumph of French policy throughout Europe."[159]

Immediately after the destruction of Izmir, the French and Italian troops withdrew their detachments from the neutral zone before Istanbul (including the Dardanelles and Çanakkale), so that Kemalist forces could more easily advance. Backed by the potential of its Empire and a Greek army in Thrace, but no longer by its dominions, London could, however, make a stand against the Turkish army.

Yet, the political price for Lloyd George's government – and for the idea of Empire generally – was high. During this Çanakkale or "Chanak Crisis," the dominions and the public expressed strong dissatisfaction with the cabinet's policy and any further costly engagement in Turkey. Nevertheless, in the armistice agreement of Mudanya on 11 October 1922, the Turkish army had to renounce on its desired immediate occupation of Istanbul and Eastern Thrace.[160] As a consequence of these events and the failure of the British-supported Greek campaign as a whole, Lloyd George's cabinet fell a month before the Lausanne Conference began.

***

In early 1922, Prime Minister Lloyd George still had sought to stem the tide of developments that thwarted the aims of his imperial cabinet for Europe and Turkey. The Paris-Geneva peace should last, but be enhanced. An economically sound and politically balanced pacification should contain resentments, reactions, and crises among those in the position of pariah groups and states, as seen from the Paris treaty system.

Initiated and led by Lloyd George, the Genoa Conference in April–May 1922 brought thirty-four nations together, including Germany and Soviet Russia, the pariahs of the Paris treaty system.[161] Relations with Berlin and Moscow should be improved. The meeting aimed at solving the major economic, financial, and political problems, when hyperinflation reigned in Germany. The meeting failed in what it had intended, but, in a sideshow, led to the Treaty of Rapallo, a city next to Genoa where German and Soviet representatives met. This Treaty of 16 April 1922 normalized the relations between the isolated countries. It enabled commercial and military relations that partly contravened the Versailles Treaty.

---

[159] WO106/1505 no. 864, 13 September 1922, quoted in Demirci, *Lausanne Conference*, 20.
[160] For the *Convention militaire entre les Puissances alliées, le Gouvernement de la grande Assemblée nationale de Turguie et la Grèce*, see FO Confidential Print 12330, 199–201. Steiner, *The Lights that Failed*, 114–119; Demirci, *Lausanne Conference*, 36–37. See also Robert M. Dawson, *The development of dominion status 1900-1936* (Oxford University Press, 1937).
[161] Carole Fink, *The Genoa Conference: European Diplomacy, 1921–1922* (Chapel Hill: University of North Carolina Press, 1984).

110   Against the Paris-Geneva Peace

Due to its failures in Europe and its insistence on the moribund Sèvres Treaty, Lloyd George's government fell in October 1922 – a month after the entry of Nureddin Pasha's army into Izmir. Until then, London had remained loyal to a tradition of British policy in Turkey that sought to meet imperial and humanitarian ends. This approach had definitively come to its conceptual and material limits.[162] While Britain was latest in letting down the main victims of a decade of extreme violence in Anatolia and Mesopotamia, it lacked not only material capacities but also faith in human equality. Outworn ideologemes of race and British exceptionalism coexisted with a rhetoric of Western civilization. In this vein, as we have seen, London and Washington had defeated a 1919 racial equality proposal as unsuitable to be part of the Covenant of the League of Nations.[163]

Consequentially, British policy, too, was finally to turn to what this book calls the West's new Interwar realpolitik. This started in earnest by integrally appeasing nationalist Turkey in Lausanne. Colonial Secretary Winston Churchill, one of the architects of late-imperial realpolitik, had initially clarified what he understood as London's interests in the Middle East at the Cairo Conference of British officials in March 1921. Two years before the Lausanne Conference, he already sought to accommodate Ankara. But he was torn between support for his staunchly anti-CUP, thus anti-Kemalist, Prime Minister George Lloyd and a traditional pro-Ottoman stance of British pre-1914 conservativism.[164] Churchill had warned in a letter to Lloyd George in March 1920, "We are leading the Allies in an attempt to enforce a peace on Turkey which would require great and powerful armies and long, costly operations and occupations. . . . [T]he Greek armies are your only effective fighting force."[165]

There had been ongoing British indecision, indeed aporia, vis-à-vis late-Ottoman Turkey. This led Churchill to later frankly admit that, "generally mystified by many contradictory voices," he and many others had, in August–September 1914, wrongly believed "Turkey had no policy and might still be won or lost"[166] – while the Young Turk regime consistently pursued a policy of domestic ultranationalism in Anatolia that Churchill grasped only years later.[167] The CUP combined this with a policy of imperial restoration of Turkey's sultanate-caliphate. The Treaty of Lausanne endorsed what, ten years earlier, had begun as the

---

[162] Michelle Tusan, *The British Empire and the Armenian Genocide, Humanitarianism and Imperial Politics from Gladstone to Churchill* (London: I.B. Tauris, 2019).
[163] Shimazu, *Japan, Race and Equality*.
[164] Warren Dockter, *Churchill and the Islamic World* (London: I. B. Tauris, 2015), 142–94.
[165] Winston Churchill, *The World Crisis* (London: Thornton Butterworth, 1929), 378.
[166] Ibid., 359–360. [167] Ibid., 404.

CUP's Turkist project for Anatolia. Then-interior minister and party boss Talaat Pasha implemented it in the shadow of European war and confusion, and his demographic engineering won over in the long run.

13 Lausanne's Ottoman Diaspora: Preparing National Futures

On the eve of the 1921 London Conference, Scotland Yard had sent Member of Parliament, Turkey expert, and spy Aubrey Herbert to secretly interview Talaat in Hamm in Germany. From his exile in Berlin, the former Grand Vizier promoted the Turkish nationalist cause in Europe, several times passing through Switzerland, a place of particularly intense political agitation at Lake Geneva. The secret police were well aware of Talaat, his contacts and interactions, and the stamps in his passport under the fake name of Ali Said that proved several entries to Italy from Switzerland.[168]

Although Talaat was prevented from personally attending the landmark meetings in Rome, he stayed in Rome and conducted important conversations in those weeks. The meetings in Rome set into motion the gradual diplomatic delegitimization of the Sèvres Treaty. The former CUP boss was fully informed and involved in the struggle for the revision of this Treaty.[169] His assassination in Berlin on 15 March 1921, during the London Conference, did not stop this process. Talaat and Ankara would have found less resonance in Europe without late-Ottoman diasporic networks that, led by ex-CUP agents in exile, served the Turkish nationalist outreach. On the margins of the Conference of Lausanne including its long eve and aftermath, there lies, therefore, a little-known, but seminal story in which Muslim Ottoman diasporas in Lausanne and elsewhere in Switzerland and Europe played roles in the fight against the Sèvres Treaty.[170]

The diasporic presence also impacted on the microcosm and atmosphere at the Lausanne Conference itself. At first sight, it appeared the

---

[168] "Talaat was once a very fat individual with long moustaches. He has lost a lot of weight and his description can now be established as follows: height 178 cm, fairly strong build, round face, slightly pointed nose, moustaches cut in the American style, dark complexion, graying hair." Confidential report by the Cantonal Police, 14 June 1920, S112/88, ACV. See also Margaret Fitzherbert, *The Man Who Was Greenmantle: A Biography of Aubrey Herbert* (London: John Murray, 1983), 232–237; 220–221; Kieser, *Talaat Pasha*, 388–389.

[169] Cavid diary, vol. 4, 187–224, entries of 5 December 1920 to 19 February 1921.

[170] For a detailed account, see Kieser, *Vorkämpfer*, or in its revised and expanded Turkish version: *Türklüğe İhtida: 1870–1939 İsviçre'sinde Yeni Türkiye'nin öncüleri* (Istanbul: İletişim, 2008).

Turkish delegation had to take a lonely and difficult stance against all the nominally Christian delegates coming from England, France, Italy, Greece, Romania, and the Kingdom of the Serbs, Croats, and Slovenes – Japan being the only non-Christian and "non-white" nation present. Apart from the fact that tensions and contradictory interests made a lasting united Allied front impossible at the Conference, the gatherings at Lausanne with all its regional Turkish and Muslim organizations could at times look like a home game for Ankara's delegation.

At the side of the first delegate Ismet Inönü, a confidant of Mustafa Kemal and military icon of the war for Anatolia – as discussed earlier – stood Rıza Nur, a staunch (pan-)Turkish nationalist. Having fallen out with the CUP, he had spent time as a member of the diaspora in Switzerland and Egypt before being summoned by Ankara's leader as minister, and had been given key diplomatic tasks. The secretary-general of the delegation was Réchid Safvet alias Kara-Schemsi – later spelled Reşit Saffet (Atabinen) – an ex-CUP agent, former secretary of Mehmed Cavid, and habitué of the Turkish diaspora in Switzerland.

From the 1890s onward, Geneva and Lausanne had become privileged places of political exile and higher education for Muslim Ottomans. These were late arrivals compared to the Ottoman Christians, ex-Ottomans from the Balkans, and, especially, the Armenians who were already firmly established alongside Russian students and activists in Geneva.[171] The Ottoman – or newly post-Ottoman – diasporas were compartmentalized and organized around ethno-national Greek, Serbian, Bulgarian, Armenian, Zionist, Albanian, and Egyptian clubs. Such clubs served as a model for the Turkish-Ottoman diaspora, which, in the 1890s, included many young and disoriented Muslim asylum-seekers who fled Sultan Abdulhamid's repression.

Emerging from fresh strong currents of Turkism under the influence of Gökalp and other mentors in the early 1910s, so-called *Foyers Turcs*, or Turkish Home Associations (*Türk Yurdu* and *Türk Ocağı*) were founded in the Ottoman Empire and abroad. Number one among them was the *Foyer Turc de Lausanne*. Starting in 1911, it met at 19 Avenue de Riant-Mont, close to the city center, and cooperated with its counterpart in Geneva in forming a new active nucleus of the Turkist movement in Europe. In spring 1913, they organized an international congress in Petit-Lancy, close to Geneva, which called Turkish elites to strive for making Anatolia a Turkish national home (*Türk Yurdu*).[172] Ten years later, the

---

[171] See H. Kieser (ed.), *Die armenische Frage und die Schweiz* (Zürich: Chronos, 1999).

[172] *Yurdcular Yasası. İsviçre'de Cenevre şehrine yakın Petit-Lancy Köyünde Pension Racine'de kurulan İkinci Yurdcular Derneği'nin muzakerat ve mukerreratı* (Istanbul: Yeni Turan Matbaası, 1914).

Kemalist delegation at the Lausanne Conference insisted on obtaining international recognition for a nation-state in line with the *Türk Yurdu* project.

The Turkish Home Associations were important places of ethno-Turkish socialization for a whole new Muslim nationalist elite, as well as a small number of late-Ottoman Jews and so-called *dönme*.[173] Initially starting out as a cultural movement, the associations soon turned political. The division between East and West, and Muslims and Christians, brought about by the Tripolitan war – the Italian invasion of Libya – in autumn 1911, affected student circles in Lausanne, Geneva, Paris, and many other places. The new Turkish Home Associations in the Ottoman Empire and abroad supported the CUP. The CUP, in turn, sponsored them and also sent students abroad with state scholarships. Turkish Home members remained largely loyal when the CUP established its dictatorial party-state in 1913, and during the Great War. After defeat and demise in 1918, they formed an intellectual backbone of Turkish nationalism, and this most notably in Europe. There they were able to move and publish freely. Neutral Switzerland was a case in point.

The main function of the Turkish Homes and associated centers and offices after the Great War was agitation, propaganda, and public diplomacy toward the West, in close cooperation with Ankara. As we have seen, Ankara's new Grand National Assembly brought together generals and comrades of Kemal, the country's Muslim notables and a new elite emerging from the Turkish Home Associations. Several young figures of this elite took office in the counter-government alongside experienced former subordinates of Talaat. Examples are Mahmut Esat Bozkurt, Şükrü Saraçoğlu, and Harun Aliçe. After studies and Turkish Home activities in Switzerland, they became deputies or ministers in Ankara by 1923.[174]

Born the son of a Muslim land baron in Izmir, Mahmoud Essad Bey, as he was then called, was a minister of economy during the Lausanne Conference, thereafter a minister of justice, and as such responsible for introducing the Swiss Civil Code in Turkey. Besides presiding over the Turkish Home Association in Lausanne during and after the Great War, he wrote a doctoral thesis at the University of Fribourg, near Lausanne, on the Ottoman Capitulations.[175] The Capitulations were premodern

---

[173] Descendants of Jews who had followed the self-proclaimed seventeenth-century messiah Sabbatai Zevi. They ended as a distinct, outwardly Sunnitized group centered in late-Ottoman Salonica, the headquarters of the CUP before it moved to Istanbul.

[174] See Kieser, *Talaat Pasha*, 411–412; Paul Gentizon, "Lettre d'Angora," *Gazette de Lausanne*, 18 October 1923, 1.

[175] Mahmoud Essad, *Du régime des capitulations ottomanes, leur caractère juridique d'après l'histoire et les textes* (Istanbul: n.p., 1928).

"contracts" or privileges which gave European nationals in the Ottoman Empire a privileged status of extra-territoriality. They constituted a major obstacle to the full sovereignty of the state, after the late-Ottoman Empire had become dependent on European Powers and the number of people benefitting from the Capitulation had exponentially increased.

For Bozkurt, Switzerland was an almost-utopian model for democracy, having achieved a constitutional revolution in 1848, remained outside the "concert of European Powers," and done so without colonies. Already for late-nineteenth century writer and activist Ali Suavi, Switzerland therefore represented Europe's only real democracy.[176] These features, together with a strong fascination among many students for the Enlightenment philosopher Jean-Jacques Rousseau of Geneva, contributed to making Switzerland an ideal place for late-Ottoman intellectuals and young dissidents, Muslim and non-Muslim. For many hundreds of them, it became an attractive place to study. Political activists appreciated the high degree of freedom that allowed them to discuss and publish political ideas, benefit from modern education, and find understanding for their cause. We have already mentioned the 1912 poem "Kızılelma," in which Gökalp imagined an educational center next to Lausanne. From there civilizational progress would stream to Turkey and make the country strong.[177]

Late-Ottoman higher education guides praised Switzerland as an ideal place for Muslim girls, arguing that sexual morality there was more generally observed than in the European metropolises.[178] One such young girl was seventeen-year-old schoolteacher Ayşe Afet Inan (later surname: Afetinan), who dreamed of completing her education at Lake Léman. Adopted in 1925 by the supreme leader, she saw her long-cherished dream realized, as she was sent to an international boarding school in Lausanne. In the 1930s, she continued her studies with Professor Eugène Pittard, a rare European friend of Atatürk, at the University of Geneva. There she completed her doctorate in anthropology. A close acquaintance of Ankara's delegation in Lausanne, a decade later Pittard facilitated a doctoral thesis by Afet Inan that entirely served the concept of a unitary Turkish Anatolia.[179]

---

[176] "Demokrasi, Hükûmet-i Halk, Müsavat," *Ulûm Gazetesi*, 2.18 (May 1870), 1083–1107.
[177] "Kızılelma," *Türk Yurdu*, 118.
[178] Serpil Çakır, *Osmanlı Kadın Hareketi* (Istanbul: Metis, 1994), 259; n.a., *Cenevre'de tahsil* (Istanbul: Mezîyet-i iktisâdiye matbaası, 1328/1912); Tunalı Hilmi, *Avrupa'da tahsil* (Genf: n.p., 1903).
[179] Ayşe Afetinan, *Atatürk'ten Mektuplar* (Ankara, TTK, 1989). See also Chapter 27.

Neither the proximity to different late-Ottoman diasporas, nor the multiple connections made with Swiss people, contributed to creating bonds for peace between Muslims and Christians, Turks, Greeks, Rûm, and Armenians. In the name of humanity and Christian faith, sympathy for the Armenians as a small, industrious yet threatened nation generally prevailed among the Swiss. But this had little impact on the country's foreign policy and Swiss commercial activities.[180]

***

During the decade before the Lausanne Conference, the Turkish Home Associations in Lausanne, Geneva, and other cities served as think tanks and laboratories for young patriots who envisioned a revolution that would lead to a "new Turkey," both socially and politically. Handwritten in Ottoman in a sturdy notebook of over 300 pages,[181] the minutes of the Turkish Home in Lausanne bear testament to almost religious Turkist convictions and a desire for national awakening.

These minutes put little emphasis on pan-Turkish visions, but focus more on a social and educational revolution that the members believed was desperately needed for the future. They put European-style education and civilization, and the exclusion of Islam from public life, at the heart of the transformation, without however questioning the public predominance of Turkish-Muslim identity. We easily recognize avant-gardist voices for a "Turkish Revolution" that would take place under Kemalist rule a few years later, although then by authoritarian means. The same voices came to the fore during Lausanne's "Turkish Congresses" in 1919–22.

From May 1919, a "Permanent Bureau of the Turkish Congress in Lausanne" organized an annual "Turkish Congress" in the city's foyer of the Café du Théâtre. After Esat Bozkurt's departure in 1919, Harun Alitché (Harun Aliçe/Aliçeoğlu), presided in Lausanne over the Turkish Home, the Permanent Bureau, and the Inter-Muslim Academic Society (Société académique inter-musulmane). These were all closely interconnected lobby organizations that came to serve Gazi Kemal's cause. They made Lausanne a familiar destination, even a place of pilgrimage, for Turkish nationalists. The activists usually met at the Restaurant de la Paix, next to the railway station. In 1920, Harun Alitché founded an Ottoman Academic League and helped found the

---

[180] Hans-Lukas Kieser, "Schweiz des Fin de siècle und 'Armenien': Patriotische Identifikation, Weltbürgertum und Protestantismus in der schweizerischen philarmenischen Bewegung," in Kieser, *Armenische Frage*, 133–157.

[181] *Lozan Türk Yurdu Cemiyeti'nin Muharrerat ve Zabt-ı Sabık Defteri*, Türk Tarih Kurumu (TTK), Y 653.

Islamic Union, both in Lausanne. The Union was committed to fighting for the independence of Muslim countries. With their concerted activism, Turkish nationalists dominated the Arab, Egyptian, and Indian Muslim diaspora, thus creating anti-Western, specifically anti-British, synergies.

In February 1921, the Permanent Bureau started the newspaper *Turkey: Monthly Organ of the Turkish Congress at Lausanne*.[182] This launch took place during the London Conference where, as we have seen, Ankara's delegation demanded the entire abrogation of the Sèvres Treaty. Published in Lausanne for English-speaking readers, *Turkey: Monthly Organ* fought for the same goal by emphasizing the utility of a renewed Turkish–British friendship. It skillfully played on the double anti-Western threat of political Islam and Bolshevism, insinuating that the Turks enjoyed excellent relations with both of these currents. "Whether the Turks be bound to the Bolshevists or separated from them depends upon the position to be taken by Great-Britain as regards the Turkish claims," it wrote.[183]

Among the most prolific agents and pamphleteers in Switzerland in the immediate aftermath of the Great War was Reşit Saffet (Atabinen) who published under the pseudonym Kara-Schemsi. He and a few others authored propaganda booklets which denied CUP mass crimes, rejected non-Turkish claims in Anatolia, and orchestrated a chorus in Europe that decried an alleged "annihilation of the Turks." They demanded a unitary Turkish state encompassing all of Asia Minor as according to the National Pact. They rejected any right to self-rule by others, even if a referendum had positively determined the wish of regional majorities for autonomy. No effort was spared to relativize, belittle, or deny the extermination of Armenians. In his main arguments, Reşit Saffet exonerated the state and "the Turkish nation" by placing the blame on Kurds and others. He made a sweeping comparison of Armenian and Muslim suffering in modern history that served to ridicule the Armenian deaths – describing them as "jokes" compared to Turkish and Muslim victimhood.[184] A former member of Talaat Pasha's circle who propagandized Gökalp's pan-Turkism, Atabinen thus perpetuated CUP denialism in a European Turkish diaspora whose youth was initially quite open to soul-searching and new democratic horizons.[185]

---

[182] Printed by Giesser & Held, located rue Caroline 5, Lausanne (close to the Restaurant de la Paix).

[183] "The Turko-Russian Treaty," *Turkey*, 6 (July 1921), 2. See also "A note from Tchitcherine to the government of Angora," no. 3, April 1921, 4.

[184] Kara-Schemsi (Atabinen), *L'extermination des Turcs* (Genève: n.p., 1919), 2.

[185] Kieser, *Talaat Pasha*, 384. For a more detailed discussion of Reşit Saffet Atabinen and the literature then produced, see Kieser, *Vorkämpfer*, 90–95, and Liebisch-Gümüş, *Verflochtene Nationsbildung*, 52–53 and 145–150.

***

The CUP politician and intellectual Ahmed Rıza is a case in point to understanding the emotionally polarizing situation in Anatolia and the European diaspora in the aftermath of the occupation of Izmir by Greeks on the long eve of the Lausanne Conference.

Turks of all strands were indignant that the Allies permitted "to a country of former *raya* subaltern non-Muslim Ottomans to occupy a great Turkish city."[186] Ahmed Rıza's booklet *La faillite morale de la politique occidentale en Orient*, published in summer 1922, is a telling lament and indictment, rich in insights into its author's intellectual biography. It is the moral denunciation of a West that allegedly crusaded against the Levant, in particular the Turks, since the Middle Ages. Ahmed Rıza included almost no introspective historical analysis. Though he knew better, he – like Atabinen – used the hyperbole of a Western "extermination of the Turks" to emotionally strengthen his argument. A democratic outlook is entirely absent.[187] Rıza knew better because in the Ottoman parliament in autumn 1915, he had courageously taken a position against a law that legalized the dispossession of the Armenian citizens after genocide. He was immediately intimidated and silenced by Talaat.[188]

Sure enough, Ahmed Rıza had a point against the biases in the Paris-Geneva peace project. But he exaggerated, making himself a temporary instrument of propaganda for Ankara whose "dictatorship" he, however, soon had to deplore. "It is certainly neither the Sèvres Treaty's Financial Commission nor the League of Nations that would be responsible for our moral and intellectual development. It would be absurd to expect from them the recovery of a nation whose disappearance they have decided to bring about," he caricatured the Sèvres settlement in 1920.[189] Ahmed Rıza's moral confusion was most manifest in Rome where he excluded Talaat from the meetings to please anti-CUP Western diplomacy, but reconciled and fraternized with this architect of genocide in private. Together, they imagined the Rûm being thrown into the sea in a war with Greece that Talaat had wanted and prepared for since late 1913.

---

[186] Grand Vizier Ferid Pasha quoted in Sforza, *Italia*, 68.
[187] Ahmed Rıza, *La faillite morale de la politique occidentale en Orient* (Ankara: Ministry of Culture, 1990, first published in Paris in 1922), 12 and 17. See also Kaynar, *Ahmed Rıza*, 816–824.
[188] Kieser, *Talaat Pasha*, 269. See also Liebisch-Gümüş, *Verflochtene Nationsbildung*, 151–153.
[189] Ahmed Rıza, "Quelques Réflexions sur le Traité de Paix Turc," in Rıza, *Echos de Turquie. Vivre au grand jour. Vivre libre ou mourir*, Paris 1920, 100, quoted in Liebisch-Gümüş, *Verflochtene Nationsbildung*, 152–153.

Cavid, too, proved of short memory after 1918, when he uncritically reengaged at Talaat's side, resharing sweeping anti-Western outrage, or even cultivating nostalgia. "In huge Turkey, in fact in the whole Near East, there is no man who can replace Talaat," he wrote in a letter to Ahmed Rıza.[190] Still, generally, he kept more intellectual distance than the others to anything ultranationalist.[191] At the Rome Conference, Ankara benefitted from Rıza's reputation among European diplomats in its first step toward recognition. After that, he was of no more use to the Kemalists and soon sidelined. In contrast, Ankara's press spoke highly of Talaat, and the National Assembly finally named a central boulevard after him. He was Ghazi Kemal Pasha's real and immediate predecessor.[192]

At the opposite side of the Turkish-nationalist diaspora at Lake Léman stood the émigré André Mandelstam, a Russian-Jewish expert of international law and dragoman at the Russian embassy in the Ottoman capital until fall 1914. He had resided at the Bosporus before moving to Geneva and Paris. There he continued to inquire into late-Ottoman history, the quest for post-Ottoman peace, and the mass crimes at the end of the Ottoman Empire. In his 1917 opus magnum, he labeled the CUP's extermination of the Armenians a "crime against humanity" (*crime de lèse-humanité*).[193] Because of his legal expertise and empathy for the Armenians, he became a bogeyman for the CUP and the Kemalists. They particularly hated him as the author of the first draft of what finally became the February 1914 Reform Agreement for seven Ottoman eastern provinces. For Turkish nationalists of all shapes, this constituted a conspiratorial step toward Armenian autonomy.

***

The city was very busy and all its hotels were almost full when Turkish journalists arrived in Lausanne in mid-November 1922, a week before the Conference began. In their understanding, the years from 1919 to 1922 were all-decisive. They had erased the past before; global history had been turned upside down with the Turkish victories in Anatolia. They resented that for others, former events, facts, and arguments, notably regarding the Armenians, still carried weight.

---

[190] Cavid, *Meşrutiyet Ruznâmesı*, vol. 4, 334, entry of 21 December 1921.
[191] Ibid., vol. 4, 203–204, entry of 8 January 1921.
[192] Kieser, *Talaat Pasha*, 406–424. Three years after the Rome Conference, Ahmed Rıza labeled the Ankara government an "ultra-revolutionary directorate" and "dictatorship" (letter to Emile Corra, 14 April 1924, quoted in Kaynar, *Ahmed Rıza*, 826).
[193] André N. Mandelstam, *Le sort de l'empire ottoman* (Lausanne: Payot, 1917), 406, 414. See also André N. Mandelstam, *La Société des Nations et les puissances devant le problème arménien* (Paris: A. Pedone, 1925).

Shortly before the Conference opening, Necmeddin Sadık (Sadak), a journalist for the daily *Akşam* (*Evening*), wrote in one of his first "letters from Lausanne":

> There are still those who talk about the modification of the Treaty of Sevres. The Lausanne Conference, in its first sessions, will see the representatives of a Turkey with a different spirit and thought, and it is possible that only then will the truth of Turkish nationalism be understood. The Swiss character, in particular, is completely alien to these ideas. Geneva and Lausanne have only heard accusations against us since the General War. They seem to be astonished by the new Turkish claims. Therefore newspapers started to publish against us. ... Against this, it is necessary to form a regular front, to wage a struggle outside the conference.[194]

Besides being an international media event, the Conference of Lausanne was to become a "school in diplomacy" for a whole generation of ambitious young men within or attached to Ankara's large delegation.[195] The future diplomat and foreign minister Necmeddin S. Sadak was one among dozens. Most knew each other from common activities in and around Istanbul's CUP headquarters. This was the case for the future ministers Celal Bayar, Şükrü Kaya, and Sadak; the future ambassadors Mehmet Ertegün and Yahya Kemal Beyatlı; as well as Atabinen, soon a deputy and "missionary" of the Turkish History Thesis; and Hüseyin Cahit Yalçın, a future deputy and influential journalist – although Yalçın had to suffer in and after Lausanne for his proximity to Cavid.

In Lausanne, the journalists performed an efficient collaboration of press and politics, learned in their years under Talaat Pasha. Lausanne also proved formative for this kind of symbiosis in the Republic of Turkey. Part III of *When Democracy Died* now turns to the Conference itself. It also pays attention to the struggles fought in the press and public sphere.

---

[194] *Necmeddin Sadık (Sadak) Bey'in Lozan Mektupları*, ed. Mustafa Özyürek (Ankara: Gece, 2019), 40.

[195] As Bilal N. Şimşir, a historian and diplomat in the service of Ankara, underlined in his article "Şair Yahya Kemal Beyatlı'nın Elçiliği ve Büyükelçiliği," *Atatürk Araştırma Merkezi Dergisi*, 23.67–68 (November 2007), 30–31. For a list of the delegation members, see Sadak, *Lozan Mektupları*, 20–21. See also the Biographical Notes in the Annex.

Part III A Protracted Conference: Redefining Turkey, Western Realpolitik

The Conference of Lausanne consisted of several months of intense interactions. Most participants arriving by or after mid-November expected, like French Prime Minister Raymond Poincaré, that it would take not more than a month to come to a conclusion.[1] It took more than eight months, including the busy interval after the Conference's first half.

Multiple exchanges took place on the shores of Lake Geneva. Some delegations or representatives who came to Lausanne were not allowed to sit at the main table, even if they spoke for indigenous groups living in, or hailing from Anatolia. This territory was now tantamount to what Turkey's National Pact demanded and the Conference was to endorse; that is, Turkey consisted of the whole of Anatolia plus a few additional parts. Other hopeful delegates spoke for neighbors or future borderlanders whose land the Conference was to divide. Others represented those many millions concerned about the future of the caliphate. Thus, there were unrecognized representations – Armenian, Assyrian, Syrian, Palestinian, Egyptian, Hashemite and Persian as well as hundreds of journalists, lobbyists, and figures of the private sector gathered in Lausanne after mid-November 1922.[2] Notable Kurdish representatives – the Kurds became main victims of the Lausanne Treaty, as their land was divided – were conspicuously absent.

To be added to Lausanne's multiple official meetings and scenes were sideshows, soirées, dance events, recreational events, and prostitution in and outside the city.[3] Published or unpublished reports, interviews, statements, or talks in backrooms, grand hotel halls, or corridors complete the picture of vibrant and expectant, at times cacophonic, and often

---

[1] *Neue Zürcher Zeitung*, no. 1517, 20 November 1922, 2.
[2] *Journal de Genève*, 22 November 1922, third ed., 2. See also Teitelbaum, *Hashimite Kingdom*, 240.
[3] Besides press report, diaries, memoirs, etc. on Lausanne's daily events, the cantonal police's daily secret reports in the file "Conférence de Lausanne 1922-23," S 112/95, ACV, are instructive. Enjoying privileged access, the highly diverse Swiss press was particularly keen to cover all aspects of the Conference.

contradictory communications. "Lausanne is swarming like a hive of bees," Cavid Bey felt; and for *Akşam* correspondent Necmettin Sadık (Sadak), "Lausanne has become a [global] center where all political and religious interests freely clash." Ankara's vice-plenipotentiary Nur scorned all unofficial delegates, including those from Syria and Egypt, and especially the Armenians. "They came to Lausanne from all over the world. A bunch of vagrants, policy buggers, poured into this city."[4]

The results of the mega-event were clear and incisive. Besides the Treaty itself and related agreements, they included historical visions, omissions or distortions that had framed the process of decision-making and would mark the understanding of generations to come. The Conference set the post-Ottoman course, including the lines of Western relations with the Republic of Turkey. The road toward the Treaty was twisted and protracted. There were poignant debates and moments in the Conference's commissions and sub-commissions, notably on the question of minorities, population transfer, the Armenian home, and highly disparate – but hardly talked out – historical understandings.

Lausanne's most tabooed topic was the "Armenian home"; its most ominous term and measure, disputed in its genesis and promotion, was "compulsory population exchange." As we have seen, international diplomacy and historiography after 1923 was to take the "exchange" as a positive, "brutal, but effective" tool that ended ethno-religious conflicts.[5] The Conference changed the architecture of the post–Great War peace and recognized a redefined Turkey. Part III combines a chronological and thematical narrative of the Conference from a global history perspective. It starts with an outline.

14 The Conference's Eve, Premises, and Grand Lines

The Swiss town of Lausanne was a neutral place in the heart of Europe with all necessary infrastructural requirements. Its train station was on the direct line of the Orient Express. It was close to Geneva, but did not carry the title of being the seat of the League of Nations that Ankara (in line with the Bolsheviks) hitherto repudiated. The Conference was enforced by Turkish nationalist success, but orchestrated by British diplomacy. Though in agreement with Paris and Rome, Foreign Secretary Curzon basically decided the Conference place, date, agenda, and time table.

---

[4] Cavid, *Meşrutiyet Ruznâmesi*, 416, diary entry of 16 December 1922; Sadak, *Lozan Mektupları*, 31; Nur, *Hayat ve Hatıratım*, vol. 2, 346–347.
[5] Historian Bernard Lewis in Lewis, *Emergence*, 250.

In early October 1922, British diplomats started to suggest Lausanne as the place for a new Near East peace conference.[6] On 26 October 1922, in the name of the allied powers, the Foreign Office invited the government of Ankara and all other prospective participants to the new conference there.[7] Ankara's National Assembly had first suggested, and for a few days kept insisting on, Izmir (Smyrna) as the conference place.[8] For the deputies, this Levantine city was the symbol of a recent Turkish victory not only over Greece, but also Europe and Christianity. For Turkish-Muslim nationalists, before its destruction in September 1922, Smyrna had represented a place of *gavur* (infidels) and scorned Levantine cosmopolitanism.

In early November 1922, Britain deferred the opening from 13 to 20 November due to the fall of Lloyd George's cabinet and new elections. From the eve to the end of the Conference, London remained in a position to set the dates and the agenda. Added to this, importantly, was its superiority in intelligence gathering thanks to intercepting telegraphic lines and, possibly benefitting from Lausanne's secret police.[9] As for telegram interception, "The information, which was obtained mainly from the British wireless intercept operation in Constantinople, did ... mean that on certain occasions they could cut their losses and know when not to push the conference to a breach."[10] Secret British knowledge of serious rifts in Ankara's National Assembly, which plagued the Turkish delegation, proved essential in fine-tuning negotiation tactics.

***

For the ex-Ottoman peoples, the negotiations in Lausanne were existential. For the main allies – Europe's national empires Britain, France, and Italy – they were crucial because of vested and new mandatory interests.

---

[6] Rumbold to Curzon, 11 October 1922, Foreign Office, *Further Correspondence Respecting Turkey, October to December 1922*, Confidential Print 12330, FO 424/255 (hereafter FO Correspondence Turkey, Confidential Print 12330), 118–161. Curzon's argument for Lausanne in his telegram to Ambassador Hardinge in Paris, 12 October 1922: "Lausanne has the following advantages: 1. It is on the direct line of the Orient Express to Constantinople (which Geneva is not). 2. It has excellent hotel accommodation and a good climate even in winter. 3. It was the seat of the peace conference between Turkey and Italy in 1912. 4. The League of Nations establishment at Geneva would doubtless be willing to assist in the arrangements for the conference at Lausanne, just as they did in the case of the Genoa Conference. They could supply a large and trained staff of typists, shorthand writers and translators in English and French, and possibly other languages. 5. The central position of Lausanne would enable foreign delegates to go to and fro with comparative ease."

[7] Telegram Curzon to Rumbold, Istanbul, 26 October 1922, FO Correspondence Turkey, Confidential Print 12330, 231.

[8] FO Correspondence Turkey, Confidential Print 12330, 54, 105, 107, 110, 118, 127, 129.

[9] The police used dozens of hotel employees and other persons for information gathering, as transpires from the reports in ACV S 112/95.

[10] Jeffery and Sharp, "Lord Curzon and Secret Intelligence," 115.

14 The Conference's Eve, Premises, and Grand Lines 123

Geo-strategically for the West, it was about separating Turkey from Soviet Russia and pan-Islamism.

Critical domestic and foreign politics met in Lausanne, including politics concerning Germany that saw its horrible year of hyperinflation in 1923. A sense of haste seized French and European diplomacy when, on 11 January 1923, the French-Belgian occupation of the Ruhr in Germany drew political and media attention away from the Oriental Question. France's primary concern and security issue was Germany. There it was ready to employ its army to extract German reparations. A serious rift existed between Paris and London on Germany and Turkey. As we have seen, the French emissary Franklin-Bouillon had early on made a deal with Ankara, the 1921 Treaty of Ankara. This had factually erased the French signature from the Sèvres Treaty. The cabinet of center-right politician Raymond Poincaré sought primarily financial and economic satisfaction in Lausanne, as France had been the biggest investor in late-Ottoman Turkey.

The Conference broke down in early February 1923, on financial and economic issues, including the related Capitulations. By then, Britain had achieved its main goals; that is, open Straits, weakened Turkish-Bolshevik ties and Mosul's delayed, but probable incorporation into mandatory Iraq. During the break, meetings of the Allies in Paris and London dealt with the remaining bones of contention, while Ankara's National Assembly experienced turbulent weeks. For some observers, it was not certain that Mustafa Kemal's circle would emerge victorious. Those weeks saw steps that set the course toward Kemalist dictatorship.

In Lausanne, the Allies were not united and not coordinating policy on important issues in Europe and the Near East. Nevertheless, during the first Conference weeks, the Turkish delegation met Allies who were less disunited than expected. This was due to Lord Curzon's clever tactics, not to a strategic consensus. Ankara's cause was underpinned by considerable ideological, diplomatic, and, above all, military power. In a remarkable hyperbole a few weeks after the signing of the Treaty, US delegate Grew talked of "probably the greatest diplomatic victory in history" that Ankara had achieved. However, it "could hardly result otherwise" if considered "that Ismet held all of the cards in his hands." Grew meant military victory, the ongoing readiness of Turkey to fight on versus the well-known Allied refusal to do so, and Allied divisiveness.[11]

The Sèvres Conference had largely ignored Ankara's reorganization of power, in particular its capacity to remobilize the army and parts of the population. This went beyond reactivating the CUP networks and

---

[11] "Informal Talk at the Consular Dinner at the Hotel Victoria," Interlaken, 2 September 1923, 3.

co-optations from the Great War. The negotiators in Paris-Sèvres were surprised by the Turkish–Bolshevik alliance. Britain feared, in particular, Ankara's proximity to Bolshevik Russia and its support by pan-Islamists in India, Egypt, and the Arab mandates. Fear of multiple illiberal alliances, if the Lausanne Conference failed, was perpetuated by independent Swiss dailies like the liberal *Journal de Genève*. "And just as only the [German-Russian] Treaty of Rapallo remained from the Genoa Conference, the Lausanne Conference would [if failed], in the final analysis, only tighten the alliance that already united Turkish nationalism and Bolshevist imperialism against the West."[12] This, however, underestimated the Kemalist will to move closer to the West at the expense of the Russian ally of convenience.

Foreign Secretary Curzon, who led the British delegation in Lausanne, had had different plans for Turkey's future than what crystalized in Sèvres, as he had outlined in three memoranda in 1918–early 1919. There he opposed the partition of Anatolia in line with the secret wartime promises to French, Italian, and Greek allies, but insisted that Istanbul "be internationalised under the League of Nations with a Commission, if possible under American chairmanship, charged with the task of keeping open the Straits and of safeguarding Constantinople as 'the cosmopolis or international city of the Eastern World.'" In particular, Curzon had been hostile to the Greek landing in Izmir in May 1919. By internationalizing Istanbul he stressed the need, in his eyes, to deprive Turkish rulers from "overweening ambitions" as a Muslim Great Power, and to deprive them of "the position to play off one Power against another, and in their jealousies and his [the Turk's] own machinations to find pretexts for his continued immunity."[13] Opposition then came from the India Office, which feared offended Muslims in India; and from the War Office that calculated in terms of military power, thus seeking conciliation with Ankara. Internal opposition increased apace until the eve of the Lausanne Conference. Ronald Graham, London's ambassador in Rome, felt the "whole sentiment" in Italy as "enthusiastically pro-Turkish" and believed the Turks to be suitable guardians of the Straits against Russia.[14]

***

Ankara's delegation in Lausanne had a threatening and imposing nationalist cause to defend. It knew what it wanted: peace with the West, particularly Britain, including full recognition and diplomatic reintegration; Allied

---

[12] *Journal de Genève*, 334, 5 November 1922, 1.
[13] Quoted in Nicolson, *Curzon: The Last Phase*, 77. For League plans with Istanbul, see Liebisch-Gümüş, *Verflochtene Nationsbildung*, 85–90.
[14] Demirci, *Lausanne Conference*, 15–16 and 29–30.

endorsement of the National Pact, that is, of a fully sovereign and unitary Turkey in the entirety of Anatolia; and the definitive rejection of any claims by indigenous non-Turkish groups related to autonomy, former dispossession, and justice.

From mid-1922, internationally, Ankara enjoyed the strong momentum of its victory in the Anatolia wars. As emphasized in this book, the general momentum of war defined the post-1918 national re-collection and re-concentration of Turkish-Muslim power in Ankara. As impactful as it proved, since it benefitted from existing CUP structures, this was double-edged. It paved the way to rapid repressive autocracy instead of gradual compromises and constitutional nation-building in Ankara. The Turkish delegation in Lausanne remained tied to the milieu and birth conditions of a National Assembly whose first common denominator had been the war against the West and indigenous Christians. Under multiform pressure, Ismet Pasha's team could not realize all of Ankara's objectives. These would have comprised a complete removal of non-Muslims; war reparations by Greece; the rejection of the Ottoman debts; the abolition of the international Debt Administration; and a maximum of national territory (including Western Thrace, Mosul, Aleppo, and several Aegean islands close to the Anatolian coast).

Within and around the delegation, we can make distinctions or even see polarization. On the one hand, there was an intransigent majority intoxicated, as it were, by successful violence and the expectation of a brilliant new Turkey; on the other hand, were those seeking, above all, good compromises in view of a respected, hopefully democratic country. Despite many blind spots, Mehmed Cavid, an insightful counselor of Ankara's delegation, stood clearly and pragmatically for the latter group. Ismet depended on those in his close proximity in Lausanne as well as on binding instructions from Ankara. To a certain extent, he could escape the tensions and contradictions of the National Assembly by corresponding directly with Chief-Commander Mustafa Kemal, the National Assembly's president and ruling spirit. This, however, meant sidelining the cabinet and Hüseyin Rauf (Orbay), Ankara's prime minister.

The direct, privileged relation thus came at the price of open debate and decision-making. It amounted to firm first steps toward an oligarchic autocracy, with the Lausanne settlement as the oligarchy's international pillar. Personal relations (i.e. loyalty, submission, and show and sharing of affections) are particularly important in oligarchic settings. Although possibly inauthentic, they cement the setting. Emotional proximity and submission transpire, illustrated, for example, by this telegram that Ismet sent to Kemal after difficult last negotiations toward the end of the Conference: "You come to me like Hızır [a prophet and angel] in my time of need. Imagine my torment for four or five days. You are a man who has done and initiated great things. My loyalty to you has increased one more time. I kiss your eyes, my dear brother, my beloved Chief."[15]

In preparation for the Conference, Cavid had several meetings in Istanbul on 8 November 1922. In a long conversation with Ismet and Nur, he was invited to be ready to be called to Lausanne. He gave an assessment of what he regarded viable and desirable compromises. He believed in an easy understanding with the new Italian cabinet under Mussolini, while he saw important questions open with France and Britain. More conciliatory than most others, he recommended not even suggesting the abolition of the Ottoman Debt Administration – a red rag to Turkish nationalists – because of Turkey's need of international loans. To aim for a special friendship with and loans from the USA was an illusion to him. The abolition of the Capitulations would take place, but require temporary compromises from the Turkish side. A settlement of the Strait issue under control of the League of Nations was to be accepted. To remain an outsider of the League would prove detrimental, even if the League had hitherto taken a critical stance vis-à-vis Turkey. To demand reparations from Greece was absurd, not least because Greece was in no position to pay anything. The same day, he became exasperated with journalists who blindly defended Ankara, while throwing all negative aspects of Turkey back to the CUP past. "Their awakening from this sleep will not be sweet."[16]

Cavid's assessments were reasonable and realistic, but not sufficiently nationalistic. They carried little weight in a political milieu where willingness to compromise appeared as treason. Already during CUP rule, Cavid had complained that expertise and competences counted less than chauvinistic bravado and personal and party loyalties.[17] At the Conference itself, Cavid grew apart from the delegation's majority, in particular from Nur, but also from Ismet Pasha whom he had appreciated in Istanbul. The Conference broke down in early February 1923 on financial and economic issues, including the related Capitulations. Cavid was dismissed. During the second half of the Conference, a more business-like atmosphere prevailed. Critical situations nevertheless emerged, because the questions of reparations, debt payments, and the rights of foreigners in Turkey involved substantial interests of the main delegations. There was still no straightforward road to a successful settlement.

In terms of involvement, we may consider Greece the fourth most important actor in Lausanne, after Turkey, Britain, and France. Without

---

[15] 20 July 1923, quoted in Kemal, *Nutuk*, 524.
[16] Cavid, *Meşrutizet Ruznâmesi*, 404–406, diary entry of 8 November 1922.
[17] Kieser, *Talaat Pasha*, 214–215.

doubt, Greece's situation was chaotic and desperate in November 1922. Added to the catastrophic defeat in Asia Minor and a million or so refugees to deal with in an impoverished country, the "September 1922 Revolution" had deposed King Constantine I and his government that had come to power after Venizelos' unexpected electoral defeat in November 1920. This government was made responsible for the catastrophe in Asia Minor. The September 1922 Revolution brought a revolutionary committee of pro-Venizelist officers under Colonel Nikolaos Plastiras to power. They called upon the exiled Venizelos to lead the Greek delegation in Lausanne, while preparing a Second Hellenic Republic (proclaimed in 1924). Five ministers and a general considered mainly responsible for the defeat and the "Asia Minor Catastrophe" were executed in Athens on 28 November, after a quick and controversial "Trial of the Six" which sent shock waves and a negative image of Greece to Lausanne. As we will see, Curzon could then deflect attention to another burning common problem, by setting Fridtjof Nansen, the League's legendary Commissioner for Refugees, and the question of population transfer on the Conference agenda.

The Second Hellenic Republic saw democratic moments, reconstruction, and industrialization, but descended into a totalitarian regime in 1936, as the Republic of Turkey had already done a few years earlier. Nevertheless, schism-plagued Greece did not suffer the same degree and continuity of illiberal authoritarianism, politics of violence, demographic engineering, and impunity that characterize the implementation of Turkish nationalism since the early 1910s. This version of nationalism – generally termed ultranationalism in this book – was to receive its diplomatic baptism in Lausanne.

15   Fascism's Historic Hour

At the weekend before the Conference started, Europe's new political star enjoyed most attention. His name was Benito Mussolini, the Italian Fascist leader and Italy's new prime minister as well as foreign minister on the eve of the Conference (see Figure 8). Both admired and controversial, he arrived at Lake Geneva Sunday, 19 November 1922, descending at Territet next to Montreux, 25 km east of Lausanne.[18] Several hundred international journalists had by then gathered in Lausanne. Dozens were already there when, a week earlier, Ankara's delegation booked in at the Lausanne Palace hotel.[19]

The Fascist agitator-turned-statesman made a show of self-importance for the international media and photographs. He snubbed French Prime

[18] *Journal de Genève*, 320, 21 November 1922, 3.   [19] Sadak, *Lozan Mektuplan*, 28.

Figure 8 Mussolini arriving in Lausanne on 20 November 1922. (Eugène Würgler, Arrivée de Mussolini au Casino de Montbenon pour la cérémonie d'ouverture de la conférence de Lausanne, carte postale, 20 novembre 1922, coll. Musée Historique Lausanne)

Minister Poincaré and British Foreign Secretary Curzon. Against expectations, he let them come to Territet to determine common ground among the main allies before the Conference. Curzon and Poincaré had arrived by special train from Paris, descended at Lausanne station, and in vain waited for the new Italian head of government. He had not participated at previous preparatory talks in Paris.[20] The outcome of the interview in Territet and Paris remained vague. The communiqué after the Paris meeting claimed allied accord on all issues pertaining to the upcoming negotiations.[21] Mussolini himself, however, sounded less optimistic. He told American delegates Joseph Grew and Richard W. Child, who met him on Monday afternoon, then in his hotel in Lausanne, that "they failed to agree on several points and M. [Mussolini] made various reservations. He ... predicts an early break-down of the Conference."[22] This latter was not to be the case. Against expectations and Turkish–Bolshevik propaganda of hopeless Western division and weakness – enforced by the downfall of Lloyd George's cabinet on 19 October and Britain's general elections on

---

[20] *Journal de Genève*, 321, 22 November 1922, 2.
[21] *Neue Zürcher Zeitung*, no. 1513, 20 November 1922, 2.
[22] Grew, *Diary*, entry of 20 November 1922, Grew papers (hereafter Grew diary), 154.

15 Fascism's Historic Hour

15 November 1922 – the allies showed considerable unity during the first weeks. Unity began to crumble in early January due to the French-British antagonism on Germany and Turkey; it left much to be desired during the second half of the Conference.[23]

After his coup d'état – the March on Rome in late October 1922 – Mussolini had immediately been given power by the king to form a new government and entered office as Italy's new prime minister. Internationally, he faced two outstanding issues: peace with Turkey and the reparations settlement with Germany.[24] Both were to play crucial roles in Interwar Europe's road away from democracy and undermined the League of Nations. The October 1912 Treaty of Lausanne – also called "Treaty of Ouchy" after Lausanne's port – had given the Italian invader Libya's Tripoli and Cyrenaica as well as the Dodecanese islands in the southeastern Aegean Sea including Rhodes. This was the start of Italy's nationalist-imperialist drive that Mussolini was to take up and realize – once he had fully established Fascism in the country itself. In 1922–3, he was little interested in the intricate matters of the Lausanne Conference, except the preservation of Italy's vested interests based on the gains in the 1912 treaty.

Nonetheless, he resented that Italy had not been entrusted with a mandate during negotiations in Paris and San Remo. For this reason, Mussolini tried a short-lived attempt at blackmail via Marquis Garroni. In early December 1922, this plenipotentiary of Italy suddenly stated to an infuriated Curzon "that unless Italy were promised some share in the mandates over territory detached from Turkey she would feel obliged to withdraw from the Conference." Two days after Garroni's unfortunate appearance with Curzon, Mussolini paid a courtesy visit to the British foreign secretary and lunched with the Curzons. This encounter apparently proved "an enormous success," according to Nicolson. Relations between Britain and Mussolini's Italy became, in fact, cordial for years to come. A telling caricature by Alois Derso and Emery Kelèn shows Mussolini with Garroni, Italy's former ambassador in Constantinople, at the Lausanne Conference. The caricaturists represent Garroni as intimidated and overpowered by the new Fascist PM – and with Garroni Italy's entire liberal-conservative cadre.[25]

---

[23] See Chapters 21–24, and Nicolson, *Curzon: The Last Phase*, 325.
[24] Alan Cassels, *Mussolini's Early Diplomacy* (Princeton: Princeton University Press, 1970), 21–45.
[25] Nicolson, *Curzon: The Last Phase*, 303–304. The caricature is in Alois Derso and Emery Kelèn, *Guignol à Lausanne* (Lausanne: A. Marsens, 1923), 15; online in the collection of the Peace Palace Library: https://cdm21069.contentdm.oclc.org/digital/collection/p21069coll14/id/4/rec/8.

In contrast to the Kemalists after Lausanne – except the open Mosul question until 1926 and Alexandretta before 1938 – Italian Fascists were by no means territorially satisfied, but felt frustrated as victors of the Great War. General Pangalos, Greece's short-lived dictator in 1925–6, sought to benefit from Mussolini's aggressive feelings in order to prepare a common war of limited reconquest against Turkey. This was an exception to Greece's otherwise modest and conciliatory foreign policy during the decade after 1923. By then, however, Mussolini would not dare to put the excellent Anglo-Italian relations that started in Lausanne at risk. In line with the policy of former Foreign Minister Sforza, an adversary of Mussolini, the "economic exploitation of the Near East" and with this a desire "to infiltrate into Asia Minor" remained an unattained goal. In the eyes of Italy's generally circumspect second delegate, Giulio Cesare Montagna, it was "a perfectly natural and logical policy." Loyal to Mussolini, Montagna believed that France and Turkey would "crumble away" within a few decades – France due to a low birth rate and Turkey as an overaged "mummy." And "when the collapse came, the other nations would be there to profit by it and Italy could not be left out in the cold."[26]

***

Though controversial, Mussolini enjoyed remarkably good press and welcoming reception by all sorts of officials and lobbying groups at, or at sideshows of, the Lausanne Conference (see Figure 9). This was typical of the zeitgeist. Years later, if in a position to do so, diplomats liked to censure themselves, as did Grew (or his editor) in the published 1953 version of his diary.

Grew wrote, "Mussolini impressed me as a simple, open, direct, strong man of the people, the patriot rather than the statesman,"[27] but not as the recent putschist. Similarly, many in Lausanne saw in Inönü the strong, frank and stubborn nationalist, not the diplomat or the representative of a political elite responsible for the worst crimes during the preceding decade of wars. Grew's colleague Child, the US ambassador in Rome and first American delegate in Lausanne, could not amend his record, as he died in 1935 when he was still Mussolini's friend and propagandist.

---

[26] Grew diary, 87–88, 30 April 1923. See also Antonis Klapsis, "Attempting to Revise the Treaty of Lausanne: Greek Foreign Policy and Italy during the Pangalos Dictatorship, 1925–1926," *Diplomacy & Statecraft*, 25.2 (2014), 240–259.

[27] Grew diary, entry of 20 November 1922, 154. For diplomatic convenience, this passage has typically been censored in the diaries' published version. See Grew, *Turbulent Era*, vol 1, 489–490. For a comparatively positive contemporary analysis of the new PM, see, for example, "Das Programm Mussolinis," *Neue Zürcher Zeitung*, no. 1515, 20 November 1922, 1.

15 Fascism's Historic Hour   131

Figure 9 Mussolini in Lausanne, November 1920 (gallica.bnf.fr / BnF)

He boasted to have promoted Fascism since his ambassadorship in Italy.[28] Shortly after the Lausanne Treaty, the *Gazette de Lausanne*, Lausanne's main daily, praised Mussolini's Fascist Italy for she "has gone back to work with a joyful heart. More than ever, she gives an impression of health, extreme activity and growing prosperity."[29]

The University of Lausanne, in whose main auditorium the final Treaty was signed, awarded Mussolini with a doctorate honoris causa in 1937.

---

[28] "Richard Washburn Child, Author-Diplomat Dies," *The Bend Bulletin*, 31 January 1935, 1.
[29] Maurice Muret, "Impressions d'Italie. Le marasme d'hier et l'ordre d'auhourd'hui," *Gazette de Lausanne* 18 (October 1923), 1.

In his former life as a pre–Great War socialist, Mussolini had agitated in Geneva, shortly enrolled at the University of Lausanne, and stood in conflict with the regional police and justice.[30] The University's political scientists honored Italy's leader at what they believed to be the long zenith of Mussolini's glory. Despite all violence and crimes committed by Fascist rule in Libya, Ethiopia, and domestically, by the mid-1930s, they and very many Westerners – including youngster John F. Kennedy, the later US president, and Britain's former prime minister Lloyd George – had reconciled themselves with authoritarian regimes in Europe.[31] Only a minority, identified with the victims and fundamentally questioned antidemocratic futures in seemingly expedient and promising dictatorships.

Right-wing, together with certain academic and commercial, circles in the Swiss canton of Vaud, where Lausanne is the capital, welcomed Mussolini in November 1922 as a prodigal son, now justly a rising star. In the same breath, the Swiss colonel Arthur Fonjallaz most prominent among them, they sought and enjoyed the proximity of the men from Ankara during the eight months of the Conference. British diplomats at the Lausanne Conference typically saw Mussolini as a rude Fascist, but thought that he was nothing more than a "provisional dictator" and of "boyish naïveté." Democracy with civil liberties was not regarded as the universal core value to be defended by all possible means, wherever democrats were threatened, wherever they called for help.

Why and how, therefore, is the Lausanne Conference a historic breakthrough of fascism in Europe, a main argument of this book? There, international diplomacy opened its arms to Mussolini, a declared Fascist. Most important, however, and little considered, is the number of proto-fascist ideas and the patterns of violence, accumulated within a decade of war and party dictatorship in late-Ottoman Turkey, that diplomacy was to approve in Lausanne, implicitly or explicitly. Although ultranationalist forces prevailed, the new government in Ankara was not fascist in 1922–3, but in the process to becoming a leader-led single-party regime. Based on the cadres of the previous CUP party-state, it evolved to a dictatorship by the mid-1920s and to a totalitarian state toward the end of the decade. Nevertheless, Ankara's rule notoriously rested on its predecessors' policies, whose genocidal achievements

---

[30] The doctorate was awarded in January 1937 on the proposal of the Department of Social and Political Sciences. Mussolini was credited for a "social order" in Italy that had "enriched the science of sociology" and would leave "deep traces" in history. Mauro Cerutti: "Mussolini, Benito," in *Historisches Lexikon der Schweiz*, version of 6 April 2010, https://hls-dhs-dss.ch/de/articles/027903/2010-04-06.

[31] John F. Kennedy, *Unter Deutschen: Reisetagebücher und Briefe 1937–1945*, ed. Oliver Lubrich (Berlin: Aufbau Verlag, 2013); Antony Levin, *Lloyd George and the Lost Peace: From Versailles to Hitler, 1919–1940* (London: Palgrave Macmillan, 2001), 89–105.

it uncompromisingly defended. At the same time, it categorically rejected any responsibility for the misery of millions, natives of the country that it claimed exclusively for itself.

Lausanne was the Bolsheviks' historic hour of diplomacy insofar as, for the first time, a delegation from Soviet Russia, Ukraine, and Georgia, led by Georgy Chicherin, made an appearance on the highest platform of international diplomacy. The Bolsheviks had been entirely excluded from the negotiations in Paris. An earlier step toward establishing ties had been the failed Genoa Conference that focused on economic issues only. Chicherin was not extended the positive welcome offered on all sides to Mussolini and ultimately to Ismet Pasha. In Lausanne, there was British irony and condescendence for Mussolini, the "schoolboy visage of the Pasha" (Ismet) and the deeply committed Marxist Chicherin, the Bolshevik chief delegate. Witty pursuit of imperial self-interest, however, helped little to seriously deal with antidemocratic powers, revolutionary claims, and records of extreme unaccounted for violence.[32]

Revolutionaries from the left and the right possessed arguable causes against the Paris-Geneva peace in general and Western capitalism in particular. This peace project favored democratic home countries. It seemed to care much less for welfare and civil, social, and human rights in other societies, giving the impression that all others were excluded from the West's privileged community of equal rights and democracy. The CUP's head Mehmed Talaat, Atatürk's predecessor, had put it this way at the eve of the Great War – in a Turkey that he was then transforming to a proto-fascist party-state: "Presently, if there is something like a rule of law, it is only for Europeans. We, like Asians, Africans, and [indigenous] Australians, are anyway people outside of and alien to Europe. The main principles of the rule of law are not [acknowledged as] valid for us."[33] A clear-sighted coming to terms with ultranationalism and early fascism in Lausanne was complicated by an Allied approach that considered rightist revolutionists potential allies in a global rivalry with Moscow. Even if not fascistic themselves, all kinds of groups and states were inclined to flirt with what seemed upcoming powers in Turkey and Italy.

***

Ankara's delegation was particularly skillful in making diplomatic use of relations at and besides the Lausanne Conference, benefitting from a Turkish diaspora at Lake Léman. Jews were a case in point and used as a favorite argument. At the negotiation table, Ismet Pasha repeatedly

---

[32] For the related view and vocabulary, see Nicolson, *Curzon: The Last Phase*, 189 and 311.
[33] Muhittin Birgen, *İttihat ve Terakki'de on sene: İttihat ve Terakki neydi?* (Istanbul: Kitapyayınevi, 2006), 179

contrasted Turkey's Jews with allegedly disloyal Ottoman Christian subjects whom imperialistic Europe had made its unfortunate agents. He thus showcased the Jews as a happy minority in harmony with a tolerant state since the late fifteenth century. Most of the minority's representatives cooperated in this show.[34]

The Permanent Bureau of the Turkish Congress in Lausanne had fabricated Turkey's Jews' full and voluntary embrace of Turkish rule.[35] The argument of Turkish–Jewish harmony went strongly on with Ankara's delegation, which counted among its members Chief Rabbi Nahum Chaim, a long-standing acquaintance of Talaat Pasha. On 11 December 1922, a newly established Turkish–Sephardic Friendship Association organized a special soirée in Geneva. Besides journalists, the invitation included Swiss cantonal and federal representatives; Ismet, Nur, and other members of the delegation, including Chief Rabbi Nahum; members of the Turkish diaspora; and special Swiss friends, notably Eugène Pittard. At this occasion, the speech of the leader of Geneva's Jews perfectly attuned to Ankara's expectations, as Turkish newspapers reported with satisfaction.[36]

Another element of pro-Kemalist lobbying in Lausanne was the Swiss Society of Friends of Turkey, founded by Colonel Arthur Fonjallaz who soon gained prominence in Switzerland as a fascist and later as a notorious pro-Nazi.[37] A visit to Asia Minor during the Greek–Turkish War had made Fonjallaz a friend of the Kemalist cause, admirer of Gazi Mustafa Kemal Pasha's military genius, and adept of the Kemalist vision of contemporary history. Ismet Pasha received him in the Lausanne Palace hotel after his arrival in Switzerland.[38] On 6 December, he was invited by the Curzons to a private dinner with Mussolini who briefly had

---

[34] This had also been the case during the 1910s against Armenian-related bad press in the West, when Talaat pushed for good Jewish public relations for his regime and his cause. Woe to those who did not fulfill the expectations set out in them. Ismet's argument rested on mythmaking by Jews eager to win favor with the late-Ottoman state. See Julia Phillips Cohen, "A Model *Millet*? Ottoman Jewish Citizenship at the End of Empire," in Abigail Green and Simon Levis-Sullam, eds., *Jews, Liberalism, Antisemitism: A Global History* (London: Palgrave, 2020), 209–231. CLA, first series, vol. 1, 161, 163, 172. See also Kieser, *Talaat Pasha*, 295–315.

[35] "What the Israelites Think of the Turkish Regime," *Turkey*, no. 2, March 1921, 7.

[36] Necmettin Sadık (Sadak), *Akşam*, 17 December 1922, 2, transcribed in Sadak *Lozan Mektupları*, 138–141.

[37] ACV, ATS: A. Fonjallaz ; Claude Cantini, *Le colonel fasciste suisse, Arthur Fonjallaz* (Lausanne: Pierre-Marcel Favre, 1983). See also "Ismet Pacha et le colonel Fonjallaz," *Journal de Genève*, 15 November 1922, 10.

[38] Colonel Arthur Fonjallaz was invited by General Ismet Pasha to visit him at the Lausanne-Palace. He had devoted articles to Turkish operations in Asia Minor in which he praised Turkish tactics and predicted the Turkish victories. "Ismet pacha et le colonel Arthur Fonjallaz," *Journal de Genève*, 15 November 1922, 10.

come back to Lausanne.³⁹ Fonjallaz's new and short-lived, but then-effective Swiss Society met for the first time on 16 December 1922, during a soirée at the Lausanne Palace hotel. Fonjallaz raised a toast and Ismet Pasha made a long speech, defending Turkish claims and flattering Swiss historic achievements. Lausanne University professor of sociology Maurice Millioud expressed agreement with Ismet and emphasized Turkey's civilizational role for the Orient. This perfectly accorded with what the Turkish delegation wanted the public to hear and what it wanted to see written in the local press.⁴⁰

Pittard participated at the soirées on 11 and 16 December, and made a lasting friendship with Ismet Pasha. During and after the Conference, he applauded new Kemalist historical consciousness, rhetorically blending Kemalist nation-building with Swiss understanding of democratic citizenship. "After the military victory, the victory of the citizen. The gods are with you! You know how much we wish that your country will rise from its ruins, and find, after so many years of hardship, suffering and injustice, an era of peace, work, justice, joy," Pittard wrote to Ismet on 28 October 1923, a day before the declaration of the Republic of Turkey. "You will become the architect of an era, and its leader. The history of Turkey will, I am sure, inscribe your name on the pediment of the present period, next to that of your comrade and friend, Mustafa Kemal."⁴¹ Pittard had had some exchanges on premodern and ancient Turkish topics with Atabinen already before the Conference. His suggestive role as a mentor of physical anthropology and ethnohistory for Atatürk's race-based History Thesis in the aftermath of the Conference proved seminal for Kemalist history-writing (see Part IV).

***

Nine months after his first appearance in Lausanne, Mussolini sent a squadron to the Greek island of Corfu, bombarded the citadel in which Armenian refugees were housed, killed sixteen children, and occupied the island. The pretext for the military action on 30 August 1923 was the killing, on 27 August, of three Italian members of on interallied commission sent to delimitate the exact border between Albania and Greece.

---

[39] "L'arrivée de Mussolini," *Journal de Genève*, 8 December 1922, 8.

[40] Ismet was also Fonjallaz's private guest on the evening of 6 February 1923, before his return to Ankara. "La conférence est suspendue," *Journal de Genève*, 7 February 1923, 10. See also *Necmeddin Sadık (Sadak) Bey'in Lozan Mektupları*, 159–163 (including references to further sources) and 298.

[41] Lettre d'Eugène à Ismet Pacha, 28 November 1923, quoted in Caroline Montebello, *Eugène Pittard, un anthropologue genevois en Turquie nationaliste (1910–1950): idéologie d'exclusion, corruption intellectuelle et logiques sociales* (Paris: EHESS, Mémoire de Master, 2016), 21.

Montagna, Italy's former delegate in Lausanne, was now minister in Athens. After Mussolini had urged on his minister the need of "immediate and exemplary punishment," Montagna suggested that the Greek government "had acted as the assassins' financier or worse." The issue was and remained an unsolved ambush by gunmen on Greek territory.[42]

Subsequently, the Greek government appealed – in full accordance with what was meant to be the new international order – to the League of Nations and the League's mechanism of conflict resolution among members as according to Covenant Article 11, "Any war or threat of war, whether immediately affecting any of the Members of the League or not, is hereby declared a matter of concern to the whole League, and the League shall take any action that may be deemed wise and effectual to safeguard the peace of nations." Yet, meanwhile, the Paris–Geneva–based international order had become a regressive Paris–Geneva–Lausanne combination that gave Great Powers, fascists, and expansionists a new scope of action. The crisis was solved not by the League as it should have been, but rather by a pre-1914 style conference of ambassadors that blamed and heavily fined Greece. League-averse Paris was in strong support of Italy, and Curzon folded at the end.[43]

Pacts with illiberal powers were the price for driving "a sharp wedge into the Russo-Turkish Alliance" and definitively safeguarding France's and Britain's mandatory interests at the Conference of Lausanne.[44] The price was high, while much scope for maneuvering was still left to Ankara in dealing with Moscow. The Corfu incident was like a last proof that after the deal-making of the Lausanne Conference, the League was no longer operational in its core function, at least not against relatively strong players. Its prestige and authority were evaporating.

Adolf Hitler's failed putsch in early November of the same year was arguably much more inspired by Ankara's radiating military and diplomatic success than by the comparably modest example of Mussolini and the Fascist March on Rome.[45] Since Lausanne, German National-Socialist leader Hitler venerated Turkey's president as a teacher and guiding star, not Mussolini. Put shortly, the new visibility of fascism on the highest level of European politics right at the start of the Conference boded ill. It indicated that the failure of the Paris peace architecture, including the League's liberal world vision, was to be definitively consummated during

---

[42] Richard J. B. Bosworth, *Mussolini* (New York: Bloomsbury, 2003), 147–165.
[43] Walters, *History of the League of Nations*, 244–55; Nicolson, *Curzon: The Last Phase*, 368–71.
[44] Nicolson, *Curzon: The Last Phase*, 313.
[45] Stefan Ihrig proposes this convincing understanding contrary to long-held Western opinions: Ihrig, *Atatürk in the Nazi Imagination*, 68 passim.

the months to come. The embrace of an already experienced and well-engrained proto-fascism was the price for going ahead with the West's national-imperial policies with related Middle Eastern mandates, and for the growing dependency on oil, in which the disputed province of Mosul was particularly rich.

16 Inauguration, Personalities, Early Imprints

When Swiss Federal President Rudolf Haab inaugurated the Conference in the late afternoon of Monday, 20 November 1922, in Lausanne's Montbenon Casino, he stressed the importance of a peace that would also satisfy the needs of the losers. This was a noble-minded and wise wish, but hardly one in accordance with the zeitgeist of the early 1920s.[46] During the first days and weeks of the Conference, the speakers aired lofty wishes for world peace, underlining the importance of reconciliation with Turkey. After more than a decade of war in the late-Ottoman world, including the Great War, peace was yearned for on all sides.

Speaking after Haab, Curzon, the chief of the British delegation, flattered the Swiss for their model of conciliation between different population groups and a peaceful, but well-armed coexistence. The allocution was in English, with translation into French by Gustave H. Camerlynck, a respected interpreter.[47] From its second day (21 November), until early February 1923 (i.e. during the first half of the Conference, before its interruption) Curzon presided over the Conference. In the plenary session of 21 November, he skillfully managed to hold, as the senior representative of the "Powers which had organized the Conference" (Britain, France, Italy), a "provisional presidency" that resulted in his presiding in all plenary sessions as well as the First Commission – the Territorial and Military Commission – until February.[48] During the official meetings, he "is the only delegate who [always] speaks in English, although he understands and speaks French."[49] (See Figure 10.)

---

[46] "Discours du président de la Confédération," *Journal de Genève*, 320, 21 November 1922, 3–4. The embassy in Paris had informed the Federal Council about the allies' wish for an inaugural speech by the Swiss president. Haab promised to his co-ministers to express "the hope that the conference would reach a peace agreement that would also permit the defeated a continued existence and to look forward to a prosperous future." Minutes of the Federal Council, 17 November 1922, BAr E1004.1#1000/9#11799.

[47] *LCP*, 1–5.

[48] "The rule was that a Conference held on Swiss territory should be presided over by a Swiss citizen. The Federal Government had been careful to renounce that honour in advance." Nicolson, *Curzon: The Last Phase*, 291; *LCP*, 5–14.

[49] Grew, *Turbulent Era*, vol. 1, 500.

Figure 10 Curzon, satisfied, after the first Conference meeting (Eugène Würgler, Lord Curzon sortant du château d'Ouchy, pendant la conférence de Lausanne, carte postale, 21 novembre 1922, coll. Musée Historique Lausanne)

The most fundamental discussions and decisions, and the most drama, happened in this first half of the Conference, when the diplomatic core issue was the coming to terms between the main opponents of the previous decade, Britain and Turkey (see Figure 11). Though brilliant with witty analyses and profound historical insight, Curzon resembled an old imperial commander in rearguard action, but with tactical advantages, who sought and eventually succeeded to protect ancient interests of the Empire. Time and again, he gave in to temptation and humbled his unexpectedly strong Turkish adversary with his superior knowledge and intellect, and with rhetoric that oscillated between wit, irony, majesty, and condescension. A conservative statesman and former viceroy of India, Curzon had traveled around the world as a young man and written historical-geographical books on countries in Asia. Though he was a celebrated figure of the British Empire, he was by no means Eurocentric. Representing the British Empire in Lausanne from April 1923, Horace Rumbold, High Commissioner to Constantinople, had a more sober and business-like style than Curzon, whom he succeeded. He signed the final Treaty on 24 July.

16 Inauguration, Personalities, Early Imprints

Figure 11 Drawn by the artist Derso, this late 1922 postcard puts the interaction of an oversized Lord Curzon and a tiny Ismet Pasha who reluctantly shake hands with each other in its center. The British-Turkish interaction dominated the first half of the Conference. (Alois Derso, Caricature représentant les délégués de la Conférence de Lausanne, carte postale, 1922, coll. Musée Historique Lausanne). A rich collection of highly original, instructive and expressive caricatures in color is in Derso and Kelèn, Guignol à Lausanne (Lausanne 1923). A number of these caricatures can be accessed online in the digital collection of the Peace Palace Library. (https://cdm21069.contentdm.oclc.org)

Ismet (Inönü) Pasha, that counterpart of the British, was twenty-five years younger than Curzon and fifteen years younger than Rumbold. He too declared himself very satisfied with the choice of the Conference's location. In his unplanned French address at the inaugural ceremony on 20 November, he picked out Switzerland's "glorious history" to make his point: "The value a noble [Swiss *or* Turkish!] nation attaches to its independence." The entirely peaceable Turkish nation, as he insisted, had now "conquered its place within civilized humankind." He stressed the suffering inflicted on Turks after 1918 during the Graeco–Turkish War and the "exclusionary [Western] spirit of extermination."[50]

---

[50] "A la séance d'ouverture: Le discours d'Ismet pacha," *Journal de Genève*, 320, 21 November 1922, 8.

140   A Protracted Conference

Ismet Pasha – as the honorific Ottoman title of "pasha" indicates – had spent his entire life as a military officer in the Ottoman Empire after graduating from the Ottoman Military Academy. He had been a leading general under Mustafa Kemal Pasha (Atatürk) during the war in Anatolia.[51] In the Great War, he had served as a high officer at Kemal's side. During negotiations with Bulgaria after the Balkan Wars in 1913, Ismet had had the chance to gain a little diplomatic experience as an advisor. He had also carried out the negotiations for the Mudanya armistice.[52]

When, in late October, Ankara received the allies' invitation to a peace conference in Lausanne, leader Gazi Kemal Pasha chose his loyal comrade as the chief delegate, nominating him foreign minister for Yusuf Kemal (Tengirşek) who had to resign.[53] Even before the allies held preparatory meetings in Paris and Territet, Moscow's Ambassador Aralov and Ismet had met in Ankara to prepare for the Conference. At this occasion, the Kemalist leadership rejected a possible ultimatum to the inviting Powers demanding Russia's full participation in Lausanne, not only on the question of the Straits.[54] It was more or less clear by now that Ankara henceforth sought less dependency on its Bolshevik midwife, the helpful guardian of Ankara's northern and eastern flank during the Anatolia wars.

Although Lausanne's imminent task of peace-making concerned the whole decade from 1912 to 1922, with his inaugural speech, Ankara's delegate hammered a narrative of national heroism and of unique Turkish suffering by the Greek invaders of 1919 into the ears of its European audience from the first day. Most related facts were comparatively well-known and published, in contrast to acts committed under the shadow of the Great War.[55] Ankara's method however was tactical and strategic. While, at the surface, it aimed at Greek reparations, it served above all to make violent policies of far greater dimensions – the politics of removal and extermination by the CUP rulers and their successors – seem insignificant. It was driven by the fear of related reparations, at least for damages suffered by allied nationals.

---

[51] Inönü and Curzon left memoirs and other writings related to Lausanne. There is instructive literature, but no scholarly biography of Inönü; for a bibliography, see the website of the Inönü Foundation: www.ismetinonu.org.tr/arastirma-kitaplari. Academic literature on Curzon is rich: see, in particular, Nicolson, *Curzon: The Last Phase* and David Gilmour, *Curzon: Imperial Statesman* (New York: Farrar, Straus & Giroux, 1994).

[52] Demirci, *Lausanne Conference*, 37.   [53] Sadak, *Lozan Mektupları*, 19–20.

[54] Aralov, *Bir Sovyet Diplomatının Anıları*, 182–185.

[55] During the meeting on 13 December, Ismet Pasha cited distressing lines from a report by ICRC delegates traveling in Western Anatolia (*LCP*, 206, quoting Rodolphe Haccius and Henri Cuenod, "Mission en Anatolie," *Bulletin Internationale de la Croix-Rouge*, 53.243, 951–971). See also the fact-finding and reflections in Arnold J. Toynbee, *The Western Question in Greece and Turkey: A Study in the Contact of Civilisations* (London: Constable, 1922). This book includes comprehensive contemporary bibliographical references.

Turkish journalists inculcated their readership at home with the same message. The outstanding Turkish sacrifice and victimhood is thus a constant trope in the "Lausanne letters" by Necmettin Sadık (Sadak) who wrote for the pro-Kemalist daily *Akşam*. Before standing close to Ankara and Ismet Pasha, he had belonged to the group of journalists and young intellectuals that orbited around Talaat Pasha in Istanbul's CUP headquarters. They all understood themselves then already, years before the rise of Ankara, as a new Turkey's national revolutionaries. In the late 1940s, Sadak became Ankara's foreign minister.[56] A passage from his letter of 20 November 1922 translates deep and lasting emotions of those now posing as righteous victors and revengers, feeling proud when Ismet Pasha stood at the lectern in the Casino Montbenon:

I felt a slowly rising pride in me. For the first time since three centuries the Turks do not come before the states as a loser to pay for their misdeeds. On the contrary, they come to demand the yield of their victory. İsmet Pasha has come to this place of reckoning all the way from [his battle victories at] İnönü, Sakarya and Dumlupınar over a Greek Army counting 200,000 soldiers.[57]

In reality, the story of Turkey's victims was very different from what the Pasha's address insinuated. It is true that the retreating Greek army destroyed villages and killed Muslim civilians but there is a question of magnitude. Outside the Greek–Turkish War, more than a million non-Turkish Ottoman civilians before 1918 and another hundred thousand or more after 1918 were methodically killed by Turkish forces. Post-1918 killings included the genocide of Pontus Rûm, the massacre of Marash Armenians, that of Kocgiri Alevis (the latter leading to vehement protests in Ankara's National Assembly),[58] and the extermination of tens of thousands of Christians in Izmir in the immediate aftermath of the Greek–Turkish War. For Ankara's delegation, any claim related to notorious previous crimes was highly sensitive, above all the claim of an Armenian homeland. Ankara's number one instruction to its delegation in Lausanne – out of a comprehensive fourteen points – therefore read: "1. The Eastern Border: an 'an Armenian Home' is out of question, if it becomes an issue, the negotiations will be interrupted."[59]

For Grew and others, Ismet's well-prepared emotional "outburst" during the inauguration ceremony was "a most tactless address,

---

[56] See Sadak, *Lozan Mektupları*, starting with his letter of 19 October 1922, 37; Kieser, *Talaat Pasha*, 329–131.
[57] Sadak, *Lozan Mektupları*, 41.
[58] Türkiye Büyük Millet Meclisi, *Gizli Celse Zabıtları* (Ankara: Türkiye İş Bankası, 1985), vol. 2, 248–280.
[59] Şimşir, Lozan Telgrafları, Vol. I (1922–1923), XIV, with reference to the Foreign Office Archives (Dışişleri Bakanlığı Arşivi, DBA, Ankara).

controversial and threatening in tone; it was not the time or the place for that kind of a speech, as the first session was purely ceremonial."Grew saw in Mussolini's face "an expression of utmost ferocity" during the Pasha's allocution.[60] As we have seen, Mussolini perceived, possibly with envy and thoughts of revanchism, the Turkish representative as a (too) successful rival. Mussolini had to remain silently seated during the simple opening ceremony that took no longer than half an hour. A "distinct young revolutionary with shaved mustache and stern face lines" in journalist Sadak's eyes, at the end Mussolini was the only one among the high representatives sitting in the first row to applaud Ismet's stern speech. Outside the Casino, an American – perhaps Child or Admiral Mark L. Bristol, the pro-Kemalist US High Commissioner in Istanbul, now member of the US delegation – also used congratulatory words for the Pasha's performance.[61]

In addition to Mussolini, Turkish journalist Sadak's attention turned time and again to Eleftherios Venizelos who sat in the same row with Mussolini, the Italian chief delegate Eugenio C. Garroni in between. Throughout his Lausanne letters, Sadak – a prospective deputy and minister of the Republic of Turkey – looked with disdain and schadenfreude on the chief delegate of Greece, a loser of the previous war, but long a favorite of Lloyd George whose cabinet had fallen in October 1922. Spirited, mercurial and cosmopolitan, Venizelos and his former national policy of Greater Greece compared unfavorably with General Ismet in Sadak's eyes. Ismet convinced the world with forceful nationalist action; Venizelos failed with his liberal-leaning projects, although he had been acclaimed by Westerners in Paris three years earlier.

The Conference of Lausanne was, for months, at "the center of attention of the public, the members of parliament, the journalists and diplomatic circles" in Ankara and whole Turkey.[62] Sadak's second letter of the opening day treated Venizelos with mortifying contempt. He quoted from Ismet Pasha's allocution in a free translation into Turkish that made clear how things were to be understood at home. In particular, he insisted both on the propaganda narrative of victimhood and the righteousness of the Turkish-nationalist cause including carnages perpetrated by Turkish forces allegedly under duress: "We suffered a lot, we shed a lot of

---

[60] The fascist leader "looked as if he wanted to spring at Ismet's throat" – perhaps not because of tactlessness, as Grew supposed, but because Ismet had stolen the show, while he had not thought to prepare a timely outburst for Italy's cause. Grew diary, entry of 20 November 1922, 155. See also *Journal de Genève*, 320, 21 November 1922; Nicolson, *Curzon: The Last Phase*, 290.
[61] Sadak, *Lozan Mektupları*, 43–44.
[62] Aralov, *Bir Sovyet Diplomatının Anıları*, 176–177.

blood." In his argument, the principles of Wilson and "civilization" warranted Ankara's total righteousness.

The first disaster agent of defeated Greece, this homeless diplomat [Venizelos] could not sit in his seat because of amazement and excitement. He looked around. He said something to the people next to him. He probably did not expect that Ismet Pasha would make a speech after Lord Curzon. He adjusted his glasses and cast a stern, yet cowardly evil eye at Ismet Pasha. Who knows what this Turkish general, who destroyed the hopes of the great Venizelos, would say, and which murders, which fires, which massacre he would strike in the face of Greece in front of the delegates of the whole world! Venizelos was not deceived in his anxiety. And from the moment Ismet Pasha started to read his speech, I noticed that Venizelos did not take his eyes off the ground. While listening to the accusations of the Turkish delegate, he was rubbing his fingers with each other nervously, he hardly restrained the shivering of his face. Ismet Pasha mentioned Wilson's principles and the deprivations and disasters that Turkey had suffered for three years, crying out to the four hundred representatives of civilization: "Sirs," he said, "we suffered a lot, we shed a lot of blood, they destroyed our country unnecessarily, we were attacked from all sides, we are victorious. Gentlemen, we want independence and freedom like all nations!"[63]

17 Pivotal First Weeks

The Conference's first weeks led to heated exchanges when fundamental questions like population transfer, minority rights, and the establishment of an Armenian home were addressed. By the end of 1922, faced with categorical Kemalist rejection, the European insistence on Armenian and other minority rights crumbled, as the Turkish delegates had rightly anticipated.[64] Public pressure against this course of things and the fact that, during the first weeks, "the conference receives daily telegrams from the various cities where the Armenians of Turkey have taken refuge, imploring the creation of the National Home which has been promised to them," did not carry critical diplomatic weight in Lausanne.[65]

The beginning of the Conference was seminal in how Curzon managed a strategy designed to reach goals according to British imperial priorities. Despite intense debates with a lofty rhetoric of peace and humanity, the main allied delegates obeyed to an unsurprising degree the pursuit of economic, strategic, and political advantage. Against these, elementary rights and historical truths, which concerned millions of natives with no or weak voices at the negotiation table, went down. In regard to collective

[63] Sadak, *Lozan Mektupları*, 43.
[64] Necmeddin Sadık, "Lozan Mektupları: 26–27 Kanûn-i Evvel 1922," in: Sadak, *Lozan Mektupları*, 193–198.
[65] *Journal de Genève*, 5 December 1922, no. 334, 2.

and individual rights of non-Turks in Anatolia, Ankara almost entirely prevailed by early January 1923, but not so in other points of primary Allied interest.

Conference president Curzon chose the delimitation of national borders in Thrace as the first topic to be discussed in the First Commission on Territorial and Military Questions, that is from Wednesday, 22 November. As other commissions began only in the second week of the Conference, full attention in Lausanne was on these first commission meetings.[66] Thrace was a topic where allied unity could easily be established and maximalist Turkish claims easily reduced to diplomatic absurdity. In line with CUP policy that had passionately sought to recover entire Thrace after it was lost during the Balkan Wars, Ismet Pasha firstly demanded entire Eastern Thrace (including a section ceded to Bulgaria in 1915 for the latter's entry into war under German pressure). He secondly proposed a referendum for the rest (i.e. Western Thrace). All allies, in particular the neighbors Greece, Rumania, and Yugoslavia (Kingdom of Serbs, Croats, and Slovenes), but also Turkey's former ally Bulgaria opposed Ismet's proposal. A third Balkan war might loom, delegates said. Western Thrace had been lost to Bulgaria in the 1913 Treaty of Bucharest, but Bulgaria had to cede it to the Great War victors (prospectively to Greece) in the 1919 Treaty of Paris-Neuilly. It was clear that coming back to irredentist CUP claims of the early 1910s was excluded. If the principle was to be adopted, Curzon insinuated with malice, referenda about national belonging might also be held in Istanbul or at other places where Turkish forces had not yet accomplished ethnic cleansing. "Self-determination cut both ways," he added.[67] Thus, the main issue was cleared, but geographical fine-tuning remained to be done.

The next comparatively uncontroversial topic in Lausanne – not in the future, as we know – were the Greek islands close to Anatolia that had remained under safe Greek control. This was dealt with in two meetings of 25 and 29 November. Understandably, Ismet stressed the near islands' "great importance for the peace and security of Anatolia." Except for the indisputably Greek, but to be largely demilitarized islands of Lemnos, Mytilene (Lesbos), Chios (Sakız), Samos, and Nikaria (Ikaria), Ismet claimed, "They must remain under Turkish sovereignty on this account [security], and also because they were situated in Turkish territorial waters."[68] Imbros (Gökçeada) and Tenedos (Bozcaada), two neighboring islands near Gallipoli which had gone to Greece in the Sèvres Treaty, went back to Turkey in the conclusion of the negotiations; the other islands close

---

[66] *LCP*, 19–94; Nicolson, *Curzon: The Last Phase*, 293–301.   [67] *LCP*, 83.
[68] Ibid., 95–96.

17 Pivotal First Weeks

to the coast were largely demilitarized, but remained Greek. Italy maintained possession of Rhodes and the other islands of the Dodecanese, based on the 1912 Lausanne-Ouchy Treaty (until the Second World War, after which the Dodecanese came under Greek sovereignty).

On Monday, 27 November 1923, when the First Commission did not sit, the Third Commission on Economic and Financial Questions started its work with a discussion on Ottoman debts. All issues of this Commission – notably Ottoman debts, commercial régime (tariffs, taxes), Greek reparations – were to last into the second half of the Conference, whereas those of the First Commission were basically solved by the end of January 1923. The First Commission, presided by Curzon, was by far the most active during the Conference's first half, holding twenty-five meetings. The Second Commission on the Regime of Foreigners – including on the Capitulations and Turkey's future justice system – held six meetings; the Third Commission only five. The results of the Second Commission, presented with additions to the Turkish delegation in the Allies' draft peace treaty of 31 January 1923, and of the Third Commission, were not acceptable to Ankara. Dissolution occurred, though it was immediately framed as an interruption after which the Conference would resume.

***

Then as now, the Straits are the maritime entrance to Istanbul from the Mediterranean as well as the Black Sea. Being in the possession of both shores of the Straits, Ankara can today easily control and close the narrow corridor between both Seas. It is nonetheless bound to the regulations of the 1936 Montreux Agreement that revised those determined in Lausanne, allowing Turkish remilitarization of the Straits. The Sèvres Treaty had foreseen an international Commission of the Straits under the League of Nations, composed by all Black Sea states plus Britain, France, Italy, and the USA, if these states had become League members (Articles 37–61, plus Annex).

On Monday, 4 December 1922, the First Commission sat in the heavily congested dining room of the Château d'Ouchy. Here is the description by Nicolson, Curzon's secretary: "The political secretaries, the military and naval experts, the economic advisers, the jurisconsults, the stenographers and the attachés of every delegation had inserted themselves behind the chairs of their plenipotentiaries." The Commission started to deal with the Straits, and a Bolshevik delegation led by People's Commissar for Foreign Affairs Chicherin was for the first time present at the negotiation table. Members in this delegation were Christian G. Rakowski, his assistant delegate (shot on Stalin's order in 1941); Vatslav Vorovski for the Ukraine (assassinated during the Conference); and Polikarp Mdivani for

Georgia (executed in Stalin's Great Purge). As usual, Commission President Curzon gave the floor first to Ismet Pasha who read with pathos – for Nicolson "with jerky and unnecessary emphasis" – a relevant passage from the early-1920 National Pact. This passage gave ample space for compromise with the West, since from late 1922, Turkish sovereignty over Istanbul was no longer disputed:

> The security of Constantinople and seat of the Caliphate must be sheltered from any attack. This principle having been laid down and accepted, the Turkish nation is ready to subscribe to any decision which may be taken by common agreement between the Turkish Government, of the one part, and the Powers concerned, of the other part, with a view to ensuring the opening of the Straits to world trade and to international communications.[69]

Most attention in the Château d'Ouchy was fixed on the Bolshevik newcomers, in particular, for Sadak, on the "hero" Chicherin, the inspired, highly erudite revolutionary representative of an up-and-coming non-Western Great Power which had helped win Ankara the wars in Anatolia. Ismet Pasha had "in short explosive phrases expressed his extreme satisfaction at the presence" of the Bolshevik delegation, as if anticipating that he was going to disappoint his former comrades-in-arms. Chicherin began by solemnly stating, "The main object of the Russian Government and of its allies in the Near East, and also in the whole of their foreign policy, is to contribute towards establishing and consolidating general peace." He went on to demand that the Straits be permanently open to vessels of commerce, but permanently closed to vessels of war; and that Turkey should be allowed to fortify the Straits against attacks.[70] The British delegation knew that Ankara no longer claimed these conditions in the spirit of the 1921 Moscow Treaty, which treated the Straits as an issue for Black Sea countries only, Russia being the hegemon among them, but would be cooperative for "opening of the Straits to world trade and to international communications," based on the National Pact. Thus, it was easy for Curzon to embarrass Ismet Pasha. When asked, the Turkish delegate was not in a position to explicitly identify with Chicherin, who thus, right from the start of the Conference, saw himself cornered.

From there, it was a comparatively direct path to a successful compromise that allowed freedom of transit in times of peace for commercial and war vessels, though subject to a few limitations in number and duration of stay for warships. The compromise included a moderate

---

[69] Ibid., 127; Nicolson, *Curzon: The Last Phase*, 307–308.
[70] Sadak, *Lozan Mektuplan*, 103; Nicolson, *Curzon: The Last Phase*, 307–311; *LCP*, 128–131.

demilitarization (to be rescinded in 1936). Curzon could not refrain from making fun (only partially maliciously) of Chicherin's proclaimed universalism and pacifism. It is true that the Bolshevik proposal would also have blocked Russian warships from passing from the Black Sea to the Mediterranean Sea, but it would also have "shut off from the world" the Black Sea and the Caucasus.

Mr. Chicherin's loudly expressed love for equality is consistent with a willingness to deny to those [Western] Powers all right of protection [in that area]. ... M. Chicherin told us that he was very much disturbed at the preponderance of the forces of any Power at the mouth of the Dardanelles. ... But he does not object to a similar preponderance in the safe seclusion of the Black Sea – provided only that it be Russian. Such is the very remarkable contribution that was made two days ago by the Russian delegation to the doctrine of the equal rights of nations and the peace and contentment of mankind.[71]

The decisive discussions on the issue then came to an end, to be followed by expert work for a fine-tuned draft of the Straits Convention.

18   "Population Exchange" and Minorities

Open Straits weighed heavily for imperial Britain, France, and the USA. More fundamental topics of the Conference's first weeks, in human terms, were those directly deciding the fate and future of millions of people, and of a prominence that set new international standards. On 1 December 1922, three days before discussion on the Straits begun, the appearance of Nansen in the eighth meeting of the First Commission caught the attention of international Lausanne. He had just come back to Switzerland from a journey of investigation in Istanbul and Greece. A world-famous Norwegian explorer and author now in the service of Geneva's League, he spoke on the topic of how to organize a mass population transfer between Turkey and Greece.

League of Nations' Commissioner for Refugees, Nansen had met with Hamid Bey in Istanbul on 31 October 1922, in order to prepare negotiations on population exchange. Hamid (Hamit Hasancan) – himself a member in Ankara's delegation in Lausanne – was Ankara's representative in occupied Istanbul under the guise of being a Red Crescent functionary (actually the Red Crescent's vice-president). In line with a decade of Turkish ethnic cleansing, including the destruction and massacre of Izmir in September 1922, Hamid told Nansen during their preparatory Istanbul meeting that he was instructed "to negotiate on the basis of a total and enforced exchange of populations, from which the

---

[71] *LCP*, 141.

population of Constantinople would not be excepted."[72] The majority in Ankara's National Assembly believed that non-Muslims had "no place in this country anymore." As a consequence, according to one deputy on 3 November 1922, as far as all remaining Ottoman Christians in the country were concerned, "There is only one thing that can be done with them: exchange of populations."[73]

Ankara's instruction to Hamid meant that virtually all remaining Christians were to be forced to leave their Anatolian home and that Ankara was ready to accept a number of incoming Muslims from Greece. This set a clear and utterly harsh threshold. Compulsory population exchanges had hitherto been a legal no-go in international relations, although the concept of ethnically homogenous nation-states loomed large – though not unchecked – among the makers or promotors of new post–Great War states in Eastern Europe and the Ottoman world. The numerically smaller nonobligatory exchanges in the Balkans, discussed and partly also concluded after the Balkan Wars and after 1918 in Paris, did therefore not represent direct precedents to what was discussed in Lausanne in December 1922.[74] One dealt with the tacit acceptance and conclusion of a scheme of expulsion and genocide that, all in all, concerned more than three million people. The Treaty of Sèvres had attempted to revert and repair this scheme, but had failed. In consequence, an "orderly completion" of a vicious ten-year scheme had to be targeted in Lausanne, in order to save lives.

In early 1914, the main actors in this issue had already expelled approximatively two hundred thousand indigenous Rûm to Greece. During the Graeco-Turkish war, they pushed many hundreds of thousands more, as well as tens of thousands of Armenian survivors, all considered foreign elements and traitors, to and beyond Anatolia's Western borders. Nansen's estimated figure of 850,000 refugees in Greece, in his report of early November, was expected to rise to much more than a million in December.[75] The Commissary for Refugees had understood during his talks in Istanbul that Ankara absolutely rejected

---

[72] "Report by Dr. Nansen," *League of Nations Official Journal*, January 1923, 127. See also Liebisch-Gümüş. *Verflochtene Nationsbildung*, 362–373. For Nansen's retrospective on the exchange and its genesis, see Fridtjof Nansen, *Betrogenes Volk: Eine Studienreise durch Georgien und Armenien als Oberkommissar des Völkerbunds* (Lepizig: Brockhaus, 1928), 23–27.

[73] Mehmed Şükrü (Koçoğlu), quoted in Lerna Ekmekcioglu, "Republic of Paradox: The League of Nations Minority Protection Regime and the New Turkey's Step-Citizens," *International Journal of Middle East Studies*, 46. 4 (2014), 657–679 (quotation p. 657–658).

[74] Stephen Lades, *The Exchange of Minorities: Bulgaria, Greece and Turkey* (New York: Macmillan, 1932).

[75] LCP, 5 3.

the return of Christian expellees. Dozens of the refugees died every day from exhaustion; many more would die during the months to come if resolute action was not taken. An expedited exchange, even if disproportional (i.e. targeting many more Christians than Muslims) and compulsory, would at least put a certain number of houses and parcels at the disposition of the refugees from Anatolia. Without exchange, Ankara would anyway pursue its removal and dispossession of Christians, but without giving anything in return.

Faced with a catastrophe that culminated in Izmir, by mid-October Venizelos had already reacted to ongoing unilateral removal of Anatolian Christians by Ankara's authorities. In a letter to Nansen, he then mooted "compulsory recourse to the exchange of Greek and Turkish populations" to alleviate the problem of housing the million or so of refugees or expellees in Greece.[76] The choice was between passive acceptance of full-scale ethnic cleansing that no Western army was in a position to stop, or at least a partly orderly and compensated last phase of an overall process of demographic, cultural, and material de-Christianization. To be clear: the negotiators in Lausanne were to endorse a coercive model of "conflict resolution" based, primarily, on the will and patterns of CUP and Kemalist decision-makers. This is why early pro-Kemalist Nazis significantly, though incorrectly, understood Lausanne's population transfer as a one-sided expulsion of Rûm.[77] The CUP's rule had made compulsion and expulsion, coercion, and violence a commonplace during five years of Turkifying demographic engineering in Anatolia. As readers have seen in Part II, this proactive, genocidal policy started after the Ottoman losses during the Balkan Wars, but its makers also referred to Muslim losses and victimhood in former conflicts.

The basic question for the practitioner Nansen – who had gained a reputation working with refugees and prisoners in the Russian Civil War – was how to save as many lives as possible and give survivors the material opportunities to reconstruct their existence in the winter and spring 1923. Time was of the essence. He addressed the Lausanne Conference on 1 December 1922, in the Château d'Ouchy, arguing:

I believe that any exchange of populations, however well it were carried out, must impose very considerable hardships, perhaps very considerable impoverishment, upon great numbers of the individual citizens of the two countries who are exchanged. But I also believe that these hardships, great though they may be,

---

[76] Venizelos to Nansen, 13 October 1922, quoted in Kévonian, *Réfugiés et diplomatie humanitaire*, 112.
[77] Ihrig, *Atatürk in the Nazi Imagination*, 86.

will be less than the hardships which will result for these same populations if nothing is done."[78]

In order not to misread the relevant minutes of December 1922, it is essential to fully take cognizance, firstly, of CUP demographic engineering inherited, defended, and continued by Ankara, and, secondly, of the immediate antecedents in October 1922 and the resulting constraints that, as all insiders at Lausanne's table knew, defined the narrow scope of negotiation right from the start.[79] There was scope to exclude certain groups, mainly the Rûm of Istanbul. Also, Turkish diplomacy had well understood before December that the intended removal of all Christians, including the remaining Armenians, was a diplomatic no-go. Thirdly, for a correct reading in light of the first two points, Nansen's enthusiastic commitment and persuasive identification with the task before the delegates must not be confounded with proactivity in the matter of transfer and removal itself. This matter hailed from the given facts; Nansen's proposals amounted to an improvised reaction to brutal facts. For the sake of survival of the homeless, he wanted to carry out the exchange, "at least in part, by the end of February, three months from now"; and made a particular effort to win the trust of Ankara for an operation under the aegis of the League of Nations. Ankara had hitherto displayed hostile distance to a League whose Covenant had been part of the Sèvres Treaty.[80]

These comments pertain also to Nansen's insistence in the Sub-Commission (or "special committee") on the Exchange of Populations, created on 1 December and presided over by the particularly capable diplomat Montagna, Italy's second delegate. Montagna stated in his report on 8 January 1923:

Although the compulsory solution was regarded by everyone with repugnance, Dr. Nansen himself felt obliged to recommend it as the only one likely to prove useful and effective in the circumstances. . . . in the course of the discussions in the special committee the question was raised afresh by a written declaration of the Greek delegation, proposing that the exchange should be voluntary. The Turkish delegation definitely opposed this proposal.[81]

One might discount such and similar statements by the Greek delegation as rhetorical. All relevant documents nonetheless leave little doubt on

---

[78] *LCP*, 115.
[79] One among many examples of misreading (because insufficiently contextualizing Nansen's and Curzon's statements) is in the chapter on the Lausanne Treaty in Philippe Ther, *The Dark Side of Nation-States: Ethnic Cleansing in Modern Europe* (New York: Berghahn, 2014), 76–78.
[80] *LCP*, 116–117.   [81] Ibid., 330.

the question which enforced the transfer of an as comprehensive number of Christians from Anatolia as possible, in exchange for a fraction of Muslims from Greece.

***

In his reaction to Nansen's presentation on 1 December, Ismet Pasha displayed surprise that the refugee problem had unexpectedly been put on the meeting's agenda. After emphasizing that to Nansen's statement "he could only attach a personal character as no official relations existed between Turkey and the League of Nations," Ismet drew attention to what he had reason to regard as the interconnection between population exchange and "the question of minorities in Turkey."[82]

Before 1914, there had existed no clear ethnic majority in the Ottoman Empire, even in the imperial core region in Anatolia where the Empire had begun in the fourteenth century.[83] There was a majority of the Muslim "element," that comprised Turks, Kurds, Arabs, and various other groups. The Ottomans used the descriptive word *unsur* ("element") for the various population groups, whereas, especially since the Berlin Treaty, Western diplomacy featured "minority" in relation with the question of equal rights and the need of protection for specific ethnic and religious groups that did not form imperial or national core groups.

The issue of equality between the existing, highly diverse elements had been the crux of late-Ottoman reforms. Both Sultan Abdulhamid and the CUP perceived the domestic and international efforts related to this postulate as a foreign conspiracy to break up the Empire by disenfranchising the Turkish-speaking Muslims. Therefore, the CUP had turned to a policy of ridding Anatolia of minorities. Questions of minorities and population transfer were therefore closely interrelated for Ankara's delegation: it was about the elimination or maximal reduction of minorities and non-Turkish rights in future unitary Turkey. For the Allies, a minimum of the League's minority concept and protection should be implemented, and population exchange should be limited as much as possible.

After the intermezzo with Nansen and the meetings on the Straits, which both led to the creation of sub-commissions, Curzon was happy to put the issue of minorities on the agenda of the First Commission. This resulted in three heated meetings from 12 to 14 December – the most intense moments of the Conference, as far as the main Commission meetings were concerned. After 14 December, the topic was left to the

---

[82] Ibid., 117.
[83] See Hans-Lukas Kieser: Minorities (Ottoman Empire/Middle East) (Version 1.1), in *1914–1918-online. International Encyclopedia of the First World War*, Berlin 2014–10–08. https://doi.org/10.15463/ie1418.10512/1.1.

Sub-Commission on Minorities. Once more, the Turkish delegation experienced the disadvantage of being little involved in the Conference's agenda-setting managed by Curzon. On the night before 12 December, Ismet wrote in his memoirs:

> After midnight, they informed us that the issue of the minorities was on the agenda of the next day. The clerk of the delegation did not wake me up because it was too late. In the morning, when I was going to get up calmly and start working because there was no session that day, they said we were going to the conference. No, there was nothing last night, I asked, since they hadn't told us about an agenda. Yes, they came after you went to bed, they said, but we didn't wake you up. They stated that the issue of minorities will be discussed. I scolded the clerk for not waking me up. At least, there was a historical study that we had prepared hastily on the issue of minorities in Ankara. I took it with me and went to the conference.[84]

For Nicolson, his chief's "essential object" in then putting the minorities question on the agenda was, as with the Straits, to widen the breach between Moscow and Ankara and to make Ankara's representative take a stand regarding the League of Nations. Curzon used Ismet Pasha's acute uneasiness in discussing the issue of minorities before an international public "to induce Turkey to enter the League of Nations. If only he could secure such adhesion, the breach between Moscow and Angora would become irreparable," Nicolson noted.[85] As we have seen, even Ankara's Bolshevik allies addressed crimes against minorities in Anatolia at times, but as the true antidote against the poison of ethnic nationalism, they proposed socialist brotherhood, not League of Nations protection.

Starting on 12 December, Curzon pressed Ankara's delegate time and again to join the League of Nations, "when once peace is concluded." On 13 December, the latter "hastened to correct" the impression that he was "disrespectful towards the League of Nations.... the Turkish Government regarded it with all due respect and consideration." On 14 December, finally, he admitted that Turkey would enter the League "as soon as peace was concluded. She would then express her opinion on this subject, and the strong desire of the Allied Powers to see her enter the League would be satisfied."[86] As mentioned earlier, this promise was not fulfilled, as Ankara adhered only very belatedly, in 1932, when the League was an almost impotent international actor without any real supervisory power in Turkey.

---

[84] İsmet İnönü, *İsmet İnönü'nün hatıraları: Büyük zaferden sonra Mudanya Mütarekesi ve Lozan Antlaşması* (Istanbul: Yenigün, 1998), 113.

[85] "It was an article of faith with the U.S.S.R. to forbid her satellites and associates to have any dealings with the 'organised impotence of Geneva which serves only to further the designs of the capitalist imperialist Powers.'" Nicolson, *Curzon: The Last Phase*, 315.

[86] *LCP*, 177, 209, 219.

Besides omnipresent considerations of Conference strategy, Curzon was able to appreciate the human dimension of the minority question in his statements, without however conceding this issue had any real priority. Still, he wanted to give it prominence, therefore transferring it from the Second to his First Commission. Garroni, who presided over the Second Commission, had intended to refer the minority question to a sub-commission; for Curzon, an approach "wholly inconsistent with importance and worldwide interest of subject."[87] Starting the meeting of 12 December, the gifted orator implored the delegates "to approach this vital question [of minorities] in a humane spirit." He kept repeating that "the eyes of the world are upon us," or "the whole world had its eyes fixed on the conference room" (i.e. Château d'Ouchy's dining room). The minorities problem, he insisted, excited more attention throughout the world than anything else, and "according as it is settled in an equitable and reasonable spirit or the reverse, so shall we [the Allies] and they [Turks and Greeks] be judged."

In vain, Curzon tried to move the Turkish delegation on this topic. He must have sensed that Ankara would be as callous on minority rights as on the related topic of population transfer. "If we break down upon this; if we have to go away after this [minority rights]; will there be a single voice lifted up for the Turkish Delegation in the whole world?"[88] The foreign Secretary was well aware that the minorities issue was only "most desirable," not essential, for his policy.[89] The solution for ethno-religious conflicts as proposed by Ankara's National Assembly and stated by Ismet Pasha on 12 December 1922, postulated: (1) the "exclusion of every kind of foreign intervention and of the possibility of provocation coming from outside"; (2) for this purpose, an exchange of populations; and (3) loyal to an allegedly progressive Turkish-Ottoman tradition in this field, the promise of modern laws and "the liberal policy of Turkey with regard to all communities whose members have not deviated from their duty as Turkish citizens."[90]

These prospects concluded a long historical speech by Ismet that used contemptuous and patronizing language, particularly for the Armenians. Now on the highest diplomatic level, Ismet framed the past in line with the pre-Lausanne writings by delegation members Rıza Nur and Atabinen. In this vision, it was removal of non-Turks that solved the problems of minorities, not the latter's recognition and rights.[91]

---

[87] Demirci, *Lausanne Conference*, 105.   [88] *LCP*, 175, 183, 215, cf. 212, 573.
[89] Demirci, *Lausanne Conference*, 54–55.   [90] *LCP*, 204.
[91] "The exchange of populations is not, as Ismet Pasha believes, a means of settling the question of minorities" (*LCP*, 184). Several delegates, among them Venizelos, insisted in vain on this point.

At the end of the Conference's most intense days and debates on 12–14 December, Rumbold concluded by again clarifying that Ankara had proactively imposed the compulsory condition of an exchange that suited its demographic policy. The Turkish delegation time and again claimed the contrary by emphasizing Greek authorship.[92] The British High Commissioner in Istanbul, Rumbold had closely followed the events:

> When the Greek population fled from Asia Minor in hundreds of thousands, the High Commissioners met to examine the problem. Dr. Nansen ... was invited to attend these meetings, and the idea of an exchange of populations [instead of ongoing unilateral ethnic cleansing and impossible return] came from him. The High Commissioners, who realised the magnitude of the problem, were of the opinion that it must be settled by the [Lausanne] conference and not by themselves. It was at this point that Dr. Nansen approached Hamid Bey, the representative of the Angora Government at Constantinople, and the latter replied categorically that the question of exchanging populations could only be considered on a compulsory basis.[93]

After the meetings of the First Commission on 12–14 December 1922, negotiations on minority rights and population exchange continued in the sub-commission led by Montagna where Rıza Nur was entrusted to represent the Ankara government. Concluding these sub-commission meetings, Montagna reported to Curzon on 9 January 1923, "The Turkish delegation, however, met all the questions put to them, whether in regard to the [collective resettlement of] Armenians, the Assyro-Chaldeans or the Bulgarian populations [from Thrace] on National Pact territory, with an absolute and clear refusal."[94] Turkey insisted on an ethnically cleansed country.

***

Nur led the Turkish delegation in Lausanne's commission and sub-commission meetings on minority rights. The resulting weak protection of the weak and the wholesale exclusion of consideration for groups outside the traditional Ottoman categories corresponded to his expectations. Ankara's delegation asserted that it would recognize as minorities only those which the Ottoman state had treated as so-called non-Muslim "millets," that is Jewish, Armenian, and Rûm communities. This notably

---

[92] Ismet Pasha and Rıza Nur underlined Greece's early readiness for exchanges, omitting that this was principally for voluntary exchange and finally, by mid-October 1922, possibly for compulsory exchange, if forced so by Ankara's ongoing ethnic cleansing. *CLA*, first series, vol. 1, 100–104, 187, 577, 606–607, 613. The Turkish interest in as complete a compulsory exchange as possible is reported by journalist Necmettin Sadık (Sadak) in "Lozan Mektupları: 28 Kanûn-i Evvel 1922," in Sadak, *Lozan Mektupları*, 258.
[93] *LCP*, 227.   [94] Ibid., 308.

excluded other non-Muslims like the Assyrians and – most importantly for the future – nominal Muslims like the Kurds and the Alevis.

Imposed by Ankara in the Treaty of Lausanne, the restricted definition of minorities contradicted and diminished that of the minority protection treaties in the Paris-Geneva peace settlement.[95] Ismet's argument in the conclusive meeting on 9 January 1923 was unsound. "There were no Moslem minorities in Turkey, for no distinction was made either in theory or in practice between the various elements of the Moslem population." But again, the Allies gave in while expressing vague hope for the best. "Lord Curzon had expressed the hope that these Moslem elements would be able to live on perfectly good terms with the Turkish population. Ismet Pasha was firmly convinced that future events would fully justify that expectation."[96] The wars against Kurdish unrest brutally falsified Ismet's argument from the immediate aftermath of the Conference.

In the final Treaty, the stipulations in the section on minority protection (Part I, Section III) were enshrined as internationally guaranteed "fundamental law," that is, the League and its Council had to keep watch over them and react in case of infraction. These stipulations were almost entirely restricted to the small number of remaining Christians and Jews. Still, a few stipulations in the Articles 38–39 of Section III clearly apply to all nationals in the country; for example, "full and complete protection of life and liberty to all inhabitants of Turkey without distinction of birth, nationality, language, race or religion"; "free exercise, whether in public or private, of any creed, religion or belief"; and "the free use by any Turkish national of any language in private intercourse, in commerce, religion, in the press, or in publications of any kind or at public meetings." The diplomatic reality in the immediate aftermath of the Treaty however not only made grievances of non-Turkish Muslims (e.g. Kurds) an impossibility, but also made those of non-Muslims, notably Armenians, hopeless. As readers will see (Part IV), the Kemalists had no inhibitions to breach in the name of the "Turkish Revolution" internationally guaranteed law.

How weak and inconsequential the Lausanne Conference's dealing with the minorities was, emerges also from Ismet İnönü's memoirs. His chapter on the "stormy session on minorities" not only incorrectly writes that his delegation had been ready to accept all standards defined by the League (in reality, it cut down the League's definition), but even

---

[95] See Articles 37–45 of the Lausanne Treaty. For the discussions, see the Conference minutes, *CLA*, first series, vol. 1, 182, 244. For the sentiment in the Turkish delegation including affiliated press members, see Necmeddin Sadık (Sadak), "Lozan Mektupları: 23 Kanûn-i Evvel," in Sadak, *Lozan Mektupları*, 191–192.
[96] *LCP*, 301.

candidly confesses that Ankara refused League supervision. "We do not consent to any control. We do not consent to the supervision of the League of Nations," the chapter concludes. This, indeed, was the spirit at the negotiation table and the reality after Lausanne. The breach of the weak stipulations for weak was quasi-inscribed to the Treaty. In the same chapter in his memoirs, Ismet also admits that he was very perturbed by the topic and feared a break, until one British senior diplomat calmed him down in private, "We [allies] have made a lot of commitments all over the world. While putting an end to all this now, why do you find it strange that there is a lot of spectacle?"[97]

In retrospect, Lord Curzon's lofty words of 12–14 December therefore appear as little more than smoke and mirrors. London became a loyal follower of Ankara's minority definition for decades. By the end of January 1923, Ismet's delegation had asserted its diminished concept of minorities pertaining only to the remaining Jews and Christian. Fifteen years later, a despairing Alevi Kurdish representative reported on an impending genocide – that eventually took place in 1938 – in Turkey's Dersim. London's then–Foreign Secretary found it opportune to inform Ankara that Britain did not give the least attention to Kurdish voices.[98]

The Convention Concerning the Exchange of Greek and Turkish Populations, signed on 30 January, terminated the age-old presence of hundreds of thousands of Muslims in Greece (with the exception of Western Thrace). Above all, however, it finished off the millennia-old presence of millions of Rûm in Anatolia. In the end, after strong insistence by the Allies, only Istanbul's Rûm residents were excepted from the removal.[99] The consequential policy of ethnically cleansing Anatolia, and the restriction of the minority definition in Lausanne, enabled suppression of any sizable recognized minority in the country. From a CUP and Kemalist point of view, Ismet was entirely right in affirming population transfer and minority issues to be related. The great fallacy of the scheme was the illusion that, as Muslims, the Kurds would be assimilable to an ultranationalist Turkey.

The minority issue had strong material and related legal aspects that partly overlapped with topics of the Second Commission (on the Régime of Foreigners). Removal of Anatolian Christians – a few them nationalized

---

[97] İnönü, *İsmet İnönü'nün Hatıraları*, 121–124.

[98] Letter of the British Embassy in Ankara to the *Eastern Department* of the *Foreign Office*, 5 October 1937, quoted in M. Kalman, *Belge ve tanıklarıyla Dersim Direnişleri* (Istanbul: Nûjen Yay., 1995), 311.

[99] For this Convention, see *LCP*, 817–27. The Convention was an integral part of the final Treaty.

as Americans, Italians, or Frenchmen – had gone along with dispossession since the aftermath of the Balkan Wars and during the Armenian genocide. It was factual spoliation, even if the government provided legal cloaks as in 1915.[100] The most recent experience of such lawlessness applied to minorities were the killings and financial misappropriations happening after Turkish entrance into Izmir in September 1922. There, the new authorities not only "destroyed confidence and made banking operations practically impossible by various measures, one of which was the sequestration of all moneys belonging to Greeks [Rûm] and Armenians in all banks," Rumbold reported in the 28 December meeting of the Commission on the Régime of Foreigners. The sober diplomat continued in an unusually sharp tone:

> They requisitioned foreign property freely, and they even threatened to apply to the property of foreigners who had left Smyrna temporarily that arbitrary measure known as the "Law on Abandoned Property." ... When we have used the example of Smyrna in the sub-commission, we have been told by the Turkish delegation that everything that has happened there has been due to abnormal circumstances. The conditions at Smyrna have been in truth abnormal for reasons with which the world is familiar [Turkey's methodical elimination of minorities]. There might have been some force in the Turkish argument if the acts of which Allied subjects so bitterly complain had been confined to matters of military necessity. But it was not so. Too many of these acts, the measures taken in regard to the banks, for instance, were of a nature to destroy any remnant of normal conditions which might remain. It was the duty and it would have been to the interest of the Turkish authorities to do their utmost to reassure foreigners. They have wholly failed to do so.[101]

Against this background, trust in the functioning of Turkish justice equalled zero on all levels. Nevertheless, Turkish delegates initially kept repeating the mantra that "all the necessary [legal] guarantees already existed in the Turkish legal system and in the Turkish administration of justice," so that absolutely no special reform, expertise, or measures, as demanded by the Allies, were required.[102] Yet, Ankara's delegation soon understood that regaining a minimum of confidence and making sound promises for legal reform was paramount for the process of negotiation, especially for the essential objective of abolishing the Capitulations. Simply insisting on legal achievements and the establishment of a faculty of law at the University of Istanbul during the last Ottoman decades did not convince anybody. Not the soundness of bold reform promises, however, as we will see, but the common interest in concluding the treaty was decisive for finally overcoming dissent in legal matters.

---

[100] Kieser, *Talaat Pasha*, 268–272.   [101] *LCP*, 487.   [102] Ibid., 502, see also 473.

This final success in the second part of the Conference again largely took place at the expense of minorities, in particular the Armenians, victims of genocide and dispossession.

19 Lausanne's Armenian Catastrophe: No "Armenian Home," No Assyrian Independence

On 6 January, the British, French, and Italian delegates argued in the Sub-Commission on Minorities for an extremely modest "Armenian home" – an autonomous province at most – under full Turkish sovereignty, a far cry from the independent Armenia projected in the Sèvres Treaty. The Sub-Commission also received an Armenian, an Assyro-Chaldean, and a Bulgarian delegation to hear their requests regarding resettlement in Anatolia or, as for the Bulgarians, in Eastern Thrace.[103]

In his memorandum dated Lausanne, 6 January 1923, Agha Petros, who spoke for the Assyro-Chaldeans, still boldly demanded an independent "Assyro-Chaldée," potentially situated between Diyarbekir, Mosul, and the Lake of Urmiah. He also still insisted, in the vein of the Sèvres Treaty, on restitution of stolen property, reparations, and support to reconvert for those forcibly converted to Islam during the genocide.[104]

Before even listening to the Armenian, Assyrian, and Bulgarian representatives in the 6 January meeting, Rıza Nur furiously interrupted the procedure and left the room with his team composed of Mehmed Münir (Ertegün), Ahmed Cevad (Açıkalın), and Şükrü (Kaya). Şükrü, a future minister of foreign affairs and of the interior, had been Talaat's director in charge of the camps for deportees in Northern Syria during the second phase of the Armenian genocide. Before exiting Château d'Ouchy's meeting room, Nur shouted, "the Allies had to make such statements as they had incited these people against the Turks and were responsible for the present situation."

While still very agitated, Nur went to delegation chief Ismet, told the story, and proposed to go back to Ankara. But the latter responded, "Well done, I congratulate you." All in all, indeed, Nur had acted according to Ankara's Conference instructions.[105] Interestingly, Nur, notwithstanding his own hard-line position, strongly felt ultranationalist pressure from

---

[103] *CLA*, first series, vol. 1, 541–549; Montagna's report is also in *LCP*, 303–308. See also "Conférence de Lausanne: La situation," *Gazette de Lausanne*, 7 January 1923, 4; "L'Arménie sacrifiée," *Journal de Genève*, 7 January 1923, 8.

[104] *La question assyro-chaldeenne devant la Conference de la paix de Lausanne, par le general Agha Petros, président du Comite exécutif national, président de la délegation assyro-chaldéenne à la Conférence de Lausanne* (Lausanne: n.p., n.d. [6 January 1923], annexes and maps).

[105] Şimşir, *Lozan Telgrafları I*, XIV; *İnönü'nün Hatıraları*, 120.

19 Lausanne's Armenian Catastrophe

Ankara, as he confessed three days later to an inquiring Antony Krafft-Bonnard. "But, please know that if we accept the [Armenian] Home here [at the Conference], we cannot go back to Angora. They would kill us there." Very present in Lausanne during the Conference, the Protestant pastor Krafft-Bonnard, himself a Vaudois, was, and remained for decades, a particularly loyal friend of stateless Armenians, and a sustained public voice for justice.[106]

Montagna, the sub-commission's president, addressed a formal protest and a request for an explanation to Ismet, asking whether he supported Nur's undiplomatic behavior. He received an evasive answer. The matter was dropped, "but left a very bad impression," Grew noted in his diary. "There is no subject upon which the Turks are more fixed in obstinacy."[107] On 27 December already, "an awkward event was concocted," a bad and disruptive joke, in Cavid's eyes. "Because of Armenian insistence at the conference, Ismet Pasha sent a memorandum to the plenipotentiaries; Rıza Nur another one to the commission, both on the same issue," both claiming that the Armenians should be entirely excluded from the Conference. Nur suggested that if the Armenians were listened to, an Irish delegation should also be invited to a hearing.[108] Nur's and Ismet's memoranda reacted to a presentation made by Noradounghian and to additional explanations by Aharonian before the same sub-commission, but without the Turkish representatives, on 26 December 1922.[109]

Nur's posthumously published private notes on the Lausanne Conference are in line with his behavior at the Conference and the beliefs

---

[106] Nur quoted in Khatissian, *Eclosion*, 413. Besides efficient humanitarian activism, Krafft-Bonnard was a prolific writer. See Antony Kraft-Bonnard, *L'Arménie à la Conférence de Lausanne* (Alençon: Foi et vie, 1923); Kraft-Bonnard, *Arménie, Suisse et Société des Nations* (Geneva: Secours suisse aux Arméniens, 1924); Kraft-Bonnard, *Arménie, justice et réparation* (Geneva: Soc. générale d'impr. 1930). See also Sisvan Nigolian and Pascal Roman (eds.), *Sauver les enfants, sauver l'Arménie: la contribution du pasteur Antony Kraft-Bonnard (1919–1945)* (Lausanne: Antipodes, 2020).

[107] Grew diary, 6 January 1923, 5. Same in the published version: Grew, *Turbulent Era*, 530–531. There is a detailed chapter on the Conference of Lausanne in Esat Uras, *The Armenians in History and the Armenian Question* (Istanbul: Documentary Publshing, 1988, Turkish edition 1950), 970–999, that largely consists of translated passages from Khatissian, *Eclosion* (i.e. from the Armenian original). The English version smooths openly derogatory sentences in Uras's "Turkish bible" on the Armenian question, cf. notably pp. 976–977 and Esat Uras, *Tarihte Ermeniler ver Ermeni meselesi* (Ankara: Yeni Matbaa, 1950), 732. Particularly instructive are the additions in the appendix of the 1989 French edition of Khatissian's book, which contain Khatissian's aide-memoirs written day by day during the Lausanne Conference.

[108] Cavid, *Meşrutiyet Ruznamesi*, vol. 4, 427-8, diary entry of 27 December 1922.

[109] For Noradounghian's presentation, see "Exposé lu par M. Noradounghian devant la Sous-Commission de la Conférence de Lausanne le 26 Décembre 1922," Folder "Délégation arménienne, Traité de Lausanne 19223," BNu. See also Khatissian, *Eclosion*, 404–405.

expressed in his *History of the Armenians*. "It is of vital interest and perfectly fair not to let any human of another race, of another language and another religion live in our homeland." For Nur, a surgeon turned politician, indigenous non-Turks and non-Muslims counted as "a foreign element, a plague and microbes." On the question of what to do with Kurdish Muslims, he answered, "With a persistent assimilation program, they must be purified of their distinct language and race."[110] His idea of a purified state came close to what the Polish sociologist Zygmunt Bauman described as a mass-murdering modern "gardener state" after the Second World War.[111]

The Allied delegates knew well that an Armenian home, even in a small part of Anatolia, had become a utopian ideal by 1922. Moreover, appointing former Turkish perpetrators as sovereign overlords over a hypothetical province composed of Armenian survivors was nothing short of preposterous. Nonetheless, the Allied delegates could not lightly abandon the topic, and it would be too simple to say that this was for show only and under public pressure. Most understood that the Armenian issue was a seminal challenge with a long, complex, and poignant history. However, the crème de la crème of international diplomacy which met in Lausanne did not see a practical solution. The topic left them in a brutal political aporia. After deliberating for at least a few intense moments in December 1922 and early 1923, they abandoned it to diplomatic oblivion, though as a "question not settled" and thus shelved.[112] Convenience joined unsolved aporia.

The "privately expressed views of the Allied representatives are that it is not possible to formulate any concrete plan which will be wise even for the welfare of the Armenians themselves," Grew noted in his diary on 6 January. All knew that Ankara flatly rejected the return of Armenians to their native land. Thus, they gave some easy credit to the Turkish delegation's "opinion that such Armenians as remain in Turkey will be useful where they are, and if not subject to foreign intrigue, will be safe and happy also."[113] History soon taught differently, as responsible participants of the 6 January meeting well anticipated and further negotiations in the second half of the Conference indicated. One of them, long-term dragoman and Istanbul resident Andrew Ryan, a member of the British delegation, regretfully emphasized in his memoirs his delegation's failure regarding minorities.[114]

---

[110] Rıza Nur, *Hayat ve Hatıratım* (Istanbul: İşaret, 1992), vol. 2, 260.
[111] Zygmunt Bauman, *Modernity and the Holocaust* (Cambridge: Polity Press, 1989).
[112] *LCP*, 305. [113] Grew diary, 6 January 1923, 7.
[114] Andrew Ryan, *The Last of the Dragomans* (London: Geoffrey Bles, 1952), 193. See also Chapter 25 as well as Part IV.

19 Lausanne's Armenian Catastrophe   161

***

From August 1922, the Armenian representatives had diligently prepared what they sensed would become a critical and definitive hour of decision during the upcoming Near East peace conference. Since the negotiations at Paris-Sèvres, they formed a united delegation composed of the delegation of the Republic of Armenia and the so-called National Delegation, the latter representing the Ottoman Armenians.

They stuck to Western promises, the League's commitment, and Lloyd George's rallying call that the Sèvres Treaty would be maintained in its substance. A legitimate party in Paris-Sèvres, they initially hoped to enjoy the same status in Lausanne. They were informed by London's foreign Office in late October 1923, "The three Principal Allied Governments regret that, owing to the adoption by the Republic of Armenia, whose *de jure* independence has been recognised, of the Soviet form of Government, they cannot see their way to admit the participation of Armenia in the approaching peace conference or her signature of the new treaty."[115]

Cavid Bey, the former CUP finance minister in Swiss exile after the Great War, was in close touch with those reorganizing Turkish power after World War defeat, but also with Armenians. Although typically ambivalent in his attitude toward claims of non-Turkish minorities, he was by no means a nationalist hardliner. In many private meetings, he frankly warned his Armenian acquaintances, notably his former CUP comrade Bedros Halajian and the former liberal Ottoman foreign minister Gabriel Noradounghian, they should not expect anything from Europe. However, once more over-optimistic in his outlook on the Turkish nationalist project – as at the eve of the February 1914 Reform Agreement and regarding the future of Rûm – he admonished the Armenian representatives to renounce on their territorial rights enshrined in the Sèvres Treaty and to put trust in a renewed Turkey. "Based on a new constitution, all provinces will be given large administrative autonomy of which the oriental provinces will also benefit; but great Armenia is an illusion." For Armenians leaving Anatolia, "there will be reparations."[116] Sure enough, as well-meant as it possibly was, Cavid's advice proved entirely built on sand.

Avetis Aharonian and Boghos Noubar Pasha had represented the Armenians during the negotiations in Sèvres in 1919–20. Members of the united delegation also participated at the London Conference in

---

[115] Curzon to British Ambassador Hardinge in Paris, 23 October 1922, FO Confidential Print 12330, 198–199.
[116] Cavid, *Meşrutizet Ruznâmesi*, 243–244, diary entry of 13 March 1921.

February–March 1921. Among these were Aharonian (president of the delegation of the Republic of Armenia), Khatissian, Garo Pasdermadjian, and Noubar, president of the National Delegation (in Lausanne, he was succeeded by Noradounghian). In London, for the first time, the notion of an "Armenian Home," *Foyer arménien*, was introduced for what Article 88 of the Sèvres Treaty had unequivocally defined as a "free and independent state."[117] The vague notion of "home" had won notoriety with the "Jewish home" in Palestine, promised in the 1917 Balfour Declaration. After the Bolshevik Revolution, this pronouncement had gone hand in hand with outspoken British commitment for an independent Armenia.[118] While the Jewish home under the protective roof of mandatory Britain rapidly evolved toward a proto-state, the Armenian home in Anatolia, left without mandatory protection, had been reduced to a ghost house by 1922.

By then, "Armenian home" was tantamount to a moral statement only, without real backing by the Powers, which liked to refer moral issues to the League, which itself was impotent without the commitment of its members. The progressive disengagement by the Allies from Armenia and the Armenians went on at the March 1922 ministers' conference with Poincaré, Curzon, and Carlo Schanzer, the Italian foreign minister: the Armenians were not invited. A passage in that conference's communiqué that introduced new critical concessions to Ankara in preparation of a post-Sèvres settlement reads: "The situation of the Armenians must be given special attention because of the commitments made by the Allied Powers during the war and the terrible hardships suffered by this people.... [T]he assistance of the League of Nations is requested in order to satisfy the traditional aspirations of the Armenians to create a National Home."[119]

The Armenian representatives did all they could to maintain momentum for their cause, at least in the League of Nations. They enjoyed strong moral and intellectual support in the League's Assembly. There, many deputies were fully aware that the vision of a future of freedom, self-determination, and rule of law depended paradigmatically on the Armenian case. The relevant passage in the motion proposed at the League's Third Assembly in September 1922, two months before the opening of the Lausanne Conference, reads, "in any peace with Turkey it should be an essential

---

[117] Khatissian, *Eclosion*, 306. The notion of the "Armenian home" under Turkish sovereignty was hotly disputed among Armenian leaders, Aharonian rejecting it, whereas Noradounghian saw no other way to Armenian survival in Anatolia after sovietization of Caucasian Armenia. For this discussion between them both on 16 December 1921, see Aharonian, *From Sardarabad to Sèvres and Lausanne*, 184–185.

[118] Jonathan Schneer, *The Balfour Declaration: The Origins of the Arab-Israeli Conflict* (New York: Random House, 2012), 261.

[119] Khatissian, *Eclosion*, 314.

condition that a National Home should be provided for the Armenians."[120] The Armenian delegates knew well however that even if "the entire civilized world stood up and demanded that the Conference meet the aspirations of the Armenians," nothing was achieved, as long as "we could not see any practical way to influence the Turks."[121]

The case of the Assyro-Chaldeans was similar, although not of the same dimension and notoriety. Their delegation remained in touch with the Armenian delegation since the negotiations in Paris-Sèvres. In contrast to the Armenians, after 6 January 1923, Agha Petros made a last serious attempt in Lausanne to get a concession from Ankara. He did this in very modest terms and related it to the question of Mosul that was soon to be negotiated. Agha Petros visited Ismet on 15 January 1923, as commented on Ismet's telegram to the cabinet in Ankara the same day.[122] Petros asked that Ankara allow the return of surviving Assyrians to their pre-1914 homes. He promised that, if Turkey facilitated Assyrian return, the Assyrians would renounce on any other claims. Furthermore, the (Assyro-)Chaldeans in Mosul would support Turkish annexation of Mosul.

The answer of Prime Minister Rauf to Ismet's telegram on 18 January was brief and clear: "It is obvious that that we will not agree to the resettlement of Assyrians and Chaldeans in our country. However, if this is beneficial, Agha Petros may be sent away from Lausanne to Ankara without any further commitments from our side."[123] From then, the Lausanne case was closed for the Assyrians. For them, and the Armenians, there remained henceforth only some – as it proved, vain – hope that the League of Nations would be able to act in their interest after the Conference.

***

Ismet's strategy in dealing with the Armenians was simple. He insisted that, diplomatically, all questions with the Armenians were settled through the 1920 Treaty of Alexandropol and the 1921 Treaty of Kars, concluded with the Republic of Armenia, the only legitimate Armenian representative. As for Anatolia, Ottoman Armenians who had survived could now stay peacefully. Chief of a delegation composed of several former collaborators of Talaat Pasha, Ismet outright rejected any CUP legacy and any relation of the Ankara government with what had happened during the Great War to the Armenians.

In Lausanne, therefore, the denied mass crimes were always the elephant in the room (i.e. in the meetings with Ismet and other members of Ankara's delegation). Ismet's deaf ear is particularly striking in

---

[120] Motions proposed at the Third Assembly, 1922, page 8, R1376/26/23251/23251, United Nations Library & Archives Geneva. See also Khatissian, *Eclosion*, 314–316.
[121] Ibid., 335.   [122] Şimşir, *Lozan Telgrafları I*, 388–389.   [123] Ibid., 400.

conversations with members of the Armenian delegation and the latter's Swiss friends. He had a deaf ear in the literal physical sense, as he suffered from hearing loss. However, he also revealed himself metaphorically deaf. Rejecting any responsibility and pretending ignorance, he abnegated the evident CUP legacy and refused to listen to his interlocutors. At the beginning of the Conference, flimsy propaganda by Ankara's Anatolia Agency sought to discredit the Armenian representatives who had come to Lausanne. Addressing a national and international public, a dispatch of 28 November spread fake news attributing evil designs to Armenian terrorists, among them members of the united delegation. In a letter to Ismet on 6 December 1922, Leon Pashalian vehemently protested in the name of the united delegation and asked for a retraction. In particular, he drew attention to the dangerous incitement that such all-too-frequent fake news stirred among the Muslim population against the remainder of Armenians still living among them.[124]

Ismet could not entirely shirk exchanges with Noradounghian, Pashalian, Sinopian, and Edouard Naville. "I know, many things happened in World War," he admitted according to his memoirs, but denied any association with the main matter. Instead, he repeated the mantra of a prosperous future after forgetting the past and that friendship would flourish with the Armenians, if henceforward they were obedient to the state.

> We [in Ankara] do not belong to those who had anything to do with the events that took place between the Armenians and the Turks, neither in the past nor during the First World War. We are new humans who kept completely aloof from the events in question. Our state is also a completely new state. It is our aspiration to live well and to have good relations with Armenians as our citizens. ... We will forget the past.[125]

Talking Ankara's new speech, he failed to name, and deal with, the critical wounds of the emergent Turkish nation-state, which consequently proved almost incurable. He went so far as to not only blame but also to make fun of the victims. In late November, Pashalian and Sinapian, a former Ottoman minister, had a conversation with him during which Ismet claimed, "the Armenians lived in Turkey contentedly and happily" and "only the discontented element left the homeland and went abroad." Pashalian and Sinapian retorted, "the Armenians were forcibly driven out of their habitat and their properties were confiscated." Ismet answered, "As you well know, Armenians love to travel. That is why they often leave the provincial cities and reach Constantinople!"[126]

---

[124] Letter Pashalian to Ismet, 6 December 1922, Box Délégation arménienne 1923, Noubar Pasha Library, Paris. See also Khatissian, *Eclosion*, 332.
[125] *İnönü'nün Hatıraları*, 114–117.   [126] Khatissian, *Eclosion*, 334.

19 Lausanne's Armenian Catastrophe

Ismet Pasha recounts in his memoirs a harsh encounter with Edouard Naville, a seventy-eight-year-old member of the central committee of the Swiss Federation of the Friends of the Armenians, a former president of the CICR, and professor emeritus of Egyptology at the University of Geneva. The straightforward Naville asked Ismet how Ankara prepared to face the ongoing injustice, trauma, misery, and aporia of Armenians who had been aggressed and dispossessed by Turks. Ankara's plenipotentiary recollects to – again mechanically – have answered, "There is no such thing as an Armenian issue for us. We are a new state, another state."[127] Karl Meyer, an insider and chronicler of the Federation, reports a related conversation of Naville and Krafft-Bonnard with Rumbold, who was frank: "We cannot wage war for the Armenians. We do not want to deny our commitments, but we are not in position to fulfil them. ... It is clear: the Armenians are sacrificed in the process [of compromising with Ankara]."[128]

In Meyer's retrospective half a century later, "The outcome of this conference is and remains unsatisfactory; for the Treaty of Lausanne is based on the fiction that Armenians do not exist. Thus, it serves neither peace nor justice. As a result, the situation of the Armenians became so tragic that it can hardly be properly imagined." A humanitarian leader, who worked among handicapped survivors in Lebanon for four decades after the Lausanne Conference, Meyer knew the conditions.

After the horrors under Turkish rule and the insecurity of the post-war years, the difficulties for homeless refugees followed: without state identity papers, without official representation in a foreign country, without money, without knowledge of the foreign language, without proper housing, in tents or barracks, without work or earnings. In addition, they were often weakened or ill due to the privations, hunger and starvation of the deportation years.[129]

Franz Werfel's meeting with Armenians in this situation during travel in Syria in the 1930 is what profoundly moved him and motivated him to write *The Forty Days of Musa Dagh*, an outstanding piece of world literature.[130]

***

A few years after the Conference, looking back to the complete diplomatic defeat in Lausanne, Khatissian of the former united Armenian delegation nevertheless displayed confidence (see Figure 12). "The catastrophe of Lausanne lacked the power to deprive the soul of the Armenian people

---

[127] *İnönü'nün Hatıraları*, 114–117.
[128] Karl Meyer, *Armenien und die Schweiz* (Bern: Blaukreuz-Verlag, 1974), 142, see also 123.
[129] Meyer, *Armenien und die Schweiz*, 142–143.
[130] Peter Stephan Jungk, "Franz Werfel – ein Weltfreund zwischen den Welten," in Knocke and Tress, *Franz Werfel und der Genozid an den Armeniern*, 13.

Figure 12 Alexandre Khatissian in front of the Armenian Church in Paris in 1927 (Courtesy ARF Archive, Boston).

of its strength, roots, sap." Convinced of the strong "moral and legal basis of our case," he trusted "that one day the political situation would change," and Bolshevism and Turkish ultranationalism come to their end – and ultimately, law- and truth-based criteria would prevail.[131] Some members of the Turkish delegation themselves had recognized the righteousness of the main Armenian claims. Dr. Nihat Reşat (Belger), Ankara's former envoy in London and member of the delegation in Lausanne, was particularly articulate in several meetings with Armenians. He was a medical doctor, but turned activist, diplomat, and journalist during those critical years.

According to the Khatissian's diary, a day after the heated meeting of 12 December 1922, Nihat Belger said him, "The atmosphere in Lausanne and in Angora is radically different. What is clear here seems obscure to the leaders there. Perched on their mountains, they do not see anything and they do not know the real situation. The number of those who think like me is increasing every day." Curzon's emphatic

---

[131] Khatissian, *Eclosion*, 325, 354, 364.

admonitions the day before had deeply impressed Ankara's delegation. "We spent all last night writing our reply to Lord Curzon's inadmissible and hurtful speech, the one in which he said: 'Your hands are dipped in blood ... ' We have today taken the important step of applying for membership of the League of Nations." Although too optimistic – or euphemistic vis-à-vis the Armenians – Nihat Reşat astutely stated, "We see that people here who did not want to hear about the [Armenian] Home, are now beginning to say that we must give satisfaction to the Armenians, if we want Lausanne to bring us not only material benefits, but also moral benefits."[132] The ultimate loss of the "moral benefits" is a defining outcome of Lausanne.

By mid-December, Belger seemed to believe that an Armenian home in Anatolia had a chance, though he drew attention to strong emotions and cleavages. "Forty people accompany our delegation, who play a great role with Ismet. All the questions are put to the vote, all the proposals too." He asserted, "the psychological argument plays a great role here [in the Armenian question]. The Armenians are so hated by a large number of Turks that it will take time to calm minds and passions."[133] He tried to inspire confidence to Noradounghian, "there will soon be elections and Angora will be rid of the fanatics and extremists who have scuttled the Armenian Question." For him, the fact that "[the] Turks have obtained in Lausanne advantages which they did not expect at all" should induce them "to make some territorial concessions to the Armenians, especially as there are not many [Armenian] people left in Turkey." For "Turkish insiders" (like himself), "the [Armenian] failure at Lausanne [so far] has not eliminated the rightness of the Armenian claim."[134]

Alas, the contrary proved to be the case: early successes made the anti-Armenian hardliners even more demanding. Nonetheless, Dr. Nihat Reşat Belger's statements are testimony to a real awareness and historical sensitivity that concerned certain members of the Turkish delegation in Lausanne who were familiar with contemporary history. They also knew the importance of ethics and moral benefits. Yet, it was not these members, but the ultranationalists – the adepts of extreme nationalism, *müfrit nasyonalizm*, as the mindful ones called them – who basically got their way, both in Lausanne and in Ankara. They prevailed in the post-Lausanne republic. Rıza Nur's hateful statements against Armenians during the same days of mid-December 1922 painfully reminded the concerned group of this reality. "There is no more any Armenian Question. It is closed forever," Nur reapplied in a private meeting in Lausanne to Talaat's notorious words of late August 1915. Nur

[132] Ibid., 394.   [133] Ibid., 398.   [134] Ibid., 418.

threatened to "kill thousands [of Armenians], just like in the past," if the Armenians dared to attack "one [Turkish] man."[135]

For an anti-Armenian anti-Semite like Nur, it was "natural" that downtrodden people like the Armenians or the Jews were denied equal collective rights and had to suffer further, allegedly self-inflicted, disasters. The hand of Nur's social Darwinist "god" himself brought this about.

> The Almighty Force, who weighs and determines the fortunes of nations, filled all sorts of ancient and eternal pages of history. In this world, he destroyed two nations forever; he moved them from diaspora to diaspora; distributed them all over the world; and condemned them to live miserably. The first of these nations is Jewish, the second is Armenian.[136]

For Nur, Jews and Armenians were and had to be "eternal nomads" (ebedî göçebe) without any rightful claim to a homeland. A homeland was reserved for capable warrior nations of fit character. "As we have now again ascertained," he wrote during the Lausanne Conference, "there is no and cannot be an [independent] Armenia," neither in Anatolia nor in the Caucasus. "The Armenians living there lack everything that would make them the lords of the land; also, they do not have the right to possess that territory."[137]

Toward foreign journalists, Nur used a language whose keywords "freedom," "true democracy," "peace," and "separation of church and state" sounded almost perfectly correct, as in a complacent interview given to the *Gazette de Lausanne* at the end of the Conference. Naïve Westerners, unsuspecting journalists, and politicians tended to take such speech at face-value.

> Our ideal was to recover our complete freedom. This was the first and essential condition of the total overhaul that we propose to attempt. Now, having peace in freedom, the new Turkey, a true democracy, which has chased away the Sultan and achieved the separation of Church and State, will be able to work productively. Turkey, having lost its non-native territories, is today within its ethnic borders, with a homogeneous population. This is the way we wanted it, and it is much better for our peace and for the tranquility of the Armenians who have a different political ideal than to return to Turkey. The antagonism which separates us is not, as has often been said, of religious origin. It is purely political and therefore irreducible.[138]

---

[135] Ibid., 417. Talaat quoted in Ambassador on Extraordinary Mission in Constantinople (Hohenlohe-Langenburg) to the Reichskanzler (Bethmann Hollweg), 4 September 1915, PA-AA/R14087.
[136] Nur, *Ermeni Tarihi*, 477.   [137] Ibid., 480 and 487.
[138] "Conférence de Lausanne: Quelques minutes avec Riza Nour," *Gazette de Lausanne*, 20 July 1923, 4.

However, the assertion of an irreducible political antagonism between Turks and Armenians must have sounded suspect to *Gazette* readers. But how could they imagine the same Nur's religiously tinted extreme racism, as entrusted to his contemporary book manuscripts in Ottoman language?

From early January 1923, the Armenian Question as a whole – not only the belated project of an "Armenian Home" instead of independence in a corner of Anatolia – remained archived as "an unresolved question." Significantly, however, Lausanne was not explicit in determining and justifying Turkey's eastern borders that Kemalist and Bolshevik troops had established in 1920 by concerted invasion. Armenian and Assyrian hope rested on League agency for a home – a last hope after disillusion in Lausanne, especially when Turkey would become a League member – but proved null and avoid.[139] Also shelved, almost buried, in Lausanne, were the ethical implications and unmet democratic challenges related to the Armenian question.

In the long term, the Armenian issue remained a historic, moral, and diplomatic Damoclean sword hanging over the new state based in Ankara. Not less, however, it was a lasting poignant reminder of the seminal failure of Western powers in matters of democracy and human rights. Ethically, the Allies had failed while Turkey backed itself into a corner in Lausanne, and remained paralyzed in this position, bereaved of the ethical benefits referred to by Nihat R. Belger. Mindful Turks were sidelined, even prosecuted or executed. Or they went into exile, like the liberal politician and sociological thinker Prince Sabahaddin. Dr. Belger left Turkey in the aftermath of the Conference to live in France and Egypt. He returned when he was personally invited by Atatürk. As a physician, he cared for the solitary and sick Turkish leader before the latter's early death in 1938.[140]

The Lausanne Conference made the small Armenian people the twentieth century's victim par excellence. Armenians were not only robbed of their homeland, their home, their possessions – and, for a million, of their very lives. For many decades, they and Anatolia's other post-Ottoman Christians were denied the public articulation of their own history, trauma, and identity, which nevertheless remained in their minds. For decades, being deprived of articulated public history was the norm internationally, at official commemoration, at universities, in school history textbooks, and especially in diplomacy. In Turkey, tens of thousands of mostly Armenian

---

[139] See notably the discussion between Aharonian and Aristide Brian in Paris, 24 September 1927. Aharonian, *From Sardarabad to Sèvres and Lausanne*, 210–211.

[140] *Atatürk Ansiklopedisi*, https://ataturkansiklopedisi.gov.tr/bilgi/nihat-resat-belger-1882-1961/?pdf=3432 (30 April 2022).

women, brought into Muslim families during the Genocide by force and through slave markets, or out of charity, were completely condemned to silence. The Lausanne Treaty thus set the course internationally for nearly a century of cover-up and conceptual acrobatics in diplomacy. It induced, as it were, the symbolic annihilation of Armenian people.

20 Mehmed Cavid, Ankara's Mindful but Sidelined Expert in Lausanne

Thanks to their peculiar character and quality, Mehmed Cavid's notes and observations play a considerable role in *When Democracy Died*. Dense and vibrant, his "ego-writing" started in the aftermath of the Young Turk Revolution, after he lost his first wife. It ended on the eve of his trial and execution three years after the Lausanne Conference. A bad historian of longer developments, but a highly sensitive observer and brilliant analyst of contemporary constellations, Cavid has left outstanding records.

Cavid (1877–1926) was a nationalist, but never a Gökalpian Turkist. An agile cosmopolitan, he did not embrace the predominant essentialist credo of Turkism internalized by most of his cohort, including leaders like Talaat, Rıza Nur, or Atatürk. Throughout his diary, Cavid took his distance vis-à-vis what he regarded as the unhealthy inflation of a mythic national ego that ambitious leaders captured at the cost of reasonable and decent compromises. For a person of his intelligence and moral sensibility, essentialist identity was a no-go. His peculiar ethno-religious background played a role for his independent-mindedness, even though he never delved into identity issues. Outwardly a Sunni Muslim, Cavid was a *dönme* of the Sabbatean tradition and therefore widely treated as a crypto-Jew, "not an authentic son of the native land," according to a reproach by fervently nationalistic journalists in late 1922. "Such news even during the conference is mischief and treason," he bitterly noted in his diary in Lausanne.[141]

After the end of CUP rule in late 1918, Cavid chose exile in Europe, mostly Switzerland. He was the only prominent CUP leader Swiss authorities permitted to stay, though under police observation. Talaat and others entered only very temporarily under pseudonyms and with false papers. In Switzerland, Cavid stood in contact with the different diasporas from the Ottoman Empire, met personalities in transit,

---

[141] Cavid, *Meşrutiyet Ruznâmesi*, vol. 4, 425–426, entry of 26 December 1922. On the *dönme*, see Marc D. Baer, *Jewish Converts, Muslim Revolutionaries, and Secular Turkish Jewish Converts* (Stanford, CA: Stanford University Press, 2010), 60.

himself undertook many travels in Europe, and kept a rich international correspondence. He came back to Allied-occupied Istanbul on 29 June 1922.[142]

Thousands of pages even in the printed version, Cavid's diaries cover the years 1909–24.[143] Of a peculiar relevance, is Cavid's both personal and political *Şiar'ın Defteri, Note-book for Şiar*. Şiar is the name of Cavid's son, born in 1924, when Cavid was 55, from his recent second marriage. In the form of letters to Şiar, which closely follow the toddler's development, this tender and family-centered writing reads like the continuation and conclusion of his diary. Its entries go from 25 October 1924 to 10 June 1926, the day of his detention in Istanbul, two-and-a-half months before his judicial assassination in Ankara.[144] For *When Democracy Died*, Cavid's diary offers insider knowledge on unofficial networks, statements, thoughts, and gatherings from both a Turkish nationalist and a cosmopolitan angle. Cavid enjoyed excellent information thanks to his various interlocutors. Among them were prominent acquaintances made during more than a decade of active political and public life in Europe and Ottoman Turkey. These comprised many personalities in, or formerly in, high positions. He enjoyed and cultivated a large network of acquaintances far beyond Near Eastern and Turkish nationalist circles. Because he mostly summarized his letters in his diary, the diary gives also insight into his rich correspondence in the wide context of the Lausanne Conference.

In many respects an ordinary Turkish nationalist rooted in the CUP – thus claiming the nation as his supreme good and declaring to serve the nation as his supreme duty – Cavid was, however, more spirited and critical, more communicative, frank, and honest than most others. Besides being a well-informed interlocutor and diarist, he also emerges as a voice of truth in critical situations. Like others in his cohort – of whom so many left memoirs, rarely, however, authentic diaries – he also celebrated his patriotic ego from time to time, emphasizing tireless sacrifices for the national cause. Since the eve of the Young Turk Revolution, he had stood close to Talaat and given in to Talaat's will when Talaat insisted. He never left the latter's orbit and never seriously sought, or was in a position, to react against the dominance of this CUP chief executive or to radically question the CUP, his political-emotional home.

---

[142] Cavid, *Meşrutiyet Ruznâmesi*, vol. 4, 373, entry of 29 June 1922.
[143] In 2014–15, a meritorious, uncensored and complete four-volume publication by the Türk Tarih Kurumu (Turkish Historical Society) in Ankara. As earlier indicated, this edition is used throughout this book.
[144] Cavid Bey, *Şiar'ın Defteri* (Istanbul: Iletisim, 1995).

Yet, he was different in that he could quite rightly claim a "treasure of honesty" (sermaye-i namus). In the seclusion of his diary, he boldly, proudly, and solemnly underlined this self-affirmation.[145] He categorically rejected entry into the Great War in autumn 1914, and felt horror at the anti-Armenian exterminatory contempt and hatred of his party comrades in 1915, making him an exception among high-ranking CUP members. Back in Istanbul from negotiations in Berlin, he accused his comrades in his diary – but nowhere else – at the end of August 1915: "Not only the political existence, but also the biological existence of an entire [Armenian] people you dared to destroy."[146]

***

Expecting Ismet's call, as agreed on during their meeting in Istanbul on 8 November 1922, Cavid arrived in Lausanne on 11 December. He had to assist as an expert counselor to the negotiations on economic and financial questions, in particular on the Ottoman debts and the Ottoman Public Debt Administration, a European-led organization, founded six years after Ottoman imperial bankruptcy in 1875.[147]

Rejecting the former imperial debts, as the Bolsheviks did and Ankara's hardliners tended to want, would have meant pariah status instead of international recognition; notably exclusion from international loans, of which the new state was in dire need. In any case, the Ottoman Public Debt Administration was a thorn in Ankara's flesh, and those in close touch with it, like Cavid, who had many friends in Paris, were suspected of enriching themselves at the expense of patriotic interests. Cavid's name does not figure among the participants of the Third Commission's relevant subcommission meetings. As transpires from his diary, he only participated at preparative informal meetings and negotiations from mid-December to the end of January. Such informal meetings however contributed substantively to the negotiations. Cavid was given little official visibility in Lausanne. According to Nur, İsmet had invited him "despite my strong and repeated objections and eventually without my knowledge."[148]

During his first days in Lausanne, Cavid participated at gatherings within the Turkish team and at meetings together with experts from other, namely the French and Italian, delegations. Besides Cavid, those from Ankara's team most involved in the debate on financial questions were the delegates Hasan (Saka) and – belatedly – Rıza Nur; the

---

[145] Cavid, *Meşrutiyet Ruznâmesi*, vol. 4, 374–375, entry of 29 June 1922. See also Kieser, *Talaat Pasha*, 161–162.
[146] Cavid, *Meşrutiyet Ruznâmesi*, vol. 3, 135.
[147] Ibid., vol. 4, 373, entry of 29 June 1922, and 406, entry of 11 December 1922.
[148] Nur, *Hayat ve Hatıratım*, vol. 2, 204.

counselors Hamid (Hasancan) and Zekai (Apaydın); and, without official mandate, Cavid's long-standing friend Hüseyin Çahit (Yalçın). Cavid expressed satisfaction over a frank and efficient four-day exchange of opinions, from 13 to 16 December, on the Ottoman debt, reparation, tariffs, and further issues, including compensation for the Ottoman warships that Britain had confiscated in August 1914.

Cavid enjoyed the reputation of a brilliant expert. He was a well-known personality, a figure of sympathy from Turkey for many in the West – much more than others in Ankara's delegation. This raised envy and fear. An early incident with the press impaired the newly arrived counselor's position after mid-December. In line with his outspokenness and also some predilection for the limelight, Cavid was so imprudent as to give optimistic interviews with the daily *Tanin* and other papers on the course of the negotiations. Though apparently not instructed by his delegation, he must, from the beginning, have known the sensitivity of public statements and the need of previous agreement.[149]

Things nevertheless looked positive to him after an internal Turkish meeting with Ismet on 21 December that reached agreement on the main financial questions.[150] This situation, and Cavid's stance in Lausanne, soured when Nur intervened in the financial discussion, accusing Cavid vis-à-vis Ismet of sacrificing Turkish interests. This happened in the delegation's internal meeting on 25 December, at which also Nur and Zekai participated. "First, they read all [debt-related] articles with rage and disgust. They left out all hitherto made modifications. ... Compared to them, Bahaeddin Şakir and Doktor Nazım – our [the CUP's] worst ultras who always used offensive and slanderous language – were mild and moderate." They repeated their mantra – "Our weapons are our defense" – and talked about attacking France in Syria. French institutions were late-Ottoman Turkey's main creditors so France was most involved in the Public Debt Administration and therefore most interested in it at the Conference. "Every minute I regret to have been drawn in this circle."[151]

From other delegates, notably Hasan, he learnt that the turn of mood was due to Nur's influence. As for the issue of Ottoman debt, Cavid committed a cardinal error according to Nur, when he pretended, "The division of the [debt's nominal] capital is technically impossible." Cavid's expert opinion contrasted with Nur's nationalist attitude that ascribed great importance to a division. In the end, however, this would not change the debt burden for Ankara. After consultation with Franz Günter – the

---

[149] Cavid, *Meşrutiyet Ruznâmesi*, vol. 4, 419–420, entry of 20 December 1922.
[150] Ibid., 423, entry of 21 December 1922.
[151] Ibid., 487–490, quotations on 487–488, entry of 25 December 1922.

Deutsche Bank's unofficial delegate in Lausanne – and Swiss bankers in Zurich, it became clear that division was possible, though expensive.[152] For Nur, Cavid was "the greatest traitor" who was working with the French enemy – and anyway a priori disqualified as "a Jew."[153]

The division of the capital meant that all post-Ottoman countries were theoretically responsible for a part of the Ottoman debt (except for debts made during the Great War, as those remained with Ankara). However, questions of currency, control, and further negotiations on concrete terms proved much more important for the amount of repayment of the Ottoman debts and interests. Still, the partition of the capital itself was of legal and symbolic importance. It also meant that at least to a certain extent, the Ankara government was considered a new state like other post-Ottoman states, and not the Ottoman Empire's successor in every respect. In reality, however, most arguments at the Conference indicated Ankara as imperial Istanbul's legal successor. In multiple ways, Ankara's delegation historically identified with and referred to its Ottoman predecessor, by, for example, "renouncing" former imperial territories, or claiming allegedly tolerant Ottoman treatment together with a restrictive definition during the minority debates.

As for Nur, he took the Conference's partition of the debt capital first and foremost as his own great patriotic exploit: "As I remember this, I actually feel my chest rise."[154] Due to Nur's insistence, as Nur himself claims in his memoirs – but also by Ismet, Mustafa Kemal, and Ankara's common will – Cavid, Hasan, Haim Nahum, and Nihat Reşat were dismissed from the delegation by the end of January 1923. Nur and others, including Ismet, argued Cavid, Nahum, and Reşat clearly had too much contact with Europeans.[155] Opportunists like Reşit Saffet (Atabinen) immediately started to avoid those now visibly fallen from grace, who had been long-time acquaintances. "He abandoned Cavid in Lausanne and was no longer even greeting him. What bad things does he not say to Ismet against Cavid in my presence! However, before I went to Ankara, he had hung the photos of Talat and Cavid on his bed in the bedroom. Cavid has been his benefactor."[156] As a result of this sidelining of comparatively moderate voices, Ankara's ultras were strengthened. By

---

[152] Nur, *Hayat ve Hatıratım*, vol. 2, 330–331. See also Jonathan Conlin, "'Nobody Writes Letters to the Dead': Deutsche Bank and Lausanne," https://thelausanneproject.com/2021/02/01/deutsche-bank-gunther, visited 23 May 2022.

[153] Nur, *Hayat ve Hatıratım*, vol. 2, 332.   [154] Ibid., 334.

[155] "Frenklerle çok temasta." Ibid., 334. Ismet endorsed the argument; see Cavid, *Meşrutiyet Ruznâmesi*, vol. 4, 493. In the diary entry of 28 January 1922, vol. 4, 496–500, Cavid details how Ismet explained the dismissal.

[156] Nur, *Hayat ve Hatıratım*, vol. 2, 268. See also idem, *Hayat ve Hatıratım*, vol. 1, 470. Reşit Saffet had been Cavid's private secretary in 1917–8.

20 Cavid, Ankara's Mindful But Sidelined Expert

early January, the local press had grasped the crisis, including Cavid's fall into disgrace among the foremost nationalists.[157]

When Cavid understood the situation at the end of December, he reacted vehemently in his diary. "How can such gentlemen with this mentality make [real] peace?"[158] In his eyes, the delegation lacked the courage to embrace reasonable concessions and a conciliatory language of trust. During those weeks, he still considered the chief delegate Ismet a honest, but somewhat helpless, broker under pressure from Nur in a delegation of forty people. Less than two years later, in his *Note-book for Şiar*, he wrote, "Against this man I nurture a limitless enmity and hate." The reason for this extraordinarily negative emotion was that Ismet brought the convenient libel of Cavid's treason in Lausanne back to Ankara. "Actually, this servile man implored me to assist him at the Lausanne Conference. But later, in order to silence an authorized voice who could expose the mistakes committed in Lausanne, he chose the easy way and accused me and another friend, Hamid [Hamit Hasancan] ... of having created problems and virtually committed treason."[159]

Inclined to conserve good ties with the European, particularly French, world of finances, Cavid may have been technically wrong about the possibility of debt partition. But he proved right when admonishing Ismet in Lausanne that for many years Turkey would have difficulties to get international loans. For Cavid, there was a question of reliability and the moral responsibility (manevi mesuliyet) for one's liabilities. An ultranationalist attitude, that is, the ideological dismantling of the Public Debt Administration in the name of sovereignty, would exacerbate the problem and have little to do with a reasonable debt management, or relief, for Turkey's common benefit.[160] But it seemed to Cavid the sacrosanct slogan of sovereignty held sway over Ankara, choking a more agile and suitable thinking of the national future. Overused at the Conference itself, as proven in the minutes, "independence" and "sovereignty" were reduced to absurdity by illiberal minds who claimed them most vocally in the name of freedom. In this vein, by late 1922, Cavid pointedly critiqued the political culture in Ankara. What to his sense predominated, were fear, personal loyalties, or enmities, and a xenophobic war mentality. There lacked trust and foresight.

In Cavid's eyes, "Most deputies and delegates only think of their responsibility before the Assembly. They do not appreciate the greater responsibility before the people, and the sin of not providing [in Lausanne] the country

---

[157] "A la Conférence de Lausanne: La crise," *Journal de Genève*, 9 January 1923, 1.
[158] Cavid, *Meşrutiyet Ruznâmesi*, vol. 4, 427–431, entry of 27 December 1922.
[159] Bey, Şiar'ın defteri, 28–30, entry of 22 November 1924.
[160] Cavid, *Meşrutiyet Ruznâmesi*, vol. 4, 453–454, entry of 6 January 1923.

with the pretty brilliant peace that is possible." Fearing the hardliners, they sought to outdo each other in nationalist intransigence. Taking as an ultimate criterium a supposedly impeccable ideological posture, not the welfare of the people, they couldn't help but lead Turkey again into poverty-stricken autocracy. "Their pervasive fear of Ankara is stronger than the true interests of the country." Some, notably Nur (see Figure 13), talked easily of a possible rupture and war, even wished so in late December. They detested compromises on then-hotly discussed topics like the Ottoman Debt, the Armenian home, and Mosul. "The second delegate [Nur] is both ignorant and impertinent."[161] "Ignorance," "impertinence," and baseless "boldness" belonged to the most negative terms in Cavid's vocabulary.

***

Success of ultranationalist demands in Lausanne, which surprised moderate members of Ankara's delegation, immediately translated into actions on the ground in Anatolia, thus perpetuating radical politics. One of these was the "damaging intervention" (in Cavid's words) in the Public Debt Administration. "They want the immediate dismissal of the Rûm and Armenian employees," Cavid noted in his diary on 10 January 1923. These (Ottoman-)Turkish nationals were to be replaced by Muslim Turks, most of whom lacked the professional and linguistic skills required in an international financial institution. "Poor country. At what unsuitable places they appoint men who abash the national self-respect. They are both bold and ignorant."[162] In September 1923, Ankara decreed the dismissal of Rûm and Armenian Debt employees working abroad, "presuming that they all were traitors against Turkey."[163]

Cavid was an adept of unitary Turkish nationalism; not a particular friend of minorities. At times he proved ambivalent or improvident on critical issues concerning non-Turks. However, he clearly rejected incompetence and unfairness, autocracy and extremism. He hated crimes and coercion against weaker human fellows. His outlook was cosmopolitan, his ideal a functioning constitutional polity. Though politically unable to translate outrage into effective action, a long line of personal writing from 1908 to 1926 testifies to a constant, morally alert, and sensitive mind. Nevertheless, historian Ozan Ozavci is right counting Cavid among early examples "of what now is called the culture of denial" in Turkish politics and public history.[164] Cavid, too, had internalized the apologetic reflex of his generation.

[161] Ibid., 427–431, entry of 27 December 1922.
[162] Ibid., 458, entry of 10 January 1923.   [163] Ibid., 582, entry of 13 September 1923.
[164] Ozan Ozavci, "Honour and Shame: The Diaries of a Unionist and the 'Armenian Question,'" in H. Kieser, M.L. Anderson, S. Bayraktar, T. Schmutz (eds.), *The End of*

20 Cavid, Ankara's Mindful But Sidelined Expert

Figure 13 "A box match out of season. Sirs Rıza Nur and Hüseyin Cahid." Rıza Nur against Hüseyin Cahit (Yalçın), a prominent journalist and Cavid's close friend, that is, nationalist hardliners against Istanbul-based, more cosmopolitan nationalists still rooted in the CUP. Hüseyin Cahit had been together with Cavid in Lausanne, but did not belong to the delegation. Like his friend, he was exposed to continued attacks during the turbulent Conference interval in Turkey. (*Akbaba*, no. 40, 23 April 1923, 2. Artist: Ratib Tahir)

Denial was due to a nationalist perception bias in general and a worm's-eye view from defeated Istanbul in particular. All contributed to the formation of an impassioned nationalistic apologia that combined the categorical claim of modern Muslim-Turkish victimhood with sweeping anti-European and anti-Christian accusations. It was additionally fueled by the harsh conditions of the Sèvres Treaty and a capital

the Ottomans: The Genocide of 1915 and the Politics of Turkish Nationalism (London: I.B. Tauris, 2019), 219.

Istanbul, seat of the sultanate-caliphate, under allied occupation. For biased minds, the apologia made the indelible outrage of genocide in a general vague picture of war, misery, and allegedly "mutual massacre" during the Great War disappear. Cavid was an excellent day-to-day chronicler in his diary. He could take intellectual distance vis-à-vis daily events and astutely comment on them, but he did not join the dots to bring longer lines into a multi-perspectival and balanced picture. Not in a position to draw fair conclusions, he dealt volatilely with the challenges resulting from the Armenian genocide, and continued loyalty to Talaat Pasha and the CUP even after genocide made valid and coherent conclusions in this regard illusionary.

A telling snapshot on this issue is a diary entry written after 17 April 1922, when an Armenian commando in Berlin had killed Bahaeddin Şakır and Cemal Azmi, two organizers of mass murder. Cavid was right in insisting that revenge and anger could not build the future and that, in this respect, "the Armenians [ARF exile leaders] march on a very bad road." However, in his personal assessment, he entirely dismissed the unrepentant role that both victims had played only a few years earlier. Instead, he honored them as uncorrupt patriots with whom "on certain issues our opinions never agreed." In human and political terms, this was a poor view of men responsible for a historic crime. What disqualified Cavid even more as a valid and serene judge of history was his almost threatening advice to Armenians to forget the past. "A curtain of forgetting must be drawn over the past – not an agreement. Otherwise, blood will drag blood, and this will again mostly victimize the Armenians."[165] He expected support from Ankara against Armenian accusations in the press that targeted prominent CUP members. "It suffices that Ankara threatens the Armenians in order to silence them."[166]

Admittedly, Cavid was shocked to learn in April 1922 that he figured on a death list of Armenian revolutionaries. At least, this is what the French police told him. He was bewildered that – as he believed – CUP leadership alone made him and others targets (i.e. even persons who had defended or saved Armenians). Thus, he quoted an anti-Armenian stereotype: "It is not for nothing that one calls the Armenians the ungrateful nation."[167] During official Conference meetings, Ismet uttered analogous libels several times.

In the changed political atmosphere after 1921, Cavid lost sight of the supreme issue of justice, reparation, and prosecution for genocide victims, although, in 1915, he had been more sensitive than the others to the

---

[165] Cavid, *Meşrutiyet Ruznâmesi*, vol. 4, 359, entry of 20 April 1922.
[166] Ibid., 365, entry of 13 May 1922.   [167] Ibid., 358, entry of 13 April 1922.

magnitude of that crime. In 1918–19, he advocated, measuredly, the return of survivors, the restitution of Armenian possessions, and a viable Armenia including parts of Eastern Anatolia. However, he rejected this inclusion after the Turkish–Bolshevik division of the South Caucasus in 1921. After 1921, he made do with admonishing the Armenians to be cautious or even silent. By and large, he followed the nationalist guideline that read, "The issue of Armenia will not be talked about." Almost without a whimper, Armenians should give up their cause and claims, including the public memory of their suffering.[168]

21 Mosul

An elitist and discreetly triumphalist British narrative of the Lausanne Conference focuses on great successes achieved by Curzon during the first half of the Conference (see Figure 14). These consisted in open Straits, weakened Turkish–Soviet ties, and an open door toward the mandatory future of Mosul. Importantly for Curzon, Mosul did not become the manifest reason for the break of the Conference in early February.[169]

All three British objectives were related to imperial geostrategy and, in the case of Mosul, also the need for oil. At issue in Lausanne was the question whether to attribute the Mosul province to Turkey or to mandatory British Iraq. It became the thorniest matter among London's priorities, because, in this case, the expectations of both sides clashed head on. Turkish readiness to nevertheless possibly conclude a separate peace with Britain in February 1923, appears in the British triumph story as an additional proof of success. It is also emphasized as a sign of supreme loyalty to the other Allies, as Curzon was by no means inclined to a separate peace. Based on the Allies' treaty draft of 31 January, the Mosul issue would have been postponed, to be settled bilaterally between Ankara and London within a year.[170] The final settlement followed and developed this line.

Bilateral Turkish–British conversations had taken place and memoranda exchanged in Lausanne since early December, after a fundamental private meeting of Curzon and Ismet on 26 November 1922. This already held out the prospect of a final settlement of the Mosul question only after the Conference.[171] In late December, the detailed and trenchant "Counter Reply to the Memorandum of the Turkish Delegation

---

[168] Ibid., 343, entry of 11 March 1922. See also Ibid., 365, entry of 13 May 1922; 368–369, entry of 5 June 1922.
[169] Exemplarily: Nicolson, *Curzon: The Last Phase*, 281–350 Similar credits for Curzon also in Dockrill and Goold, Peace without Promise.
[170] Ibid., 346.
[171] "A la Conférence de Lausanne: La frontière d'Asie," *Journal de Genève*, 29 November, 1.

Figure 14 Lord Curzon going to the Château d'Ouchy, the main meeting place of the Conference (gallica.bnf.fr / BnF)

concerning the Question of the Vilayet of Mosul" plunged the Turkish delegation into depression, fueling rumors of a Conference break and of an anti-British insurrection in Mosul.[172] Open debate started in the First Commission on 23 January 1923. That day – with its two meetings, one at 11am, the second at 6pm – turned out to be one of the most heated days of the Conference. Besides a few strong points for his position, Ismet's argument revealed critical flaws, among them the racial definition of the Kurds as "Turanians," and thus as Turks for the matter in question. As dealt with in earlier sections, such definition rested on a flawed Turanian vision of history into which Nur had delved most fervently and copiously. While the British consideration for Mosul "smelt oil," oil was not the priority for Curzon. Imperial strategy and mandatory commitment however were.[173]

With the habitus of a victor at least on a par with all others, Ismet faced in Curzon a blunt and historically pertinent plenipotentiary whose knowledge of the region excelled that of the others. This intellectual superiority led

---

[172] *LCP*, 381–387; Cavid, *Meşrutiyet Ruznâmesi*, 428, diary entry of 27 December 1922; "Insurrection dans le vilayet de Mossoul?" et "Recul des troupes britanniques?" *Journal de Genève*, 3 January 1923, 3, and 9 January 1923, 4.

[173] Jonathan Conlin, "An Oily Entente: France, Britain, and the Mosul Question, 1916–1925," *Diplomacy & Statecraft*, 31.2 (2020), 246–249.

Ismet time and again to hyperbolic reactions and contentions. Champion of the Turkish nationalist antithesis to the Paris-Geneva system, he insisted almost mechanically on full parity vis-à-vis the "European imperialist" Curzon. When he felt at an impasse, Ismet took the habit "to speak like an automaton."[174] The competition for hegemony in historical argumentation went along with a pretentious claim to equivalence in matters of democracy. Ismet suggested that full-fledged, exemplary democracy existed in Ankara where Kurds sat in the National Assembly. Any trouble of the government with Kurds in recent history "was due to incitement by certain consuls." The Kurds had "always enjoyed all the rights of citizens" and "always collaborated with the Turkish Government"; there was "not a single Kurd" who wished autonomy warranted by Europe in exchange for unity with Turkey.[175] This was fake and fiction.

Throughout 23 January, Ismet remained stubborn in his contentions. In a world of alternative facts, as it were, the National Assembly

> was composed of the real and freely elected representatives of the Turkish people. All the inhabitants of Turkey, including both Turks and Kurds, were equally entitled to the franchise and enjoyed the same rights in the Grand Assembly, which thus afforded the world the most striking example of a nation being directly administered by those best qualified to represent it.[176]

Curzon's response was pointed. "Is there a single [Kurdish] one who was elected by a popular constituency? It is notorious that they are all nominated men."[177] At the end of the evening meeting, Ismet again doubled down on his account. The handpicked Kurdish deputies, he insisted, "had been elected under conditions of liberty and independence equal to those of all other countries."[178]

While reacting to felt or real condescension from the British side, Ismet's pronouncements, all in all, reflected more the contemporary doctrine in Ankara than situational reactions and emotions. The Turkish claim of Mosul rested on the First Article of the National Pact:

> Inasmuch as it is necessary that the destinies of the portions of the Turkish Empire which are populated exclusively by an Arab majority, and which on the conclusion of the armistice of the 30th October 1918 were in the occupation of enemy forces, should be determined in accordance with the votes which shall be freely given by the inhabitants, the whole of those parts whether within or outside the said armistice line which are inhabited by an Ottoman Moslem majority, united in religion, in race and in aim, imbued with sentiments of mutual respect for each other and of sacrifice, and wholly respectful of each other's racial and social rights

---

[174] Cavid, *Meşrutiyet Ruznâmesi*, vol. 4, 503, entry of 30 January 1923.
[175] *LCP*, 344–346, 23 January 1923. [176] Ibid., 396. [177] Ibid., 357. [178] Ibid., 404.

and surrounding conditions, form a whole which does not admit of division for any reason in truth or in ordinance.[179]

From Ankara's point of view, this statement made two strong arguments for a Turkish Mosul. First, the province of Mosul was not yet occupied by 30 October 1918. Second, it was preponderantly "inhabited by an Ottoman Moslem majority, united in religion, in race and in aim." The second argument was valid – if the Kurds were included in its definition of the Turkish nation, and if the common Turkish-Kurdish will for a Gökalpian future was insinuated. Hailing from the early 1910s, Gökalp's definition mixed religion, culture, race, and the ideal of Turkey's great modern future. Myths of grandiose military and political achievements by (proto-)Turks since times immemorial underpinned this projection of the future.

Tantamount to "Great Turkey," Gökalp's catchword "Turan" had, until 1918, been a main label for the new vision of the past and the future. Discredited after CUP war defeat, "Turan" survived in the nationalist vocabulary, but moved from the center to more discreet zones of articulation. As just mentioned, Ismet declared Turks and Kurds to be from the same Turanian race and therefore to have been living in perfect harmony since the dawn of time. Ethnographically, according to him, Erbil and Kirkuk were to be recognized as entirely Turkish places. In nationalist argumentation since the late 1910s in general and in Lausanne in particular, "race" weighed heavily. "[R]acial considerations suffice to prove that the Mosul Vilayet must return to Turkey," concluded the Turkish reply, dated 23 December 1922, to a British Memorandum regarding the Mosul Question. The reply added the bold argument of the general popular will to the racial contention. "The Turks and Kurds, who constitute the great majority of the population of the Mosul Vilayet, are firmly determined to obtain the union of their countries to Turkey; no doubt is possible on this point." Ismet insisted in his accompanying letter that the "Turkish Government cannot for a moment consider abandoning its sovereign rights over Mosul, which forms an integral part of the Turkish mother country."[180]

Thus, in the critical meetings of 23 January 1923, Ankara's plenipotentiary argued, "the origin of the Kurdish people is Turanian," and "as regards manners, usage and customs the Kurds do not differ in any respect from the Turks, and that these two peoples, while they speak different languages, form a single unit in respect of race, religion and manners."[181] A bit derisive, a bit acerbic, Curzon's targeted, fine-grained response took

---

[179] Translation in Toynbee, *Western Question in Greece and Turkey*, 207–210.
[180] *LCP*, 372 and 374–375.   [181] Ibid., 342–343.

one hour and a half. "It was reserved for the Turkish delegation in one of their papers to discover for the first time in history that the Kurds were Turks. Nobody has ever found it out before. The origin of this people is somewhat obscure." It was an easy game to tear down the Turanian argument and the pretended Turkish–Kurdish union by referring to recent facts, experiences, and recognized scholarship. "It is a matter of general [scholarly] agreement that the Kurds are a people of Iranian race. They speak an Iranian language, their features are entirely distinct from those of the Turks, so are their customs and their relations with women. I have been in the Kurdish country myself; I have stayed with the Kurds."[182]

Curzon's arguments were fashioned not to serve the truth or the cause of democracy, but rather to achieve success in negotiation. This became clear with the question of a plebiscite that Ankara wanted, but Britain feared. There were good reasons to consider a referendum in the province of Mosul not viable and subject to Ankara's manipulation by way of bribes, bullying, and (temporary) population transfer. It was again easy to expose Turkish inconsistency in wanting a referendum there, but refusing it at any other place in Anatolia and Istanbul. In any case, however, Curzon's successful argument against a plebiscite in the province of Mosul proved the loss of confidence in one of the League's most innovative instruments for decision-making. Ismet took this rejection as "the most convincing proof of the weakness of the case brought forward against Turkey."[183]

During the first half of the Conference, Curzon succeeded in preventing rupture because of Mosul, as this would have been seen as Britain's fault. He could rally the Allies, including the USA, behind his position, and leave the matter in a suspense that was to Britain's advantage. Mosul became the most salient failure of Ankara's initial strategy of dividing the adversary camp. On 23 January, 7.20 pm, Curzon could thus conclude the evening meeting saying, "I regret very much that the Turkish delegation have resisted the advice that was given to them with so much authority by M. Bompard ... and by the heads of the Italian and Japanese delegations." Himself a sceptic of the League, he nevertheless claimed "the opinion of the world" for Britain's imperial cause. "I think that Ismet Pasha will be somewhat surprised when he sees what the opinion of the world, to which he has appealed, is upon this matter."[184] In any case, the League of Nations, not the British Empire, was the recipient and guardian of "world opinion."

Curzon warned Ankara with Article 11 of the League Covenant, according to which a conflict, which was likely to disturb international

---

[182] Ibid., 356. See also Nicolson, *Curzon: The Last Phase*, 337. [183] *LCP*, 397.
[184] Ibid., 404.

peace, was to be dealt with by the League's Council and could lead to sanctions or an international intervention. This was notably for a scenario in which Turkish troops would enter Northern Iraq. The argument with the League served London's plenipotentiary as a means to put pressure on Ankara. "I have stated on behalf of my Government the action which I shall be compelled to take, and I shall take it without delay," he said in his very last sentence at the end of the 23 January meeting.

Agreed on in the second half of the Conference, the final settlement de-escalated the situation: if within one year after conclusion of the Treaty the matter could not be solved bilaterally, it would be decided by the League of Nations (Treaty Article 3). Thus, on Mosul, London prevailed provisionally at the Conference and ultimately in 1926. In late January 1923, Ismet already had privileged compromise with Britain on Mosul, that is, deferral to the League despite the high probability of loss, because for him a constructive relationship with British world power was primary. Though willing to compromise with Britain, Nur, in contrast, pursued a more Asia-centric vision of Turkey's future. This went hand in hand with his negative attitude toward Kurds and Armenians: "Mosul is very necessary for us with its oil, and thus essential for the prosperity of the country. Also, losing it means causing a scourge of Kurdistan, which will make us vulnerable from the flank. Kurdistan may unite with Armenia. Losing Mosul will cut us off from our future, the Orient."[185] Nur's arguments bode ill for a time when post-Kemalist rulers in Ankara were to look at Mosul with a renewed "neo-Ottoman" or pan-Turkish desire for irredenta, as since the 2010s.

22 Diplomatically Framing History, "Civilization," Rule of Law

The Conference of Lausanne became a defining moment for history writing and a related understanding of "civilization," including law. The copious debates framed, in particular, the worldwide perception of the contemporary history of Turkey and the Middle East. For the emerging Republic of Turkey, the Conference involved a first, comparatively comprehensive and coherent articulation of Kemalist historical concepts, beliefs, and taboos. Of these, crucial elements have been touched on in the previous sections dealing with the deliberations on population exchange, minorities, the Armenian home, and Mosul. It goes without saying, that diplomatic exigencies thus conditioned fields that scholarship and democracy want to be independent.

---

[185] Şimşir, *Lozan Telgrafları I*, 449–450, 443, 27 January 1923, Ismet Pasha to Rauf Bey.

The way history was framed at Lausanne's negotiation table therefore impacted on the new Western visions of the post-Ottoman area. During the remainder of the twentieth century, Anatolia's modern history in particular, was by and large looked at through Kemalist lenses by mainstream Western academia and diplomacy. In this vision, Atatürk looked benign and unique among totalitarian Interwar autocrats. He led a model dictatorship committed to the best development of its country (i.e. secular Western-oriented civilization), and to peace with the world. Lausanne-anchored, this discourse overlooked the cohesiveness of Turkey's foundation from 1913 to 1939. It white-washed contemporary history and turned a blind eye to Turanianism. Thus, it left out or minimized manifest racialist shortcomings and sidelined the dark sides and genocides, notably those of the pre-1923 decade.

The racial and ethnographic Mosul argument by Ankara's delegation was, as we have seen, not situational or due to a temporary debate in Lausanne. Present in prepared memoranda and various statements, it was rooted in the minds of the leading cadres, going back to their thorough Turkist and "Turanian" socialization during the 1910s. This fact is manifest in Rıza Nur's writings and also in the already-discussed March 1923 speech by Mustafa Kemal, in which Ankara's supreme leader contended that Turks and Turanians had always been the predominant population in Asia Minor and beyond. Thus, he labeled all others invaders and framed the mediaeval invasions and immigrations from Central Asia as the coming of "brothers from the Turkish race" who "restored life to its true [Turkish] origins." After the wars and finally in Lausanne, Ankara just had to ensure that the country "was confirmed in the hands of its original owners."[186]

Military victory and diplomatic affirmation went hand in hand with a Turanian master narrative. Negotiation at Lausanne therefore consistently comprised, and was prejudiced by, historical arguments. Even if they were manifestly fictitious, but politically impactful, the Lausanne Conference let them stand, making no serious effort to rectify them. Thus, they were up to no good for a century.

***

In the aftermath of World War defeat in view of a new global order, all sides produced historical arguments, particularly the victims or losers of the war. On the Turkish side, we have mentioned Atabinen and Rıza Nur. Their arguments were largely based on established tropes of the previous CUP party-state, at times even of Hamidian diplomacy. In a departure

---

[186] *Atatürk'ün Söylev ve Demeçleri*, vol. II, 130–132.

from the decade before, however, the Turkish historical argumentation in Lausanne clearly preferred race over religion. It almost felt Islam as an embarrassment, although from 1911 to 1922, wars had been fought in the name of Islam. Kemal Pasha himself was explicitly honored as an outstanding *Gazi*, or warrior of Islam (i.e. of *gaza* raids and jihad), a title that was internationally in use during the whole 1920s.

Promoting Turkishness and repressing Anatolia's ethno-religious alterity, the new prominent argument in Lausanne both prefigured the Turkish History Thesis and prepared the Kemalist turn to assertive secularism after the Conference. The years before Lausanne saw writing and publication of several race-based histories of Turkey by historian-politicians, including besides Nur, Ahmed Ağaoğlu and Mehmet F. Köprülü.[187] During the 1910s, Islam still had played an explicit and dominant role for national – until 1918 national-imperial – self-definition, namely by the predominant ideologist Ziya Gökalp. From the early 1920s, however, Ankara's diplomacy felt the need of concepts and boundaries for a "new Turkey" based on ethno-racial history. This kind of history-writing comprised, and increasingly centered on, premodern, ancient, and prehistoric times.

As we have seen, there were many potential stumbling blocks at the negotiation table depending on how history was worded. Not only the meetings of 12–14 December 1922 on minorities (though these in particular), delved extensively into historical arguments and narratives. Ismet Pasha's long speech on the 12 December amounted to the government's diplomatically convenient framing of minorities. He actually read, in French, a study prepared in Ankara.[188] To this defining paper must be added Ismet's responses and statements of 13 and 14 December, his statements on the Armenian Question on 31 December 1922, and his speech on Mosul's history on 23 January 1923, as well as statements by Rıza Nur and other members of the Turkish delegation during or outside Conference meetings.

Many of Ismet's statements and speeches resulted from concerted efforts within the Turkish delegation, starting on the eve of the Conference, possibly edited by Atabinen. Other members able to

---

[187] Köprülüzade, *Türkiya Tarihi*; Agayef, 'Türk medeniyeti tarihi'; Agayef, ' Mukaddime' to *Pontus Meselesi* (Ankara: Matbuat ve İstihbarat Müdüriyet-i Umumiyyesi, 1922), quoted in Can Erimtan, 'Ottomans and Turks: Ağaoğlu Ahmed Bey and the Kemalist construction of Turkish nationhood in Anatolia', *Anatolian Studies* 58 (2008): 141–171. In this vein, an annex to the December 1921 Treaty of Alexandropol, in addition to minimizing Armenian population figures, denied an authentic Armenian culture, insisting that "the Armenian music had Turkish origins" (quoted in Khatissian, *Eclosion*, 279).

[188] Reproduced in *LCP*, 190–204. See also *İnönü'nün Hatıraları*, 113.

22 Diplomatically Framing History

contribute were the Sorbonne-trained counsellor Yusuf Bayur, legal counsellor Mehmet Münir (Ertegün, Talaat Pasha's advisor during the conference of Brest-Litovsk), and last but not least Rıza Nur. There were others who also had a say among the forty or so people belonging to the Turkish team. They frequently met, in varying configurations, late in the evening or at night. Important team members with an articulate historical say were the military advisor Mehmet Tevfik Bıyıklıoğlu, later a founding member of the Turkish Historical Association; Baha Said Bey, Talaat's and Ankara's expert for ethnic and confessional groups; and members of the press team like Necmeddin Sadık (Sadak), Hüseyin Çahit (Yalçın), Yusuf Nadi (Abalıoğlu), and Nihat Reşat (Belger).

Relevant national history regarding minorities began, according to the 12 December 1922 paper, with the heroic conquest of Constantinople in 1453 and the supreme tolerance of the victorious sultan vis-à-vis minorities. On the minority issue, the Kemalists by and large thought in terms of Sunni imperial elites. Ismet's paper has to be placed against the background of pre–Great War intervention by Europe in favor of non-Muslim minorities in general and the Entente's 24 May 1915 declaration to prosecute the anti-Armenian crimes against humanity, in particular.[189] Armed or purely diplomatic intervention in the name of minority protection had started with actions in the late eighteenth century. During the last Ottoman decades, they were based on articles of the 1878 Berlin Treaty.

Ankara's delegates stressed two arguments against European insistence on minority rights in new Turkey: First, European efforts in favor of minorities had amounted to making them harmful and treacherous agents of foreign, in particular Russian power. The Powers had thus misused the argument of minority protection for their own interests against Ottoman Turkey. Second, Ottoman politics had displayed an exemplary treatment of minorities and thus anticipated the progress that was much later enshrined in the League's minority protection treaties. Ankara could therefore do without any lessons or oversight from Europe. Both arguments mirrored the experiences and wide-spread mindset of late-Ottoman imperial elites. Labelled an "objective examination," the assertions the Turkish delegation made in Lausanne were considered authoritative and set the main lines of Ankara's official history in textbooks, diplomacy, and publicly for decades.

On 12 December, Ismet taught his audience the "striking [Ottoman] tolerance" vis-à-vis minorities (i.e. non-Muslim *millet*) throughout

---

[189] "Notes du Département à l'Agence Havas," Paris, 24 May 1915, in Arthur Beylerian (ed.), *Les grandes puissances, l'Empire ottoman et les Arméniens dans les archives françaises (1914–1918): Recuil de documents* (Paris: Publications de la Sorbonne, 1983), 29.

history, claiming Europe's post–Great War minority rights and protection were an old liberal Ottoman achievement, because "the rights of minorities ... sought to assure in the twentieth century under the guarantee of the League of Nations, were spontaneously accorded to the non-Mussulman elements of the Ottoman Empire," beginning with Mehmed the Conqueror. Thus, Turkey had always been a factor of high civilization and progress. "Foreign instigations," foremost by Russia, caused "mutual distrust and the unhappy events" (i.e. massacres). Ottomans lived in a harmonious "great empire which the incessant attacks of malevolent neighbours had already appreciably weakened" by the late-eighteenth century. Blaming bygone Tsarist Russia was costless and spared self-critical introspection. As for the Armenians: "Up to the middle of the 19th Century the Armenians had lived at peace and at full liberty in Turkey." In the "unhappy events," there was no fault whatsoever with "the Turks" and their state. "Turks have never failed to acknowledge the rights of the non-Moslem elements so long as the latter did not abuse the generosity of the country in which they lived in comfort for centuries."[190]

For convenience, during the minority discussion, Ankara's delegation also used the argument of loyal Turkish-speaking "Orthodox Turks," in contrast to Rûm close to Greece. Yet, significantly, these Turkish Christians, too, were not offered any future in the Republic of Turkey, but included in the population transfer. Much more than Orthodox Turks, the Jews served as a model minority. Ismet Pasha went regularly to play the "Jewish trump card." Supporting the imperial order before 1918, the model of the Jews had now to foster unitary nationalism. "The example of the Jewish community, which [for four centuries] has not up to the present had to complain of any inhumane act on the part of the Turkish Government or people, would suffice to show that the blame for the distressing events in the case of the Greeks and the Armenians falls entirely upon themselves."[191]

At Lausanne's table, that was a convenient way of whitewashing history: a powerful blueprint for the blaming of the weak and the victims for being destroyed. It mirrored the arguments in Nur's *History of the Armenians*. Curzon made do with sarcastically asking whether the Armenian Ottoman community had killed itself. The assembly of delegates was, however, far from any concerted front against this kind of social-Darwinist, proto-fascist discourse. Ismet's verbal display of continued good will and tolerance toward Christian natives, if only they behaved as the state expected from them, stood in disconnect with what Ankara did and actually wanted, namely, their removal. Again, the

[190] *LCP*, 190–204. [191] Ibid., 201

reaction was little more than a short sarcastic comment. "Why were hundreds of thousands of Armenians now fugitives in every country in the world, when all they had to do was to return to the cordial embraces of the Turkish Government?"[192]

Readers of *When Democracy Died* easily recognize that Ismet's 12 December historical argumentation took up Atabinen's 1919 trope of the contemporary "extermination of the Turks" by the West, when he asserted that "the Turks of the Morea and Thessaly, are confronted with certain extermination," so, according to Ankara, population exchange was urgently required.[193] Countering Venizelos on Armenian suffering, Ismet turned the table saying "the last Government in the world which should dare to express in public its pity for the fate of the Armenians was the very Government which had been the direct cause of their misfortunes." This meant that the Greek campaign had made Armenians suffer in the first place, not the previous CUP genocide and the defense of the gains from this genocide by the CUP's successors.

Hyperbolic rhetoric completed the self-righteous, at times grotesque, presentation of Turkish history on 12 December 1922. After nearly a decade of mass violence against Ottoman conationals in Anatolia, perpetrated predominantly by forces related to the Turkish state, Ismet lamented: "The pity, generosity and tolerance of the Turks always recoiled upon them to their disadvantage."[194] No fault lay on the Turkish side in this view, either of premodern or contemporary history. The generalized culpability of defeated Greece served as an inflated criterion for historical and moral judgments, according to which Ankara now counted as a force of civilizational progress, whereas with Greece "all the reactionary, mediaeval elements in the country were roused against the intellectual and enlightened classes" of the Turkish nation in 1919–22.[195]

Ankara's chief delegate kept on denying any continuity with the former CUP party-state to which members of the current government and of the delegation had actively belonged, asserting, "the hands of the Turks now at work in their own country, which had been devastated and ruined by foreign invasion, were quite peculiarly clean. Those hands had never violated, invaded or devastated any foreign country."[196] Persians, Kurds, Armenians, Assyrians, Rûm, and Arabs had totally different stories to tell about devastation of their land by invading Turkish forces or by local forces related to the state during the previous decade. They were not given access to the Château d'Ouchy.

***

---

[192] Ibid., 208, 211–212; cf. Halide Edip Adıvar, *Memoirs* (London: Murray, 1926), 372.
[193] *LCP*, 203.   [194] Ibid., 189.   [195] Ibid., 206.   [196] Ibid., 219.

Backed by the intellectually alert Venizelos and the Serbian SHS delegate Miroslav Spalaikovitch, Curzon countered some of Ismet Pasha's most fantastic allegations.[197] The French chief delegate Camille Barrère remained silent, but, on 14 December, complimented Ankara's delegation for "a highly interesting discussion" that had "arisen out of the minorities problem." He was "glad to see that very real progress towards conciliation had been made. ... Ismet Pasha and the Turkish delegation had approached this question with true regard for equity and justice."[198] From the beginning of the Conference, the French delegation sought to preserve gains of a special relationship with Ankara based on the 1921 Accord. In the privacy of hotel rooms, it suggested that the displayed official approach did not equal the real French attitude and offered concessions. Cheapest were those on the backs of minorities.[199] Nevertheless, the French strategy largely failed, as we will see when we examine the second half of the Conference.

On burning topics of contemporary history, Ankara's watchful and well-prepared delegation was questioned – but by no means defied – in Lausanne, because the Allied diplomats pursued other objectives as according to their current exigencies and constraints. Dubious or clearly unacceptable contents, proffered in the Château d'Ouchy, were not diligently addressed and clarified. These contents and related patterns of behavior ended hushed up, ready to be reproduced in later policies. In all their heatedness, the relevant discussions thus remained restrained. Framing the past and the history of minorities the way Ankara's delegation did, justified the forceful – implicitly, the exterminatory – removal of minorities and the compulsory "exchange" of those remaining. Removal stood in direct relation with the Armenian question. Lausanne's Convention concerning the Exchange concluded a ten-year policy that had targeted the erasure of any potentially autonomous Christian presence, particularly and primarily, the erasure of an Armenian home in parts of Eastern Anatolia.

Curzon was articulate, yet brief, on the topic of the historic meaning of compulsory population transfer. In the meeting of 13 December 1922, he "deeply regretted that the solution now being worked out [for Anatolia's Rûm] should be the compulsory exchange of populations – a thoroughly bad and vicious solution, for which the world would pay a heavy penalty

---

[197] Remarkably enough, they continue to be used, at times verbatim, in Turkish media until the present. See, for example, Alev Coşkun, "Ermeni iddiaları: Üç önemli belge," *Cumhuriyet*, 2 May 2022.

[198] *LCP*, 225.

[199] Jeffery and Sharp, "Lord Curzon and Secret Intelligence," 117; Demirci, *Lausanne Conference*, 95.

for a hundred years to come. He detested having anything to do with it." Knowing the root cause of the transfer proposal, he added that "to say it was a suggestion of the Greek Government was ridiculous." As explained in Chapter 18, the proposal was, by and large, "a solution enforced by the action of the Turkish Government in expelling these people from Turkish territory."[200]

Curzon was intellectually able to grasp and articulate the meaning of a gigantic population removal conditioned by a decade of ultranationalist demographic engineering. Yet, for him, too, it was finally about forgetting the past and finding a "solution for the future" by viable compromises according to his British-imperial terms. Thus, though "he deeply regretted to hear the repeated charges in the speeches of the Turkish delegation against the Greek population and array, when similar and much greater charges could easily be brought against the Turks," he quickly called, "Let not the scene be darkened." The overall "purpose of the conference was to make a solution for the future."[201]

In sum, the Allied delegates eluded critical controversies over history. They left a diplomatically framed, utterly blurred and whitewashed history to generations after them. Historical clear-sightedness proved onerous, terminological clarification uniquely acrobatic after Lausanne. For Germany – the CUP regime's senior war ally which had taken responsibility for the future of the Ottoman Armenian with its commitment to the 1914 Reform Agreement[202] – it took more than a century (until 2016) to simply recognize and openly name the extermination of Armenians in Anatolia. For the USA, it took a few years more (2019). Great Britain, a great beneficiary of the Lausanne Treaty, still lags far behind the pioneer France (2001).

***

Framing history and boasting of civilizational exploits in the past went hand in hand. "Civilization" was a key argument in Lausanne related also to legal discussions that ranged from civil to international law. The promise of a transition to modern secular law codes and of Turkey's prompt adherence to the League of Nations proved critical for the compromises struck during the first two months of the Conference, especially regarding minorities.

The claim of an age-old Turkish or Turanian civilization went hand in hand with bold reform promises at the negotiation table. Anything barbaric (i.e. anything that referenced the extermination, dispossession, and expulsion of Ottoman Christians), was completely disregarded. Ankara's

[200] *LCP*, 212.   [201] Ibid.   [202] Kieser, Polatel, and Schmutz, "Reform or cataclysm."

delegation displayed both (alleged) age-old Ottoman tolerance and secularizing late-Ottoman reforms as its credentials.[203] In addition, it held out the prospect of things that anticipated groundbreaking Kemalist steps. But in the same breath, it claimed existing full-fledged achievements, as Ismet did in a commission meeting "on the Régime of Foreigners" in late December 1922: "The present state of Turkish law is such as to meet all the requirements and necessities of modern life."[204] He displayed little or no sense for what concrete rule of law meant.

US delegation member Admiral Bristol – who was "very pro-Turk and very anti-British and for that reason ... his talks with Ismet carr[ied] weight"[205] – tried to explain to Ismet Pasha in a private meeting that there were manifest defects in the justice system: lack of confidence in the judges; necessity of recodification of the legal codes, notably eliminating inequality provisions due to the sharia; lack of transparent laws on court procedures and the admission of evidence; lack of laws on the inviolability of domicile and habeas corpus; need for modern prisons and prison regulations. However, "Ismet did not refute these arguments but he would not admit that reforms in the present juridical regime were necessary for the good of Turkey."[206]

In contrast to the internationalist approach to law, nationalists in general and Ismet and his cohort in particular, understood "the law" primally as "an expression of sovereignty. In principle, each state exercises its sovereignty over all persons and objects located in its territory."[207] Law was therefore not about universal standards that might be checked from the outside. Atatürk confirms this stance in his *Nutuk* where he mentions those "who were alleged to have persecuted or mistreated Armenians and British prisoners." This refers to a failed agreement at the 1921 London Conference that would have exempted such culprits from a prisoner exchange (they were not exempted in the end, as Britain gave in). "Our government, of course, could not approve and ratify such a deal. Because to ratify such a deal would be to confirm the jurisdiction of the foreign government over the actions of Turkish subjects within Turkey."[208]

Ankara in Lausanne is a typical, though particularly radical, case of judicial nationalism. For the Turkish delegation, the notion of "sovereignty" was paramount during all debates in Lausanne. At the hand of an ambitious, but not democratic-minded leadership, this notion did not

---

[203] *LCP*, 473.   [204] Ibid., 489, 28 December 1922.
[205] Grew diary, 22 January 1923, 20–27.   [206] Ibid., 17 January 1923, 20–21.
[207] Cemil Bilsel, "Medenî Kanun ve Lozan Muahedesi," in *Medenî Kanunun XV. Yıl Dönümü İçin* (Istanbul: Kenan Matbaası, 1944), 21.
[208] Kemal, *Nutuk*, 391.

designate the sovereignty of Anatolia's people(s) or a "sovereignty of law," to be evidenced by constitutionality and independent justice. For Ankara, it meant supreme Muslim-Turkish rights (*Türk hukuku*) in the whole of Anatolia, as represented by Ankara's National Assembly, at the exclusion of any other rights of self-determination by the groups specified in the Sèvres Treaty. Importantly, it also meant the abrogation of any penal prosecution for crimes against humanity perpetrated by representatives of those included in the nation. Legal sovereignty was thus, in other words, a matter of the will to unrestricted rule, which the late-Ottoman national-imperial cadres enforced. They easily succeeded against non-Turkish minorities that were weakly backed by ageing European imperialists.

On all sides, the delegations pursued imperially biased interests on the backs of those excluded from Lausanne's main table. By January 1923, the Allies had definitively given up insisting on substantial rights of Anatolian non-Turks. The abandonment of the Armenian home was the central piece of this legal volte-face and the number one priority for Ankara. Other aspects were the weak rights of the recognized Christian and Jewish micro-minorities; the diminution of the Genevan standard definition of "minorities"; and the abolition of the capitulations. In exchange, as it were, for the volte-face on fundamental legal issues, Ankara promised modern equal law and declared itself a model electoral democracy. In order to immediately achieve full sovereignty at the Lausanne Conference, the nascent state thus raised a mortgage of the claim on rule of law and democracy that it never was able to pay off.

As we have seen, the reduction of the status and meaning of minority meant that only the former Ottoman millets were to benefit from all minority rights laid out in the Treaty, and even this conditionally. Thanks to impending reforms in "new Turkey," the delegation insisted, some of these rights would soon become obsolete, along with the capitulations that the final Treaty abolished for good.[209] In the second half of the Conference, Ankara's delegation accepted foreign legal advisors for a five-year transition to a new justice system that would introduce full legal equality based on modern (i.e. European), law. It declared Turkey "prepared to have an investigation made and to cause the [legal] situation to be studied with a view to the institution of such reforms as may be rendered advisable by the development of manners and civilisation."[210] Justice Minister Mahmut Bozkurt, who was in charge of the reforms from

---

[209] "Memorandum read by the Turkish Delegate at the Meeting of December 2, 1922, of the Commission on the Régime of Foreigners," *LCP*, 471–480.

[210] "Draft Declaration Relating to the Administration of Justice in Turkey," 801. This draft was the basis for the Declaration signed on 24 July 1923, quoted here. www.mfa.gov.tr

1925, put it this way: "When we abolished the capitulations in the Lausanne Peace Treaty, we took it upon ourselves at the same time to establish a whole new Turkish judicial organization with a new legal system, new laws and new courts."[211]

In this vein of promises, a recognized modern civil law in line with previous reforms under Talaat Pasha would, in the near future, more than compensate the abrogation of the millets' own family laws.[212] The related Article 42 of the Lausanne Treaty remained therefore a paper tiger:

> The Turkish Government undertakes to take, as regards non-Moslem minorities, in so far as concerns their family law or personal status, measures permitting the settlement of these questions in accordance with the customs of those minorities. These measures will be elaborated by special Commissions composed of representatives of the Turkish Government and of representatives of each of the minorities concerned in equal number. In case of divergence, the Turkish Government and the Council of the League of Nations will appoint in agreement an umpire chosen from amongst European lawyers.

Readers will see in Part IV, how Ankara circumvented this provision in the context of its "Turkish Revolution."

23 Conference Break – Interval – Continuation

January 1923 was critical for the abandonment both of Armenia and of substantial rights for non-Turks in or from Anatolia. This development coincided with a crisis in Europe related to the issue of German reparations, French occupation of the Ruhr, and France's insecurity vis-à-vis Germany in general.

Germany was in turmoil. Hyperinflation accelerated. Militants both from the far right and a Bolshevik left saw the situation in the Ruhr as an opportunity for violence. Mid-June 1922, the German-Jewish foreign minister Walther Rathenau had been murdered. Politicians of the Weimar Republic like Rathenau, Matthias Erzberger (assassinated by far-right militants in 1921), and Gustav Stresemann were considered lame, unpatriotic "Erfüllungspolitiker" by radical German nationalists. In September 1923, when "traitor" Stresemann succeeded Wilhelm Cuno as the Reichskanzler (before becoming foreign minister), he ended

---

/xi_-declaration-relating-to-the-administration-of-justice.en.mfa. This site includes the Treaty and its related Conventions, Declarations and Protocols (14 June 2022).

[211] Mahmut Bozkurt, "Türk Medenî Kanunu nasıl hazırlandı?" in *Medenî kanunun XV. Yıl Dönümü İçin* (İstanbul: Kenan Matbaası, 1944), 8.

[212] Kieser, *Talaat Pasha*, 323; Osman B. Gürzumar, "Die Übernahme westlichen Rechts in der Türkei vor 1926," in H. Kieser, A. Meier, W. Stoffel (eds.), *Revolution islamischen Rechts: Das Schweizerische ZGB in der Türkei* (Zürich: Chronos, 2008), 43.

Berlin's politics of obstruction in the Ruhr and sought reconciliation with France. This and a brilliant Turkish role model of ultranationalist success contributed to triggering the Hitler Putsch (Munich Beer Hall Putsch) in November 1923.[213]

The January 1923 crisis sharpened existing French–British rifts regarding both Europe and Turkey. Arousing both national egoisms and solo actions, the tensions negatively impacted on the quality of the Lausanne Conference. Western unity on fundamental issues was even more weakened; the concentration on a calm, thorough, and persistent work of peace disturbed. In the last third of January, even for the hitherto optimistic Montagna, "under the present weak position of the Allies and with all possible concessions already made, there is little hope of continuing satisfactory negotiations."[214] On the eve of the Mosul debate, there were rumors and suspicions of a separate French–Turkish peace. Curzon had his reasons to complain that "the French had let him down completely; that they were weakening on every issue ... and that they had disclosed all the conference plans to the Turks."[215] Yet, he exaggerated, as a day later, on 23 January, the French delegation stood on Britain's side during the Mosul debate. Again, a day later, on 24 January, Maurice Bompard, France's new plenipotentiary after Camille Barrère's sudden resignation, found Curzon's methods "peremptory" and Curzon's time table overhasty: "There was no use in trying to hurry matters by handing in an unnegotiated treaty to the Turks and setting a definite date for departure."[216] Bompard was considered closer to Ankara than Barrère; he had been France's ambassador in Istanbul before the Great War.

On 31 January 1923, Curzon formally presented Ankara's delegation the draft treaty which they had informally received two days earlier. The same day, 31 January, a telegram from Paris shocked London's delegation. In a note to the British ambassador, Poincaré considered France not bound not to sign a separate treaty with Ankara. Poincaré's argument was remarkable: the renouncement of a commitment not to sign a separate peace concerned only the World War and the Istanbul government, not the current negotiations with Ankara. "France would reserve all rights to negotiate and sign a separate treaty after the British left Lausanne if it were found impossible to sign one en bloc."[217] After having supported Britain on Mosul – what Ankara's delegation strongly resented – France feared its hopes dashed as far as an advantageous financial and economic outcome of the Conference was concerned. France's demands were not

---

[213] Ihrig, *Atatürk in the Nazi Imagination*, 68–107.   [214] Grew diary, 28, 22 January 1923.
[215] Ibid., 27, 22 January 1923.   [216] Ibid., 32, 24 January 1923.
[217] Ibid., 41, 31 January 1923.

yet met and of uncertain destiny, though included in the partly unnegotiated draft treaty.

Britain had factually attained her specific imperial goals by late January: free passage through the Straits and, pending further negotiations or a League of Nations decision, annexation of Mosul to mandatory Iraq. In early February 1923, Nur made a private advance to Nicholson for a separate Turkish-British peace. "He leered a pink grin. He took me aside. He said: 'Look here, why not make a separate peace with us?'"[218] This was out of the question for Curzon.

An elderly woman acting behind the official scene, Madame Bompard, the wife of the new French chief-delegate, tried to pressure the notorious hardliner Rıza Nur during a banquet. In blunt and direct language, she embarrassed him publicly, calling him a hindrance in the search for peace and holding him responsible for Ankara's hesitation vis-à-vis the Allied proposal. She was therefore given the name "Madam Whip." In those weeks, French and English papers drew very unfavorable portraits of Nur, whereas the nationalistic press in Germany and Austria praised him.[219] Nur was in tune with the sentiment and rhetoric reigning in the National Assembly when writing from Lausanne in late January, "The newly emerged draft agreement is not in a form that will give Turkey political and economic independence and the capacity of [full sovereign] life. The idea of Turkey having the capacity to live has not yet entered the minds of Europeans."[220]

***

In the atmosphere described above, the Allies' plan to bring the Conference to a good end by late January 1922, plus perhaps a few additional days, failed, and there remained suspense and expectations until the last hour on Sunday, 4 February. It was "a fateful day" with an evening "full of electricity" in the air, but looked also like "a carnival" (see Figure 15).[221] Curzon's ultimatum-like presentation triggered a rush of interactions on all levels, without leading to successful final compromises. The result was the Conference's rupture, which the main delegates quickly interpreted as a temporary interruption. Nicholson has described in his diary the day of British departure from Lausanne by train on 4 February 1923, with the historic last meeting in Lord Curzon's room at the Beau Rivage hotel late on that afternoon:

Pack in the morning. We are all tense and depressed, awaiting the next Turkish move. At 1.30 it comes in the form of a Note. It accepts practically all the British

---

[218] Nicolson, *Curzon: The Last Phase*, 346.
[219] Nur, *Hayat ve Hatıratım*, vol. 3, 182–185.
[220] Şimşir, *Lozan Telgrafları I*, 449, no. 443, 27 January 1923, Ismet Pasha to Rauf Bey.
[221] Grew diary, 56, 4 February 1923.

23 Conference Break – Interval – Continuation

Figure 15 "Lausanne turns to a carnival. The British: Do not be embarrassed, gentlemen, our return [to London] coincides with the carnival." During the first half of the Conference, the British delegation all in all reached its main goals, although the situation in late January, early February 1923 looked hectic and chaotic, resulting in the Conference's rupture. (*Akbaba*, no. 17, 1 February 1923, 2. Drawn by Ramiz)

claims, but holds out over economics and capitulations. At 2.40 Bompard comes, embarrassed and solicitous (when I *think* of his patronising attitude during the early stages I see red). He begs Curzon to make some further concessions up on *our* points. The Marquis [Curzon] throws in the ships [Ottoman warships confiscated on 1 August 1914] and the appeal to the League over Mosul. Bompard, Rumbold and Montagna then go up to the Lausanne Palace to find out what the Turks really mean about the economic clauses. They come back at 4.0 [sic] and the allies meet again in Curzon's room. We talk together till 5.20 when Ismet is summoned. He arrives at 5.40. From then on the scene becomes emotional and confused. Ismet is unhappy and embarrassed. He twists about in his chair, mops his forehead, dabs at his lips with his handkerchief and is very unhappy and nervous.[222]

For Ismet, those days were extremely stressful. On 28 January, he even turned to sidelined Cavid for advice. Cavid saw no other resort for the Turkish delegation than, for the moment, to leave without fracas and to expect a continuation in the near future.

"He [Ismet] is very anxious. The feeling of having lost his cause heavily weighs on his conscience and idealism. He ruminates all the time." "Who is considered responsible [for the impending rupture]?" "Above all Curzon because of his impatience," Cavid responded. Did the other delegations also see faults on the Turkish side? "Yes, because our politics is obstinate even in minor issues."[223]

At an official dinner to the Turks by the US delegation on 29 January, Ismet "smiled broadly" saying "I am absolutely content," while he looked to Grew manifestly "depressed throughout dinner."[224] According to Ismet's memoirs, "the time when I felt lowest spirits [in Lausanne] was 4 February, the day of the conference rupture."[225] That afternoon, Ismet and Nur retired from Curzon's room for deliberation, after being implored by Curzon, who used "every tone – cajolery, despair, menace, authority," to make them accept the amended draft. Here is how Nicholson continued his narrative of the last day with Curzon in Lausanne:

I accompany them out into the passage. Our luggage and our documents are being gathered together on the landing, and carpenters ... are hammering at packing-cases. The passages are blocked by journalists who have crept upstairs. We push through these encumbrances and I guide Ismet into Crowe's [another delegation member's] room. I return to the Marquis. ... At 6.45 Ismet returns. He accepts all our own conditions but refuses the economic paragraphs. ... Bompard and Garroni, with the Marquis' superb support, bombard Ismet with appeals and menaces. ... Ismet is obdurate. For once he loses his temper. He says, "I shall return to Angora and tell my people that the conference, under the Presidency of Lord Curzon, desired war ... " "No! No! No!" they all shout. ... Ismet dabs his handkerchief against his lips. ... "Je ne peux pas," he mumbles wretchedly, "Je ne peux pas." It is very painful. ... The Marquis, who likes Ismet, is obviously distressed.[226]

Although Curzon may have liked Ankara's young and inexperienced plenipotentiary, he lashed out at him after Ismet had ultimately rejected

---

[222] Nicolson, *Curzon: The Last Phase*, 346–348.
[223] Cavid, *Meşrutiyet Ruznâmesi*, vol. 4, 497, entry of 28 January 1923.
[224] Grew diary, 39, 29 January 1923.   [225] İnönü, *İsmet İnönü'nün Hatıraları*, 67.
[226] Nicolson, *Curzon: The Last Phase*, 347–348.

23 Conference Break – Interval – Continuation

the draft treaty and left Beau-Rivage. "That little nincompoop of an idiot has wrecked the peace of the world over a few matters of insignificant detail," he shouted before the Allied delegates. Bombard and Montagna, and after them the US delegates drove to the Palace hotel, where the Turkish delegation stayed. They tried to sway Ismet, who raised the specter of "financial and industrial slavery" if Turkey signed the current treaty. Still, he went to offer small concessions.[227] Grew noted in his diary that day that he had "no very high opinion of Ismet's intelligence." For him, Ankara's plenipotentiary "had little grasp of the details of the negotiations .... At times he has seemed dull of comprehension, almost stupid. I believe he would have gone much farther in meeting the position of the Allies had it not been for Riza Nour who was obstinate from the start."[228] Both Ismet and Nur, however, strongly depended on the instructions from and atmosphere in Ankara; the former being closer to Mustafa Kemal's circle, the latter to the hawks in the National Assembly.

Nicholson describes in detail 4 February's "Je ne peux pas" scene that invoked war. For him, this was a personal emotional outburst by Ismet. But Ismet was familiar with war. Wars had enforced the Lausanne Conference. "Lausanne was a campaign for me, like that of Anatolia," he himself confessed shortly after the Conference to a Swiss journalist in Ankara.[229] Cornered by the Allies into compromises on 4 February, he thus could not but refer to war (i.e. the basic logic of violence and might that underpinned the Conference), being Ankara's most trenchant argument in Lausanne.

Ankara's delegation knew that only Britain, the strongest at the table, would, though reluctantly, be in a position to wage war, possibly alongside Greece. All others, France and Italy in particular, explicitly shied away from any armed confrontation with Ankara. This was the main reason why the deal with Britain had priority for Ismet and Nur, and why Curzon attained more than the others in Lausanne. Ismet however knew well that, having reached its main goals by late January, Britain would not go to war, at least as long as Ankara refrained from adventures in Iraq.

Ismet's "losing his temper" on 4 February 1923 was therefore not less rhetorical and theatric than it was authentic. In any case, it was effective. It strengthened Ismet's image as a frank, honest, and committed soldier-patriot with whom (i.e. a strongly nationalist, but predictable Turkey, for which he seemed to stand) Britain would go to build up mutually beneficial relations. A pact of bilateral interests was therefore bourgeoning, despite impending interruption. The Allies would be ready for further compromises.

---

[227] Grew diary, 57–58, 4 February 1923.   [228] Ibid., 60, 4 February 1923.
[229] Gentizon, "Lettre d'Angora," 1.

Here is the end of Nicholson's 4 February entry:

> We get up and say good-bye. They leave the room sullenly, out into the corridor thronged with journalists and packing-cases. Among them is [Conference Secretary-General] Massigli, armed with the final Treaty ready for signature. Ismet descends in the lift. I go with him. He recovers his composure. He leaves the hotel as if nothing very serious had happened. Bompard and Montagna are sent after him to suggest a new formula about capitulations. We telephone to the station and stop the Orient Express for half an hour. We snatch some dinner. At 9.15 we leave the hotel. There is a crowd at the station and many police. We lean out of the train hoping that at the last moment Ismet will relent. Bompard, fussy and out of breath, dashes up the stair-case. "No good," he says. "Nous partons," I say to the station master. Slowly the great train slides into the night.[230]

The US delegation came a few minutes too late to the station, hoping to tell Curzon about Ismet's last concessions. Thus, the "First Lausanne Conference," as many called it, was definitively dissolved. The delegations returned home for further consultation in view of a continued, or "Second," Lausanne Conference.

***

The Conference interval was particularly turbulent in Ankara where Ismet faced heavy criticism by hardliners and maximalists in the National Assembly. Also, the interval proved critical in view of the transformation of the Assembly government to a single leader-led Kemalist dictatorship. This transformation took place during the second half and the aftermath of the Conference. *When Democracy Died* argues that, in 1923, the making of "peace" and dictatorship, of the Lausanne Treaty and the inherently autocratic rule in Ankara, were two faces of a same coin. We come back to this Lausanne-related development in Part IV.

Lausanne saw the delegations and their retinue return at the eve of 23 April 1923, when the Conference reopened. All needed and wanted a final deal, a "peace," that would relieve the protracted strain and uncertainty. Most desperate of all was Ankara: its state-building depended on the Lausanne "birth certificate." The *Journal de Genève* struck a chord when summarizing at the end of the Conference interval: "The authority of Mustafa Kemal himself was undermined, so much so that he had to dissolve the Great Assembly of Angora, which had become too indocile, and mobilize his supporters for new elections. The famous nationalist regime, about which people in the West sometimes had strange illusions, was maintained only by arbitrariness and violence."[231] Though correct in

---

[230] Nicolson, *Curzon: The Last Phase*, 348.
[231] "A la Conférence de Lausanne: Le second acte," *Journal de Genève*, 111, 24 April 1923, 1.

assessing the lack of democracy and thus, in final analysis, a building on sand, this statement was too derogatory. It underestimated Western weakness and divisiveness that in turn empowered a fervent and resolute nationalism. It did not count on the diplomatic scope and skills, and the potential of disruption, of a well-armed oligarchy in times of international crises.

One telling tactical move during the interval was the Chester concession that the National Assembly approved on 9 April 1923. It conferred railway construction from the Black Sea to Mosul and beyond to a private US syndicate, with the rights to all the resources, including oil, within a large zone on each side of the railway lines. It comprised further rights like that to build ports. Even if this gigantic project failed because it lacked sufficient finances and was not backed by the US State department, it caused trouble among the Allies; particularly for the French delegation that claimed conflicting pre–Great War concessions. In Ankara, it raised temporary hope that Mosul was not lost, but that the staggering concession would prompt US support for the Turkish claim. The loss of Mosul and other regions was a specter raised by members of the so-called Second – Kemal-critical – Group in the Assembly. Those who chose a maximalist interpretation of the National Pact furiously refused to compromise on these territorial issues.

The most tangible achievement of the Chester move was probably the growing proximity between Ismet and Grew, the US chief delegate during the second half of the Conference. Against the background of intensified British–American economic competition in the Middle East, Curzon was upset by the Chester concession and hardly accepted the presence of US delegates in the second half of the Conference. US–Turkey proximity went hand in hand with Ismet's efforts to conclude a Turkish–American treaty even in advance of the main treaty, thus putting the Allies at a great disadvantage.[232] Chapter 24 explains how the Lausanne Treaty finally came about. Chapter 25 comes back to the separate negotiations that led to a treaty signed on 6 August 1923 between Turkey and the USA, thirteen days after the main Treaty was concluded.

24 After a Long Last Mile, the Treaty

In contrast to the first half, the second half of the Conference was no longer dominated by Turkish–British interaction. By and large, Britain had achieved what it wanted, having made her rapprochement with Ankara at the cost of Turkish–Soviet friendship, put the future of Mosul in a favorable suspense, and all in all restored British prestige

---

[232] Demirci, *The Lausanne Conference*, 159–162.

in the East and respect among Turks. A comprehensive military operation during the Conference interval tightened the mandatory power's control over Mosul and over the inhabitants of Southern Kurdistan, thus preventing Turkish interference. Henceforth, for Foreign Secretary Curzon, a more important battle was still to come, "with an adversary more potent and more skilled than any Ismet, than any Mustapha Kemal. It remained to restore ... our credit in Europe."[233]

Although the Turkish–British divide and the fundamental issues of minority rights, population exchange, and the Armenian home were settled, final peace was by no means easily made from April to July. The unsolved financial and economic questions touched the heart of French and Italian interests in Asia Minor (see Figure 16). Principal understandings reached in the first half had to be finalized, like those on Mosul, amnesties, and boundaries. A few other seemingly minor, but tricky conflicts remained to be solved. The Allied draft treaty of late January as well as the Turkish counter-proposal[234] made during the interval served as a basis for discussion. The conference stood two, three times again at the brink of rupture. The outbreak of a renewed Greek–Turkish war was not excluded.

Six main questions were to be addressed in Lausanne's sequel: reparations; the Capitulations; the Ottoman public debt; concessions to Western companies; amnesty and return; and the Allies' evacuation of Istanbul. For Ankara, this evacuation and the Capitulations had priority, though the refusal of any return by Armenians and the perpetuated confiscation of their properties was also highly important. The Turks were advantaged insofar as Britain, the only great power still principally ready to use force against Ankara, chose not to do so on the issues that remained to be settled. Most open questions concerned France, Greece, and Italy in the first place. As from the Conference's genesis itself, brute power continued to define Lausanne's negotiations. "I know it is humiliating to give way to the Turks," commented Rumbold in June 1923, "but if we are not going to use force, we must take the best bargain we can."[235]

From the Conference's restart in late April, the issues of reparations, Capitulations, as well as again – far-reaching, but less prominent and between the lines – the return and/or dispossession of surviving

---

[233] Nicolson, *Curzon: The Last Phase*, 351–352. See also Demirci, *The Lausanne Conference*, 165–166.
[234] *LKT*, vol. 4, 21–62.
[235] Telegraph of 19 June 1923, quoted in Demirci, *The Lausanne Conference*, 199, see also 185, 193.

Figure 16 "The question of interests. Would you allow me to put this gold bracelet on your arms as a souvenir of the conference?" The European diplomats – in this picture represented by General Pellé, head of the French delegation – want to trick the diplomat and general Ismet Pasha. The good, superior type of a soldier patriot, Ismet however stands firm in his national mission to win full, including financial and economic sovereignty for Turkey, and to minimize interest payments for the Ottoman debts. (*Akbaba*, no. 54, 11 June 1923, 1. Artist: Ramiz)

Armenians to Anatolia loomed heavily. The Allies agreed on the end of the Capitulations. But – as mentioned in Section 21 with regard to a "diplomatically framed" understanding of rule of law – they still had to negotiate the transition period, the issue of judicial advisors, and the requirement of independent justice. In the 25 April meeting of the Third Committee,[236] Ismet hastened to emphasize, the "Turkish courts would by no means remain under the influence of the Turkish government."[237]

---

[236] The "Commissions" of the first half were called "Committees" in the second half of the Conference.
[237] *LKT*, vol. 5, 17.

204   A Protracted Conference

Again built on Turkish prospects and promises, an adjustment was reached in June. Its prospective character is underlined in Grew's related statement in the First Committee: "[T]he really important consideration is the largeness of spirit in which the entire judicial system of Turkey is to be administered in the future."[238] Hopeful conjecture is omnipresent in Lausanne; for example, according to Grew, Ankara is "determined apparently to reorganize its government and the fabric of its society along modern and democratic lines," and therefore committed to peace.[239] The adjustment related to the abolition of the judicial Capitulations is recorded in a Declaration Relating to the Administration of Justice and a Convention respecting Conditions of Residence and Business and Jurisdiction. These two documents are among a total of sixteen diplomatic instruments signed and added to the proper Treaty of 24 July 1923. At the end, Treaty Article 28 solemnly declared, "Each of the High Contracting Parties hereby accepts, in so far as it is concerned, the complete abolition of the Capitulations in Turkey in every respect."

Ankara tied the renewed demand of Turkish reparations by Allies with its demand of reparations from Greece, against which the Greek delegation battled fiercely. This conflict carried the risk of renewed military hostilities by way of a Greek advance through Eastern Thrace toward Istanbul. A combat-ready army and their revanchist leaders were prepared for such action during May 1923 (see Figure 17). The conflict in Lausanne was aggravated by the notoriously bad treatment by Turks of Greek prisoners and the continued expulsion of Rûm. The tensions nearly lead to a rupture of the Conference. There was "no doubt whatever that at one moment the conference hung on the brink of rupture and Europe on the brink of war." This was the "most serious development in the second phase of the Conference," said Grew.[240] With Grew and Montagna's special diplomatic skill, an adjustment was reached in late May: Ankara's delegation took a slight territorial correction in Thrace (Greek cession of Karagatch, a suburb of Edirne) as a compensation; and the Allies renounced any claim for reparations. By the same token, there emerged the risk, or chance, of a separate Greek–Turkish peace deal, while the other issues and the outlook of a final treaty remained stuck in early June.[241]

---

[238] "Statement made by Mr. Grew at the meeting of the First Committee on June 4, 1923, with regard to the Judicial Declaration," Grew papers, 1923.
[239] Untitled statement made on 26 May 1923, Grew papers, 1923.
[240] "Informal Talk at the Consular Dinner at the Hotel Victoria," Interlaken, 2 September 1923, 24.
[241] "Conférence de Lausanne et affaires d'Orient: Le conflit gréco-turc: La rupture est évitée," *Journal de Genève*, 27 May 1923, 10; "Conférence de Lausanne: Marasme," *Journal de Genève*, 7 June 1923, 10; Demirci, *The Lausanne Conference*, 179–191.

24 After a Long Last Mile, the Treaty

Figure 17 "In the Lausanne concert, Greece plays 'harp,'" [Lozan konserinde Yunanistan "harp" çalıyor – the word "harp" means "war" in Turkish.] "The World to Venizelos: Do not disturb the harmony!" World peace was again at stage when rupture threatened in late May 1923 because of Ankara's reparation demands from Greece. (*Akbaba*, no. 48, 21 May 1923, 1. Drawn by Ramiz)

The assassination of the Soviet delegate Vatslav Vorovsky on 10 May 1923, brought additional drama to the resumed Conference and highlighted other contemporary forces. All in all, the Conference sided with Italian Fascists and Ankara's nationalists, but sidelined Soviet communism, although conceding it a minor place in international diplomacy. The murderer was Maurice Conradi, a Russian Swiss whose grandfather had founded a chocolate factory in St. Petersburg that was nationalized by the Bolsheviks when Conradi's uncle was killed by the Red Guards. After fighting in the White Armies, Conradi moved back to Switzerland where he socialized with Russian émigrés. He took the presence of a Soviet delegation in Lausanne as an opportunity to take his revenge. The same year, the trial took place before a court in Lausanne and turned into an indictment of Bolshevism. In this sense, it was comparable to the trial of Talaat's murderer in Berlin in 1921 that had evolved into the indictment of Talaat's genocidal regime. Although accused of murder complicated by premeditation, Conradi was acquitted by the popular jury. Théodore Aubert, the defense attorney, published his plea in several languages and founded in 1924 the International Anticommunist

Entente. The Entente saw its mission accomplished when, twenty-five years later, anti-communism became an official US doctrine.[242]

France, the main investor in the late-Ottoman Empire, had to face heavy losses, and could not count on much sympathy in a zeitgeist that condemned Europe's pre-1914 capitalism. Revolutionary nationalists and communists believed in a reset of world affairs, a historic "hour zero," after Europe's Great War. The French delegation was headed by General Maurice Pellé, the former French high commissioner in Istanbul. It was weakly supported by Allies who had their own priorities and were competitors in the Levant. It wanted to reach compromises that satisfied the considerable number of French debt holders, investors, and concessionaires. Because of them, a satisfactory outcome in Lausanne on economic and financial questions – including the question of the currency of the interest payments for pre-1914 debts – carried domestic political weight for Paris. Related negotiations lasted from April to July. Britain feared the creation of "another Ruhr question at Constantinople" by Paris' insistence in matters related to the Ottoman debts. In early July, the French were isolated and had to give in.[243] At the end, French expectations were largely frustrated, especially in the long term.

The Treaty Articles 46–57 defined some conditions and principles on Ottoman debt repayment, but details were to be determined by a commission after conclusion of the Treaty; and possible disputes to be dealt with by an arbiter of the League of Nations. The commission had to include a representative of the Council of the Ottoman Public Debt. In 1928, this organization – which reminded everyone of late-Ottoman fragility and dependence, but also international cooperation, notably with CUP finance minister Cavid Bey – was converted into the Distributed Public Debt of the Former Ottoman Empire (Dette Public Répartie de l'Ancien Empire Ottoman). The Kemalist authorities obstructed it systematically, doing everything to reduce, postpone, and finally, in the late 1930s, annul debt payments. Ankara was helped to do so by its geostrategic value for Western diplomacy, while, from the late 1920s, it could refer to problems related to the global economic crisis. "Despite the signing of the [post-Lausanne] contract, the holders'

---

[242] "Le procès Conradi-Polounine à Lausanne," *Journal de Genève*, 17 November 1923, 4; Bernard Degen, "Conradi-Affäre," in *Historisches Lexikon der Schweiz (HLS)*, 2010, https://hls-dhs-dss.ch/de/articles/017335/2010-12-02; Caillat Michel, Cerutti Mauro, Fayet Jean-François, and Gajardo Jorge, "Une source inédite de l'histoire de l'anticommunisme: les archives de l'Entente internationale anticommuniste (EIA) de Théodore Aubert (1924–1950)," *Matériaux pour l'histoire de notre temps*, 73 (2004), 25–31.

[243] Demirci, *The Lausanne Conference*, 193–207, Rumbold quotation p. 204.

24 After a Long Last Mile, the Treaty

associations could only note the absence of payment by Turkey of the annual instalments due," a recent study concludes.[244] In sum, Turkey disregarded the Lausanne-based repayments, though not entirely. In contrast to Bolshevik debt rejection, in Lausanne, Turkey declared itself liable for the debts of the Ottoman predecessor state, but subsequently failed to gain the trust of international creditors.

The issue of concessions, too, was by no means solved according to the wishes of Paris and – in this case – also London. Ankara's and Washington's delegations pulled together. The Americans strove against monopolies and for their Open Door policy. They therefore discreetly, but resolutely, backed a Turkish delegation who rejected, as much as possible, the insertion of pre-1914 obligations vis-à-vis Europeans into the treaty. They largely succeeded, as important concessions and rights given in the chaotic period on the eve of the Great War were not beyond all legal doubts. Besides concessions to French companies, this also concerned a concession promised in 1914 to the predominantly British, partly German, Turkish Petroleum Company. Related open questions were finally left to bilateral talks with Ankara, while Germany had no say in Lausanne. At least, a Protocol relating to certain Concessions granted in the Ottoman Empire, signed together with the final Treaty, upheld the rights, including claim for indemnity, of a French company concessionary of the Samsun–Sivas railway.[245]

This was the Conference's last prominent crunch point. It was solved at the last negotiation meeting on 17 July 1923, when all three Commissions had to meet a last time, one after the other. Several other points had also to be finalized, including a particular sensitive one, regarding the Armenians, to which we will come back. The meeting of the Third Commission dealing with the concessions lasted until late into the night. The days before 24 July served to prepare all relevant documents.

On the afternoon of 24 July 1923, a simple ceremony started at 3 in the auditorium of the university in the Palais de Rumine (see Figure 18). Swiss Federal president Karl Scheurer invited the delegates to sign the documents. After that, in a pithy speech (see Figure 19), Scheurer insisted:

We Swiss know from experience what dangers lie in differences of race, language and creed ... but we also know that it is possible to live in peace and friendship in

---

[244] Andrea Gennai, *La Question d'Orient: La gestion multilatérale de la Dette Publique Ottomane* (University of Geneva: MA thesis, 2015), 95–98, quotation p. 98.

[245] *Treaty Series: Publication of Treaties and International Engagements registered with the Secretariat of the League of Nations.* vol. 28, 203–213. See also Joseph Grew, "Informal Talk at the Consular Dinner at the Hotel Victoria," Interlaken, 2 September 1923, 32–40; Demirci, *The Lausanne Conference*, 207–212.

Figure 18 Signing the Treaty, 24 July 1923, as seen from where (in the foreground, from right to left) Ismet (Inönü), Rıza Nur, and, probably, Reşit Saffet (Atabinen) sat. (Gaston de Jongh, Signature du Traité de Lausanne au palais de Rumine, photographie, 22 juillet 1923, coll. Musée Historique Lausanne)

spite of all these differences and to make them a source of progress and beneficial development ... from the clash of weapons the most bitter pains arise for humankind, from the clash of ideas the light arises.

Militantly democratic, his words concluded the Conference of Lausanne.[246]

The editorial in the *Neue Zürcher Zeitung*, Switzerland's leading daily, offers a glimpse of how the host country's civic and bourgeois intelligentsia received the outcome in Lausanne, the next day:

It would be daring to claim that the Peace of Lausanne has definitively settled and cleared up the "Oriental question." ... The new treaty has too many gaps

---

[246] *CLA*, vol. 5, 155–175, 259–267 and 377–392 (minutes of 17 July 1923), 525–530 (minutes of 24 July 1923). Scheurer's speech in German in *NZZ*, 25 July 1923, 2; in French in *Journal de Genève*, 25 July 1923, 2.

24 After a Long Last Mile, the Treaty

Figure 19 Karl Scheurer, president of the Swiss Confederation, speaking at the conclusion of the Lausanne Treaty, 24 July 1923. (Eugène Würgler, Signature du Traité de Lausanne au palais de Rumine, carte postale, 24 juillet 1923, coll. Musée Historique Lausanne)

and unresolved problems for that. ... In Lausanne, for the first time since the disastrous example of Versailles, no dictatorial peace was concluded. ... In sum, the Turkey created in Lausanne can enjoy the undisputed possession of the Asia Minor Peninsula. Politically, this possession includes the obligation to protect the Christian minorities living in this area, especially the Armenians, for which, unfortunately, Turkey has so far given anything but sufficient guarantees.[247]

***

Though diplomatically "shelved" in January 1923, the Armenians remained present not only in press and public memory, but also during the second half of the Conference itself. However, most delegates were anxious to henceforth avoid the word "Armenian" as it displeased the Turkish representatives. In the end, to prevent further trouble, they invoked the need for generosity vis-à-vis Ankara and appealed to the goodwill of a partner who was by no means inclined to any goodwill for the Armenians.

---

[247] *NZZ*, 25 July 1923, 1.

The return of survivors and the Anatolian possessions of Armenian-Ottoman nationals defined portentous questions that still loomed – and that Ankara feared. They loomed during and beyond the second Conference, reemerging in Interwar, particularly League, diplomacy, and with claims in US courts again in the twenty-first century. In 1923, many Armenian-Ottoman nationals or their descendants lived outside their Anatolian home country where they could not return, out of fear or because they were not permitted to do so by the authorities. Even during the Conference itself, many survivors and post-1918 returnees were compelled to leave the country. Of course, there was no longer any question, as of December 1922, of a return to an autonomous province, but only to the "new" and unitary Turkey.

Rumbold was outspoken in the 19 May meeting of the First Committee.

> The Turkish authorities are already forbidding the return of the Greeks and Armenians of Constantinople who have recently left their homeland. Moreover, these authorities consider everything that these unhappy people cannot take with them as abandoned property; thus, these people, who cannot be there because of the same authorities who do not allow them to return, are also deprived of their property.

As for the Armenians, he did of course not limit his remark to Istanbul, the place where "Greeks" (Rûm) enjoyed exclusion from the population exchange. He bluntly asked Ismet if prohibition of return cum dispossession was Ankara's policy. The other delegates backed Rumbold. But, again, they ended embracing wishful thinking. General Pellé "firmly believed that the Turkish Government, in the restoration of peace, will allow these refugees to return to their homes ... inspired by the Declaration on general amnesty." It was easy game for Ismet to give a vague response, "wanting the Conference to believe that he will act [in Ankara] in this matter in the direction of appeasement."[248]

In a Declaration of 31 May 1923, the sub-committee dealing with amnesty issues, however, left no doubt "that it could not usefully discuss the question whether certain persons who had left Turkey, in particular Armenians, should be entitled to return freely to their homeland under the general amnesty provisions."[249] When the discussion was continued in the First Committee on 4 June, Rıza Nur made Ankara's stance more concrete. The "Turkish Government, like any other Government, reserves the right to take security measures against subversive elements, revolutionaries, assassins and, in general, evil elements." He meant

---

[248] *LKT*, vol. 5, 121–122. [249] Ibid., 170.

24 After a Long Last Mile, the Treaty

Armenians in general, as did Ankara's unrelenting policy of de-Armenization since Talaat's rule. Ismet backed Nur and repeated, "Those who do not stir up trouble will be free to return to Turkey." Again, besides Rumbold's display of "astonishment and sadness," the Allies were content with "taking as a deed the words of İsmet Pasha" – though knowing that, in the end, this left an unwilling Ankara a free hand for continued ethnic cleansing and confiscation.[250]

The issue was again raised on 11 July, and a last time in the evening of 17 July, during the very last meeting. Rumbold then felt "compelled to return once more to the Declaration on general amnesty" (the Amnesty Declaration was to be added to the final Treaty) and the question of the return of hundreds of thousands of Armenian survivors, made stateless. Ismet concluded the renewed debate with a long declaration. He rejected any link between the comprehensive general amnesty and the return of refugees. Return to Turkey would be "subject to the permission of the Turkish Government, and this permission will be granted only to those who ... have not been guilty of bad behavior in the past." – What was "bad behavior" vis-à-vis brutal persecution by state authorities, still most recently experienced in Izmir in September 1922? – Permissions would be individual and exceptional, never collective. This is what Ismet made clear in his declaration. Amnesty, however, would be comprehensive, as commonly agreed also in the case of Greece.[251]

Clear (verbal) resistance came at the end only from Rumbold. Grew meanwhile contented himself with admonishing, crediting intentions, and conjuring better futures. He did so in his statement in the final meeting of the First Committee on 17 July. "The present moment ... calls for generosity, for an assuring expression which shall declare the spirit in which the Turkish Government purposes to conduct its affairs." They all would "confidently expect equally practical and constructive measures on the part of the Government of the Grand National Assembly to remove this problem [Armenian refugees, properties] from the realm of international anxiety and concern."[252] This was tantamount to conveniently outsourcing an international problem to a broker known to be dishonest on the relevant matter.

At the end, however, as part of the Treaty, the Amnesty Declaration had the quality of superordinate law. This is how André Mandelstam and other international lawyers argued with the League in favor of the Armenians. In the aftermath of Lausanne, they explicitly referred to Ismet's declaration of 17 July 1923. For them,

---

[250] Ibid., 157–158. [251] Ibid., 188–192.
[252] "First Committee Final Meeting July 17, 1923," Grew papers.

Lausanne's superordinate law, in this case the Amnesty Declaration, safeguarded both the citizenship and the Anatolian possessions of the amnestied Armenian absentees. Turkish law could not denaturalize them and declare their goods abandoned property.[253] But legal arguments proved of no use vis-à-vis a League that more and more sided with governments, not law, to avoid trouble; Turkey being a case in point in this respect (see also Part IV).

The League could not repair the damage done in Lausanne, where the Powers recognized an unambiguously exclusionary – in its early phase, exterminatory – nationalism and gave in to a pioneering policy of de-Armenization cum dispossession. The policy's exterminatory and violent phases, starting in late 1913, were completed by 1922, but not their material, cultural, and – in the wake of Ankara's judicial nationalism – legal follow-ups. The Conference thus tacitly endorsed that more than a million Anatolian Armenians and their descendants where dispossessed (from 1915 into the aftermath of Lausanne) – while, for example, Britain made Turkey renounce on the repayment for the "warships ordered in England by the Ottoman Government which were requisitioned by the British Government in 1914" (Treaty Article 58).

In retrospect, this and similar discrepancies appear almost obscene. Ankara's delegation had to make a few concessions, not on fundamental rights or any matter of democracy, but on those that referred to the oil-rich region of Mosul, the Straits, reparations, the debts, former European investments, and even minor Western interests. Economic and strategic goals by Britain and France, Turkey's new mandatory neighbors, turned out to create the most protracted conflicts during the Conference – not the fate of Anatolian natives or the refugees dying in the winter of 1922–3. Nonetheless, this urgent refugee issue had sped up the decision-making on the compulsory population transfer.

Andrew Ryan sadly remembered that "Our greatest defeat" in Lausanne was "our failure, in spite of strong efforts on Rumbold's part, to get any guarantees worthy of the name for the treatment of non-Moslem minorities." Tellingly, they succeeded however, as Ryan adds, in obtaining "a minimum of satisfaction" where Western interests were involved, that is, "the treatment of our [British] schools and other

---

[253] *Confiscation des Biens des Réfugiés Arméniens par le Gouvernement Turc*. Gilbert Gidel, Albert de Lapradelle, Louis Le Fur et André N. Mandelstam, eds. (Paris: Massis, 1929). See also, among many League files, the correspondence with the Central Committee of the Armenian Refugees, Paris (since 14 December 1925)," R1694/41/48393/37912, and a memorandum of this Committee presented in 1925 to the President of the Council of the League of Nations, R1694/41/45767/37912, all in the LNA and online at https://libraryresources.unog.ch/lontad. See also the files in DNA (Délégation Nationale Arménienne), Serie Complémentaire 5, 1922–1925, BNu.

similar [notably American] institutions."²⁵⁴ Again tellingly, Britain ratified the Treaty a year after Turkey on 6 August 1924: this was also the day when Britain confidently referred the still unsettled Mosul question to the League of Nations.²⁵⁵ National interest, but nothing of an elementary higher human level, was safeguarded in Lausanne vis-à-vis a resolute ultranationalist power. This outcome helped prepare the ground in Europe for the Shoah a decade later, ending in the Holocaust of 1941–5. The Nazi perpetrators were fervent admirers of Ankara since Lausanne.

There were no "guarantees worthy of the name." The League's petition and minority protection system was never to have a chance in post-Lausanne Turkey. It became clear, "the minorities procedure adapted for the European States does not give the desired result when applied to Turkey," the League wrote in 1927. Moreover, the small remainders of non-Muslim minorities were put under pressure not to petition Geneva.²⁵⁶ It took eight decades until relevant Armenian experiences could more openly come to the fore in the post-genocidal country, and that grandchildren of (forcibly) Islamized Armenian girls found the courage and public opportunity to speak out on their real family history.²⁵⁷ It took about the same length of time to concede to the Armenian experience a place in academic and public history in the West. Lausanne indeed helped silence almost all things Armenian. It inspired Adolf Hitler to aggressively shout "Who still speaks of the Armenians today?" in order to deprive his assembled generals of any moral scruples in their upcoming onslaught on Poland in September 1939.²⁵⁸

---

²⁵⁴ Ryan, *The Last of the Dragomans*, 193.
²⁵⁵ Demirci, *The Lausanne Conference*, 214.
²⁵⁶ Minority Commission Director Colban, 1 May 1927, to Secretary-General Drummond, quoted in Martin Scheuermann, *Minderheitenschutz contra Konfliktverhütung?* (Marburg: Herder-Inst., 2000), 367. See also Part IV.
²⁵⁷ *Anneannem*.
²⁵⁸ Hitler's 22 August 1939 Obersalzberg speech before invasion into Polen. There has been protracted scholarly debate on the authenticity of this quote since the Nuremberg trials (i.e. of the so-called L-3 document of the minutes from which it is taken, a document transmitted by the journalist Louis Lochner). Like most current experts, I do not follow the assessment of conservative German historians in the second half of the twentieth century who well admitted this document to origin from high German officers, but believed it to be a propaganda version by Hitler's adversaries for foreign use, because of the document's particularly harsh language. This argumentation is unconvincing, not only regarding the immediate context of the speech, but also because the assessment hails from a time when scholarship knew little about early Nazi identification with Ankara and a very lively Nazi reception of Turkish nationalism, Lausanne, and the Armenian experience. During the second half of the twentieth century, the Armenian genocide was denied or almost entirely silenced in German academic and public history. See also Richard Albrecht, "'Wer redet heute noch von der Vernichtung der Armenier?':

25 The US Lausanne Treaty: A Paradigm Shift in the Middle East

US diplomacy was eager not to miss the post-Ottoman train, as assembled at Lausanne from spring 1923. The seeds for post-Lausanne American–Turkish friendship and a related official vocabulary of political appreciation, optimism, and euphemism were arguably sown in those months. During the Lausanne Conference, the USA turned from a century of prevailing missionary, educational, developmental, and humanitarian engagement to more governmental, economic, and finally military footprints in the Middle East. Humanitarianism continued, but was more staged and put in the spotlight as a sideshow to other main objectives, no longer as part of an overall mission, ideal, and commitment.

The vocabulary of political friendship and economic opportunities replaced power-critical Protestant utopias for the Levant. American and internationalist missionaries had spread them since the early nineteenth century through schools, colleges, the press, and organizations all over the late-Ottoman Empire. Their network of institutions was largely owned by the Boston-based American Board of Commissioners for Foreign Missions (ABCFM). Modern Protestant utopias longed for a Levant-centered republic of Jesus (a democratic version of the biblical "kingdom of God") on Earth, to be built up by faith, "moral force," democratic tenets, and modern education according to best (secular) Western standards. Ottoman Armenians played a central role, because they proved most open to the opportunities offered by the new missionary education and institutions since mid-nineteenth century.[259]

Democracy, collaboration, and federation, and, after 1918, a Near Eastern Federation under the League of Nations, marked the political thought of Protestant internationalism that rejected exclusionary nationalisms. The ABCFM strongly supported the League and US membership. The Introduction and Chapter 11 have mentioned missionaries involved in Turkey and at the Paris Peace Conferences. Present in Lausanne during the first half of the Conference was James Barton, the leading ABCFM secretary, a former missionary in Ottoman Turkey. How could Barton stomach the paradigm shift of 1923? Besides leading a nongovernmental organization with global outreach, he had been engaged in publicly documenting the destruction of the Armenians during the Great War and in building up the Near East Relief, the hitherto

---

Adolf Hitlers Geheimrede am 22. August 1939: Das historische L-3-Dokument," *Zeitschrift für Genozidforschung*, 9.1 (2008), 93–131.

[259] Kieser, *Nearest East*, 15–115; Michael B. Oren, *Power, Faith, and Fantasy: America in the Middle East 1776 to the Present* (New York: W. W. Norton, 2007), 101–502.

biggest humanitarian organization rooted in an organized missionary response to genocide in September 1915.[260]

The shift of 1923 had not only far-reaching practical, but also theological consequences, as it meant the abandonment of a century of basically optimistic Protestant post-millenarism. It also meant the destabilization of the assertive democratic liberalism that these internationalist missionaries or college teachers had advocated in education and politics. It left the vast field of eschatology almost entirely to evangelical pre-millenarism; and practical work in the Levant to well-paid, unpolitical temporary employees of humanitarian organizations. For efficient and rapid fundraising, these now more than ever put their work on stage, making ample use of the new cinematic means.[261]

When the project of an Armenian home, which the ABCFM supported, proved to be a chimera in January 1923, Barton stated in a letter to Boston that the ABCFM had to restart "from the established facts and consider what can be done to make the most of an almost intolerable situation. There can be no advantage in reviewing the past. We must face forward and proceed." He knew the situation on the ground and could therefore "not advise any Armenian to return or to stay in Turkey."[262] A success-oriented pragmatist, Barton sought to adapt to the new situation and to maintain the ABCFM's considerable pre-1914 investments in Turkey. Benefitting from them, he now intended to make a Gospel-inspired (not Gospel-explicit) impact among Turks. In a painful process, the ABCFM institutions thus accommodated to Kemalist Turkey. Not everybody agreed. In its January meeting in 1923, an ABCFM meeting in Istanbul drew up a "statement of attitude sternly condemning the massacres and horrors of the past, and giving repentance as the one hope for a better day in Turkey." Although aware that "such a stern rebuke of the actions of the government would

---

[260] James L. Barton, *Story of Near East Relief (1915–1930)* (New York: Macmillan, 1930). For a new exploration of contemporary humanitarianism in general, see Davide Rodogno (2021). *Night on Earth: A History of International Humanitarianism in the Near East, 1918–1930* (Cambridge: Cambridge University Press, 2021), on the Near East Relief in particular, 72–105.

[261] This is notably true also of the time-honored Red Cross. See Lukas Straumann, *L'humanitaire mis en scene: La cinématographie de CICR des années 1920*, internal CICR study (Geneva: CICR, 2000); Enrico Natale, et al. *Humanitaire et Cinéma : Films CICR des Années 1920 = Humanitarian Action and Cinema: ICRC Films in the 1920s* (Genève: CICR, 2005, DVD and booklet). For a fine exploration of the Robert College in Istanbul in the early Republic of Turkey, see Erik Sjöberg, *Internationalism and the New Turkey: American Peace Education in the Kemalist Republic, 1923–1933* (Cham: Springer, 2022). On pre-millenarism (premillennialism) and post-millenarism (postmillennialism), see Kieser, *Nearest East*, 8–12, 63–100.

[262] Barton to ABCFM, Boston, 20 and 21 January 1923, quoted in Kaley M. Carpenter, *A Worldly Errand: James L. Barton's American Mission to the Near East* (Princeton: Theological PhD Dissertation, 2009), 370–371.

probably result in the summary closing up of all our work," some members submitted a motion to present the statement to the Ankara authorities, regardless of results. But the motion was voted down.[263]

Nothing could hinder the 1923 paradigm shift toward almost pure US interest politics. It is true that the failure of the Chester project seems to suggest that the "time of effective alliance between the State Department and American businessmen was not yet at hand." But soon after it was. Grew's embrace of a Kemalist future in spring 1923 prepared it.[264] "The United States and Turkey had much in common. We ourselves had struggled for our newly won independence and we sympathized with Turkey in her present national aspirations. We had our George Washington: Turkey had her Mustapha Kemal," Grew told Ismet, back in Lausanne, in late April 1923.[265] In 1939, Ankara printed stamps that united the flags and main icons – Atatürk, Inönü, Washington, Franklin Roosevelt – of both countries.

As early as 26 April 1923, Grew and Ismet addressed the Chester concession and the plan of a Turkish–American treaty in a "conversation which was cordial throughout." Grew was from then seen as pro-Turk by the Allies in Lausanne, as Admiral Bristol had been during the first half of the Conference. In critical situations during the second half, Ismet sought Grew's advice and support. In particular, the Turkish interest in getting rid of pre-1914 obligations and the US policy of an economically "Open Door" in the Middle East overlapped, thus fostering backdoor cooperation during the relevant negotiations.[266]

What impressed Grew and many diplomats after him, was that – though not democratic, at times even brutal, and clearly anti-minority – "Turks were logical and frank in their methods. They knew at the start what they wanted."[267] The Allies, Americans included, knew less clearly what they wanted. This offered scope of action for Ankara and gave way to terminological ambivalences. Inauspicious ambivalences came to the fore with the emerging new course of US diplomacy with Ankara, in line with a growing personal sympathy between Grew and Ismet. In its wake, the term "democracy" was repetitiously used in relation to "new Turkey" and got entirely blurred. "Democracy" applied by no objective assessment to really existing Kemalism, be it in 1923 or ten or twenty years

---

[263] Riggs, *A.B.C.F.M. History 1910–1942: Section on the Turkey Missions*, chap. 4, 20–21, Ms. Hist. 31, ABC, Cambridge: Houghton Library, Boston.
[264] John A. DeNovo, "A Railroad for Turkey: The Chester Project, 1908–1913," *The Business History Review* 33.3 (Autumn 1959), 300–329, quotation p. 300.
[265] Grew diary, 83.
[266] Ibid., 81, 85 (26 April 1923) and, in retrospect, "Informal Talk at the Consular Dinner at the Hotel Victoria," Interlaken, 2 September 1923, 21 and 32–42.
[267] Grew, *Turbulent Era*, 603.

later. Without giving the matter proper thought, representatives of Western democracies adopted vocabulary that Ankara's delegation implanted in Lausanne.

On 16 December 1922, Rıza Nur was the first to explicitly promise "the establishment of an entirely democratic regime" in Turkey. He did so in a meeting of the sub-commission on minorities to argue against any special rights for minorities.[268] In a similar meeting two days later, he boldly declared, "Turkey has made a great revolution, pronounced the separation of the Caliphate and the State and put an end to the theocratic monarchy in its country; by doing so, Turkey has become a modern and secular State in the full sense of the word, and, as a consequence, it has definitively separated religion and State." Thus, well before the abolition of the caliphate and the introduction of the Swiss Civil Code, Ankara's representative claimed the quality of "a modern and secular State in the full sense of the word," that is, a state that democratically separated religion and politics, offering free space to both. "State protection [of minorities] would be contrary to the principle of secularism [laïcité] which the new democratic Turkish Government has accepted," Nur argued, making a comparison with France.[269]

The reality of the upcoming (rather than already made) "great revolution" was total submission and control of religion by the state. Again and again, Ismet or Nur deliberately confused imagination and reality, using a rhetoric of hope on constitutional secular democracy to push their points at the negotiation table. "Turkey intends that her future acts shall speak even louder than her words," Ismet boldly trumpeted, when Grew emphasized the need of vested minority rights in the separate Turkish–American treaty-to-be. Ismet played this need down and Grew gave in at last.[270] Since the Conference of Lausanne, the claim of secular democracy established in Ankara has wafted through Western public diplomacy.

Ankara's delegates promised legal institutions according to Western standards, while de-emphasizing Islam and jihadism, both in Turkey's recent past and future. The claimed or prospective endorsement of high standards helped appease Turkey's adversaries at the negotiating table and contributed in particular to toning down international safeguards for minority rights and legal rights of foreigners. In 1925, the claim of European modernity and conformity became Ankara's main argument to make minorities renounce on their autonomous civil law rights enshrined in the Treaty. The mortgage taken in Lausanne led Ankara to introduce the Swiss Code of Obligations and Civil Code in 1926 – the

---

[268] *LCP*, 322 and 333. For the claim of democratic futures, see also 335 and 348.
[269] *CLA*, vol. 1, 451.   [270] Grew, *Turbulent Era*, 589.

backbone of Kemalism's assertive secularism. The ambitious timing and radical contents of reforms after the Conference, therefore, were conditioned by the diplomatic-discursive matrix at Lausanne. But, the Kemalist policy had nothing to do with building up a democracy.

When, in early August 1923, Grew was talking about recent changes in Turkey's "system of Government and in her political ideas," he concluded "it seems fitting that these changes, which consist essentially in the adaptation and working out of ideals and principles of democracy, should furnish the occasion and the fundamental reason for the conclusion of treaties with the United States."[271] In reality, the recent changes from April 1922, as we will see in Part IV, strengthened oligarchy and one-man rule. A rhetoric of appreciation and vague prospects prevailed. This stood in contrast to a sober and modest language that faced facts, findings, and the unequivocal recent record of ultranationalism. For decades, self-interested American representatives euphemistically described post-Lausanne Turkey as an existing democracy on the path to further development.

***

This spirit marked the immediate aftermath of 24 July 1923, when Grew hastened to finalize the separate bilateral treaty, fearing an early return of Ismet to Ankara. Readers should note that the US delegation had been invited as observers and discussants to Lausanne, but not as a contracting party, because the USA had not entered war against Turkey. Therefore, Grew did not sign the Treaty of Lausanne on 24 July 1923. US diplomacy, however, identified with this Treaty.

Negotiations with Ankara's delegation for a separate but analogous treaty had begun in April 1923, but took longer than expected. Unsurprisingly, Armenian- and ABCFM-related issues – to which the American public was particularly sensitive – like naturalization and property claims as well as a solid declaration on minority and foreigners' rights were onerous again. Grew's team relented on these points and signed a bilateral Treaty of Amity and Commerce, analogous to the Lausanne Treaty, on 6 August 1923 (see Figure 20). This is the American Turkish Lausanne Treaty that Washington and the American world of business highly welcomed. Barton, too, backed it and even publicly lobbied for Washington in protracted efforts to successfully ratify it by the Senate. Despite flaws in the Treaty, he now saw recognition of Kemalist Turkey in the interest of both the ABCFM and US trade.[272]

---

[271] Ibid., 600. [272] Carpenter, *A Worldly Errand*, 372–380.

25 The US Lausanne Treaty

Figure 20 Reşit Saffet (Atabinen), Ismet (İnönü), Joseph Grew, and Rıza Nur in a photo taken in Lausanne in early August 1923. (Bibliothèque de Genève)

The same day, 6 August 1923, Grew wrote to Secretary of State Hughes that the outcome was

far from what I should have wished to have it. It represents a considerably greater number of concessions on our part to meet the Turkish point of view than concessions on their part to meet ours. Among other concessions we have given up the articles on naturalization and claims, we have failed to obtain the desired modifications in the Judicial Declaration and ... any provision whatever with regard to minorities. ... Our obtaining most favored nation treatment ... was perhaps the most important principle gained.[273]

In Europe, the national parliaments rapidly ratified the Treaty, and even the Soviet Union ratified the Treaty's Straits Convention that it had signed. In a significant, though ultimately symbolic, difference to the signatories of the Lausanne Treaty in Europe, in 1927, the US Senate rejected the long-delayed ratification of the US–Turkish Lausanne Treaty: the opposition by the population, lobbying groups,

[273] Grew, *Turbulent Era*, 601.

humanitarian NGOs, and the press in the name of Anatolia's disfranchised Christians was too strong. It was finally an exchange of notes that normalized Turkish–American relations. In 1917–27 official relations had been interrupted, although Admiral Bristol remained a semi-official representative of the USA during most of this time. However, even though the deed itself was not ratified, the contents of the Lausanne Treaty and the preceding negotiations proved a paradigm shift for US policy in the Middle East.

Grew was appointed the first US Ambassador in Ankara in 1927. He had continued to serve as US ambassador in Bern, before he was promoted under-secretary of state in Washington, in 1924.[274] In Ankara, he negotiated and signed a Treaty of Commerce and Navigation in 1929. A Treaty of Establishment and Sojourn (1931), a claims settlement on Turkish violations of American persons and property 1914–22 (1934), and an extradition agreement (1934) followed.[275] However, post-Lausanne US diplomacy, too, failed to claim the property of naturalized US citizens which – despite being US citizens – the Republic of Turkey had expropriated, because they were ex-Ottoman Christians. No consensus was found on the nationality issue either. This again concerned expropriated ex-Ottoman Christians, above all Armenians, who had acquired US citizenship, but were not permitted to return to Turkey (and claim their properties), or had no realistic opportunity to do so.

Race and religion defined politics, making whole groups scapegoats. It was about having "fully liquidated a past which [they] all wanted to consider finished and buried," as the second delegate of the negotiation team at the US embassy in Ankara put it. Bowing at last to the Turkish prejudice against Armenians, Washington accepted a fundamental discrimination among US citizens. Therefore, it annulled rights of Armenian Americans that other US citizens or organizations retained, in this case those – like the ABCFM – which had suffered damages or lost properties during Turkey's Great War. These only benefitted from the 1934 property settlement.[276] Figures like Chester, Bristol, Grew, and – to a lesser degree – Barton, stand

---

[274] As the chairman of the foreign service personnel board, managed to exclude African Americans from promotion. See Michael Krenn, *Black Diplomacy: African Americans and the State Department, 1945–69* (New York: Routledge, 2015), 45.

[275] John A. DeNovo, *American Interests and Policies in the Middle East: 1900–1939* (Minneapolis: University of Minnesota press, 1963), 236–240; Armaoğlu, *Belgelerle Türk-Amerikan münasebetleri*, 110–116.

[276] Juliet Davis, "The New World and the 'New Turks': The American-Turkish Claims Commission and Armenian-Americans' Contested Citizenship in the Interwar Period," *Journal of Genocide Research*, 19.3 (2017), 299–317, quotation p. 307; Kemal Kirişci, "National Identity, Asylum and Immigration: The EU as a Vehicle of Post-National Transformation in Turkey," in Kieser, Hans-Lukas (ed.), *Turkey beyond Nationalism* (London: I. B. Tauris, 2006), 184.

for the turnaround in which the USA began to throw in its lot with the winners of the political game in Asia Minor. They wanted America to gain economic and other advantages in its competition with the European powers. During the same years, oil began to play a central role for US Middle East diplomacy, and oil companies penetrated into post-Ottoman territories like Iraq and Saudi Arabia. From diplomacy, they demanded an "open door," which became "now the cornerstone of American policy in the Middle East."[277] Fossil fuel began to heavily damage ecology and political relations.

Barton was an active part of the paradigm shift. Still, he felt deep regret with the outcome in Lausanne when he wrote his "Autobiographical Notes" a decade later, shortly before his death. Looking back at the Conference, he recognized once more the gaping chasm between a universal moral judgment and the time-bound, but fatal, assessment by contemporary peers. The latter's endorsement of Ankara's exclusionary nationalism made Anatolia's Armenians definitively "wanderers upon the face of the earth with no home" in their homeland.

In spite of the most sincere endeavors of our representatives, every moral issue was lost. The Turks had won ... the right to expel their non Christian citizens, to abrogate treaty agreements entered into it by the preceding government, to eliminate forever any future discussion of the so-called Armenian question. ... I contended that the Turkish case was officially closed. That it had been tried in a court of its peers and ... no indictments were established against it. ... The moral judgment of the world had spoken with no uncertain voice, but that voice had been drowned in the greed for gain and in the clamorous rivalries of European powers and the insistent demand at home that American shall make no sacrifice for the moral settlement of eternal wrongs in the Near East. We must accept the conclusion of the Lausanne Conference as final. ... [T]he Armenians are wanderers upon the face of the earth with no home within the bounds of Turkey.[278]

---

[277] In 1928, a US consortium was able to participate with the Anglo-French Iraqi Petroleum Company that, before 1927, had been called the Turkish Petroleum Company and been a major issue in Lausanne. DeNovo, *American Interests*, 196 and 202.
[278] "Autobiographical Notes," ABC 11.4,12 (Cambridge: Houghton Library, 1936), 305–308. Quoted in Carpenter, *A Worldly Errand*, 371.

Part IV Post-Lausanne Turkey: Most Favored Dictatorship?

Part IV focuses on post-Lausanne Turkey, analyzing the rise of an internationally acclaimed "model dictatorship," a modernizing unitary nation-state after the Conference. *When Democracy Died* has emphasized the need to understand the Lausanne Treaty by considering the whole decade of transformative politics, wars and violence that preceded the Conference. It has stressed proactive planning by Turkish leaders in the context of the European and global crises of the 1910s and 1920s. It has insisted on a mutual shaping: the Conference fundamentally shaped the nascent Republic of Turkey, while the delegation from Ankara's National Assembly government marked the Lausanne Conference and defined the Allies' (i.e. the West's) new realpolitik.

Turkey's course was keenly observed in a Middle East that had had no say in Lausanne. As previously emphasized, Arab and Persian neighbors and other non-Turkish Muslims had been excluded from the Conference, although they had tried to sit at the table. Their reactions to the outcome and the domestic "Revolution" in post-Lausanne Turkey were mixed. Middle East historian Amit Bein recently summarized it thus:

> For some in the region, Mustafa Kemal's leadership and accomplishments offered useful examples for emulation in their own societies, whether in order to secure complete liberation from foreign rule or to modernize them by doing away with restrictive local customs, traditions, and institutions. For others, Kemalist Turkey set an alarming precedent for other Muslim-majority countries, whether because of its secularizing and nationalist policies, or because of its nondemocratic form of government.[1]

Analyzing the Conference and the precedents of the Conference has clarified the rationale of republican Turkey's foundation. The republic was declared after the conclusion of the Treaty, in the aftermath of the first general elections, which, significantly, were held in an atmosphere of intimidation. Henceforth the West's most-favored dictatorship, as it were, Turkey enjoyed a wide degree of international approval, even twenty-seven years before NATO membership. Support was most

---

[1] Amit Bein, *Kemalist Turkey and the Middle East: International Relations in the Interwar Period* (Cambridge: Cambridge University Press, 2017), 139.

enthusiastic by the revisionist far-right in Germany. For the Nazis, Turkey became the positive role model for effective nationalist politics, having asserted itself militarily vis-à-vis the victors of the Great War after having concluded a pact of interest with the Soviets. Apart from the temporary mandatory powers, the Republic of Turkey was now the politically and militarily predominant state in the post-Ottoman Middle East, and a middle-sized power in the global perspective.

Part IV first goes back to the Lausanne Conference interval that set the lines for single-party rule in Ankara. After that, it follows Mehmed Cavid Bey's personal trajectory in post-Lausanne Turkey. Targeted as a traitor in Lausanne because his expert opinion contradicted ultranationalist convictions, this prominent adept of the 1908 constitutional revolution remained not only sidelined, but suffered a sham trial and execution that equaled a judicial murder. No doubt, there were also constructive rudiments of the new republic. What it called the "Turkish Revolution" was a radical transformation from above, carried out by young idealistic cadres and welcomed by segments of society. A few of these innovations were Lausanne-induced, first of them the "Revolution of Law" with its new civil code. This is the topic of Chapter 28. Translated into Turkish from the Swiss original, the new civil law underpinned Kemalism's assertive secularism. It abolished the sharia in the legal core area of family law. This also contributed to more gender equality in professional life.

The dark side of the "Turkish Revolution" has to do with the antidemocratic nature of the nationalist state-building endorsed in Lausanne. Lausanne/*Lozan* is an omnipresent argument in Atatürk's vindicatory *Nutuk*, the Kemalist bible of contemporary history. Together with the post-Lausanne Turkish History Thesis, the *Nutuk* forms the religion-like historical doctrine of Kemalism. Both apogee and aporia of Kemalist weltanschauung, the speculative and extremist History Thesis owed most of its elements to a world of thought that we have already encountered with Rıza Nur, Ankara's senior diplomat in Lausanne. In a logical coincidence, Ankara pushed the History Thesis most forcefully during the 1930s, when it undertook its genocide in Dersim.

The dark side was marked by the continued ideal of a "pure" ethnonation, cleansed by supposedly functional and salutary violence. In 1926, when the Kemalist dictatorship was established, the leading nationalist journal *Türk Yurdu* celebrated: "Finally, with the foundation of the new Turkey, all [social Darwinist] knowledge and truth has shone on the points of the bayonets. The Turkish nation gave, as it should, its response with the fist, and not with arguments, to what was nonsense and sophistry. Finally, we are by ourselves." Baha Said, the author of these words, was an influential hero of the Turkish War of Independence, a counselor at the Lausanne Conference, and a former collaborator of Talaat Pasha and Ziya Gökalp in Istanbul's CUP headquarters. For him, "the eyes" the nation "wanted to see happy, were happy, the bodies it wanted to be destroyed, were destroyed." Thus "the Hearth [the Turkish nation-state] lit up. ... Finally, we are by ourselves."[2] The last Chapter of this Part, finally, will deal with the abolition of the caliphate eight months after, and in correlation to, the Conference.

26 Establishing "Peace" and Dictatorship in Republican Turkey

Ismet was left without the authorization by Rauf (Orbay), the head of government, to sign the Treaty after the last meeting of 17 July 1923. This was a protest against Ismet and Mustafa Kemal, the ultimate decision makers, resulting from Rauf's critical experiences in Ankara during the Lausanne Conference. Feeling politically sidelined, Rauf retired from politics and left the upcoming capital. Gazi Kemal, the supreme leader, not the head of the Assembly's cabinet, sent a telegraph that allowed the delegation to sign on 24 July.[3] As described in Chapter 25, Ismet and a core of the delegation remained in Switzerland for further talks on the treaty with the USA. They returned only toward mid-August.

According to the Treaty's Protocol relating to the Evacuation of the Turkish territory occupied by the British, French, and Italian Forces, the ratification of the Treaty in Ankara had to precede the departure of European troops. This was a strong incentive to ratify as soon as possible. After unfree elections in June–July 1923, the Assembly was brought into line, though not yet entirely. After the opening on 13 August and subsequent debates, several deputies rejected on the Treaty in the voting, among them, interestingly, also the delegation members Şükrü (Kaya) and Yahya Kemal (Beyatlı).[4]

Kemal's long inaugural speech at the reopening of the Assembly on 13 August 1923 enabled him to summarize his achievements. "Indeed, our four-year struggle for independence has resulted in a peace worthy of the glory of our nation." His later *Nutuk* took up several phrases and

---

[2] Baha Sait, "Türkiye'de Alevi Zümreleri," *Türk Yurdu*, September 1926 (new ed.: Ankara: Tutibay, 1998, vol. 11), 105. See also Markus Dressler, *Writing Religion: The Making of Turkish Alevi İslam* (New York: Oxford University Press, 2013), 126–133.

[3] Demirci, *The Lausanne Conference*, 212–213.

[4] Ahmet Demirel, *Birinci Meclis'te Muhalefet: İkinci Grup* (Istanbul: Iletisim, 1994), 511–531; Tayfun Mater, "Bugünden bakınca Lozan ve İsmet Paşa," www.bianet.org, 2020. See also Nurullah Ardıç, *Islam and the Politics of Secularism: The Caliphate and Middle Eastern Modernization in the Early 20th Century* (London: Routledge, 2012), 294.

26 Establishing "Peace" and Dictatorship

historical arguments of his August 1923 speech, for example, "the accounts settled in these peace negotiations were not the legacy of four years, but of a four-hundred-year period." As in the impressive number of speeches given all over the country during the Lausanne Conference, he pulled out all rhetorical stops before the reunited Assembly, including religious, ideological, and historical ones.

> The new Turkish State is the manifestation and realization in this country of that great and mighty idea [of revolutionary liberation] that dominates the world. Born out of the social and political necessities of the world and the result of thousands of years of Turkish history, our state possesses all the qualities and conditions of continuity and stability. I pray to God Almighty that your Assembly will be successful in ensuring the happy development of these conditions.[5]

Tevfik Rüştü (Aras), the rapporteur of the foreign affairs committee, praised the Treaty as a historic outcome and asked for rapid ratification. For him, "the most important of our national achievements" was the abolition of the capitulations (Article 28). They were

> incompatible with our independence and dignity. . . . This article is a great victory that demonstrates that the blood shed by our nation for the sake of independence and all the hardships and sufferings it has endured have resulted in a positive and beneficial outcome . . . . It will perpetuate the memory of the sacrifices of our heroes and of our brothers fallen on the field of honor.

Aras understood the "blood" successfully "shed by our nation" as the real fundament of the Lausanne settlement. At the end of his speech, he clarified that, for him, "peace" meant Turkish national unity and strength. "This treaty is the beginning of our peace. Peace will be established and consolidated only through the good preservation and development of our national unity and power, which have brought it [the Treaty] about."[6]

***

Gazi Kemal's looming dictatorship required compromising and appeasing Western powers in order to safely establish itself. Lausanne's dealmakers agreed not to bother each other in their spheres of rule and interest, and to maximize common benefits. From this mutual need resulted what this study calls the enduring Lausanne deal between ageing imperialists; that is, Europe's Middle Eastern mandate-holders, and late-Ottoman national-imperial cadres reorganized in Ankara. Claiming anti-imperialist liberation, these cadres in Lausanne asserted their ultranationalist notion of

---

[5] "İkinci dönemi açarken," 13 August 1923, *Atatürk'ün Söylev ve Demeçleri*, vol. 1, 330, 335.
[6] Tevfik Rüştü Aras, "Lozan Muahadesinin tasdikı hakkında Türkiye Büyük Millet Meclisi Hariciye Encümeninin Ağustos 1923 tarihli esbabı mucibe lâyihası," in Aras, *Lozanın izlerinde* (Istanbul: Akşam, 1935), 3 and 13.

sovereignty. More than ever, henceforth a political vocabulary of civilizational progress prevailed. "The successes we have achieved so far have only paved the way towards progress and civilization.... The duty of us and our descendants is to advance on this path without hesitation," the supreme leader emphasized in his August 1923 speech.[7] Before long, his political practice within the coordinates of Lausanne led to a dictatorial party-state.

The outcome in Lausanne was, as we have recognized, a deal on the back of millions of indigenous victims and scapegoats – abandoned, disfranchised Armenian and other Christians in the first place. The deal sacrificed not only the project of a plural society with intact justice, minority rights, and penal prosecution for crimes against humanity, but also democracy generally. Ankara's National Assembly had started in 1920 on the agreement to fight against the Paris-Geneva peace and against indigenous groups in Anatolia that it considered foreign agents. By 1921, this had taken the main form of a Greek–Turkish war in which many domestic non-Muslims stood on the Greek (i.e. Allied) side. From 1921, Mustafa Kemal had secured considerable personal power by insisting that the power of the National Assembly, which he controlled, was absolute, thus consistently rejecting any checks and balances. He also insisted on remaining commander-in-chief, to control the army and assert the army's support. He identified himself with the Assembly, which, in turn, represented the nation. The nation's absolute sovereignty was his own sovereign power.

In critical situations, the upcoming supreme leader applied (or threatened) violence, as in the case of the abolition of the sultanate before the Lausanne Conference. That moment of decision in the Assembly was typical (i.e. entirely antidemocratic), according to his own, doctrine-like recollection in the *Nutuk*. After he had set forth the idea on the separation of sultanate and caliphate, he presented the deputies with a fait accompli: "If those assembled here, the parliament and everybody see the matter in its natural light [i.e. as presented by the speaker], in my opinion we shall all agree. Otherwise, again the truth will properly come to the fore. But probably some heads will be cut off." Gazi Kemal "naturally" identified with violent ways of seizing power, believing these to be scientifically proven necessities. "Sovereignty and sultanate are not given to anyone by anyone, through negotiation, through discussion. Here is a scientific constraint. Sovereignty and sultanate are taken by force, strength and compulsion."[8] Against such a background and mental world, which seamlessly joined Talaat's and sultanic methods, democracy was not the

---

[7] "İkinci dönemi açarken," 13 August 1923, *Atatürk'ün Söylev ve Demeçleri*, vol. 1, 336.
[8] Atatürk, *Nutuk*, 459. See also Mango, *Atatürk*, 332–333 and 363–364.

only thing that had no chance in the bourgeoning new state by 1922–3. Finding common ground and trust for honest compromises proved very difficult during peace-making in Lausanne as well.

The National Pact left room for conflicting, including maximalist, interpretations. It was by no means a democratic social contract. From 1920, war, armed resistance, and enemy images had been a far stronger common denominator than the project of Anatolia's reconstruction and the labor of negotiated constitutional consensus. Suspicion of European plots and insufficient steadfastness by Turkish delegates were omnipresent in the press and in and around the National Assembly from the eve of the Lausanne Conference. Suspicion culminated during the Conference interval. Already in December 1922, the correspondent of the daily *Akşam* wrote from Lausanne:

> If Ismet Pasha leaves Lausanne without signing a peace, every Turk and Muslim must know without any doubt that Europe, the merchant of money and self-interest, has still in no way offered to the Turkish nation a peace that does not sacrifice its future or sully its honor and betray the sanctified memory of the martyrs [*şehitler*] that we gave during the last three years.

In tune with predominant nationalist rhetoric, Sadak thus preemptively put any possible blame on Europe.[9] Many feared to lose the caliphate for good or to see it even more reduced after the Conference. They considered it unacceptable to compromise on Mosul, Iskenderun, Thrace, and several Aegean islands, claiming them as part of the Turkish motherland.

Alarmist and rejectionist voices came to the fore in the discussions of the draft treaty in the National Assembly during the Conference interval.[10] Members of the then so-called Second Group, to which Nur was close, stood at the forefront of fear and critique, among them Ali Şükrü, Atatürk's adversary in the Assembly, a gifted orator. Their accusations included statements like "They [Ankara's delegation] sell Mosul"; "We have to take back by bayonet the places ... from Basra [Iraq] to Shkodër [Albania]"; "They [the Europeans] want to erase the caliphate and the caliphate's impact on the Islamic world"; "With this document, ... we lose the religious principles ..., we accept policies informed by the Christians ..., we put Turkey's future in danger and make it materially weak. ... May God keep me off from permitting such an agreement"; "Have we been cheated?"[11]

---

[9] Necmeddin Sadık, "Lozan Mektupları: 27–28 Kanûn-i Evvel 1922," in *Lozan Mektupları*, 197–198.
[10] On the first Assembly and its end in July 1923, see Demirel, *Birinci Meclis'te Muhalefet*, 483–605.
[11] *TBBM Gizli Celse Zabıtları* (Türkiye İş Bankası, 1985), vol. 3, 1320–1323 (27 February 1923); *Açık ve Gizli Oturumlarda Lozan Tartışmaları: TBMM'de Lozan Müzakereleri Tutanakları*, Taha Akyol and Sefa Kaplan (eds.) (Istanbul: Dogan Kitap,

The Kemalists wanted to secure safe futures in power; hence they were ready to compromise internationally and nationally. During the Conference interval, both they and the Allies feared that hardliners would take the lead in the National Assembly and obstruct the road toward the treaty. During the turbulent interval, Gazi Kemal and his loyal entourage therefore set the course toward authoritarian oligarchy in the name of peace, national sovereignty, and republican renewal. British diplomacy welcomed these steps aimed at crushing the opposition. From communist Mustafa Suphi and his comrades (1921) to oppositional deputy Ali Şükrü (1923) and prominent dissenter Mehmed Cavid (1926), Gazi Mustafa Kemal did not refrain from having adversaries and dissenters murdered, be it by hitmen like Topal Osman or by trumped-up trials. Sure enough, he accepted that the road to supreme power passed via elections, even if unfree and manipulated, and that he had to mobilize the people, soldiers, and local notables in his favor.[12]

Renewed military conflict or domestic conflagrations were possible in 1923. Risky tensions arose as far back as 6 February, when an ultimatum by the National Assembly demanded that all foreign warships bigger than 1,000 tons had to leave the harbor of Izmir (the so-called Izmir Incident). In order to appease hardliners – among them militarists close to Mustafa Kemal, like field marshal Fevzi Çakmak – London partially accommodated Ankara's demands in late February. In a turn of tides due to the Lausanne Conference, Britain meanwhile enjoyed the prestige of a friendly power with Turkish nationalists even if the Mosul question still loomed large, whereas France and Italy were accused of wanting to enslave Turkey economically and financially, according to Ankara's reading of the Allied treaty proposal in February 1923.[13]

Gazi Kemal aspired to much more than being a primus inter pares. Via control of the National Assembly by an elitist oligarchy, he sought supreme power, not democracy. As Ankara identified with the cadres and legacy of the CUP party-state, democracy became, from the beginning, a utopian no-go option for Kemalist Turkey. Ankara held to the spoils of genocide in Anatolia together with what it claimed was the "Defense of National [Muslim] Rights in Anatolia and Rumelia" (Anadolu ve Rumeli Müdâfaa-i Hukuk) since the 1919 Sivas congress. Overwhelmingly led by loyal collaborators, the organization of this name (Anadolu ve Rumeli Müdâfaa-i Hukuk Cemiyeti) underpinned Gazi

---

2014), 576, 583, 586, 613. See also Nurullah Ardıç, "Abolition of the Caliphate," in Ardıç, *Islam and the Politics of Secularism: The Caliphate and Middle Eastern Modernization in the Early 20th Century* (London: Routledge, 2012), 241–309.

[12] Mango, *Atatürk*, 381–384; Demirci, *Lausanne*, 154.

[13] Demirci, *Lausanne*, 139–147.

Kemal's power, and its handpicked members filled the ranks of the National Assembly from 1920. In 1923, it became his party and the new republic's unique party, now named Republican People's Party (Cumhuriyet Halk Fırkası/ Partisi, CHP). Mustafa Kemal was the pivotal figure of the transition of power from CUP Istanbul to CHP Ankara. He wanted supreme power in an Anatolia that he – an immigrant from Salonica – had adopted as his country and field of commitment. Anatolia's Muslims served him as his "ego-nation" or "self-nation."[14] A successful political leader and commander-in chief, he was highly popular among them by 1922–3.

Might underpinned Gazi Kemal's claim to sole power. He knew himself solidly backed by the army. Nonetheless, the relationship with the still-mobilized army needed careful attention by 1923. In contrast to superficial Western portraits of an (allegedly) serene elderly statesman Atatürk, the young Gazi Kemal well knew to use ringing phrases and to play the Turkist and Islamist keyboard of populism, as readers already know with his 16 March 1923 talk in Adana. When he toured the country from January to June 1923, addressing soldiers and civil audiences in many towns of western and southern Anatolia, he spread his vision of a new state underpinned by a new Popular Party (Halk Fırkası). His performance combined charisma with eloquence, and nationalist fervor and pride with self-righteous blame of others (i.e. perceived domestic and foreign foes).[15]

This is also true of his opening speech of the economic congress in Izmir, when, on 17 February 1923, he referred to the Lausanne Conference "that probably absorbs the attention of us all" and attacked "the real enemies," those who prevented a fully, politically, *and* economically sovereign Turkey. Calling for a "National Pact of Labor," he exposed the vanity of "our New Turkey" based only on military and political success. This would be the case if it continued to be only a well-protected place for foreign capital as in late-Ottoman times, without significant Muslim productivity. In the footsteps of Talaat Pasha, and hand in hand with Minister of Economy Mahmut Esat (Bozkurt), the initiator of the congress, Gazi Kemal campaigned for a national (i.e. Turkified) economy.

Gazi Kemal's talk exclusively addressed the Muslim Turks, "the founders and proper basis of the Ottoman state, the true people of this country." This ego-nation – which he identified with himself, as its aspiring supreme leader – was "resolute and brave." It no longer accepted making "any

---

[14] Hülya Adak, "National Myths and Self-Na(rra)tions: Mustafa Kemal's *Nutuk* and Halide Edib's *Memoirs* and *The Turkish Ordeal*," *South Atlantic Quarterly*, 102.2/3 (2003), 509–527.

[15] Paul Gentizon, "Lettre de Turquie: Moustapha Kemal et ses adversaires," *Gazette de Lausanne*, 3 April 1923, 1; Dermirci, *Lausanne*, 146–147.

concession in its will to full independence and national sovereignty." It was destinated to be a military, political, and economic power following the example of Japan. However, the Allied negotiators in Lausanne "have not yet understood" this fact. They have "begun to settle a bill of three hundred, four hundred years, but not yet the bill of [the last] three, four years." These outstanding years under his victorious direction had created, he claimed, a completely new situation and the prospect of a state that accomplished millennia of Turkish history by making Anatolia – allegedly proto-Turkish since times immemorial – entirely Turkish and sovereign.[16]

In spring 1923, there were still a few rival generals with political ambitions, or at least with objections against one-man-rule in Ankara. But as long as they could not unite with others, they were no match for Gazi Kemal. In order to eliminate this risk, he prompted the dissolution of the National Assembly on 1 April 1923, and prepared for general elections on 28 June. The opposition boycotted the vote of 1 April. "This decision by the [reduced] Assembly constitutes an important point in the history of our revolution. Because, by making this decision, the Assembly showed that it had admitted the illness that had afflicted it and that it had realized the anguish thus induced to the nation," the supreme leader stated in retrospect in his 1927 *Nutuk*. He perfectly mastered a political discourse that pled the good of the nation for what he wanted, claiming his perfect union with the nation. "The whole nation fully embraced the principles I had proclaimed, and it became clear that those who would show opposition to the principles and even to myself could no longer be elected as deputies by the nation."[17]

In the parliamentarian interim, the existing Assembly formally still existed, but was nonoperational, which gave Gazi Kemal and his followers free scope for action. These first general elections in Ankara-ruled Turkey took place in a climate of growing intimidation. The opposition deputy Ali Şükrü was murdered on 27 March 1923. A new "law on the intangibility of national sovereignty," reported Paul Gentizon, a Swiss journalist in Turkey, denounced all public critics of "the current regime as traitors to the country." He referred to an amendment of 29 March 1923 to the High Treason Law of 1920 (Hiyanet-i Vataniye Kanunu). This amendment made any opposition to the Grand National Assembly illegal, particularly any propaganda for a return to the sultanate. By 15 April,

---

[16] Mustafa Kemal Atatürk, "İzmir iktisat kongresini açış söylevi," in *Atatürk'ün Söylev ve Demeçleri*, vol. 2, 103–116. See also idem, "İkinci dönem açarken," in *Atatürk'ün Söylev ve Demeçleri*, vol. 1, 330–339, and Gentizon, "Lettre de Turquie: Moustapha Kemal et ses adversaires," 1.

[17] Kemal, *Nutuk*, 483–484.

when the revised High Treason Law was put in force by the Assembly, the Second Group was crushed.[18]

In light of Gentizon's own lively experience of democracy in which he had grown up, "the atmosphere of the current elections is by no means impregnated with this invigorating oxygen called liberalism," he wrote in June 1923. "Whoever acts against the thought of Angora is considered traitor and punished on the spot."[19] The law thus served as a weapon against any dissent at the eve of a "new Turkey's" first elections. It provided for an obedient Assembly in view of the ratification of the Lausanne Treaty and the subsequent declaration of the republic. As for Gentizon, he lost his democratic roots in the coming years. He ended up identifying with what he finally praised as "the Orient on the move" under Mustafa Kemal's brilliant leadership. A correspondent of mainly the French daily *Le Temps*, he changed from Turkey, where he worked from 1922 to 1928, to Rome where he manifested strong sympathies for Mussolini. In 1923, Gentizon was initially more critical than Arthur Fonjallaz, both born in the Canton of Vaud in the late nineteenth century. But finally, both added identification with Fascism and Nazism to their identification with Kemalism.[20]

Eurocentric analyses of Interwar fascism and totalitarianism have for decades taken the claim of a "new Turkey" by Ankara's delegation in Lausanne at face value, without considering the nonsimultaneity of developments; that is, the anteriority of ultranationalism, single-party rule, and genocide by Young Turks after 1913. The National Assembly (i.e. the Ankara counter-government founded in 1920) rested on this fundament – including the CUP cadres and an exclusionary Gökalpian nationalism with its essentialist religious-racial tenets. To a large extent, and despite a rhetoric of democracy in Lausanne, all these defining ingredients entered the post-1923 political project. Ankara's post-Lausanne project, in other words, is embedded in a formation of the nation-state that started in the early 1910s and that – as *When Democracy Died* suggests – well might, and should, be named proto-fascist.

---

[18] Paul Gentizon, "Lettre de Turquie: La campagne électorale," *Gazette de Lausanne*, 20 June 1923, 1; Gentizon, "Moustapha Kemal et ses adversaires"; Mango, *Atatürk*, 370–376. See also Demirci, *Lausanne*, 153–154, and Ryan, *The Last of the Dragomans*, 204.

[19] Gentizon, "Lettre de Turquie: La campagne électorale," 1.

[20] See Paul Gentizon, *Mustapha Kemal ou l'Orient an marche* (Paris: Bossard, 1929). See also Olivier Decottignies, "Un correspondant de presse en Turquie: Paul Gentizon ou l'Orient en marche," in Güneş Işıksel and Emmanuel Szurek (eds.), *Turcs et Français: Une histoire culturelle, 1860–1960* (Rennes: Presses universitaires de Rennes, 2014), 195–211.

27 Cavid's End

Cavid never developed sympathy for extreme nationalism and fascism. He was a child of the 1908 Young Turk Revolution in which the best minds combined their patriotism with strong convictions of constitutional rule. After 1918, he remained among those who believed that the work started in 1908 had not yet been completed.

In the 1910s, Cavid's constitutional ideal had become other-worldly within the CUP regime, with which he closely colluded. However, as his diary proves, time and again, he felt deep unease, but he kept loyal to Talaat Pasha, the CUP's informal head. Under Ankara's increasing power from 1920 and its growingly authoritarian, leader-centered rule from 1923, the Turkish polity again quickly descended into a partisan autocracy, as chronicled in Cavid's diary. In this case, again, his opposition remained basically unspoken and limited to a private expression of opinion in his diary and in small circles of friends, and he no longer engaged in active politics. Nevertheless, this time, dissent drew him to the gallows.

In contrast to his relation with Talaat, ties with Mustafa Kemal and his entourage in Ankara were strained and marked by mistrust. Since the early aftermath of the World War, there was of course the specter of the CUP's revival (ihya) of which Cavid wrote hopefully on several occasions in his diary, at times expecting a fusion or open cooperation of the unofficially ongoing CUP with Ankara's "organization in Anatolia."[21] In terms of cadres and main tenets, this CUP-Kemalist continuity and unity was the case right from the start of the national movement in 1919. Mustafa Kemal's "we" in many letters and statements during these years rested on the CUP, of which he even pretended to be a founder and main architect.[22]

But this self-assertive narrative served to claim the leadership of a unitary post-CUP power organization, and to establish his own emerging new single party as the only legitimate one. A late-Ottoman soldier without life outside the army, he never had experienced politics beyond a leader-led state and hierarchical environment. In other words, Kemal's problem with prominent CUP members based in Istanbul was his fear of capable rivals not entirely subdued. His exclusionary claim to power induced him to eliminate them over time. This had nothing to do with seeking more democratic ground or to morally dissociating the new state

---

[21] Cavid, *Meşrutiyet Ruznâmesi*, vol. 4, 326, 336.
[22] Ahmet Emin (Yalman), "Mustafa Kemal'in Ahmet Emin'e Verdiği Mülâkat," *Vakit*, 10 January 1922, 1, transliterated version in *Atatürk'ün Söylev ve Demeçleri*, vol. 3, 39–50. See also Cavid, *Meşrutiyet Ruznâmesi*, vol. 4, 339–340, entry of 5 February 1922.

27 Cavid's End 233

from the main tenets of the former CUP policy in Anatolia. Kemalist political style was again ruler- and party-centered; its way to treat dissent was through antidemocratic repression.

Protracted dictatorships stand for the failure of dealing with and benefitting from human diversity, capacity, and competences. The first half of the Lausanne Conference, including the following break, was arguably the critical crossroad that made Cavid appear as an enemy and traitor to Ankara's post-Lausanne establishment. In September 1923, Cavid noted, "Freedom of opinion amounts to treason for the rulers. 'If you do not think like me, you are a traitor and paid agent.'"[23] Cavid felt that what was wanted was not "efficient professionals, but subservient henchmen." He inquired among close acquaintances of Mustafa Kemal and learnt the arguments circulating against him. Besides his lack of subservience, there was the argument "that he had not adhered from the start to the national movement." He responded that this was not due to him but because at that time they rejected cooperating with him, and Talaat Pasha did not act according to his suggestions. But this explanation did not help.[24]

As already alluded, the Conference break from February to April 1923 saw a cluster of coercion, violence, and preparatory electoral manipulation along critical steps toward dictatorship in Ankara.[25] For admirers of Atatürk's genius, these were necessary acts by a strong but constructive man of unique intelligence who prepared incisive reforms. For more constitutionally and democratically minded people, including Cavid, there loomed sultanic despotism – enlightened or not – reenacted in republican garb. Inspired by Nur, who then still supported Mustafa Kemal, propaganda spread in Ankara against the moderate delegation members.[26] During these same weeks of the Conference break, several meetings of long-standing political friends took place in Cavid's flat in Istanbul. In contrast to various other critics or enemies of Ankara's leader, most participants of these meetings were reform-oriented modernists ready to support Mustafa Kemal, without however wanting to totally submit to him. After several debates in Cavid's flat, in a meeting of 8 April 1923 they agreed on a reformist and comparatively liberal vision of the new nation-state whose capital should remain Istanbul.[27] Though not published, these views competed with Mustafa Kemal's election manifesto of April 1923.[28]

As proven by his post-1924 diary, the *Notebook for Şiar*, Cavid enjoyed a mostly private life, though his political temperament lived on. He

---

[23] Cavid, *Meşrutiyet Ruznâmesi*, vol. 4, 580, entry of 10 September 1923.
[24] Ibid., 578, entry of 6 September 1923.
[25] See Chapters 28–29, and also Mango, *Atatürk*, 378–387.
[26] Cavid, *Meşrutiyet Ruznâmesi*, vol. 4, 513, entry of 17 March 1923.
[27] Ibid., vol. 4, 522–523, entry of 8 April 1923.   [28] Mango, *Atatürk*, 447.

frequented his friends and Western personalities in Istanbul. He commented on the contemporary political developments in the *Notebook* vis-à-vis his son, the representative of a future generation. "In this era, which they label democratic and republican, we experience worse days than under the most horrible and accursed [sultanic] despotism. ... I hope that in your time there will be no longer such a fake republic and false democracy."[29] In the intimacy of a dialogue with his baby, this testimony is written in an emotional, subjective, at times hyperbolic language.

> On the occasion of the Kurdish uprising [of Sheykh Said] they have started to strangle the people's tongue [free speech and press]. ... What a pity that the high and noble concept of [national] sovereignty has been perverted in our [Turkish] hands to a vile caricature. They have now opened Tribunals of Independence. The government deprives the newspapers and the associations of their rights.[30]

In Cavid's emphatic words, the voices of truth lapsed into silence. Everybody feared the politicized justice operationalized by speedy special trials. As under Sultan Abdulhamid, people were again hurrying to burn any literature or personal notes that could be used against them by the police and the travesty of justice performed by the special courts. Cavid destroyed possibly compromising letters and brought his pre-1924 diaries to a secure place. He even feared for the "mini-notebook" that he was writing for his son, but decided to take it with him "until the last minute." He urged his son to always abstain from injustice and dirty intrigues. "Truth and justice shall be your emblem [şiar]."[31]

Three years after the Conference break, a trial took place in Ankara where Cavid was the indictment's key figure (see Figure 21). The prosecutor presented Cavid as the head of a secret committee and the meetings in Cavid's flat three years earlier "as a sinister plot to undermine the new state."[32] Against any evidence, but manifestly politically motivated, the court insinuated Cavid to be the brain behind an assassination plot against Mustafa Kemal in Izmir in June 1926. Cavid was hastily hanged before midnight on 26 August 1926, the day of the verdict. The Ankara trial was a sequel to a trial in Izmir that had sentenced three men to death based on concrete evidence, and thirteen more by guilt of association or suspicion – all executed at public places in Izmir in 13 July, the day after the final verdict. According to Andrew Mango's detailed and authoritative Atatürk biography (which seems however still tangibly fascinated by the great leader), the

---

[29] Cavid, *Şiar'in Defteri*, 86, entry of 16 April 1925.
[30] Ibid., 74–75, entry of 8 March 1925.   [31] Ibid., 75–76, entry of 9 March 1925.
[32] Erik J. Zürcher, *The Unionist Factor: The Role of the Committee of Union and Progress in the Turkish National Movement 1905–1926* (Leiden: Brill, 1984), 155. See also Mango, *Atatürk*, 447–453.

27 Cavid's End

Figure 21 Cavid Bey after arrest, during the Independence Tribunal, summer 1926 (Marmara University, Taha Toros Arşivi, http://hdl.handle.net/11424/141615)

supreme leader "spent the evening following the executions in his usual manner, drinking with his [subservient] friends. The anodyne effects of alcohol did not come amiss that night."[33]

The CUP- and Soviet-inspired 1926 trials unraveled promises made in Lausanne for a law-based independent jurisdiction. Repression and annihilation as a way of dealing with intellectual and political opposition went along with a growingly authoritarian, finally totalitarian rule that emerged in the decade after the Conference. The birth conditions of republican Turkey, diplomatically underpinned in Lausanne, blocked the road toward democracy. For a turn toward democracy, the foundational doctrines and acts of those in power would have to be thoroughly studied, questioned, and overcome by scholars in synergy with those willing to implement democracy in the country. Certainly, international diplomacy, too, has to be examined as far as its history with Ankara is concerned.

---

[33] Mango, *Atatürk*, 453.

Contemporary Kemalist intellectuals argued that violence in the name of "the nation" was imperative against "the enemies of the revolution." Committing or condoning violence in the name of abstractions amounts to intellectual and legal surrender to brute force. Of this, Cavid's judicial murder is an exemplar and corner stone of the new republic. In the retrospective of Falih Rıfkı (Atay), "It is a pity that the authority of the new regime rested on the scaffolds of Izmir and Ankara. However, this definitive purge ... gave Mustafa Kemal the opportunity to complete the revolution that he had started."[34] Atay was among the journalists who had made Cavid a target of ultranationalism in Lausanne in December 1922. He remained close to Atatürk throughout the latter's presidency, spending many nights drinking with him in the presidential Çankaya mansion.

No doubt, revolutionist ultranationalism devoured its own children during the 1920s, together with many more innocents. Was there an inherent or "compensatory justice" in the execution of former CUP leaders or operatives like Dr. Nâzım, Ismail Canbolad, Kara Kemal, Nail, and Hilmi? It is true that several participants in the April 1923 meetings – like Dr. Nâzım, Ismail Canbolad, and Kara Kemal – had been deeply involved in Talaat's anti-Armenian policy. But there is no consolation or higher logic in this thought. Ex-CUP cadres like Şükrü Kaya, Tahsin Uzer, Mustafa Abdülhalik, Feyzi Pirinççizâde, Ali Cenani, and Celal Bayar, who closely collaborated with Mustafa Kemal in top positions, had been not less involved. The arguments on CUP misrule, proffered by the prosecutor in Ankara, were purely instrumental; they strike as particularly out of place in the case of Cavid who stood in the center of the court's concoction.

Given its use of dosed terror and manipulated jurisdiction, the Ankara trial was an example of post-Lausanne Turkey's justice system. In its autocratic use of courts, it pointed to developments in the twenty-first century. It can also be regarded as the final step in the pioneering making of a Western-approved Interwar dictatorship. Contemporary to Fascist Italy, Ankara's Turkey was actually ahead of the latter in crushing the opposition and building an indoctrinated party-state. Turkey demonstrated how far it was possible to go with political violence, while still being courted by the nominally liberal-democratic world. Of crucial geostrategic importance, but economically weak, Ankara lived for decades from this power-supporting interaction.

In 1926, Western observers well understood that Ankara's travesty of justice liquidated dissenters. However, having secured Mosul for mandatory Iraq by a treaty in June 1926, Britain, notably, played the game of

---

[34] Atay, *Çankaya*, 470–471.

Middle Eastern autocracy, entirely disregarding domestic human rights issues, from then on. Western diplomacy enjoyed the benefits of the pact struck in Lausanne. The press in Interwar Europe admired audacious reforms by men of action more than it pondered rule of law and democracy. Post-Lausanne Ankara thus took the road to autocracy with the West's collusion, often admiration. In Lausanne, Western powers had definitively dismantled the rudiments of a constitutional construction of the post–Great War Middle East, as based on the main principles of the Paris-Geneva Peace.

It is ironic that Nur, himself an ultranationalist luminary, put this circumstance into the following frustrated terms: "At least the capitulations, these filthy instruments, would have been good to prevent some forms of [Ismet's and Mustafa Kemal's] despotism, but they were abolished with the Treaty of Lausanne."[35] With "capitulations," in a general sense, he meant internationally imposed limitations to Turkey's jurisdiction, for whose complete abolition he had fought so hard in Lausanne. Nur chose exile after the execution of Cavid and other dissenters, because he feared for his own life. He shamed the trials as a "scandal" and a "disgrace" of the Turkish judiciary.[36] However, three years before the trials, he had been a leader of the defamation of Cavid. In his memoirs, he did not or could not join the dots.

For Ismet Pasha, Turkey's plenipotentiary in Lausanne and president after Atatürk, Cavid's "fate" just represented "the worst possibility implicit in the nature of politics" – not the need to rethink a political culture that he naively took as "natural."[37] The experience of the honest dissenter Cavid, a private citizen after Lausanne, mirrors the making of a dictatorship that had bid its goodbye to residual democratic virtues. Sovereignty won in Lausanne required oligarchy at home, in order to be maintained within the labile compromises struck at the Conference.

28 "Revolution" in a Restive and Coercive, but Courted Country

While not fully convinced that reforms according to Western standards would be "for the good of Turkey," by January 1923 the head of Ankara's delegation in Lausanne had well understood the diplomatic expediency of bold reform prospects:[38] they served the overarching goal of attaining absolute sovereignty, because sovereignty was believed to be an attribute of "civilized countries."

---

[35] Nur, *Hayat ve Hatıratım*, vol. 3, 348.   [36] Ibid., 334.
[37] Quoted in Mango, *Atatürk*, 452.   [38] Grew diary, 17 January 1923, 20–21.

Ankara's civilizationist boldness displayed during and after the Lausanne Conference, by far topped the modernizing outlook promised by representatives of Anatolia's Christian minorities three years earlier in Paris.[39] To a large extent, the Kemalist or "Turkish Revolution" in the aftermath of the Lausanne Treaty served the will to make Turkey a country of European civilization. It must not be forgotten, however, that the assimilation of "universal (Western) civilization" had already been the goal of the CUP party-state under Talaat Pasha and his ideologist Ziya Gökalp. Also defining the Kemalist understanding, Gökalp had counterbalanced the embrace of civilization with a radically nationalist affirmation of Turkishness (i.e. Turkish identity and culture).

Although the ambition of national sovereignty and civilization amounted to more than a concentration of power in the hands of the country's new ruling elite, in many respects, it got stuck on this. In Lausanne, Ankara had raised a mortgage of the rule of law that it failed to pay off, in the short- and the long term. By the time of *Nutuk*, after the mid-1920s, "democracy" was nothing more than an empty phrase. What counted was the "Turkish Revolution," the main goal after the Conference. According to then–Minister of Justice Bozkurt, "The most important task of the Turkish revolution is to eradicate the past and all ideas of the past."[40] Kemal Pasha himself quoted Bozkurt in his *Nutuk*: "The Turkish nation is waiting for this [revolution] like a sword drawn in the name of democracy."[41] Bozkurt later stated that when Atatürk reigned, the nation reigned, and there was perfect "authoritarian democracy," with the chief taking his authority from the nation.[42] Nation, revolution, and leader formed an organic whole in Bozkurt's perverted notion of "democracy."

A former president of Lausanne's Turkish Home Association, Bozkurt owed his exalted devotion of powerful leadership to Gökalp who had been the mentor of both Talaat's regime and the Turkish Home Associations. Arguably, Gökalp was also "the philosopher of the Atatürk Revolution," as states Robert Devereux, a Turcologist and one of Gökalp's leading translators.[43] Atatürk himself is said to

---

[39] Laura Robson drew attention to the arguments of ancient nationhood, racial distinctiveness, opposition to Muslim power, and commitment to modernization in the narratives of those diaspora Christians. Laura Robson, *States of Separation: Transfer, Partition, and the Making of the Modern Middle East* (Oakland: University of California Press, 2017), 155–156.

[40] *Açık Söz*, 26 Juni 1928, 1, quoted in Şaduman Halıcı, *Yeni Türkiye devleti'nin yapılanmasında Mahmut Esat Bozkurt, 1892–1943* (Ankara: Atatürk Araştırma Merkezi, 2004), 538.

[41] Mahmut Esat Bozkurt as quoted in Kemal, *Nutuk*, 588.

[42] Mahmut Esat Bozkurt, *Atatürk ihtilali* (Istanbul: Kaynak, 1995; first ed., 1940), 107.

[43] Robert Devereux, "Preface," in Ziya Gökalp, *The Principles of Turkism*, transl. R. Devereux (Leiden: Brill, 1968), x.

28 "Revolution"

have referred to Gökalp as "the father of my thoughts" – which appears plausible, even if he modified Islam's place in Turkism. Therefore, some later Kemalists attempted to construe principal differences between both.[44] Atatürk "warmed late, but powerfully up to Ziya Gökalp," writes Falih Rıfkı Atay, who became the leader's confidant in the aftermath of the Lausanne Conference.[45]

A national chorus in which the international press, diplomacy, and academia largely joined, praised the post-Lausanne reforms by the Kemalists – "the Turks' revolution" in contemporary Ankara's diction – as a great civilizational progress. Imposed from above, the reforms were radical indeed. They Westernized law, alphabet, and calendar. They suppressed Islamic references. They abolished the caliphate as well as autonomous religious institutions and schools (*tekke, mektep*). They submitted all religious and communitarian institutions to strict state control; including, notably, Sunni Islam, the majority religion, which the state henceforth administered and financed by its new Directorate of Religious Affairs. A substitute for the administration of the sheykhulislam under the Ottoman sultan-caliph and for the Ministry of Sharia and (Islamic) Foundations, this Directorate was established the same day as the caliphate was abolished. Although serving Sunni Islam, it was henceforth funded by all taxpayers. The same day, 3 March 1924, the Law on the Unification of Education completed state control by the ministry of education of all aspects of education; and the Ministry of Sharia and Foundations (Şerriye ve Evkaf Vekaleti) was abolished.

These were the key elements of the Turkish or "Atatürk Revolution" that took place in a fearful and submissive political atmosphere. The following lines are representative of a predominant Western outlook on the Kemalist reforms:

> The successful efforts of the Turks to traverse overnight ... the difficult and usually long road between a backward Oriental state and a modern Western one, exemplified most vividly in the radical remolding of the country's social fabric by what are generally called the Atatürk Reforms, have attracted ... the undisguised admiration of the West. ... it would be difficult to cite an example which involved less brute force to accomplish. ... Ataturk's regime was a benevolent one, even if a dictatorship.[46]

Written by Devereux in 1968 and typical for the twentieth century after Lausanne, this view wore both "orientalist" (in Edward Said's sense) and "occidentalist" Kemalist glasses. It was blind to the role of violence in

---

[44] Şerafettin Turan, *Atatürk'ün düşünce yapısını etkileyen olaylar, düşünürler, kitaplar* (Ankara: TTK, 1999), 18.
[45] Atay, Çankaya, 429 [46] Devereux, "Preface," ix.

Turkey's formation from 1913 and to the real needs and conditions of life in the country, particularly in the eastern part of Asia Minor. Devereux could have known better, as by then, millions of Turkey's nationals had already voted by foot. Starting in the 1950s, they sought better conditions of life by migrating within the country and increasingly abroad to Europe.

***

Less noted in the West, the post-Lausanne "Revolution" Turkified the language, public history, and virtually all place, personal, and family names. It "purified" the economy, national and international companies, and public institutions from "foreign" elements, as far as "non-Turkish" personnel (i.e. foreigners or non-Muslim Turkish nationals) and the use of languages other than Turkish were concerned. It massively infringed on minority rights enshrined in the Treaty. It continued to disfranchise and marginalize non-Muslims and non-Turks.

In this political line, after aggressively repressing "reactionary" Kurdish unrest during the fifteen years post-Treaty, it committed a final genocide against Alevi Kurds. All this cost the life of tens of thousands of Kurds during the Interwar period and displaced many hundreds of thousands more, some of them fleeing to mandatory Syria. The new borders unmade communities and decomposed formerly continuous spaces, but they also acted as a shield that prevented further persecution of dissident individuals and groups by Turkish forces.[47] Lausanne's "Signatory Powers or any other Power, a member of the Council of the League of Nation" (Lausanne Treaty Article 44) were not inclined to act in favor of those persecuted on a diplomatic level. After the Second World War and despite (or because) of Ankara's new NATO membership, Lausanne's signatory powers were even less ready to defend human and minority rights.

A central prospect promised at Lausanne's negotiation table had been an independent justice system based on best contemporary standards. In this context, the most important element was civil law as referred to in Article 42 in Part I, Section III of the Treaty. As we have seen, the Articles in this Section on the Protection of Minorites were "obligations of international concern ... placed under the guarantee of the League of Nations." Theoretically, they could "not be modified without the assent of the majority of the Council of the League of Nations." However, by introducing the translated Swiss Civil Code in 1925–6, Justice Minister Bozkurt and Ankara's whole leadership considered Treaty Article 42 to be obsolete; the minorities were compelled in 1925–6 to "voluntarily"

---

[47] Seda Altuğ, "The Turkish/Syrian Borders and Politics of Difference in Turkey and Syria (1921–1939)," in Matthieu Cimino (ed.), *Syria: Borders, Boundaries, and the State* (Cham: Springer, 2020), 47–73.

renounce on rights the Lausanne Treaty theoretically guaranteed.[48] Still, as we have seen, Ankara had to accept foreign legal advisors during transition to the promised new justice system.

Well-treated as guests, the advisors had very little say in a process they were at any rate to rubber-stamp for diplomatic convenience. University of Geneva Law Professor Georges Sauser-Hall, the number one of four foreign advisors, emphasized the lack of roots and maturation of reforms that were primarily politically motivated. While publicly displaying obligate optimism on "progress," he cautiously made clear in the 1930s that only the distant future would permit a "definitive judgment."[49] In his memoirs, Ismet Pasha was keen to emphasize that the foreign legal advisors had no say in Turkey's legal reforms. Ultimately, they served to "admit that the Turkish courts were working properly, as in all civilized countries, and that Turkish judges were competent in their duties."[50] In the "Law Revolution" (Hukuk Devrimi), particularly regarding civil law, there was no question of consent-finding together with concerned groups and League representatives on how to codify and best implement new laws, as according to the Treaty Section on minority protection. Without seriously consulting with foreign expert moderators, Bozkurt transferred and implemented entire legal codes from Switzerland, Italy, and Germany.

It would be unjust to belittle the emancipatory will, momentum, and idealistic commitment of many Kemalist lawyers.[51] The problem was that the Law Revolution obeyed an overarching concept of national – not legal – sovereignty, and thus the desires of rulers. Democracy, with its supranational legal outlook, was missing. In final analysis, this amounted to a deep-seated contempt for law in its universal, supranational dimension. Right from the immediate aftermath of the Treaty, Turkey did not respect the inviolability of fundamental law in the Treaty Articles 38 to 44. In particular, there were systematic breaches of Article 39, paragraph 4, with regard to Kurds and other groups of non-Turkish mother tongue not included in Lausanne's restricted minority definition: "No restrictions

---

[48] Reyhan Gülşen, "Türkiye'deki Musevilerin Lozan'daki Haklarından Feragatı ve Hahambaşılık Makamının Yetkilerinin Kısıtlanması," *Avrasya İncelemeleri Dergisi – Journal of Eurasian Inquiries*, 10.1 (2021), 1–38. See also Gottfried Plagemann, "Die Einführung des ZGB im Jahre 1926: Das neue ZGB als Bedingung eines sökularen und souveränen Nationalstaats," in H. Kieser, A. Meier, W. Stoffel (eds.), *Revolution islamischen Rechts: Das Schweizerische ZGB in der Türkei* (Zürich: Chronos, 2008), 21–34.

[49] Georges Sauser-Hall, *La réception des droits européens en Turquie* (Geneva: Faculté de Droit de l'Université de Genève, 1938), 38.

[50] İnönü, *Hatıraları*, 54–55.

[51] See notably Bilsel, "Medenî Kanun ve Lozan Muahedesi," 21–71. See also Ernst E. Hirsch, "Vom schweizerischen Gesetz zum türkischen Recht," *Zeitschrift für schweizerisches Recht* 95.3 (1976), 229–232.

shall be imposed on the free use by any Turkish national of any language in private intercourse, in commerce, religion, in the press, or in publications of any kind or at public meetings." Very often, Article 39, 5 has also been disregarded: "Adequate facilities shall be given to Turkish nationals of non-Turkish speech for the oral use of their own language before the Courts."[52]

As preordained by Ismet's discourse in Lausanne, Ankara's approach to recognized non-Muslim minorities in the second half of the 1920s remained "imperially biased." They enjoyed the "right to establish, manage and control at their own expense, any charitable, religious and social institutions, any schools and other establishments for instruction and education, with the right to use their own language and to exercise their own religion freely therein" (Article 40). But they had always to prove that they were grateful "good citizens" (factually subjects) in order to be tolerated.[53] Despite humbling themselves before the authorities and mainstream society, time and again they were harassed, intimidated, or even heavily discriminated against – as in the case of the 1942 Capital Tax and the related labor camps. They lived under permanent observation. In their schools, they had to employ and pay Turkish-Muslim co-directors – that is, state controllers who were a hindrance to school life itself – as well as Turkish teachers for history and language lessons. Also, they suffered professional discrimination, and were excluded from many positions and promotions, and deprived of freedom of movement because they were non-Muslims. Considered racially and religiously "non-Turkish," these nationals of Turkey did not count as equal citizens.

Ankara's policies thus made a mockery not only of the Treaty's minority rights, but also of its few own, hesitant steps toward a civic-territorial, not religious, racial, or partisan (Kemalist) conceptualization of nationhood, as notably in the Republic's 1924 constitution (Article 88).[54] On paper, there were strong international guarantees by the signatory powers for the rights of the recognized minorities (Article 44). For diplomatic reasons – in the logic of Lausanne's pact of national self-interest – the Western powers did not keep watch over these minority rights, and, given sovereign mastery, Ankara methodically breached them. Among the countries with League minority regimes, Turkey was the champion of ignoring these commitments right from the start. Since

---

[52] "Prof. Baskın Oran, 99. yılında Lozan Antlaşması'nı anlatıyor," media platform t24. https://t24.com.tr, 24 July 2022. See also Baskın Oran, *Türkiye'de azınlıklar*, 63–82.
[53] "Statement read by Ismet Pasha," *LCP*, 12 December 1922, 203–204.
[54] Oran, *Türkiye'de azınlıklar*, 83–108 and 151–162; Yeşim Bayar, "In Pursuit of Homogeneity: The Lausanne Conference, Minorities and the Turkish Nation," *Nationalities Papers*, 42:1 (2014), 108–125.

Lausanne, the League's Minority Commission was not so much concerned with enforcing the content of the treaties, but with finding those compromises that met with the least resistance by recalcitrant states. In particular, it sought to avoid onerous disputes over the admissibility of petitions and, above, all confrontations between powers; for example, between Britain and Turkey in the case of Turkish violence against Assyrians in 1926.[55]

Denaturalization and the prohibition of return were among the most efficient means to deny justice. Stripped of their citizenship, tens of thousands of Armenian survivors of the genocide simply did not count as national beneficiaries of minority and other fundamental rights. This Turkish practice constituted a lever to perpetuate the material transfer generated by the Armenian genocide and further ethnic cleansing. As we have seen (Chapters 24 and 25), this outcome was inherent in Ismet's declaration on 17 July 1923, at Lausanne, concerning amnesty and return to Anatolia. The League judged petitions by minoritarians, who were natives of Anatolia but were not considered Turkish citizens, inadmissible. At the same time, members of minorities living in Turkey were intimidated and did not want to appear disloyal by turning to Geneva. There are dozens of files and thousands of pages in the League of Nations Archive on Armenian petitions referring to the Lausanne Treaty. The petitioners' legitimate cause was hardly ever addressed. In particular, they did not get back their property. Subject to the Commission's positivist and formalist legalism, which disregarded the legitimacy of fundamental human rights, individual or collective petitions from Armenian survivors from all over the world were disregarded.[56]

***

In 1922–3, the delegation of Ankara's National Assembly craved immediate recognition as the representative of a modern, sovereign, civilized, and law-based state *in spe*. But since the founders of the republic treated law as an instrument of national power and sovereignty – not as a respected universal reference and instance beyond nationalism – they did not recognize the value of the separation of powers and the acceptance of fundamental, verifiable law.

---

[55] See, comparatively and with statistics, Scheuermann, *Minderheitenschutz*. For the Jebel Tur case, see *Minderheitenschutz*, 451.

[56] For tables on Turkey-related petitions, see Scheuermann, *Minderheitenschutz*, 449–453 and 489–494. See also Kévonian, "La pratique pétitionnaire"; Ekmekcioglu, "Republic of Paradox." As for relevant League files, see, among many, notably "Confiscation of Armenian Property by the Turkish Authorities – Correspondence with the Central Committee of the Armenian Refugees, Paris (since 14 December 1925)," R1694/41/48393/37912, LNA.

Post-Lausanne Western diplomacy remained bound by its primacy of appeasement and its hopeful and admiring, though superficial, welcome of Western legal reforms. In particular, it almost entirely ignored Kurdish unrest and uprisings, which met with continuous military repression by Ankara and, in line with previous CUP policies, forced relocations. In the case of Kurdish-Alevi Dersim with its surviving Armenians, resistance met genocide, because Kemalism destroyed what it could not assimilate to its unitary idea of state and society (see Chapter 29). Western diplomacy and the League ignored desperate letters from Kurds, Armenians, and Assyrians with cries for help. All this provides essential background for a self-declared revolution and a post-Ottoman justice system that was to remain notoriously dependent on arbitrary rule. Ninety years later, in the late 2010s, arbitrary power has reached a new peak; this makes for a devastating experience for those jurists in Turkey who still believe in the "Law Revolution" and embrace secularism, while understanding themselves as servants of law, not of rulers and ideologies.[57]

Since Lausanne, Ankara knew that Western diplomats would put a good face on legal and minority matters that did not directly touch on foreign interests. The dialectics of Western needs and expectations – and of Kemalist premises, promises, and desires – thus determined political developments. Based on this dialectic, the Lausanne Treaty remained remarkably stable as a pact of elite interests that impacted on the perception both of the Treaty itself and the Republic of Turkey to which this Treaty gave birth and which it integrated internationally. Therefore, for a majority of contemporaries in the Interwar West, and for generations after them, the optics of Lausanne made Turkish-style ultranationalism look like an energetic, benign, and enlightened authoritarianism, in contrast to fascism, Nazism, and Bolshevism next door. Above all, thanks to Lausanne and, twenty-nine years later, NATO, Ankara appeared to be a Western Power, even if it was not democratic. The post-Lausanne Republic started actually as a dictatorship, constructed on the unrecognized genocidal ground of the last Ottoman decade. But why still to care about complex pasts? Even if proto-fascist and genocidal, weren't these pasts buried in Lausanne, supposedly forever?

---

[57] See, for example, the assessment by former First President of the Court of Cassation Prof. Dr. Sami Selçuk in an interview with The Arrested Lawyers Initiative on 20 July 2022: "Former President of Supreme Court of Appeal: Turkey is an Eastern Country in Terms of Law, a Failed Country," https://arrestedlawyers.org/2022/07/20/turkey-is-an-eastern-country-in-terms-of-law-a-failed-country (as of 21 July 2022).

29 Reassessing Lausanne-Based Kemalism: Lofty Claims, Clashes with Reality

If we reassess "Atatürk's Revolution," it is not simply about audacious reforms and certain shadows, but about a well-attuned combination of international diplomacy and face-lifting that went hand in hand with ultranationalist policies, coercion, and indoctrination at home. Despite Mustafa Kemal's unmatched country-wide popularity, Kemalist policies could not win over the hearts of a still poverty-stricken population outside the metropoles. In 1930, the unexpected success of a short-lived experiment with an opposition party led by Fethi Okyar, an old friend of Mustafa Kemal, as well as the anti-Kemalist riot in Menemen (near Izmir), were disillusioning eye-openers for Ankara and its Turkish Revolution. They depressed the supreme leader himself, becoming one reason more for his feverish search to legitimize his political course by historical arguments (see Chapter 30).

As for Menemen, Gazi Kemal was infuriated and revengeful, especially because parts of the population apparently sided with the rioters. He hardly calmed down when conferring with his prime minister Ismet (İnönü), defense minister Zekai (Apaydın), and interior minister Şükrü (Kaya), all former members of Ankara's delegation at Lausanne. They finally decided to deport the local population, not to destroy Menemen completely. As a further deterrent, they executed nearly thirty persons who had nothing directly to do with the shooting of an officer. Derviş Mehmet, the man responsible for the riot and of the lieutenant's murder, had already been killed on the spot. He had declared himself mahdi (i.e. eschatological leader of the ummah), and, applauded by the participants, decapitated the dead officer in the mosque. Sunni mahdism, social protest, and societal readiness to violence in the name of Islam met in Menemen.[58]

For the supreme leader in Ankara, this was the disturbing irruption of a world he believed suppressed and overcome by his enlightened Revolution. He had to learn that among Anatolia's Sunnis, his main power basis, many Muslims did not share in his eschatological Turkist claim that, based on the historic triumph in Lausanne, the new state in Anatolia represented the fulfillment of millennia of Turkish history. Not only radical and violent mahdists like Derviş Mehmet, but also more modest and seclusive Muslims like the sympathizers of Said Nursi,[59] and other large segments of the society, particularly on the countryside, had by

---

[58] Hamit Bozarslan, "Le madhisme en Turquie: L'"incident de Menemen' en 1930," *Revue des mondes musulmans et de la Méditerranée*, 91–94 (2000), 297–320, http://journals.openedition.org/remmm/26; Mango, *Atatürk*, 475–477.
[59] Of later fame as the founder of the ongoing worldwide *Nurculuk* movement.

no means assimilated Kemal's credo and doctrines, even if they had to undergo public Kemalist education and a new calendar of annual celebrations. In a time of global economic crisis, Ankara's new "command economy" (Etatism) could only partly address the existing economic problems and the loss of value of crops for export from its all-important agricultural sector. The fantastic plan to transform Turkey into a hub of transcontinental railway transit failed.[60]

As *When Democracy Died* insists, there had never been any serious attempt at forging a countrywide democratic social contract or at facing the violence that the authorities had stirred up among Sunnis in the name of religion during a long decade of internal and external struggles until 1922. From 1920, Ankara's fragile unity rested on warfare against non-Muslims and non-Muslim claims in Anatolia, as according to the National Pact goals that Lausanne endorsed. Since Ankara lacked the experience and knowledge to democratically deal with conflicts, it stiffened even more from 1930. Fear prevailed on all sides. The early Republic's domestic policies led to instances of extreme violence, physically and symbolically. These represent the darkest side of Kemalism. Because of their unequivocal, unrevoked character and thus their lasting impact, coercive domestic policies and indoctrination have defined the course of Turkish nationalism.

***

Unsurprisingly, Ankara's self-image and its show in diplomacy differed from this assessment. If we take seriously the difference between a repressive dictatorship and a democracy with civil liberties, there is little consolation or relativization in the fact that many other, notably socialist dictatorships labeled themselves democratic. In the late 1930s, when Kemalist dictatorship had turned to domestic totalitarianism, Foreign Minister Aras proudly stressed before the National Assembly the "increasing importance of democratic and republican Turkey as an agent of peace and order among nations," as recognized by growing participation in the League of Nations (of which Turkey became a member in 1932).[61]

Kemalist Turkey displays a peculiar combination of a circumspect, nonrevolutionary foreign policy with a fascism-like transformative regime domestically. This is why, for example, we see Ankara win international praise for the 1930 Ankara Convention with Greece that prepared the 1933 Entente; the 1934 Balkan Pact (Entente); and the 1937 Saadabed Pact with Iran, Iraq, and Afghanistan. The Saadabed Pact targeted

---

[60] Bein, *Kemalist Turkey and the Middle East*, 138.   [61] Aras, *Lozan*, 106.

primally Kurdish unrest and those made "border-landers" by the Lausanne Treaty, allowing the neighbor states a military hot-pursuit beyond borders. During the same years, state authorities and the press, all entirely brought into line, prepared the Dersim genocide and led vicious campaigns against "the Jew" Werfel, author of *The Forty Days of Musa Dagh.*

Sure enough, the Balkan conferences in 1930–3 and the related friendship with Greece – which implemented a pre-1914 concept of common security among Balkan states and Turkey – were constructive steps. They testified to a desire for peace, stability, and pragmatism among neighbors. They were supported by the League and inspired by the League's language of hopeful, peaceful, transparent international cooperation.[62] It would be wrong to deny the longing for peace and will to openness even among ultranationalist actors. "I have every confidence that the union of the Balkans, which today, even in its present form, gives us all satisfaction, will one day take the final form which many people have never even dreamed of. ...The bright days we expect are probably not far away even from us." Atatürk used these words when commenting before journalists on the Balkan Entente.[63] In the long term however, the promising steps proved built on sand, not only because of the Second World War and disruptive Great or Super power politics, but because these Ententes lacked democratic underpinnings.

Solid Greek–Turkish friendship, in particular, could not be achieved on the basis of the Lausanne Treaty, the European thaw after the Locarno Treaties (1925), and a temporary affection between Prime Minister Venizelos and President Gazi Kemal in 1930 (or a few years later, between the new dictator Ioannis Metaxas and his Turkish counterpart). An early toast of Foreign Minister Tevfik Rüştü (Aras) on 10 June 1930, in view of the emerging Convention, sounded wonderful but had a short expiration date. "Sirs, the foundations of a full and sincere alliance between these two countries were laid at Lausanne by two great statesmen, İsmet Pasha and Monsieur Venizelos."[64]

To a certain extent, cooperation in this alliance was once more diplomacy on the back of victims – that is, the "exchanged" Anatolian Rûm refugees or exchangees who never saw fair compensation after being transferred to Greece, and who had now to renounce on any remaining

---

[62] See R3844/3D/16109 of 14 September 1933; S666/96/24 of 9 February 1934; R3875/3D/36435/36435 of 27 April 1938, League Archives, Geneva.
[63] "Balkan Antantı hakkında bir konuşma," 27 February 1938, in *Atatürk'ün Söylev ve Demeçleri*, vol. 2, 329–330.
[64] "Mübadele hakkındaki Türk-Yunan itilâfının imzası münasebetile 10 Haziran 1930 tarihinde irat edilen nutuk," in Aras, *Lozan*, 92.

claim. Poor and despondent, they increasingly turned to the left for support.[65] During the second half of the twentieth century, violent conflicts erupted regarding Cyprus, the Aegean islands, and the Rûm community in Istanbul. Since the 2010s, diverging Treaty interpretations, which concern territorial stipulations on the islands close to the Anatolian coast (Articles 12–15), have led an aggressive and expansionist Ankara under Erdogan to the brink of war with Athens.[66]

Antidemocracy and global crises prevailed in Greater Europe in the 1930s. It would nevertheless be wrong to disregard the element of promise in post-Lausanne foreign policy. Tevfik Rüştü (Aras) stressed this before the National Assembly in early 1931, when he praised the Greek–Turkish Convention and referred to Lausanne and the 1925 Locarno Treaties, and used League vocabulary:

> This treaty [Convention] is the result of the policy initiated at Lausanne with Ismet Pasha and M. Venizelos and pursued by both sides with persistence and perseverance. It is a promising forerunner of the new era that has opened between the two neighbors. By accepting and ratifying this treaty, the Grand Assembly ... will also have set before the international world a good example that will serve to preserve peace in the region where both states are located. Doesn't the interest and congratulations by the general public of the world towards this treaty show this clearly? ... it [Greek-Turkish friendship] has reached this stage in seven years by following the development of public opinion of the two sides in the new and fresh air that started in Lausanne.[67]

The Treaty of Lausanne indeed stands in the center of Turkey's formation as a restive nation-state. But we can only understand and assess this formation and its individual elements if we take the formation as a whole. This means a foundational period lasting from 1913 (the establishment of the CUP party-state), the 1915 genocide, and the alliance with the Bolsheviks, to Lausanne, the early 1930s Ententes, the Kemalist destruction of Dersim and the incorporation of Antakya – when Ankara made the historic Syrian city of Antakya a fictitiously proto-Turkish "Hatay" (see Section 30).

A few dozen key figures predominated in Turkey's formation. Of these, besides Talaat Pasha and Gazi Kemal themselves, many were delegation members at Lausanne and/or had already worked under Talaat in the CUP party-state (on them, see Parts II and III, and the Biographical Notes in the Annexe). Personalities with specific roles in foreign policy

---

[65] Gallant, *Modern Greece*, 215.
[66] Christian Schaller, *Streit im östlichen Mittelmeer – Griechenland, Türkei, Zypern Eine seevölkerrechtliche Einordnung* (Berlin: SWP-Studie, February 2022). See also "Miçotakis'ten Devlet Bahçeli'ye harita tepkisi," *Cumhuriyet*, 11 July 2022.
[67] "Türk-Yunan Dostluk Muahedesinin tasdikı münasebetile 12 Şubat 1931 tarihinde Büyük Millet Meclisinde irat edilen nutuk," in Aras, *Lozan*, 112.

were, of course, Rıza Nur, Ismet (Inönü), and Reşit Saffet (Atabinen). Added to these, we have to mention Mehmet Münir (Ertegün) and Tevfik Rüştü (Aras). Like Nur, Aras was a medical army doctor and CUP member, but he served also in the party-state, and as a hygienic expert during the Armenian genocide. Subsequent to the decisions in Lausanne, he was the rapporteur on the Lausanne Treaty in the National Assembly, chaired the Population Exchange Commission, and headed Ankara's foreign ministry from 1925 to 1938.[68]

Münir Ertegün, legal counselor in Lausanne, deserves particular attention because of his prominent role as an ambassador in Washington during the 1930s. Part I briefly mentioned his resolute fight against Werfel's *The Forty Days of Musa Dagh*, an influential book on the Armenian genocide in the form of a novel. Shelved in Lausanne, but ultimately not suppressible, the memory of the Armenian genocide early on revealed the political limits of a restive nation-state that combined a largely cautious and conformist foreign policy with dictatorial transformation, coercion, and indoctrination at home. Given time and conjuncture, truths of the magnitude of crimes against humanity, even if diplomatically silenced, again come forcefully to the fore. This happened the first time after the Lausanne Conference with the late 1933 publication of *The Forty Days of Musa Dagh*, a well-researched German novel of more than a thousand pages that made a mess of Turkish nationalist denial. Ankara and its press reacted furiously. A Western world in crisis, however, after the Nazi rise to power, felt compelled to accommodate Turkey. This is how denial could internationally succeed in Kemalist Turkey's "first denialist crisis" in the 1930s.[69]

In this case, not only did Nazis and Turks work hand in hand, but to a certain extent also Western authorities. First, the journalist Falih Rıfkı Atay – readers know him as targeting Cavid Bey in Lausanne – and his colleague Burhan Asaf Belge, both voices of the regime, strongly reacted. The latter was, like Aras, a temporary (post-1918) Turkish communist converted to Kemalism. Atay and Belge tore Werfel's book asunder as a fabricated story that denigrated Turks as barbarians. The Turkish press then translated a long denialist article taken from the Nazi journal *Der Völkische Beobachter* against the Jew Werfel and his allegedly slanderous book. In early 1934, the press rejoiced that Joseph Göbbels, Germany's education and propaganda minister, interdicted the "immoral novel" that had already been among the books publicly burnt by Nazis in 1933.

[68] Taner Akçam, *A Shameful Act: The Armenian Genocide and the Question of Turkish Responsibility* (New York: Metropolitan, 2006), 363–364.
[69] As labeled by Emmanuel Szurek in Szurek, "Autodafé à Istanbul: La première crise négationniste de la Turquie nationaliste (1935)."

Göbbels claimed to do this in the name of "German–Turkish friendship."[70]

Hollywood planned to make a film of *The Forty Days of Musa Dagh*. In Turkey, this led to a renewed flare-up of the denialist crisis that lasted more than two years in total. It culminated in both anti-Armenian and anti-Semitic incendiarism that served as a means to pressure US diplomacy. Foreign Minister Aras made clear to US ambassador Skinner, Grew's successor in 1933, that Turkey's Armenians would probably have to suffer if the film was made. Ertegün, in turn, threatened a boycott of all US films. It took renewed attempts, but finally Aras' and Ertegün's pressure succeeded. Made aware by the State Department, Hollywood gave in. In addition, the contemporary American translation of Werfel's novel was sanitized by the American publisher's self-censorship. The basest and saddest part of the crisis was a performance of self-denial to which the decimated, intimidated Armenian community in Istanbul was compelled in late 1935. It had to publicly burn Werfel's picture and book in a church. The nationalist press reported on this "autodafé" by emphasizing the "indignation of Armenian and Jewish citizens." They were said to reject the defamation of Turkey by the "hateful" and "greedy Jew" Werfel in what they described as a Jewish-Armenian plot abroad against Turkey.[71]

30   Lausanne and Atatürk's History Doctrine

The disregard for historical truths and the "othering" – sidelining, denigration, extermination – of non-Turks and non-Turkish identities in Anatolia is an intrinsic element of what the Lausanne settlement endorsed. Built-in to the pact of mutual interests between the signatories, it paved the path to unchecked post-Ottoman dictatorship. The settlement allowed the founding fathers of the republic – many of them, like Atatürk, immigrants from the Balkans – to suppress and silence the identity, rights, history, and victimhood of indigenous Anatolians In other words, they excluded alterity from their understanding of polity, thus disabling democracy itself. They enshrined this stance in a sacred national history. Elaborate official history-writing was therefore urgently called for, in order to "scientifically" secure what was achieved by the late 1920s, militarily, diplomatically, and by domestic coercion.

---

[70] Ibid.
[71] Rıfat Bali, "Bir Tarih Romanının Filme Çekilememe Serüveni. Musa Dağ Kırk Gün'ün Hikâyesi," in Bali, *Musa'nın Evlatları. Cumhuriyet'in Yurttaşları* (Istanbul, İletişim, 2001), 109–140.

A seminal author in this vein and context, though not properly a historian, was Gökalp, the acknowledged spiritual father of Turkish nationalism. During the Lausanne Conference, shortly before his death, he published his summa *Türkçülüğün Esasları* (Principles of Turkism) in Ankara. The spirit of this book is formative for the historical weltanschauung of a nationalism that Lausanne failed to fully appease and domesticate. Parts of the book conflict with the nature of the state promised and the boundaries fixed at Lausanne, because Gökalp had not entirely given up on his pan-Turkish thought. According to *Principles of Turkism*, Anatolia's Turkification – achieved in Lausanne – had to be followed by the Oghuz union (Oğuz birliği); that is, unification with the Turkmen in the Caucasus, Iran, Turkistan, and, implicitly, Iraq and Syria. The union of Turan was the third and last step; it would encompass all Turkic peoples – "Turanians" – as far as north-western China.[72]

Ankara's national history had three main wings: ancient, premodern, and contemporary, the first and the third wing being the most formative. In the earlier pages of this study, we have made abundant reference to Nur's vision of national history. This vision contained many elements that entered the official "Turkish History Thesis." Atatürk personally pushed this Thesis with much commitment during the last decade of his life. The vision of contemporary history is defined by his *Nutuk*, a multiday speech in October 1927 before the members of his ruling Republican People's Party. This was less than two months after the judicial murder of Cavid, which Kemal Gazi's speech concealed. *When Democracy Died* has already several times referred to the *Nutuk*. From the late 1920s, the printed *Nutuk* served as the bible of Kemalist understanding of how contemporary history was to be configured and of how the Republic was founded. *Lozan* occupies a central place in the *Nutuk*. Many other texts and speeches by Kemal or members of his cohort complete what I call here Ankara's doctrine of history.

This doctrine comprises visions of Ottoman and pre-Ottoman history that still – though less than under the imperial CUP – identify with the powerful sultans of the fifteenth and sixteenth centuries. Kemalism rejects late-Ottoman history as cosmopolitan and decadent. It emphasizes the efforts by the founders of the republic to save the Turkish nation from Ottoman abuses. *Nutuk* put it this way: "The issues discussed at the Lausanne peace table did not belong to and were not limited to the new period of three or four years [1919–23]. Age-old accounts were being settled. Of course, it was not going to be so simple and easy to get out of

---

[72] Ziya Gökalp, *Türkçülüğün esasları*, ed. Salim Çonoğlu (Istanbul: Ötüken, 2014; first ed., Ankara, 1339 [1923]), 28, 32.

such old, so complicated, so dirty accounts." *Nutuk* underlines two evil foes: the corrupt palace and the foreign powers (i.e. Europe). Europe favored the Ottoman Christians and – as *Nutuk* states sweepingly and incorrectly – prevented any Ottoman development.

> It is well known, gentlemen, that the Ottoman Empire, which was replaced by the new Turkish State, was under the captivity of a number of capitulations under the Old Treaties. Christian elements enjoyed many privileges and exceptions.... The Ottoman Empire was also prevented from resorting to the means that would ensure that the Turkish nation, the main element that had established it, could live with human dignity. It was not free to develop the country, to build a railway or even to build a school. In such cases, foreigners would immediately intervene. The Ottoman rulers and their relatives, in order to ensure their lives of pomp and splendor, had not only drained all the sources of wealth of the country and the nation, but had also made many loans, sacrificing all the interests of the nation and sacrificing the dignity and honor of the state. The Ottoman Empire, of which we were heirs, had no value, virtue and dignity in the eyes of the world. It ... was considered as if it was under protection and guardianship.[73]

Whereas *When Democracy Died* has problematized the period from spring to summer 1923 as Ankara's turn toward oligarchy and dictatorship, with first general elections held in an atmosphere of repression, *Nutuk* paints a rosy picture of transition toward glory: "The second election period of the Grand National Assembly of Turkey coincided with a happy transition period in the history of the new Turkish state. Indeed, our four-year struggle for independence ended with a peace worthy of our nation's glory."[74]

Greatly satisfied, Kemal Pasha summarized the main conflicts settled in the Lausanne Treaty, comparing them to what the Sèvres Treaty stipulated. Many times, he thus could state, "There is no mention," "Of course it was not brought up," "Naturally, it was rejected by us," or "This issue has been eliminated" – notably in the case of an Armenian home, Kurdistan, the Capitulations, the question of Greek sovereignty over Izmir (he concealed the planned referendum), the restitution of property, and the prosecution of crimes related to war and "deportation" (tehcir).[75] He ended his presentation with superlatives:

> I am of the opinion that there is no need to compare the principles contained in the Lausanne Peace Treaty with other peace proposals. This treaty documents the destruction of a great assassination that had been prepared against the Turkish nation for centuries and was thought to have been completed with the Treaty of Sevres. It is an unprecedented political victory with regard to the Ottoman period![76]

Large parts of the *Nutuk*'s ego-narrative settle accounts with Gazi Kemal's early companions who came to oppose his supreme leadership and related

---

[73] Kemal, *Nutuk*, 466–467. [74] Ibid., 498. [75] Ibid., 498–510. [76] Ibid., 510.

choices. The settling of accounts went along with critical decisions, notably that of abolishing the caliphate (to which the Chapter 31 returns). *Nutuk's* elaborate personal attacks contributed to a political tradition in Ankara of targeting persons and perpetuating ideologically charged personal conflicts, instead of democratically dealing with and solving problems.

***

In multiple ways, Ankara's delegation in Lausanne had prefigured what became a doctrine of history within a decade. It used the Turanian argument, and most delegates probably believed in Turanianism to a certain degree. The delegation explicitly demarcated itself from empire, palace, dynasty, and Young Turk rule, while insisting on, and claiming, a Turkish nationally framed Ottoman history. It blared forth an alleged age-old history of Ottoman victimhood at the hands of Europe, while boasting over the successful defense of Turkish rule over Anatolia. In conformity with the later *Nutuk*,[77] it held that the crucial and enduring plot of modern history consisted of an anti-Turkish conspiracy of Europe aided by domestic agents. These had deserved punishment for treason. The nationalist narrative had enabled Kemal to reframe select core claims advanced in Lausanne: Ankara's unrestricted sovereignty; weak minority rights; and the rejection of any autonomy for non-Turkish natives, in particular of any Armenian home.

Thus, the Lausanne Conference contributed to the writing of modern and contemporary history, and set also main pillars for what became the Turkish History Thesis. It was influenced by a new national understanding of history that had burgeoned since the early twentieth century and gained pace in the 1910s.[78] Members of the Conference delegation were, or later became, prolific history writers or ethnographers. Readers have already encountered most of them: Rıza Nur, Reşid Saffet Atabinen, Yusuf Hikmet Bayur, Mehmet Tevfik Bıyıklıoğlu, Baha Said, and (possibly an unofficial delegation member) Ahmet Esat Uras. Less than a decade after the Conference, Atabinen and Bayur, as well as Mehmet Tevfik and Uras, joined the Turkish Historical Society under Atatürk's close supervision in Ankara.[79] Moreover, Bayur also took a leading role in the obligatory teaching of the History of the Turkish Revolution at new Institutes of the

---

[77] Ibid., 510.
[78] H. L. Kieser, "Die Herausbildung des türkisch-nationalen Geschichtsdiskurses (spätes 19.–Mitte 20. Jahrhundert," in Markus Krzoska and Christian Maner (eds.), *Vom Beruf zur Berufung. Geschichtswissenschaft und Nationsbildung in Ostmittel- und Südosteuropa im 19. und 20. Jahrhundert* (Munster: Lit, 2005), 59–98.
[79] First Committee (1930), then Association (1931) for the Study of Turkish History (Türk Tarihi Tetkik Cemiyeti); in 1935, renamed Türk Tarih Kurumu, Turkish Historical Society.

Turkish Revolution.[80] The delegation's official translator was Hüseyin Bey (Pektaş), a Sorbonne-trained historian and, from 1935, the Turkish-vice-president of Robert College and the American College for Girls. He led the Turkification of these formerly prestigious internationalist institutions.[81] Uras's book, *The Armenians in History and the Armenian Question*, reacted against Stalin's reactivation of the Armenian Question for Soviet-imperial goals. It became the apologetic and denialist Turkish bible on the issue during the second half of the twentieth century.[82]

Once solidly installed at the head of a party-state, the supreme leader Mustafa Kemal wanted to be not only the maker, but also the writer of national history. The *Nutuk* made him the main protagonist of the making of the Republic and put him at the center of a new field of contemporary history that was taught at so-called Institutes of the Turkish Revolution. The contemporary part of the history doctrine took as its starting point Turkey's "national salvation" in the dark wake of defeat in the Great War. Leader-centered, its narrative emphasized Turkey's national salvation through war; its recognition at the Lausanne Conference; and its construction as a sovereign nation-state. It posited Turkey as of the West, but not under the West – ultimately, in the vein of Gökalp's exalted Turkism, even superior to it.

Countrywide mass celebrations on new national memorial days followed a new official calendar based on the Kemalist epic of national salvation. Although celebrated every year in the press and also often at memorial events, *Lozan* and 24 July were not an explicit part of this calendar, but *Lozan* is the moment of official addresses and other events of commemorations every year, thus offering the occasion and a strong reference for

---

[80] From 1933, Bayur made Atatürk's narrative of national salvation the vanishing point of his monumental *History of the Turkish Revolution*. He started with the late nineteenth century, thus covering the immediate pre-history (1877 to 1918) of Kemal Atatürk's ego-history. Y. H. Bayur, *Türk inkılâbı tarihi* [History of the Turkish Revolution] (Ankara: Türk Tarih Kurumu, 1991; first ed., 1940), 10 vols.

[81] John Freely, *A Bridge of Culture: Robert College – Boğaziçi University: How an American College in Istanbul Became a Turkish University* (Istanbul: Boğaziçi Üniversitetisi Yayinevi, 2012), 272–275. See also Sjöberg, *Internationalism and the New Turkey*.

[82] Esat Uras, *The Armenians in History and the Armenian Question* (Istanbul: Documentary Publications, 1988; Turkish ed., 1950). Although there is no doubt about Uras's strong involvement in all historical issues regarding Armenians from Talaat Pasha to Kemal Atatürk, the Swiss police lists and the list in *Lozan Mektupları*, 20–21, do not confirm the official presence of Uras in Lausanne. The civil servant Uras, who knew several languages including Armenian, had been the CUP's expert for Armenian issues and Talaat's close collaborator in the ministry of the interior. See Ali Çankaya, *Yeni Mülkiye Târihi ve Mülkiyeliler* (Ankara: Mars Matbaası, 1968–9), vol. 3, 1040–1041; and German journalist von Tyszka to the Undersecretary of State in the Foreign Office, Zimmermann, to the Undersecretary of State in the Foreign Office, Istanbul, 1 October 1915, German Foreign Office Archive, DE/PA-AA/R14088.

political statements.[83] *Lozan* was implicitly inscribed to the Republic's main new celebration days, which included, first, National Sovereignty Day on 23 April, referring to the establishment of the National Assembly on 23 April 1920. Second, Victory Day, on 30 August, commemorates the ultimate military success against the Greek army at Dumlupınar on 30 August 1922 which had opened the road to the recovery of Smyrna and the destruction of its non-Muslim quarters and populations. Third came the Feast of the Republic on 29 October, referring to 29 October 1923, the date the Republic of Turkey was declared.[84]

Although outshining it, the new commemorative calendar did however not cancel what had begun as the Young Turk narrative of national-imperial salvation. The stations of this narrative were the Young Turk Revolution (1908), the recovery of Edirne (1913) and the defense of Gallipoli (1915). Significantly, the Feast of Liberty (Hürriyet Bayramı) on 23 July, in commemoration of the Young Turk Revolution on 23 July 1908, lost importance. During the 1920s, it was reinterpreted with Atatürk as its allegedly main hero, but its celebration was cancelled in 1935 and the related 1909 law abrogated. Official public history thus insisted even more on the novelty of post-Lausanne Turkey and on an inaccurate historical distance of the Kemalists from the Young Turks.[85]

***

From the late 1920s onward, Mustafa Kemal Atatürk personally led a small circle of Turkist academics in the making of the History Thesis. Early in 1930, he commissioned a group of intellectuals from the Turkish Home Society (Türk Ocağı) to transform his thoughts on the origins of the Turkish nation into a scientific doctrine. His twenty-two-year-old adopted daughter Afet Inan sat on the historical committee as his spokesperson. This committee shortly afterwards became the Turkish Historical Society (Türk Tarih Kurumu).

The Turkish History Thesis represents the apogee and aporia of a Turkism that rested on "naturally" given, identity-building Turkishness, not a democratic social contract. It modified Gökalpian Turkism by insisting exclusively on racial identity. The decisive turn took place in Lausanne, as we have seen: to be recognized as "modern" and "civilized," national identity had to rest on history, race, and ethnicity – not Islam, one of the main pillars of Gökalpian Turkism. The racial History Thesis thus serves as

---

[83] In 2022, for presidential verbal attacks against Greece, see "Yunanistan Lozan Antlaşması'nı aşındırıyor," *Deutsche Welle*, 24 July 2022.

[84] Sara-Marie Demiriz, *Vom Osmanen zum Türken: Nationale und staatsbürgerliche Erziehung durch Feier- und Gedenktage in der Türkischen Republik 1923–1938* (Baden-Baden: Ergon, 2018).

[85] Ibid., 95–98.

a corollary to the Turkification of Anatolia and the diplomatic triumph in Lausanne. It had to give a deeper sense and legitimacy to a violent formation. It had to fill the void created by the brusque post-Lausanne dismissal of Islam. Islam had underpinned national identity and – as jihad and *gaza* – justified war and violence on a popular level. Ethnic nationalism alone now had to legitimize the formation of the nation-state, the removal of non-Turks, and a life's work of the supreme leader. Not imperial Islam, but ethnohistory, based on physical anthropology, had to prove the Turkish claim to Asia Minor and Turkish excellency in the history of humanity.

The main three ingredients of the thesis had already met in Ankara's discourse in Lausanne: a Turanian-Turkish understanding of history, the endeavor to minimize Islam, and the explanation or denial of the eradication of the Armenians and other Anatolian Christians. These three items now fully underpinned and motivated an ethnocentric view of history that racial anthropology should prove. In 1928, Kemal Atatürk met with Pittard, a professor of anthropology whom readers already know from his presence at sideshows of the Lausanne Conference. The president invited the professor to do research in Eastern Asia Minor that remained closed to other travelers. In the autumn of the same year, the Turkish press published Pittard's discoveries, writing extensively about the visit of "an old friend of Turkey."[86] Following his return, Pittard himself published his findings in the European press and in scientific journals. They contained two elements: the first was the discovery of the previously denied existence of Paleolithic civilization in Anatolia;[87] the second (based on his own craniometrical measurements of soldiers at a military camp) resulted in the hypothesis that Anatolian Turks were the descendants of a "brachycephalic race." At the time, "brachycephaly" was generally associated with Indo-European, Aryan, and culture-bringing characteristics.[88]

---

[86] According to newspapers *Akcham*, 25 September 1928, and *La République*, 28 November 1928; both articles Bibliothèque Publique et Universitaire de Genève (BPU), Ms. fr. 6313. See also H. L. Kieser, "Türkische Nationalrevolution, anthropologisch gekrönt. Kemal Atatürk und Eugène Pittard," *Historische Anthropologie*, 14.1 (2006), 105–118.

[87] Eugène Pittard, "Découverte de la divilisation paléolothique en Asie Mineure," *Archives suisses d'Anthropologie générale*, 2–5 (1928–9), 135–165.

[88] Pittard also reported that the so-called *indice nasale* suggested greater "racial homogeneity" among the Turks in Anatolia than among those in the Balkans. Eugène Pittard, "Contribution à l'étude anthropologique des Turcs d'Asie Mineure," *Türk Antropoloji Mecmuası*, 8 (September 1929), 3–29, here 3, 10, and 19. Ironically, in *Les races et l'histoire*, which included the categorization of races as dolicho- and brachycephalic (long- and broad-headed, respectively), Pittard had not yet listed the Turks as brachycephalic, whereas the Armenians were already included. Pittard, *Les races et l'histoire: Introduction ethnologique à l'histoire* (Paris: La Renaissance du Livre, 1924), 47.

In addition to these two findings, Pittard made conjectures which he said needed further research, but they were immediately circulated as authoritative statements in the Turkish press: Anatolia was primarily inhabited by peoples of the same "race" and was clearly separable from the "Asian block" and assignable to the "European block" of races.[89] Pittard suggested to his Western readers that the practice of keeping domesticated animals, and many of "our" cultivated plants – even "we," as "white Europeans" – possibly came from this region where the domestication of animals had taken place: the greatest social revolution of all time, as he put it.[90] He also suggested a continuity of the Turkish race starting in the Mesolithic and Neolithic eras and continuing via the Hittites, Sumerians, and even the ancient Hellenic inhabitants of Asia Minor up to the present day. Kemalist renewal, he stated, corresponded entirely to the spirit and the genius of the Turkish race as evidenced in its continuity and its civilizing role throughout history.[91] Pittard's reference to the puzzling origin of the Etruscans in Italy was also suggestive – "Turkish," was the categorical answer of Kemalist historians, who loved to claim the Etruscans as proto-Turks.[92]

The theory of culture-bringing Turanian immigration into Europe had first been expressed by Leon Cahun, a Turcophile amateur historian in late-nineteenth-century France.[93] In 1930–1, the historical committee drafted history books written in the new spirit with record speed and published an 1873 speech by Cahun in Turkish. The First History Congress in Ankara in 1932 formed the climax of this foundation-laying phase and bestowed the History Thesis with an official seal. The Second History Congress in Istanbul in 1937 was attended by Pittard himself. As a Dean of the Faculty of Science at the University of Geneva – of which he was soon to become President – he appeared to provide the Thesis with international scientific approval. This second congress was held as

[89] Illustré 22 Novembre 1928, BPU Ms. fr. 6313; Pittard, *Visage nouveau*, 24.
[90] Pittard, Visage nouveau, 12–15. Also very clearly in Eugène Pittard, *Les origines de l'humanité et les bases préhistoriques de la civilisation*, brochure from *Actes de la Société Helvétique des Sciences Naturelles* (Berne, 1942), 9 f.
[91] *Hakimiyet-i Milliye*, 10 December 1928, BPU Ms. fr. 6313.
[92] Pittard, "Contribution," 29; Pittard's own notes record that he said the following at one of his conferences in Turkey: "What are the racial characteristics of the Neolithic Europeans? They came from Asia. They created the *Homo alpinus*. They are our ancestors and our brothers. Therefore Anatolia is sacred land [Terre sacrée]." Handwritten notes, BPU Ms. fr. 6290/3.
[93] Léon Cahun, "Habitat et migrations préhistoriques des races dites touranienne," in *Congrès international des orientalistes. Compte rendu de la première session*, vol. 1, Paris 1874, 431–441, quoted in: Copeaux, *Espaces et temps de la nation turque: analyse d'une historiographie nationaliste, 1931–1993* (Paris: CNRS Ed., 1997), 36 f. See also Léon Cahun, *Introduction à l'histoire de l'Asie. Turcs et Mongols des origines à 1405* (Paris: Colin, 1896).

a congratulatory celebration of undiscussed preconditions. The congress publication, with his portrait photo emblazoned on the cover, was dedicated to the "greatest son of Turkish history."[94] Atatürk, the spiritus rector of the endeavor, was present at both historical congresses.

A further salient element of the History Thesis was the physical measurement of 64,000 Turkish soldiers. Collected by the army, these measurements provided extensive data for Afet Inan's tellingly titled dissertation *Anatolia, the Country of the Turkish "Race"* supervised by Pittard (who was certainly responsible for the quotation marks around "race"). Afet Inan wrote that her aim was "to write the definitive history of this corner of the earth."[95] This bold pretense stands in line with the bold claims in Lausanne; it is the convenient historiographical corollary or addendum to diplomacy there. Of a meeting with Atatürk in summer 1937, Pittard wrote:

> When I came to speak of the problem that concerned him so much, namely the origins of the Turkish race and civilization since prehistoric times, I was able to please him immensely by informing him that, without invasion from Asia Minor in the Neolithic period, Europe would most likely have been unable to overcome this phase of the Stone Age.[96]

The idea that – in terms of contemporary anthropology – (proto-)Turks may have been indigenous to Anatolia and proved pioneers of civilization gave immense relief to the ageing dictator.[97]

Pushing Islam aside, the History Thesis thus integrated Turks into "Europe," which, according to Kemalist understanding, epitomized the white, civilized, Aryan West. At the same time, it made Turkish prehistory the cradle of human civilization, and Asia Minor a land inhabited by pre-historic Turks. Thus, it provided the notion of exclusive Turkish control of Anatolia with ethnohistorical credentials, while portraying the disappearance of others – Armenian, Greek, and Assyrian non-Muslims – as a natural and logical historical process. We have encountered this same argument already in Nur's much earlier *History of the Armenians*. The Thesis was not the aberrant pet project of an otherwise outstanding and

---

[94] *İkinci Türk Tarih Kongresi: Istanbul, 20–26 Eylül 1937; kongrenin çalışmaları, kongreye sunulan tebliğler* (Istanbul: Kenan Matbaası, 1943).
[95] Afet Inan (=Ayşe Afetinan), *L'Anatolie, le pays de la "race" turque: recherches sur les caractères anthropologiques des populations de la Turquie, enquête sur 64.000 individus*, preface by Eugène Pittard (Geneva, 1941), 3. See also Ayşe Afetinan, *Atatürk'ten mektuplar*.
[96] Eugène Pittard, "Quelques souvenirs personnels sur Ataturk," *Journal de Genève*, 14 November 1938, 1.
[97] Closely linked to the idea of proto-European Turkish high culture was the concept of Turkish as the mother of all languages. This developed into the so-called Sun Language Theory. See Jens P. Laut, *Das Türkische als Ursprache? Sprachwissenschaftliche Theorien in der Zeit des erwachenden türkischen Nationalismus* (Wiesbaden: Harrassowitz, 2000).

internationally courted leader. It lay close to Atatürk's political heart. In nucleo, it had underpinned the Turkish argumentation in Lausanne. It "proved" that the victims of genocide, expulsion, and dispossession were aliens to Anatolia and therefore rightfully sidelined and forgotten.

This historical thought enabled intellectual and diplomatic escapism on the highest level. It failed to ostracize exterminatory language of hate and contempt, thus making genocide repeatable. The projection of a grandiose Turkish past in general, and unto Anatolia in particular, served as a pretext for not coping with dramatically failed relationships between disparate cultures and ethnicities. Little noticed in the West, the Thesis is a monument to the denialist fragility of post-Ottoman Turkey. It reflects the fact that the new state in Asia Minor was not based on a democratic contract among the country's inhabitants – as had been the dream of the adherents of constitutional Turkey in 1908 – but on violent and exclusionary policy.

Atatürk's History Thesis certainly also arose from well-justified efforts to open up the scope of history, geographically and chronologically, and to valorize non-Europeans. This ultimately led, however, to a dead end. The illusion of an Archimedean point removed from Eurocentrism remained captive to highly problematic notions of contemporary Europe. Its anthropological and ethnohistorical alibi, as it were, evaded the difficult questions of recent history – most importantly, that of constitutionality. Nationalistic boasting of high culture and pretended original settlement was wide-spread and went to extremes throughout Interwar Europe and the Levant. In the case of Turkey, however, these extremes remained in place after the Second World War. The untenable escapism of this ultranationalist Thesis set the course for the powerful twenty-first-century return of pre-Lausanne ghosts once considered as filed away in the past.

31 Dersim Genocide: Apex of Ultranationalism

The Kemalist doctrine is deeply indebted to Gökalp. In the name of nonnegotiable "eternal" references – Islam and Turkishness – Gökalp had envisioned a country with one language, culture, mentality, religion, and morality, and one central ruler. This concept did explicitly without a democratic contract.[98] Although the History Thesis replaced Gökalp's Islamic pillar with modern scientism and physical anthropology, the

---

[98] Gökalp, "İslamiyet ve asrî medeniyet," *İslâm Mecmuası*, 51–52 (1917), English translation in N. Berkes, *Turkish Nationalism and Western Civilization: Selected Essays of Ziya Gökalp* (New York, 1959), 214–223.

essentialist and supremacist prefiguration remained unchanged. It actually reached its peak in the post-imperial framework of the early Republic of Turkey.

We must stress the logical and chronological coincidence of the Turkist apogee taking place in Atatürk's history doctrine with the exterminatory massacres in central Dersim in 1937–8. According to current international terminology and legal practice, the military campaign of those years constitutes a well-prepared genocide. A Law of Settlement on 21 June 1934 had legitimized the depopulation of regions in Turkey for cultural, political, or military reasons. This was done with the very Gökalpian intent to create, as then–Minister of the Interior Şükrü Kaya stated, "a country with one language, one mentality, and unity of feelings."[99] We have encountered Kaya as a counselor in Rıza Nur's team at the Lausanne Conference. During the Great War, Kaya had been a director in Talaat's ministry of the interior, responsible for the Armenian concentration camps in Syria.

Between March 1937 and September 1938, non-state-controlled parts of the province of Tunceli (renamed from "Dersim") were subjected to a military campaign that resulted in a particularly high death toll; many thousands of civilians fell victim to the violence. Contemporary officers called it a "disciplinary campaign" (*tedip harekâtı*, a term also used by the official military historian, Reşat Halli, in his 1972 account).[100] Politicians and press described the campaign as a civilizing mission in line with the vocabulary practiced in Lausanne. "We open Tunceli to civilization," read the title of one book by a contemporary Kemalist.[101] In contrast to the 1921 Koçgiri-Dersim uprising in the wake of the Sèvres Treaty, which had promised Kurdish autonomy, and the 1925 repression of the Kurdish Sheikh Saïd rebellion, which had reacted against the establishment of the unitary, secular state after the Lausanne Treaty, the Dersim campaign took place when the Republic of Turkey was fully consolidated. It was not a short-term reaction to a concrete uprising, but had been prepared well in advance.

The campaign against the partially autonomous central part of Dersim completed a more than forty-year cycle of violence, including genocide, against non-Turkish civilians within late Ottoman and early republican Turkey. Since genocide was by no means penalized and ostracized in

---

[99] Quoted in Erol Ülker, "Assimilation, Security and Geographical Nationalization in Interwar Turkey: The Settlement Law of 1934," *European Journal of Turkish Studies*, 7 (2008), http://journals.openedition.org/ejts/2123.

[100] Reşat Halli, *Türkiye Cumhuriyetinde ayaklanmalar (1924–1938)*, ed. by the Directorate of the General Staff for Military History (Ankara: Genelkurmay Basımevi, 1972).

[101] Naşit H. Uluğ, *Tunceli Medeniyete açılıyor* (Istanbul: Kaynak, 2007; first ed. 1939).

Lausanne, it remained an option that the state cadres had internalized, many of them remained steadily in positions of power from the 1910s to the 1930s and beyond. Genocide in political thought seeks to destroy that which does not bow to its rule and ideology, and thus cannot be brought into line. Therefore, targets of genocide are branded as troublemakers and scapegoats, to be destroyed or forcibly assimilated. Political thought in the early republic not only remained imperially biased, because it adopted the idea of elite leadership over the nation and subjected groups. It also remained social Darwinist and exterminatory, as under the CUP war regime. It separated those it wanted to dominate and incorporate into its one-party state – those it considered assimilable into the body of the state – and the others it believed it had to destroy or at least remove.

The targets of genocidal violence before the Lausanne Conference included Christian groups, above all the Armenians and, after that, the Alevi Kurdish region of Dersim, where a considerable number of Armenians had escaped genocide and remained alienated from the state along with the Alevi majority. Increasing economic strangulation and the traditional asylum system in Dersim added to what contemporary newspapers disparagingly highlighted as Dersim's poverty and banditry. In 1937–8, many families, not only men and boys, became victims of extermination. If we go by official figures, the death toll was almost twice as high as in the 1995 Srebrenica massacre, which the International Court of Justice considered a genocide, citing eight thousand exclusively male victims. In addition, there were systematic massacres of relatives on the outskirts or outside Dersim in 1937–8; the unlawful, hastily brutal execution of the main, also spiritual, head, Seyyid Rıza, and of eighty-four other leaders; and the resettlement of well over ten thousand people in western Anatolia. An unknown number of children, especially girls, were transferred to Kemalist families. Others wandered for months, even years, in the devastated, emptied Dersim.[102]

Although the Dersim campaign was about incorporating the independent mountain region of central Dersim into the unitary state, it resulted in a genocide: the intended eradication both of a despised culture and this culture's human support. Within this predetermined logic, it was then also a matter of putting down predictable armed resistance with superior force. In 1930, former Minister Mahmut Esat (Bozkurt) spoke of a war between two races, Kurds and Turks, and went so far as to say, "All,

---

[102] See Halli, *Türkiye Cumhuriyetinde ayaklanmalar (1924–1938)*, 463–465; Şükrü Aslan, *Herkesin bildiği sır: Dersim* (Istanbul: Iletisim, 2010), 411; *NTV Tarih*, December 2009, 61. For a documentary novel of the ordeal of a young mother and her child, see Haydar Karataş, *Butterfly of the Night*, transl. Caroline Stockford (London: Palewell Press, 2021).

friends, enemies and the mountains, shall know that the Turk is the master of this country. All those who are not pure Turks have only one right in the Turkish homeland: the right to be servants, the right to be slaves."[103] In October 1935, Italy began a brutal invasion of Ethiopia, in which it used chemical weapons and killed hundreds of thousands of men, women, and children. Even though Turkey's and Italy's foreign policies contrasted, Mussolini's fascism as well as Nazism were, according to Bozkurt – by then a Professor of the History of the Turkish Revolution in Ankara – nothing other than new versions of Kemalism.[104]

The sequence of Resettlement Law (İskân Kanunu) in 1934; Tunceli Law in 1935; new police and military infrastructure under military rule (Inspectorate General) in 1936; arrest and execution of elites; and the campaign in accordance with the Council of Ministers' decision on 4 May 1937, attest to the facts and logic of a planned extermination. Presented by Kaya, the Tunceli Law labeled the region a zone of "illness" that needed "surgery."[105] The Kurdish attack on a new police station in March 1937 served as the occasion to trigger the plan. Eradication policy came first, insurrection second. The minutes of the meetings of the Inspectorate General in 1936 testify to the effort to erase non-Turkish languages, cultures, and histories in Dersim as elsewhere in the country, and to a veritable intellectual raid that attributed Anatolia's cultural assets, achievements, and diverse human identities all to Turkishness.[106]

***

Nur's openly racist and xenophobic thought, as in his *History of the Armenians*; the absence of credible and enforceable minority rights in the Lausanne Treaty; and the total appropriation of Anatolia in the history doctrine are all part of an exclusionary and, in extremis, exterminatory nationalism. The new nation-state's formation came to an end with Atatürk's death and the genocide in Dersim in 1938. In contrast to the death of the supreme leader, the genocide roused no international echo.

After the mid-1930s, Lausanne's signatory powers were absorbed with the rise of Nazi Germany. They feared German–Turkish rapprochement so they became ready for increased connivance with, and new concessions

---

[103] *Son Posta*, 20 September 1930, quoted in Halıcı, *Yeni Türkiye*, 348. For a similar statement of the prime minister at the time, Ismet Inönü, on the Turks' exclusive "ethnic and racial rights" in Asia Minor, see *Milliyet*, 31 August 1930.
[104] Bozkurt, *Atatürk ihtilali*, 107.
[105] Beşikçi, *Tunceli Kanunu (1935) ve Dersim Jenosidi*, 17; Ülker, "Assimilation, Security and Geographical Nationalization," 8; Halli, *Türkiye Cumhuriyetinde ayaklanmalar (1924–1938)*, 390–391 and 491.
[106] *Umumî Müfettişler Toplantı Tutanakları*, ed. M. Bülent Varlık (Ankara: Dipnot, 2010), 72–73.

vis-à-vis Ankara. Since the resolution of the Mosul dispute, Britain did all it could to deepen its new proximity, whose roots went back to the first half of the Lausanne Conference. Although aware of what went on in Dersim, and of "methods similar to those used against the Armenians during the Great War,"[107] London chose to ignore the genocide and to flatter Ankara's dictatorship. It was about preventing any outmaneuvering by Berlin like that in 1914. The League of Nations – of which Turkey was a member since 1932, and Stalin's Russia since 1934 – had lost any agency against antidemocracy. In the international crises of the 1930s, Ankara's dictator had used the opportunity to expand Turkey's scope of action and also to reaffirm nationalist pride and grandeur in a domestically worsening economic situation. As mentioned earlier, Turkey simply disregarded private agreements, which were based on the Lausanne Treaty, regarding the repayment of the Ottoman Debt.[108]

An important and well-prepared international step was the initiation of a conference in Montreux near Lausanne in 1936. Necmettin Sadık Sadak – readers know him as a former journalist in Ankara's team at the Lausanne Conference – served as Turkey's delegate in Montreux. In those years, he was also the permanent representative at the League of Nations in Geneva.[109] The Montreux Convention permitted Turkish remilitarization of the Straits, thus revising Lausanne's related stipulations.[110] Of even greater impact was the incorporation – a thinly veiled annexation – of a considerable part of northwestern Syria with Iskenderun and Antakya ("Hatay") in 1938. France, the mandatory power, and the League gave in to a well-prepared scheme. The bullying regional power exploited the then-international system for its tolerated expansionism by way of manipulation. This included a rigged referendum after a previous mass transfer of Turks into the region.

The result was an enforced mass exodus of oriental Christians, notably Armenians, who had found refuge and protection under the mandatory roof.[111] The drive to reverse compromises enshrined in the Lausanne Treaty, in order to implement a maximalist interpretation of Ankara's 1920 National Pact, is inherent in the Lausanne settlement and anticipated in the debates of the National Assembly in 1923. It is not only built

---

[107] British consul in Trabzon to Ambassador Percy Loraine, 27 September 1938. Quoted in David McDowall, *A Modern History of the Kurds* (London: I.B. Tauris, 1996), 209.
[108] Gennai, *La Question d'Orient: La gestion multilatérale de la Dette Publique Ottomane*, 98.
[109] Mustafa Özyürek, "Giriş," *Lozan Mektupları*, 14.
[110] *League of Nations Treaty Series*, vol. 173 (1936–7), 214–241.
[111] Berna Pekesen, "The Exodus of Armenians from the Sanjak of Alexandretta in the 1930s," in H. L. Kieser (ed.), *Turkey beyond Nationalism* (London: I.B. Tauris, 2006), 57–66. Stéphane Yerasimos, "Le sandjak d'Alexandrette: formation et intégration d'un territoire," *Revue de l'Occident musulman et de la Méditerranée*, 48–49 (1988), 198–212.

into a settlement that amounted to a pact of elites in powers. it also derives from an inherently restless and expansionist, because myth-based and nondemocratic, Gökalpian nationalism. Its main expansionist stations after Lausanne are 1938 (Antakya), 1973 (Northern Cyprus), and – more assertively than ever since 1923 – the current period with invasions, armed interventions, and aggressions in Northern Syria, Iraq, Libya, the Caucasus, and the Aegean. The state-sponsored pogrom against the Rûm in Istanbul in 1955, which led to the exodus of this group exempted from the 1923 population exchange, is further testimony to Ankara's inherent Lausanne revisionism. Another example is Hatay.

In the 1930s, the supreme leader used Ankara's diplomatic and military means to incorporate "Hatay," the pretended place of ancient proto-Turkish Hittites. Underpinned by the Turkish History Thesis, the fiction of a Turanian or proto-Turkish past of Anatolia and Mesopotamia now loomed even larger than in the early 1920s. Beyond rhetoric, the incorporation of Syrian Antakya thus obeyed a historical mental map that Atatürk wanted to be recognized public history. The making of the History Thesis has revealed how close this – also international – recognition and justification was to the heart of the ageing and by then (due to alcohol) terminally ill dictator.

Full of admiration for Atatürk's diplomatic shrewdness, the narrative of Turkish historian Nur Bilge Criss reads as follows:

> Atatürk ... patiently waited until the Hatay plum ripened. Between March 15, 1923, when he mentioned Hatay (the Sandjak of Alexandretta) as having been Turkish land for 4000 years, and the mid-1936 signing of the Montreux convention ... Ataturk cautiously waited and helped the Turks of Hatay to pave the way for its incorporation into Turkey. Finally in October 1936, Ataturk, noticing the international environment was favorable for such a move took the initiative. By suddenly leaving for Adana to inspect the troops, he made sure that the French would understand his readiness to resort to military means if the Hatay problem was not solved in favor of the Turks.[112]

32   Lozan Myth: Turkey's Betrayed, to Be Restored, Sultanate-Caliphate

After the deal struck in Lausanne, Ankara's forced modernization and absent democratization failed to pacify the country in a peaceful way. Society in Anatolia had emerged in 1922 transformed by a decade of wars and demographic engineering. Coercive and violent transformation continued from 1923. However, besides continued disfranchising of the remaining non-Muslims, it was now mainly about completely subduing

---

[112] Nur Bilge Criss, "Turkish Foreign Policy toward the Middle East," *Middle East Review of International Affairs* (January, 1997), https://ciaotest.cc.columbia.edu/olj/meria/meria97_criss.html.

two critical allied forces from the preceding wars: the Kurds and political Islam. For a century to come, these forces proved highly restive.

At the end of the twentieth century, many contemporaries believed, "the whole era of ideological rivalries which began in 1917 came to an end" when the Soviet empire collapsed in 1989.[113] It is true that the collapse of the Soviet Union was followed by an interval full of liberal hope for constructive peace for Eastern Europe, Israel-Palestine, and other hotspots; a little later also for a Turkey turning to the European Union; and finally for the short Arab Spring. Yet at the same time, since the 1990s, critical pre-Lausanne polarizations in world politics came again to the global fore, though in updated shapes: a would-be restoration of the caliphate by Al-Qaeda, the "Islamic State" and related organizations, as well as, since mid-2010s, a new edition of a Russian–Turkish alliance (i.e. of two meanwhile clearly antidemocratic states). The expansionist competition between these cooperating autocracies claims (without foundation) to be anti-imperialism.[114]

All these actors follow an ideologically loaded agenda that refers to religion and former empires. They oppose liberal and leftist democracy. As far as Turkish and non-Turkish Islamists are concerned, they all have absorbed revisionist claims on the Lausanne Near East Peace that they often amalgamate with the Sykes–Picot agreement. For them, the Lausanne settlement and the subsequent abolition of the caliphate are closely related. In final analysis, this statement is not wrong. However, conspiracy theories abound in these circles about Lausanne's alleged secret deals or complots, concocted to the detriment of the Muslims and the caliphate. The exclusion of Arabs and other non-Turkish Muslims from the Conference table facilitated such imaginings. Caliphate nostalgia and militantism have however also found a rich breeding ground in Turkey itself. This religious and emotional reservoir has proved instrumental for current President Erdoğan's buildup of personalized autocracy. He benefitted from the revisionist potential by having the Hagia Sophia converted to a mosque and the public space marked with insistent and intrusive references to revered sultan-caliphs.[115] To these Turkish circles, too, the Lausanne Treaty is a red rag or at least a target of criticism.

---

[113] Mazower, *Dark Continent*, xi.

[114] Bozarslan, *L'anti-démocratie*. See also Annette Werberger, "Putin stilisiert sich zum Weltrevolutionär. Der Kreml betreibt ein Revival des sowjetischen Internationalismus. Lenin und Stalin werden zu Stichwortgebern," *NZZ*, 10 August 2022), 32.

[115] For example, the new Bosporus bridge named "Yavuz Selim" and the aggressively operating drillship "Abdulhamid Han." For rich analytical context: Nikos Christofis (ed.), *Erdoğan's 'New' Turkey: Attempted Coup d'état and the Acceleration of Political Crisis* (London: Routledge, 2020). See also Hakan Yavuz, "Erdoğan and the Hagia Sophia: Nostalgia for the Ottoman Empire," *Berkeley Forum*, 21 July 2020; Hany Ghoraba, "Erdogan's Neo-Ottoman Aspirations Inspire Islamists and Endanger World Peace," *The Algemeiner*, 10 August 2020; Cynthia Lardner, "Erdogan: Self-Proclaimed Caliphate?" *International Policy Digest*, 27 June 2017.

This is not the place to present the various post-Lausanne caliphate movements and attempts at international reorganization,[116] nor to delve into conspiracy theories and current caliphal ambitions. This Chapter will only try to shed light on the links of such movements with regard to the Lausanne Conference. First, it shortly analyzes the event of the abolition, and also inquires how far caliphate issues emerged during official Conference meetings at all.

***

Lozan myths emerged in two opposing contexts: as a hyperbolic narrative of Kemalist Ankara's diplomatic triumph over centuries-old inimical foreign intrigues; or as the lament of the betrayed Ottoman sultanate-caliphate and other interests of Turks, Arabs, and Muslims in general. In this latter vision, the caliphate awaits its restoration by a new cohort of Islamic or Islamic-Turkish saviors, who reveal and foil allegedly secret agreements made behind the scenes of the Lausanne Conference.

Many of these wild speculations, especially since the formation of the state of Israel, are blatantly anti-Semitic, while still conserving the anti-Armenian tenets of the early 1920s. The negative correlate of the Kemalist *Lozan* myth is the so-called Sèvres syndrome – the specter of Turkey's partition by inimical Western powers allied to "domestic agents" (indigenous liberals and Christians).[117] Not properly part of the Sèvres syndrome, but closely related in Kemalist argument, is fear of a caliph who could be used by enemies of the Kemalist project.

The Ankara government abolished the sultanate shortly before the Conference, in order to prevent the invitation of another delegation from the still-existing sultanate-caliphate with its seat in Istanbul. It thus separated sultanate and caliphate. Although not on the Conference's official agenda, the abolition of the caliphate in the aftermath of the Conference stood in line with the prospect presented by Ankara's delegation during negotiations: the promise to establish a modern, secular, and democratic republic. After declaring the republic on 29 October 1923, three months after signature of the Treaty, Ankara started to undertake reforms that comprised abolishing the caliphate and the sharia.

---

[116] See Mona Hassan, *Longing for the Lost Caliphate: A Transregional History* (Princeton, NJ: Princeton University Press, 2016), 142–252; Reinhard Schulze, *Islamischer Internationalismus im 20. Jahrhundert: Untersuchungen zur Geschichte der Islamischen Weltliga* (Leiden: Brill, 1990).

[117] Oran, *Türkiye'de azınlıklar*, 160–162.

During the Conference, however, there was no mention or discussion of a possible abolition of the caliphate. The "seat of the Caliphate" to "be sheltered from any attack" – as according to the National Pact – was mentioned several times during meetings on the Straits. It was not questioned from any side (see Part III). Nur asserted the establishment of "an entirely democratic regime" thanks to the separation of caliphate and state. This served him as an argument against minority rights and for the removal of the ecumenical patriarchate from Istanbul.[118] When caliphal possessions were discussed, the Turkish delegation insisted on the independence of the caliph so that no one neither the Ankara government nor, a fortiori, the Allies had any say in this issue. "In short, the solution to every problem concerning the religion of the Muslims lies with the Muslims alone," Şükrü (Kaya) apodictically stated.[119]

A prominent object of dispute was the sacred articles removed from Medina by the Ottoman army in 1917. On behalf of Muslims worldwide, the Allies argued that these were "objects of supreme veneration to Moslems in every country." They demanded that Ankara at least declare its willingness to restore the objects.[120] The Turkish side answered evasively and got entangled in contradictions. It notably claimed property of, and restitution for, the Hedjaz Railway that connected Damascus and Medina. It argued that this Railway belonged to the Caliphate. It did not want to renounce on caliphal "properties bringing in revenue to the State [Ankara]."[121] Ankara's desire to speak in the name of all Muslims and to possess the caliphal properties and possessions transpires unambiguously from the conference minutes, but there is no direct or explicit hint that it would decide on abolition less than a year later. Still, in late 1923, Prime Minister Ismet used threatening language in the Assembly: "If, at any time in history, a caliph has the desire to interfere in the fate of this country, we will definitely cut off his head!"[122]

The sudden end of the caliphate on 3 March 1924 was a shock to Muslims worldwide. Haste, fear, and verbal violence accompanied the abolition itself. Dragoman Ryan (familiar to the readers from his presence at the Conference) again stayed in Istanbul in 1924. He recollected the event as follows:

Within a few hours of the adoption of the laws [denationalization of the imperial family, confiscation of imperial property], the decision of the Assembly was notified to the Caliph. This was done late at night ..., and in the early morning

---

[118] *LCP*, 322, 333, 337.
[119] Sub-commission meeting of the Second Commission, 25 January 1922, *LKT*, vol. 2, 200.
[120] Second Commission, 27 January 1923, *LCP*, 528–530.
[121] Third Commission, 27 January 1923, *LCP*, 601.   [122] Atatürk, *Nutuk*, 560.

of the next day, March 4th, he was hurried off by car to Chatalja to be entrained for Switzerland in the evening.

The goal was to get rid of the dignitary "without leaving time for any opposition to make itself felt."[123] So-called Courts of Independence again ensured intimidation. Coerced by a representative of Ankara, a member of the Swiss Union in Istanbul had signed the passport of the ex-caliph Abdulmecid II on Tuesday afternoon, 4 March 1924.

A week after his arrival at Territet near Lausanne, Abdulmecid was welcomed by the chief of police of the canton of Vaud. On 12 March, he published a message to the "Muslim world," referring to "an impious decision of the present majority of the National Assembly" and calling for an international congress to determine the future of the caliphate. Secretary Traversini of Bern's ministry of foreign affairs visited Abdulmecid and his private secretary Salih Bey twice, on 9 and 14 March. In defense of Abdulmecid's high office, they insisted that the election and upholding of his caliphate had been agreed both by the National Assembly and, tacitly, "the Muslim world." In his second visit, Traversini imposed on them that "total abstention of any act of political or religious propaganda" was Bern's condition of the ex-caliph's continued stay in Switzerland. "It is the prison, then," Salih responded. On 17 March, having arrived in Bern for Ankara's foreign affairs committee, Şükrü Kaya expressed his satisfaction at the attitude of the Swiss government.[124]

A long letter by the Swiss legate in Rome informed Bern of an interlocution with London's ambassador Ronald W. Graham. The British diplomat expressed satisfaction over Abdulmecid's expulsion. Britain welcomed "the emergence of other caliphs at other places in order to deprive the Muslim world of this central institution.... Several caliphs are much better than one from the point of view of the interests of Europe." As for Switzerland, she should not fear any damage with hosting the deposed caliph: this was, on the contrary, "a moral privilege."[125]

***

---

[123] Ryan, *Last of the Dragomans*, 213–214.

[124] "Texte integral du message remis par le Calife," 12 March 1924; two reports by secretary Traversini, 11 and 14 March 1924. "Auszug aus dem Protokoll der Sitzung des schweizerischen Bundesrats," 18 March 1924; letter by Ernest Mamboury to Foreign Affairs, Berne, 22 March 1924; letter by Mr. Märklin to Foreign Affairs, Berne, 24 March 1924. All documents: BAr, E 2001 (B), vol. 18 E 2001 (B), vol. 18. – There was no official Swiss legation in Turkey before 1928. This is why the Swiss Union under its president Ernest Mamboury fulfilled certain consular functions in an honorary capacity.

[125] Swiss legation in Rome to Bundesrat, Bern, 13 March 1924, BAr, E 2001 (B), vol. 18, no. 5.

The ümmet had formed the main popular basis in Anatolia for the continued struggle after the World War. The CUP had fought this war in the name of the ümmet and the ümmet's head, the sultan-caliph who enjoyed worldwide esteem among Muslims. In Gökalp's 1910s-version of Turkish nationalism, the caliph played a major role, and he continued to do so among many early collaborators of Ankara's supreme leader Mustafa Kemal (Atatürk) who fell out with the latter during or after Lausanne. Rıza Nur was among them, notwithstanding the fact that Nur also had wanted the separation of the caliphate from the new state at the eve of the Conference.

The majority of Muslims all over the world had believed that the Turkish nationalists under Gazi Kemal Pasha struggled for a continued and re-empowered sultanate-caliphate in Istanbul, as proclaimed by representatives of Ankara's Assembly. Most Muslims applauded and identified with Ankara's victories in what they considered jihad, and with Turkey's subsequent diplomatic re-empowerment in Lausanne. Among the strongest sympathizers were those in Afghanistan and India (including today's Pakistan).[126] Shortly after Lausanne, they suddenly felt alienated. Informally represented by an envoy in Lausanne, Hussein bin Ali did not see any support in 1923 for his volatile desire of a restored Arab caliphate, neither by British nor Turkish interlocutors. The British did not stand in Ibn Saud's way to expand Wahhabi power on the Arab peninsula at the expense of Hussein, their former ally. The Saudis built up a large independent power base, but did not aspire to the caliphal position.[127]

"Al-ghazi's [Atatürk's] speeches left no doubt that Turkey initially revolted in order to defend Islam and the caliphate, and to assert solidarity to the Muslims and hundreds of millions of Arabs," wrote the Lebanese notable Shakib Arslan in 1933. "But as soon as the Lausanne Treaty was concluded," he continued, "they regarded Islam as a 'detrimental' principle that must be abolished, because inappropriate for a civilised nation."[128] Mostly agitating in Europe, Arslan had been a loyal collaborator and propagandist of the Young Turks beyond 1918, including in denying or justifying the Armenian genocide. A prominent pan-Islamic

---

[126] Gail Minault, *The Khilafat Movement: Religious Symbolism and Political Mobilization in India* (New York: Columbia University Press, 1982).

[127] Teitelbaum, *The Rise and Fall of the Hashimite Kingdom of Arabia*, 240–241 and 278–282. In contrast to Hussein, the Saudis did not descend from the Quraysh (the tribe of Muhammed).

[128] Arabic journal *Al-Fath* 8/353 (1933), quoted in Mehdi Sajid, *Muslime im Zwischenkriegseuropa und die Dekonstruktion der Faszination vom Westen. Eine kritische Auseinandersetzung mit Šakīb 'Arslāns Artikeln in der ägyptischen Zeitschrift al-Fatḥ (1926–1935)* (Berlin: EB-Verlag, 2015), 336. See also Teitelbaum, *Hashimite Kingdom*, 240.

and anti-colonial propagandist until 1922, he was an unofficial Egyptian delegate at the Lausanne Conference. Remaining in Switzerland, he raised an Arab voice from Geneva against Kemalism and, as an ally of the Mufti of Jerusalem Amin al-Husayni, for the Palestinian cause.[129]

A few early congresses, among them the Caliphate Congress in Cairo in 1926, all failed in their attempts to reestablish the caliphate on an international Islamic basis.[130] Hasan al-Banna, the Egyptian founder of the Muslim Brotherhood in 1928, acknowledged that the shocking loss of the Ottoman Caliphate had motivated him to found the new seminal organization from which later hailed various Islamist movements. Despite the common central idea of a restored caliphate, this could not be effectively revived during the twentieth century. The most explicit effort to date is that by the "Islamic State" (IS) in 2014, a quasi-state that excelled by an unprecedented level of extreme public and publicized violence. Controlling large territories from Syria to Iraq, its leaders declared to be a caliphate, pronouncing one of them, Abu Bakr al Baghdadi, caliph in Mosul's Grand al-Nuri mosque. Mosul was liberated from IS in 2017.[131]

In post-Lausanne Turkey, it took four decades before an articulate Islamist critique of the Lausanne Treaty appeared to the public. From the 1950s, Islam generally regained visibility and influence in the country. Revisionist Islamist history books were published, notably those of Necip Fazıl Kısakürek. The theologically most important reference for fundamental critique was Said Nursi (alias, before 1923, Said Kurdî). Although hardly touching on other than religious or personal matters in his large correspondence and conversations with groups of followers, Nursi incidentally coined harsh terms for the post-Lausanne state like "republic of absolute despotism," "regime of absolute perversion," "law for arbitrary force," and "civilization of absolute debauchery." He also had made eschatological interpretations that Kemalists resented as a threat; this is why they took him to court. In contrast to epigones like Kısakürek and Mısıroğlu after the Second World War, Nursi neither longed for a restored caliphate nor delved into historical revisionism based on anti-Semitic conspiracy theories. He rejected inflated narratives of Muslim-centered victimhood, abstained from anti-Armenian tropes, and was a long-standing critic of ultranationalist Turkism.[132]

---

[129] William L. Cleveland, *Islam against the West: Shakib Arslan and the Campaign for Islamic Nationalism* (Austin: University of Texas Press, 1985); Kieser, *Talaat Pasha*, 405 and 409.
[130] Ardıç, *Islam and the Politics of Secularism*, 300–302; Ryan, *Last of the Dragomans*, 215.
[131] Hassan, *Longing for the Lost Caliphate*, 253–260.
[132] Ibid., 244–252; Rasim Özdenören, "Necip Fazıl Kısayürek," in *Modern Türkiye'de siyasi düşünce: İslâmcılık* (Istanbul: Iletisim, 2004), 139–149.

32 Lozan Myth

Turkey's Sunni mainstream critics of Lausanne sought revenge for the lost caliphal empire, and for the hardships pious Muslims suffered under the Kemalist regime. They shared the dream of a greater Turkey and the denial of the Armenian genocide with ultranationalists. Their critique of Lausanne owed its concrete insights into the Conference to Nur's memoirs, which combined self-appraisal with regret and resentment. As observed in Parts II and III Nur had found fault with compromises struck at the Conference. His abundant writings in exile became posthumously accessible in the 1960s. His prominence as well as his personal victimhood in the eyes of his sympathizers, made him a central reference for Lausanne Treaty revisionism. Nur's memoirs underpin Turkey's main revisionist libel in three volumes – titled *Lausanne: Victory or Defeat?* – that was composed by Kadir Mısıroğlu, one of the editors of Nur's memoirs, also in three volumes. Both works were published in the second half of the 1960s.[133] Since the 1960s, the mainstream critique remains close to Nur, thus to a religiously tinged racial Turkism that resents the imperial losses in Lausanne and desires a restored caliphate. In this vision, the Lausanne Treaty was not the due recompense for Turkey's previous victories and did not reward the blood shed by martyrs from 1911 to 1922. These critics cultivate the (factually wrong) sentiment that the Kemalists were duped by Europe at the Conference and that conspiracies prevented a better outcome after a decade of late-Ottoman wars. Since the 2010s, such tenets have entered the ruling ideology in Ankara.

"It is surprising that many contemporary Islamists forget the dark side of previous caliphates, including that of the Ottomans," historian and anthropologist Madawi al-Rasheed wrote shortly before the rise of IS in her book, *Demystifying the Caliphate*. She linked failure in delivering an equitable constitutional framework for government with the nostalgia about the caliphate. At issue, in other words, is democracy; that is, the challenge to conclude democratic social contracts that underpin effective constitutionality and pragmatic peace in society.[134] The Islamists, who came to power in Ankara eighty years after the Lausanne Treaty, have no less failed the challenge, and squandered the opportunity, to focus on democracy than the Kemalists before them.

---

[133] Kadir Mısıroğlu, *Lozan: Zafer mi, hezimet mi?* (Istanbul: Sebil, 1992; first eds., 1965–1979), vols. 1–3.

[134] Madawi al-Rasheed, "The Wahhabis and the Ottoman Caliphate," in al-Rasheed and Marat Shterin (eds.), *Demystifying the Caliphate: Historical Memory and Contemporary Contexts* (London: Hurst, 2013), 134.

In Lieu of a Conclusion
Time for Democratic Social Contracts

The Conference and Treaty of Lausanne offer invaluable insights into the state of the world, Europe, and the Middle East at a crossroads in the early 1920s. Main lines drawn in this last settlement of the Paris-Geneva peace system have for a century defined the post-Ottoman space, Western relations with post-Ottoman countries, political behaviors, and far-reaching paradigms of "conflict resolution." There was the challenge of "world peace," as repeatedly invoked. Understandably, Lausanne failed to meet this almost utopian challenge.

But the Conference also gave up on the more concrete ambitions of the time, as argued in *When Democracy Died*. It gave in to antidemocracy in substance, if not in name. This is why this last treaty constitutes a fundamental watershed. This book has clarified that for Curzon, Poincaré, and other representatives of time-honored democracies, democracy and constitutionality were by no means a priority. Not only their commitment to, but also their understanding of, democracy was weak in critical regards. At the negotiating table in Lausanne, they gave Ankara what it wanted in return for getting what they wanted: reasserted national-imperial power, an exploitable Arab Middle East, working relations with potentates, and a politically sidelined Russia.

Studying a pivotal peace such as the Lausanne Near East Peace Treaty requires a reflection on what peace actually is. Is it pacification from within? What would it mean to overcome violence – to not let violence win – and make this replicable? How does one provide for the healing of wounds? Required is a peace rooted as much on the ground, among the people living in the region itself, as on a level of temporary international interactions. It is, in the terminology of this book, about democratic social contracts with which, as this author takes it, no organized peace can dispense. This closing section is not the place for an elaborate philosophy (for which this author does not feel qualified). It only serves to make transparent a number of thoughts that have accompanied and underpinned the writing of the book.

Dismantling Antidemocracy

The publicly declared ambitions of the Western powers during the Great War and for the Paris-Geneva peace were, on the one hand, the liberation of formerly subordinate peoples, in particular of those brutally victimized during the Ottoman long Great War; on the other, building up a League- and law-based framework for all, small and large. In particular, this concerned the crisis-ridden world that the West has since then called the Middle East. The failure to meet these ambitions amounted to the collapse of the core message and moral that had driven Western commitment during and at the end of the First World War. In the late- and post-Ottoman world, this collapse resulted in the ultimate disintegration of the hopes for constitutional futures that had vigorously come to the fore during the 1908 Young Turk Revolution and reemerged after 1918.

This double collapse and defeat was inherent in Lausanne's pact of power and interest, struck between Ankara's ultranationalists and Western Europe's remaining national empires. Lausanne thus opened the door for antidemocratic far-right currents in high politics and diplomacy, starting with Turkism and Italian Fascism, and profoundly impacting on Nazism. Ankara's National Assembly reestablished and rehabilitated leading forces that had carried Istanbul-based Turkey in the 1910s – a then-pioneering experience in imperial and genocidal single-party rule. Recognized by Lausanne, where it played a key role, Ankara's National Assembly government became the first regime among Interwar antidemocrats to be fully embraced by international diplomacy.

Ankara used its multiple relations with, and its belated membership in, the League of Nations as a means to domestically realize and internationally rubber-stamp its notion of state and society. This pioneering ultranationalist concept amounted to a radically homogenized, unitary, and, by the early 1930s, totalitarian nation-state. The League-supported "population exchange" of 1923 was the pivotal step toward the League's open abandonment of previously defended basic rights and principles, including freedom for small peoples on their own soil. It prejudiced the League's future to be less a beacon of humanity than a proxy of contemporary potentates, although dedicated democrats working within or associated to the League still stood for their constitutional and internationalist convictions.

Hopeful and substantial steps of a "new Turkey" and Turkey's "revolution" after Lausanne are not to be denied. But the persistence of antidemocratic patterns in political life is now, in the 2020s, and was then, after the Conference, a defining issue of the country. Lofty hopes and promises, diplomatically promoted in Lausanne and on many further occasions, were time and again falsified by antidemocratic behavior and open contempt for law. Set during and after the Lausanne Conference, the prevailing lines are detailed in *When Democracy Died*. A hundred years later, R. T. Erdogan's devastating autocracy has increased the interest in, and sharpened the analytical look on, the relevant historical conditions. A century after Lausanne, this president embodies what went wrong from a democratic perspective. Lausanne encouraged personalized partisan rule and unseparated powers. Its failure to clarify basic issues of contemporary history – such as dispossession and extermination – made the birth certificate it issued to Turkey fragile. It left recent history demagogically exploitable. The suppression and lack of fact-based clarification fuelled conspiracy theories and presaged a return of the repressed. All this contributed to the emergence of myths on late-Ottoman history and a politically powerful nostalgia for a renewed Turkish-Muslim empire.

Turkey's rapprochement with the European Union in the 2000s has to a large extent dismantled the antidemocratic legacy of a Kemalism that has long enjoyed almost universal recognition. By the same token, it at least partly dismounted a pact of interests enshrined in post-Lausanne Kemalism. From the 2010s, the long decade before 1922, which had led to Lausanne, has therefore moved to the center of critical interest. Erdogan's "neo-Ottoman" autocracy comes in multiple ways back to the late Ottoman era and questions the Lausanne Treaty. Its ideologemes smell not only of imperial nostalgia, they also bring to the political surface late-Ottoman Islamist and pan-Turkish forces that the Lausanne Conference seemed to have domesticated. If we want to understand the meaning and impact of the Treaty, Lausanne as a whole – including the preceding and conditioning decade of wars, genocide and ideology production – must be analyzed and disassembled. Appeasement after a decade of extreme violence on the backs of the weak, minorities, genocide victims, human rights, freedoms, and democratic requirements did not stand the test of time. Lausanne proved costly.

All democratic openings in the Republic of Turkey have hitherto failed to consolidate, be this during twentieth-century Europe's major democratic moments – the aftermaths of the First and Second World Wars, and of the Cold War[1] – or during peculiar moments like the 1960 constitution or the hopeful approach to the European Union in the 2000s. If, by and large, correct and free, elections and a multiparty system – as in Turkey since the mid-twentieth century –are important achievements. But they by no means suffice for a functioning free democracy. The repeated

---

[1] Timothy Snyder, *On Tyranny: Twenty Lessons from the Twentieth Century* (London: Bodley Head, 2017), 11.

practice of a multicausal antidemocracy is challenging for historians. It compels us to dig deep and distrust appearances. A knowledgeable political scientist has recently argued that any reform or opening, as pragmatic as it may appear, would end in a new radicalism, as long as "the antidemocratic logic, which has underpinned the Turkish Republic since its foundation, was not called into question."[2] The exploration of this Lausanne-related logic lays at the heart of *When Democracy Died*.

I have become acquainted with modern Turkey – its people, history, and politics – over four decades, enjoying the privilege of being treated as a "Turkish brother-in-law" (Türk eniştesi), for which I am very grateful. I have stayed in almost all corners of the historically rich, geographically beautiful country. From my encounters, I have learnt a great deal and had the chance to establish life-long relationships and friendships. Facing realities of antidemocracy willy-nilly has challenged me, however; it has impacted on my historical studies of which many explore the question of what is required for viable democratic life.

In this book, I have subsumed these requirements under the title of "democratic social contracts," taking them as fundamental factors and units of real peace and repaired relations. These requirements imply "honest history"[3] and implicate the question of the destiny of the former Ottoman conationals. What about the latter's post-Lausanne trajectory? What does it take to repair relations that were profoundly damaged in the social Darwinist context of the Lausanne Conference? The rights and cause, pain and memory of Lausanne's disfranchised victims or "losers" do not fade away: Armenians, Assyrians, Rûm, Kurds, Turkish dissenters, and very many others directly or indirectly affected by Lausanne's spirit and prescriptions. *When Democracy Died* can certainly not do justice to all of them in its narration. "More truth and democracy!" is, however, its underlying, future-oriented response. This response may deserve here a few further historical, philosophical, and theological thoughts.

Lausanne's Open Door for Fascisms

As earlier mentioned (Part I), Turkey was by no means an exotic or eccentric entity at the margins of Europe, but a pioneering and defining factor of Interwar antidemocracy. Phase one of Turkey's formation as a unitary nation-state in Anatolia took place between 1913 and 1922; that

---

[2] Bozarslan, *Anti-démocratie*, 247–248.
[3] I owe this term to the Australian "Honest History" Association that did important work related to the centenary of the Gallipoli campaign and the involved ANZAC; see https://honesthistory.net.au.

is, first under CUP rule allied to Wilhelmine Germany, and then under the ex-CUP counter-government in Ankara. The Conference of Lausanne endorsed the sole claim of this new government of a National Assembly, established by a formerly imperial Turkish-Muslim elite. Most of them were former CUP members led by Gazi Mustafa Kemal (Atatürk), who early on aspired to supreme leadership. Brought together by the will to defend previous privileges, benefits, and "Islam," the government in Ankara successfully waged war against non-Turkish indigenous claims in Anatolia. Lukewarmly underpinned by the Great War victors, the Sèvres Treaty had enshrined these claims and the project of a plural Anatolia, but also tried to satisfy imperial desires of Allies in that area.

Based on Lausanne, phase two of Turkey's formation saw the construction of a modernizing party-state led by the supreme leader Kemal Atatürk. In line with prospects drawn and the discourse held in Lausanne in 1923, he set on Western civilization, but without democracy. Related to his radical turn to Western civilization in the public sphere, he renounced the Islamic political credentials that had abundantly co-determined phase one. The former imperial elites in Ankara thus definitively implemented in Lausanne what this book has labeled the "third" modernist option; that is, an illiberal and rightist "revolutionary" road out of the Great War. This political way can be named ultranationalism or "another fascism" on late-Ottoman Islamic ground.

What unmistakably won in Lausanne, was not negotiation, consent, and the pursuit of an inclusive common good for all in the country – what underpins democratic thought – but an organization of coercive and military power that was able to effectively mobilize a critical mass of stakeholders in its own country against the Paris-Geneva peace. Their success surprised contemporaries who were not sufficiently aware of the Young Turk prehistory of Ankara, or wrongly regarded Turkey's political actors as eccentric. What therefore paradigmatically prevailed in Lausanne was the successful application of violence and compulsion for revisionist ends and a modernist dictatorship. This antidemocratic outcome was the consequence both of Ankara's resolute agenda and the inherent imperial bias in the Paris-Geneva peace.

What was defeated in Lausanne, was the common identification with an internal and external peace according to the League of Nations and the League's initial democratic thought. The victors of the war in Asia Minor spoke in the exclusive name of Turkish Muslims, who by then had been forcibly made the large majority in the country. Based on demographic engineering, genocide, and final military success, their representatives were in a position to claim unrestricted unitary rule. The League of

Nations had suffered from imperialist-colonialist bias in its mandates. With Lausanne, it became, to a certain extent, the agent and accomplice of ultranationalist nation-building.

Nothing defines fascism as sharply as the embrace of force combined with an exterminatory contempt for small peoples on Earth, and for weaker "others" in society – minorities, scapegoats, nonconformists, or "invalids." Fascism in this core sense triumphed in Lausanne. The Young Turks and their inheritors in Ankara were early-Interwar Europe's masters not only in violent demographic engineering, but also in invalidating minority rights. Over years and decades, Ankara performed an unequaled diplomatic powerplay whenever there was any question of these rights or of openly addressing those they had abused, deported, and murdered. Ankara's belated adherence to the League of Nations hardly helped any "international domestication" in a democratic sense. Though internationally again more connected and adapted, republican Turkey remained rooted in her original political soil: the belligerent imperial CUP party-state. The new other, international root perhaps inspired the Kemalists to, at times, espouse democracy as an ideal, even though this was a very distant ideal, and one which, whenever it was about to become concrete, they considered dangerous for themselves.

What effectively distinguished the Kemalists in Ankara from various fascists in continental Europe was not their domestic policies or a reluctance to be labeled dictatorial, but their insertion in a revised post–Great War system thanks to the Treaty of Lausanne. Most of them former CUP cadres, they had behind them their Great War phase of expansionist dreams of empire, which had gone hand in hand with extreme violence. In the Lausanne Treaty, they had no price to pay, no reparation to make for the crimes committed during that period against conationals. As we have seen in Part II, they successfully enforced the revision of the punitive Sèvres Treaty, with critical support from the Bolsheviks. This is why their political practice and theory were far ahead of continental Europe's fascists in the early 1920s.

Lausanne taught seminal lessons of appeasement vis-à-vis assertive ultranationalism years before the notorious Munich Agreement between Adolf Hitler and Neville Chamberlain. These lessons came from Britain's foreign minister Austin Chamberlain, Neville's half-brother. Against the advice of his ambassador in Turkey, and against the letter of the Lausanne Treaty, he refused to bring issues of dispossession and discrimination suffered by Turkish-Armenian citizens before the League, arguing that this would create mistrust with Ankara. "The fact appears to be that the Turks have now practically achieved their original object, that is, the elimination of all non-Turkish element in Anatolia. The process of what may be called racial purification or simplifications seems almost complete," he stated in early 1925. Giving priority to the Mosul issue in line with the British choices in Lausanne, he was entirely resigned to the comprehensive scheme of genocidal policy implemented by the Young Turks and completed by the Kemalists.[4] How could a defeatist Europe, as it evolved after Lausanne, seriously resist "racial purification" by genocide in Europe itself; that is, against the Shoah and the Holocaust?

Ernest Bovet, the Lausanne-born secretary of the Swiss Society for the League of Nations and a former professor at the University of Zurich, saw himself accused by Ankara for being "an enemy of the League of Nations," after he had dared to write an article on the ongoing dispossession of Turkey's remaining Armenians in *Les Minorités Nationales*. This was the bulletin of the International Union of Societies for the League of Nations, in particular of this Union's Permanent Commission of Minorities.[5] The Commission, the Union as a whole, and many of the country organizations are proof of a loyal, competent, and high-spirited commitment to the League's principles by lucid personalities. At the end of the 1920s, they still fought for a League of Nations true to its origins, bracing themselves against the rationale deployed in Lausanne by the main contracting powers.[6]

In Lausanne, the West's recipe for the Middle East was stability before democracy; short- and mid-term interests before long-term prospects; and thus appeasement before truth, justice, and law. Such distortion can never lead antidemocratic governments to self-democratize themselves, or party-states to turn pluralistic. Lausanne left this major and essential part of peace-making – soul-searching, justice, and repair – to future generations. While some democratic openings happily occurred in Ankara's post-Lausanne nation-state, they always remained brief. Time and again, political life fell back into entrenched patterns of leader-led authoritarianism, partisan autocracy, and violent polarization. Vocal in Ankara's National Assembly during the Conference of Lausanne, the rallying rhetoric of xenophobic nationalism and politicized Islam emerges repeatedly.

---

[4] Quoted in Liebisch-Gümüş, *Verflochtene Nationsbildung*, 378.
[5] Ernest Bovet, "Les biens des Armenéniens en Turquie," *Les Minorités Nationales*, 3.1 (1930), 9–14; "La Commission des Minorités de l'Union Internationale: Session de Bruxelles 23–24 février 1930," ibid., 26–27.
[6] This was not the case with the Turkish Society for the League of Nations, founded in April 1922. Subservient to Ankara's needs in the context of Lausanne, the Society's members negated the League's faith in coexistence in Anatolia and were absent among those fighting for elementary minority rights. Handpicked by the government, they voiced statements in line with Gökalp's organicist and essentialist doctrine of the nation. See Liebisch-Gümüş, *Verflochtene Nationsbildung*, 355–356.

Ruling individuals and parties in Ankara, then and now, ended up capturing the state apparatus, in particular the justice system. In doing so, they continued traditions already entrenched during CUP single-party rule from which almost all cadres in Ankara hailed. Not as one-offs, but methodically, they have disenfranchised countless innocent people, put untold people into prison, and brought many of them to unaccounted for deaths. Domestically, their politics have functioned by polarization, intimidation, and enemy images. Internationally, based on supposed geostrategic constraints, they continue to take recourse to nuisance, disruption, and extortion in critical situations. From the 1920s to the 2020s, this is most notoriously implemented by the ominous threat that the security of foreign nationals or minorities, Jews, and Christians, would or could no longer be guaranteed.

A concomitant enabler of this kind of political tradition is war, mythologization of war, and religiously dressed up hero worship. Thus, time and again in post-Ottoman Turkey, it is not the common good, but nationalist bluster that meets in the political arena of the National Assembly. Male egos dominate a polity that, right from the start, was based more on war, coercion, violence, and genocide than negotiation, democracy, and fundamental law. Power-hungry persons claim to represent "the nation" that they monopolize and spoil. They inflate themselves by this claim, both instrumentalizing and violating democracy in ways that "otherize" rivals and whole groups. The voices of the wise and peaceful are drowned out or laughed down in the process. The rights of otherized individuals and groups, innocent or not, count for nothing. Who really cares today (2022) in national and international politics about Osman Kavala and the tens of thousands more or less nameless conationals jailed according to autocratic will, not in breach of law?

As long as business functions on the levels in which foreign governments and companies are interested, Western democracies have hitherto not effectively cared about repeated domestic destruction that resulted in millions of migrants and hundreds of thousands of political asylum seekers. With its last update in June 2022 (the Turkish-Swedish-Finnish deal), NATO's ongoing appeasement of antidemocracy in Turkey is a case in point. In the footsteps of a realpolitik defined in Lausanne, it exemplifies how a state in the clutches of autocracy manages to stay afloat thanks to the skills of an ever-changing leadership to play the game of relevant partnerships. For generations, the sad price for this kind of relationship is the suffering of prominent dissenters and of millions of sidelined indigenous people who are bereft of the rule of law and efficient international solidarity.

A main victim since 1923, however, is the credibility of human rights–based democracy itself. The Lausanne settlement provided a kind of international stability by condoning "facts of power." It is time to face related *facts of history* that carry more weight in the long term. Lausanne made internationalism in the form of the League of Nations and the ICRC largely subservient to a realpolitik that disemboweled the League's political and the ICRC's humanitarian philosophy. Let us make this statement abundantly clear: Lausanne contributed to pave the way for Europe's fascisms and the Shoah. The Nazis understood Lausanne as a revisionist blueprint. They took the violent means, which had proved successful, as reproducible and flexible for their ends.

"Overcoming Lausanne" by Democratic Social Contracts

The Lausanne settlement needs to be thoroughly revisited and overhauled, as far as its inherent violence and antidemocratic spirit is concerned. We cannot separate the question of peace and the reduction and outlawing of violence from that of democracy, and for good reason. *When Democracy Died* recognizes democratic social contracts as fundamental factors and units of real peace. It has taken seriously the notion of a modern democratic social contract and the post–Great War investment in the Covenant of the League of Nations. In contrast to all other treaties of the Paris system, I have insisted, the League's Covenant vanished in the Lausanne Treaty.

This conceptual approach was helpful to elucidate the deeper realities – beneath and beyond the diplomatic surface – of the Lausanne Conference, including its antecedents and its consequences. It has clarified the distinction between democracy, illiberal currents, and a nominal liberalism that condoned its negation, as in Lausanne's realpolitik. "Peace" concluded at the Lausanne Conference followed the lines of a new "law" founded not by a covenant, but by victory – that is, by violently enforced "new conditions," as Walter Benjamin's 1921 *Critique of Violence* has put it (without referring to Ankara).[7] Might now explicitly made right.

When Democracy Died has argued that the Lausanne Treaty was a turning-point in the evolution of the West's post–World War peace and democracy project. From late 1922, the League and its associates, among them the Geneva-based ICRC, became facilitators of a new type of realpolitik. They well maintained their supranational ideals, continued innovative and constructive forms of action and cooperation, and successfully built up expert pools for international topics ranging from health and labor to disarmament and justice. But the League's core

---

[7] Walter Benjamin, "Zur Kritik der Gewalt," in Benjamin, *Gesammelte Schriften* (Frankfurt: Surkamp, 1999), vol. 2.1, 179–204. Benjamin's essay dates from 1920–1.

project – peace, constitutionality, democracy – was no more. The League's 1919 Covenant had been intended as the revisable and improvable fundament of consensual order worldwide; that is, as a potentially global social contract among democratizing nations. To this goal, the League – its apparatus, its members states, and their citizens in the League's Friendship Associations – would lead the way. But the Covenant found itself more and more reduced to a dead document. Far from evolving toward more democracy, the League's internationalism was submitted to the constraints, and served the requirements, of what this book calls a new species of Interwar realpolitik fully emerging at the Lausanne Conference. This went along with the establishment of antidemocracy.

What is democracy? Codified in a nondiscriminatory constitution, a democratic social contract defines the political and legal system. We might call "full-fledged" a democracy that implements a functioning free and general electoral system; institutional balances in favor of minorities or weaker parts of society; civil liberties and universal human rights that prevent alienation (in the Marxist and in the general sense); social solidarity and security; and elements of popular decision-making ("direct democracy" vs. elitism). A full-fledged democracy – a mature social practice of liberty and human dignity – is a utopia that comes to full fruition only if it finds strength by interconnecting with, and being checked by, other democracies.[8]

After the Second World War, the League's successor, the United Nations Organization, continued the anti-Axis war alliance, so that it counted autocracies among its members right from the start. In the executive Security Council, the superpowers, among them Stalin's dictatorship, were offered unchallengeable positions. This was "facing facts of power" in the post-1945 way – a little more than two decades after the Lausanne Treaty. The UNO rested much less than the post-1918 League on a covenant among growingly constitutional and democratic members as hoped for in the late 1910s. It built directly on the power relations resulting from the Second World War. Victory over Nazism morally underpinned them – not a democratic project or a universal credo. Might, anti-Nazi might, stood first. Second stood the covenant-based understanding of a global future, voiced in the British–American Atlantic Charter, the Charter of the United Nations, and the UN Charter's Preamble, as well

---

[8] The noncommittal interconnection by Internet is revolutionary for global interaction. But it by no means replaces the practical affirmation of being, feeling, and politically practicing to be human in democratic societies and internationally. For a reflection on intersubjective realities beyond fictive capacities and belief in science, see late philosopher Gernot Böhme's salty essay on what he calls Yuval N. Hariri's new master narrative of human history: "Wie es mit dem Menschen zu Ende geht," *NZZ*, 15 January 2022, 36–37.

as later UN conventions. Implementing right not over, but in agreement with, might, is therefore still a utopian ideal in the twenty-first century. During the nearly eighty years of its existence, the UNO did not rise above the ambivalent birth conditions that made it both a cartel of power, including dictatorships, and a global institution insisting on human rights, equality, and democracy. Double-faced right from the start, the UNO could logically never enjoy broad civil-society support in the vein of the League of Nation's friendship associations.

Deals struck and organizations acting over the heads of concerned humans violate the common good. The same is the case with national pacts in the name of exclusive groups, defined according to essentialist identities, enemy images, and the interests of power cartels. Deals and pacts in this vein lack an effective affirmation of universal values. They sideline, exploit, or scapegoat those excluded, marginalized, or subordinated. Because they want to preserve the predominance of the group or cartel that their deals and pacts underpin, they are condemned to repeat their foundational patterns of behavior. Much needs to be in place for effective and lasting peace to stand a chance of survival domestically and internationally. Good democratic peace opens the opportunity for proficient polities, underpinned by stable institutions, egalitarian rule of law, and a participative political culture.

Post-imperial Turkey set out a grandiose ethnocentric doctrine, including history-rewriting, while it failed "in trying to practice a little democracy," as Grew noted in October 1930. Sadly, "the Gazi" preferred "carrying on monologues on the ancient history of the Turks until all hours of the night at Tchan-Kaya [presidential palace in Çankaya] with a group of sycophants."[9] Autocratic regimes rest on dictatorial doctrines of a leader-led revolution or the exalted identity of a mythic community or nation. Exalted identities and myths of grandeur compensate for the daily lack of democratic achievement and common welfare. Settlements in the vein of Lausanne are best approached *ex negativo*: as a (partial) failure, and a kind of ersatz for peace. In contrast to other dictators of his time, Atatürk and most Kemalists disliked the explicit dictatorial label, at least if this was critically addressed by Westerners.[10] In this respect, they longed for horizons beyond those in which they had immured themselves.

During the emergence of the League of Nations in the late 1910s, many Eastern Europeans and Middle Easterners referred to Switzerland as a real democracy that integrated ethno-religious diversity and facilitated

---

[9] The later so-called Turkish History Thesis resulted from Atatürk's ethnocentric obsession starting in the late 1920s, but its roots reached back to earlier years (see Chapter 30). Grew, *Turbulent Era*, 874.
[10] Grew, *Turbulent Era*, 869; see also 860–863, diary entries from 1930.

peace-making. Mostly, they used (and misused) the recourse to an idealized example to promote their national ambitions.[11] The effort to display democratic and peaceful credentials was, as we have seen, also an explicit factor for Turkey's introduction of the Swiss Civil Code in the direct aftermath of the Treaty of Lausanne. In matters of democracy, some Kemalists continued to refer to Switzerland, and it happened that they did this disarmingly self-critically even in the late 1930s.[12] This was another sign for longing beyond the walls of ultranationalism.

In the case of Ankara after Lausanne, diplomatic triumph vis-à-vis ageing European national empires left little incentive for subsequent genuine democratic development. Quite the contrary, it enabled the establishment of a dictatorial Kemalism that, in US ambassador Joseph Grew's words, equaled "Fascism translated into Turkish."[13] Lausanne had recognized Ankara's Turkey in the undemocratic way it had emerged victorious during the Anatolia wars. This military success followed by diplomatic triumph fixated the initial patterns of behavior and the self-understanding that had enabled triumph. Sure enough, partners of deals and pacts must fulfill the expectations of the other partners, otherwise they cannot continue to reap the pact's dividends. But because they lack solid constitutional ground domestically, they fear democracy and create dependent, manipulable institutions at home. Repression and societal polarization, crises, wars, and the exploitation of international rivalries become their lasting breeding ground.

All modern social contracts, namely those coded in the constitutions of existing nation-states, are more or less deficient, or start being so (i.e. they carry some traits of pacts or deals struck over the heads of others). A much referred to example is the USA with its exclusion of slaves, native Americans, and female political participation. Strongly affirmed universal values, human equality in particular, as in the American constitution, are however driving progress. They thus enable the overcoming of initial exclusion and scapegoating. Where universal values are absent, or are not convincingly affirmed, myths and lies of origin (e.g. denial of genocide), prevail for generations. If based on universal values – that is, human rights and duties – democratic contracts form vital communities of law that possess the capacity to revise inherent wrongs, even if this takes long struggles.

If, however, mass crimes in the category of crimes against humanity are built in, but denied, we have to do with pacts or cartels of power rather than something close to a democratic social contract. These still prove

---

[11] See Michael Havlin, *Die Rede von der Schweiz: Ein medial-politischer Nationalitätendiskurs in der Tschechoslowakei 1918–1938* (Frankfurt am Main: Lang, 2009).
[12] Bozkurt, *Atatürk ihtilali*, 73.
[13] Grew, *Turbulent Era*, vol. 1, 880, diary entry of 27 January 1931.

community-building to a certain extent, however of communions in crime in the first instance, not of societies united in the constructive affirmation of a common good. Denied or justified misdeeds underpin a union in crime with common interest in related profits and privileges. But they block a society's evolution toward real and prosperous democracy. This remains out of reach, if the basics – the understanding of a nation's foundation and foundational values – are not revised and seen in a new light.

Among crimes inherent in the foundation of modern states and national empires are genocide, slavery, land-grab-based settler colonialism, as well as murderous plundering in a revolutionary class struggle. Structural injustices like the repression of indigenous peoples, and systemic phenomena like recurring pogroms, lynching, and exploitation, as well as discriminations related to imperial, religious, or racial biases are to be added. Most of them are potential crimes against humanity. A much broader notion than the hyponym genocide, these designate crimes that violate the affirmation of humankind as one superordinate society, held together by a utopian universal social contract and common fundamental law; and the recognition of one main home of humankind, the earth, that offers many various habitations for diverse groups, nations, and individuals.

The destructive impact of racial and ethno-religious nationalism in Europe during the era of the World Wars determined the genesis of the term genocide, as conceived and coined by Raphael Lemkin. In contrast, crimes against humanity, first codified in the 1945 Nuremberg Charter, are closely related to the thinking and development of the positive notions of human rights and the common good.[14] Today, they are primarily defined by the 1998 Rome Statute of the International Criminal Court. They encompass murder and other crimes "when committed as part of a widespread or systematic attack directed against any civilian population, with knowledge of the attack" (Article 7 of the Rome Statute).[15] Thus, they clearly include attacks against non-ethno-religious victims; for example, politically, socially, or economically defined groups of civilians – groups excluded from the UN definition of genocide.

***

---

[14] On the making of the complementary and competing notions "crimes against humanity" and "genocide," see Philippe Sands, *East West Street: On the Origins of "Genocide" and "Crimes Against Humanity"* (New York: Alfred A. Knopf, 2016). See also Daniel M. Segesser, "Die historischen Wurzel des Begriffs 'Verbrechen gegen die Menschlichkeit,'" *Jahrbuch der Juristischen Zeitgeschichte*, 8 (2006–7): 75–101; Antaki Mark, "Esquisse d'une généalogie des crimes contre l'humanité," *Revue Québécoise de droit international* (April 2007), 63–80, www.persee.fr/doc/rqdi_0828-9999_2007_hos_1_1_1393.

[15] See https://legal.un.org/icc/statute/romefra.htm.

Peace seeks and enables the common good. It is not only the absence of war and violence, but also the effective presence of consent, cooperation, justice, and welfare. "Peace quality" of human life and societies thus contrasts not only with war, but also with a possibly enduring, but crisis-ridden and violence-prone "bad peace" underpinned by pacts and cartels of power. These benefit only select groups and are the soil for autocracy, kleptocracy, corruption, partisanship, and repeated crimes.

Bound by a pact with autocrats (e.g. for geostrategic value or the exploitation of fossil fuel), nominally democratic partners remain captive to connivance and to the sacrifice of their values. Their cooperation with antidemocracy supports systems that cannot survive without manipulating state institutions, public opinion, and the understanding of history. In this vein, the Treaty of Lausanne concluded a lasting "pact of silence" on non-Turkish versions of public history as experienced by Kurds, Armenians, and many others.

International *and* societal peace, ultimately, points to the supreme challenge of functioning, multiform commonwealths bound by jointly affirmed rights and duties. This utopian perspective leads us back to the late 1910s. Real peace, indeed, is about a covenant following the example of what the League of Nations initially intended – but beyond Western racial civilization and identification with the Anglo-Saxon empire. Real peace depends on functioning democratic contracts underpinned by human rights and duties; that is, a strongly affirmed and defended truly common good. Turkey, whose birth was certificated by the Lausanne Treaty, did by and large without the "soft values" of justice, freedom, democracy, and historical truth. In Lausanne, these all were subordinated to the supreme good of national sovereignty and the need for a deal. Although a noted diplomatic achievement, the settlement at Lausanne thus perpetuated a setting that lacked the main ingredients for peace.

Violence, Peace, and Democracy: Dialectical Progress or Aporetic Spiral?

The call and command to respect the rights of others, and the belief in the inviolability of life, human dignity, and historical truths are more than "soft values." They are deeply inscribed in texts that history has left us from humankind's best spirits. Whether we call them basic, natural, or divine laws, or human rights, the idea and challenge of universal fundamental norms have existed for millennia and left seminal traces in written history. Some may argue that modern human rights and genuine social contracts – as opposed to scapegoat-based pacts or deals, as explained in the following – hail from the Abrahamitic belief in a covenant between humans and one good and true God, a God of equal humans in his/her image. Others may more emphasize debate- and dialogue-based urban democracy in ancient Greece, or may refer to other ancient experiences, achievements, or experiments.

The democratic challenge is about concrete self-government of a community that considers itself bound to norms that it recognizes and believes to be universally human or divine, thus valid for any human. Beyond pure thought and vision, the implementation of universal norms had to start in an organized, geographically limited community. Ancient Israel under Mosaic Law, including the Decalogue, is the historically earliest and best-known example in this vein. The Decalogue's "Love your neighbor as yourself" and the related ancient "Golden Rule" enshrine the inviolable human dignity of others. The animals, nature, and environment are not foreign to this attempt at universality. The prophets in the Hebrew Bible invoked a covenant, or God-given social contract, among the tribes of Israel – a covenant that comprised for them a global promise and a peace-bringing mission to humankind and the Earth.[16] They were voices of a critical spirit, perceiving the gap between promised potential and social-political realities in which they lived.

However, the Hebrew Bible also contains what a prominent Holocaust scholar has called "genocide commands" against those considered enemies or dangerous outsiders.[17] This reflects ancient experiences during Israelite conquest of the land Canaan with calls to locally exterminate Canaanites, men, women and children. The early, paradoxical link between biblical utopia and extreme violence has often appeared as a scandal and stumbling block. It is indeed (notwithstanding comparable accounts of – less radical – destruction of whole communities in the Iliad). However, as far as the bible is concerned, it has to be understood within a larger whole of dialectical progress toward establishing the common good, based on the individual good and dignity and the relation to God. This dialectical history comprises the later "scandal of the cross" with which it theologically struggles.

The anthropologist René Girard has insisted on the polity-founding role of common violence in general, scapegoating in particular, and the role of Jesus in the Gospel in unmasking scapegoat mechanisms of human

---

[16] Mark G. Brett, "Narrative Deliberation in Biblical Politics," in Danna Nolen Fewell (ed.), *The Oxford Handbook of Biblical Narrative* (New York: Oxford University Press, 2016), 540–549; and Brett, *Political Trauma and Healing: Biblical Ethics for a Postcolonial World* (Grand Rapids, MI: W.B. Eerdmans, 2016).

[17] Yehuda Bauer, *Rethinking the Holocaust* (New Haven, CT: Yale University Press, 2002), 19–20.

self-organization.[18] Ancient foundational myths about exclusion and victimization end with the justification of, or at least resignation to, the viewpoint of a perpetrating majority. The Gospel narrative, in contrast, clearly exposes the crucifixion of an innocent individual whose side it persistently takes. No self-righteous narrative of success, it untypically insists on the "loser's" (i.e. Jesus's) ultimate justification. It does this against national opinion leaders who had framed the execution as just and necessary, the victim deserving of his fate, vis-à-vis undecided imperial Roman overlords of his time.

To conclude with Girard and many others before him: in the long aftermath of the much-pondered "scandal of the cross" (Paul in 1 Corinthians 1:23), any use and justification of scapegoats for community- or nation-building is metaphysically condemned. It is reactionary and criminal wherever it happens. Theologically speaking, with Paul, the scandal of the cross once for all put an end to a pre-Jesus era of bloody sacrifices; thus of a blood-based understanding of purity and community-founding pacts.

Turkey's staunchest nationalists, and they are numerous, still today venerate Talaat Pasha, the main architect of the Armenian genocide. They praise this direct predecessor of Atatürk as a great patriot and loving father of the nation.[19] For them, a *génocidaire* statesman like him acted rightly, audaciously, and effectively. Shedding the blood of scapegoats and dispossessing them, he purified and enriched the nation. Even more thoroughly tied by religion and race, the Turkish-Muslim nation was thus renewed and recreated – and thus fitter, as Talaat's and Atatürk's cohort believed, for the modern world. The antipodes of, and antidote against, this kind of blood-based national pacts or concepts are democratic social

---

[18] For Girard's anthropological theory on violence, the scapegoat, and the sacred, see his *La Violence et le Sacré* (Paris: Grasset, 1972); and *Le Bouc émissaire* (Paris: Grasset, 1982). For a succinct introduction, see Chris Fleming, "Mimesis and Violence: An Introduction to the Thought of René Girard," *Australian Religion Studies Review*, 15.1 (2002), 57–72. For a connection with Emmanuel Levinas's ethics of otherness and encounter, see Sandor Goodhart, "The Self and Other People: Reading Conflict Resolution and Reconciliation with René Girard and Emmanuel Levinas," *Journal of Philosophy: A Cross-Disciplinary Inquiry*, 7.16 (Fall 2011), 14–25. See also Emmanuel Levinas and Jacques Rolland, *Ethique comme philosophie première* (Paris: Payot & Rivages, 1998). For Levinas' indebtedness to the Protestant theologian Karl Barth in thinking "the other," see Liisi Keedus (2020) "'The New World' of Karl Barth: Rethinking the Philosophical and Political Legacies of a Theologian," *The European Legacy*, 25.2, 167–185; and Samuel Moyn, *The Origins of the Other* (Ithaca, NY: Cornell University Press, 2005), 113–163.

[19] In full accordance with Ziya Gökalp's panegyric poem for Talaat during the genocide, "Tal'at Bey," *Tanin*, 1 September 1915, 2. Social media are full of proofs; see, for example, the comments to a critical lecture on Talaat: www.youtube.com/watch?v=g9n p14O0eKs (as of 11 March 2022).

contracts that appreciate others as equals, locally and globally. They break down autocratic patterns, national myths, essentialist notions, and millennia-old cycles of violence. Turkey's present deplorable situation in terms of democracy, economy, and human rights hails from a dictatorial state-building on genocidal ground which was sealed with the Treaty of Lausanne.

Bound to universal standards and an intact concept of the human being, the members of democratic contracts, in contrast, are prompted to negotiate the common good and interest locally and globally. Battling for their interest, democracies defend their inclusive polity and outlaw any scapegoating or "otherizing." In the long term, they are much more efficient, crisis-proof, and prosperous than are blood- and pact-based states. Certainly, macro-history weighs heavily on the performance of democracies, and grey zones abound. In a world of autocracy, plutocracy, aggression, and structural injustices, existing democracies often compromise much more than necessary to survive – as in the case of the imperially biased Lausanne Conference. Nonetheless, their own raison d'être makes them, sooner or later, insist on their core values. The inviolability of facts and historical truths is among these values. These profound challenges related to democracy make the work of a historian so incisive, tireless – and serene.

Annexes

Select Biographical Notes: Ankara's Lausanne Team

As explained in the book, the Conference of Lausanne proved a formative "school" for generations of Turkish diplomats. (Figure 22.) Besides this impact on diplomatic cadres, Lausanne was an incisive experience and reference for those who participated in person or were involved, though based in Turkey. Exploring this cohort amounts to a historical sociology of the Turkish "Lausanne elite" in which previous CUP elites and pre-Conference nationalist diaspora networks in Switzerland and Europe joined. They thus acquired political credits for their futures as republican elites. Most of those in Ankara's Lausanne team took high positions in the early Republic, many of them, including Ismet Inönü, Hasan Saka, and Cemal Bayar, far beyond the Second World War.

The select list here includes two thirds of the approximately forty delegation members during the first half of the Conference.[1] A number of them arrived after the Conference started, like Cavid Bey, and/or participated only until February. There were also a few persons close to Ankara's delegation who were at times present in Lausanne, but not registered as delegation members, notably the journalists Hüseyin Cahit (Yalçın) and Yunus Nadi (Abalıoğlu). These too, like most others, hailed from the CUP.[2]

---

[1] Information for the short biographical notes are taken from this book (see also index) plus from Harris, *Atatürk's Diplomats*; Sadak, *Lozan Mektupları* Tayfun Mater, "Bugünden bakınca Lozan ve İsmet Paşa," www.bianet.org, 2020; Bilal N. Şimşir, *Bizim Diplomatlar* (Istanbul: Bilgi, 1996); *TBMM Albümü (1920 – 2010)*, ed. Sema Yıldırım and Behçet K. Zeynel (Ankara: TBMM, 2010), 4 vols, https://www.tbmm.gov.tr. The Swiss police list of the Turkish delegation arriving on the evening of 12 November 1922, displays twenty-eight names, that of 26 April 1923, twenty-four names, ACV S112 95.

[2] A member of the National Assembly close to Gazi Kemal, Nadi was tasked to found the Kemalist newspaper *Cumhuriyet* in 1924. In the 1930s, he became notorious for his pro-Nazi and anti-Semitic stance.

Figure 22 The original contemporary caption for this photo taken in the entrance hall of the Palais de Rumine reads: "This is the delegation of Turks which was sent to Lausanne. It is a fair type of the men who are governing Turkey to-day" (shortened). Taken probably on 24 July 1924, the photo shows on the first row sitting, from the left: Reşid Saffet (Atabinen), Mehmet Zülfü (Tigrel), Rıza Nur, Ismet (Inönü), Aziz Zekai (Apaydın), Veli Saltıkgil, Ahmet Muhtar (Çilli), Mehmet Münir (Ertegün). First row standing, from the left: Mehmed Atıf (Esenbel), Yahya Kemal (Bayatlı), Ruşen Eşref (Ünaydın), Mustafa Şeref (Özkan), Tahir (Taner), Mehmet Tevfik (Bıyıklıoğlu), Seniyettin (Başak), Zühtü (İnhan), Yusuf Hikmet (Bayur), Fuat (Ağralı), Hüseyin (Pektaş, the person farthest to the right). Second row, standing: Cevat (Açıkalın, behind Yahya Kemal and Ruşen Eşref) (Library of Congress, Digital ID: cph 3c02035, http://hdl.loc.gov/loc.pnp/cph.3c02035).

Delegates

Ismet Pasha (Inönü),[3] 1884–1973. Born in Izmir. Graduate from the Ottoman Military Academy in 1906, four years after Kemal (Atatürk). Served under General Kemal (Atatürk) on the eastern front in 1916. Like many other former officers, he

---

[3] Family names introduced in 1934 in parentheses.

worked for the nationalist underground while serving at the Ottoman War Office in 1919–20. He was appointed chief of the general staff; commander of the western front under commander-in-chief Gazi Kemal (Atatürk); made foreign minister shortly before the Lausanne Conference, where he led the Turkish delegation as the first delegate and plenipotentiary. First prime minister of the Republic of Turkey, October 1923–November 1924; prime minister again, 1925–37. Succeeded Kemal Atatürk as president of the Republic, 1938–50. Again prime minister 1961–5.

Rıza Nur, 1879–1942. Born in Sinop (Black Sea). Graduated from the Ottoman Military Medical Academy in 1903 where he joined the CUP. Became a professor of surgery in 1907. Elected CUP deputy in the Ottoman Parliament that reopened after the Young Turk Revolution, he fell out with the CUP, briefly joined the Liberal opposition, and then lived in exile in Switzerland and Egypt, 1913–19. There he started to write the racialist works *Ermeni Tarihi* (History of the Armenians) and *Türk Tarihi* (History of the Turks) in which he exalted the Turks while strongly depreciating the Armenians, Jews, and other non-"Turanians." Was a co-founder of the National Assembly in Ankara in 1920, and Ankara's envoy for the Treaty of Moscow with the Bolsheviks in 1921. Minister of education 1920, minister of health 1921–3. Second Turkish delegate (vice-plenipotentiary) at Lausanne Conference. Deputy until 1927, when he chose exile because of his dissent with Gazi Kemal (Atatürk) and PM Ismet Inönü. His memoirs and other writings are crucial references for pan-Turkism, anti-Kemalism and Lausanne Treaty criticism.

Hasan (Saka), 1886–1960. Born in Trabzon. Graduated from the School for Civil Service (Mekteb-i Mülkiye) in 1908, and from the Paris Institute of Political Studies (Sciences Po) in 1912. Professor at the Mülkiye until 1915, when he started to work for the CUP state first in the ministry of finances and then as an economic director. He was elected to the last Ottoman Parliament in 1920, but joined the opening National Assembly in Ankara. Minister of Finance 1921–2, again 1925–6, minister of economy 1923, foreign minister 1944–7, president of the Republic 1947–9. He was number three among Ankara's delegates in Lausanne, but was back to Ankara in January and February 1923.

Chief secretary and advisor **Reşit Saffet (Atabinen)**, 1884–1965. From Istanbul's Sunni upper class like Necmettin Sadık (Sadak), see below. Both socialized during the 1910s in the CUP headquarters in Istanbul, side by side with Ziya Gökalp, Fuat Köprülü, Yusuf Nadi (Abalıoğlu), and Hamdullah Suphi (Tanrıöver), minister of education in 1925). CUP Finance Minister Cavid's secretary during financial negotiations in Berlin and Vienna. Ex-CUP agent and pamphleteer in Switzerland after 1918. Member of the National Assembly in Ankara. Founding member of the Turkish Historical Society. Nazi sympathizer. Internationally prominent as a propagandist of the Turkish History Thesis and as a prolific denialist under the pseudonym of Kara Schemsi in regard of state crimes against the Armenians.

Translator: **Hüseyin (Pektaş)**, 1884–1970. Grandson of a sheikh of the Bektaşi dervish order. In 1903, the first Muslim graduate of the Robert College in Istanbul. Worked as a military censor for the CUP before joining the faculty of Robert College and becoming head of its Turkish department. In the 1930s, his close connections to the regime helped him to rise to the position of a vice-president of the Robert College and the American College for Girls. He successfully pushed for the Turkification of these American institutions and the dismissal of dissenting professors.

Ismet's aide-de camp (among further military officers): **Âtıf (Esenbel)**, 1895–1951. Born in Istanbul, from Istanbul's Sunni upper class. Graduate of the War School. Cavalry regiment commandant. Aide-de-camp of the prime minister. Deputy for twelve years.

Further members of the delegation in alphabetic order according to later surnames, if existing:

Secretaries

Açıkalın, Cevat, 1902–70. From Istanbul's Sunni upper class. Rıza Nur's secretary at the Conference of Lausanne. High diplomat and official in the Republic. As an extraordinary envoy in Antakya, instrumental in arranging the process that made this Syrian province the Turkish province of Hatay in the late 1930s. Ambassador to London from where he contributed to Turkey's accession to the NATO.

Kıran, Süleyman Saib, 1892–19??. Graduate from the Galatasary Lyceum. Entered Ottoman government service in 1918 and Ankara's foreign ministry in 1922. Diplomat.

Türkgeldi, M. Emin Ali, 1890–1955. From Istanbul's Sunni upper class. Entered the foreign ministry when CUP single-party rule began in 1913. As the first secretary in the Ottoman embassy after 1918, he secretly worked for Ankara's Paris representative Ferit (Tek). Secretary in Ankara's delegation at the Mudanya Armistice negotiations. Diplomat and ambassador.

Advisors

Apaydın, Zekâi, 1880–1947. Born in Bosnia. Graduate from the Mülkiye. District governor under the CUP Interior Minister Talaat in Mersin, Kayseri, and Eskişehir. His brutal rape of a chambermaid in Lausanne covered up by a sum of money. Deputy and three times a minister in Ankara. Ambassador to London and Moscow.

Bayar, Celal, 1883–1986. Born in the province of Bursa as the son of a mufti. Secretary of the CUP branches in Bursa, then Izmir. Close collaborator of Interior Minister Talaat. Co-organizer of ethnic cleansing of Rûm in the Izmir region in spring 1914; organizer of guerilas against the Greek forces and returning Rûm in 1919. Ankara's minister of economy in 1921, acting foreign minister in spring 1922. Advisor during the first half of the Lausanne Conference. Minister of exchange of population, construction, and resettlement in 1924. Co-founder (1924) and director of İş Bankası, the Kemalist single-party's Business Bank. Minister of economy in 1932, prime-minister in 1937. Co-founder of the Democratic Party. President of Turkey in 1950, leading Turkey into NATO.

Bayur, Yusuf Hikmet, 1891–1963. Born in Istanbul, from Istanbul's Sunni upper class. Graduate from Galatasaray Lyceum and studies at Paris-Sorbonne. Teacher at Galatasaray Lyceum. To Ankara in 1920, director of political affairs in the foreign ministry. After Lausanne, general director of political affairs. Ambassador. Secretary to the president. Deputy. Minister of education 1933–4, introducing obligatory course on Turkish Revolution History at high schools and universities. Professor of history at Ankara University.

Bıyıklıoğlu, Mehmet Tevfik, 1891–1961. Born in Çanakkale. CUP officer. Director of the Operations Branch of the Western Front Command Headquarters 1921–2. Military advisor at the Lausanne Conference. Secretary to the president (Gazi Kemal [Atatürk]) 1924–7. Ambassador. Founding member of the Turkish Historical Society.

Cavid Bey, 1875–1926. Born in Salonica (Thessaloniki). Leading member, deputy and finance minister of the CUP. Constitutional-minded; critic of the CUP's minority policies. He hoped that after World War defeat, a territorially slimmed-down Turkey would at last implement constitutional rule, as according to the initial expectations of the 1908 Young Turk Revolution. Critic of what he called Ankara's extreme nationalists. Victim of judicial murder in 1926, accused of collaboration in the Izmir assassination attempt against Gazi Kemal. Left important diaries.

Cilli, Ahmet Muhtar, 1871–1958. Born in Trabzon. Worked as an engineer and a director for the Hejaz Railway, and was a counsellor in the ministry of public works in the CUP state. Was shortly a deputy in the Ottoman Parliament in 1919; became a deputy of the National Assembly immediately after the Lausanne Conference; and a minister of public works during the first year of the Republic. Was a founding member of the short-lived oppositional Progressive Republican Party, 1924–25.

Ertegün, Mehmet Münir, 1883–1944. Born in Istanbul. A practicing Muslim from Istanbul's Sunni upper class. Studied law at the Istanbul University from which he graduated in 1908. Legal advisor to the grand vizierate in 1913; with Talaat Pasha at the Brest-Litovsk negotiations in 1918. Joined Ankara in 1920 as a legal advisor to the foreign ministry; active as such at the 1921 London and the Lausanne Conferences. Chief Legal Advisor in 1924. Ambassador in Bern, London, Washington. Successfully obstructed the American movie version of Werfel's *The Forty Days of Musa Dagh* in the 1930s.

Kaya, Mehmet Şükrü, 1883–1959. Born on the island of Kos. Graduate from Istanbul Law School and Paris Law Faculty. Under Minister of the Interior Talaat, was Director for Settlement of Tribes and Migrants from 1914, responsible for the destruction of Armenian survivors from Anatolia concentrated in camps in Northern Syria. Member of Izmir's Defense of (Muslim) Rights Association after World War defeat. Exiled to Malta. In Lausanne during the first Conference half. Mayor of Izmir. Foreign minister 1924–5. Minister of the Interior 1927–37, and involved in a leading role preparing the exterminatory Dersim campaign in 1937–8.

Özkan, Mustafa Şeref, 1884–1938. Born in Burdur. Graduate from Istanbul Law School. Ottoman deputy for the CUP. Minister of trade and agriculture 1916. Joined Ankara's movement in 1920 and was involved in border talks with mandatory Syria in 1922. Stayed as a liaison officer in Lausanne during the conference interval. Deputy in Ankara 1923. Minister of economy 1930–2.

Saltıkçı/ Saltıkgil, Veli, 1880–1935. Born in Burdur. Graduate from Mülkiye and Paris Law Faculty. CUP deputy from Aydın. To Ankara in 1920; Burdur deputy in the National Assembly, member of the Independence Tribunal. After the Lausanne Conference, Professor at the Istanbul Law Faculty and advisor to the foreign ministry.

Tahir, Taner, 1883–1962. Graduate from the Istanbul Law Faculty and the Paris Sorbonne Law Faculty. Director of Criminal Affairs 1913, and Professor of Criminal Law at the Istanbul Law School 1918. After the Lausanne Conference, dean of the Istanbul Law School.

Tigrel, Mehmet Zülfü, 1876–1940. Born in Diyarbekir. Local politician and CUP deputy, side by side with Feyzi Pirinççioğlu/Pirinççizâde. Interned in Malta. Deputy in Ankara from 1921. Founding member of the Republican People Party in 1923.

Press Team

Bayatlı, Yahya Kemal, 1884–1948. Born in Skopje. Poet. Graduated from Sciences Po in Paris. Professor at Istanbul University. Deputy in Ankara from 1923. Ambassador.

Baydur, Hüseyin Ragıp, 1890–1955. Born in Rhodos. Graduate from the Law Faculty in Istanbul. General secretary of the Turkish Hearths (Türk Ocağı) 1913. Inspector of education of the CUP government for students in Europe 1918. Chief-editor of *Hâkimiyet-i Milliye*, the Ankara government's major newspaper 1921, and director of press in Ankara's foreign ministry. Ambassador 1925–55.

Belger, Nihat Reşat, 1882–1961. Graduate of the Military Medical School in Istanbul and the Paris Medical School.

Advisor to Bekir Sami's mission to London in 1921 and the subsequent negotiations with Yusuf Kemal (Tengirşek) in London. Figures variously as a political advisor, secretary, and member of the press team in Lausanne. Returned to Turkey in 1936 to become Atatürk's private physician. Deputy of the Democrat Party in the 1950s.

Sadak, Necmettin Sadık, 1882–1953. Born in Isparta. Graduate in humanities from Lyon, France. Professor of sociology at the University of Istanbul, succeeding Ziya Gökalp in 1916; inspired by the latter's Turkism. Co-founder with Falih Rıfkı Atay and Ali Naci Karacan of the daily *Akşam* 1918. Deputy in Ankara 1927. Delegate to the League of Nations 1931. Nazi sympathizer. Foreign minister 1947.

Ünaydın, Ruşen Eşref, 1892–1959. Born in Istanbul. Graduate from Istanbul University's Literature Faculty. Journalist, CUP member. Editor of *Hâkimiyet-i Milliye* 1921. Deputy 1923. Founding member and secretary of the Turkish Language Association 1932. Secretary of the presidency (Atatürk). Ambassador.

Select Chronology

The Conference of Lausanne was to conclude more than ten years of almost uninterrupted warfare in the Ottoman world. Chagrins, wars, traumas, and losses had followed the very hopeful constitutional Young Turk Revolution of 1908. This chronology therefore starts with 1908 and details the subsequent war decade. It then focuses on the Lausanne Conference and lists the Conference's main structure, debates, decisions, and incidents in and outside the Conference rooms. Finally, it mentions a few elements of the still-enduring "post-Lausanne era." Though Lausanne- and Turkey-centric, it also looks at other areas in order to make visible the simultaneity, connection, or interaction of events and currents that defined the Conference.

Like the other post-Great War treaties concluded in or near Paris (Versailles, St. Germain, Neuilly, Trianon, Sèvres), the Treaty of Lausanne dealt with the Great War starting in 1914. However, the Lausanne Conference negotiated with a loser of the First World War which had won subsequent wars in Anatolia. Ankara's delegation systematically highlighted this fact, while seeking to leave the years 1914–18 in oblivion. Furthermore, a number of issues from the Ottoman wars before 1914 (the Balkan Wars and the Libya War starting in 1911) still needed discussion and negotiation in Lausanne. Thus, the Lausanne Treaty was distinctive and opened a new era in interwar diplomacy, while concluding the Paris treaty system. The Paris–Geneva peace and its early dismantlement in the Caucasus and Anatolia overlapped with Ankara's wars in Anatolia, which ended the Ottoman war decade. This development decisively altered the West-centered Paris–Geneva peace process.

1900s: Hope for Constitutional, Progressive, Internationalist Futures

Constitutional revolutions *in Russia 1905, Persia 1906, Ottoman Turkey 1908, and China 1911. Specific hubs for revolutionaries are the South Caucasus, Macedonia, Eastern European "Yiddishland," and Switzerland* *(a center of exile, education, and agitation for young elites from the Russian Empire, the Balkans, and the Ottoman Empire).*

1907 Hague Convention for the Pacific Settlement of International Disputes. Stuttgart Congress of the Socialist International (Second International) with manifesto against militarism.

1908 The Young Turk Revolution reinstalls the suspended Ottoman constitution of 1876, thus ending three decades of autocratic Islamist rule by Sultan Abdulhamid II. It raises hope on a democratizing, consolidating, possibly shrinking Ottoman state; in other words, a peaceful solution to the notorious international "Eastern Question."

Any territorial shake-out is, however, out of the question, both for imperial Islamists and the leading Young Turk party (CUP), particularly after suffering losses in late 1908: Bulgaria proclaiming its independence; Austria annexing Bosnia and Herzegovina; Crete declaring adherence to Greece.

1909 Reactionary coup in Istanbul; anti-Armenian massacres in Adana; anti-constitutional agitation country-wide (April 1909). The CUP stiffens, losing faith in constitutional rule and Ottoman coexistence based on equality. The imperative of imperial sovereignty and restoration prevails among Sunni elites. From the early 1910s, a powerful ethno-Turkish nationalism (Turkism, pan-Turkism, Turanism) is added to imperial Islam. It determines the CUP and, even more, from 1920, the nascent Kemalism.

The Long Final Ottoman War Decade (1911–22)

***This "long decade" includes** Italian invasion in Libya and the Balkan Wars, the First World War, the CUP party-state, genocidal demographic engineering in Asia Minor, the 1917 Bolshevik Revolution, and CUP defeat in the First World War. It continues with the post-1918 Anatolia wars won by the direct heir of the CUP (the new Ankara government), allied to Bolsheviks, against the Paris treaties.*

1911 The Italian invasion of Libya results in an Italian–Ottoman war and Italian conquest of the Dodecanese. Peace concluded at the Conference of Lausanne-Ouchy in 1912.

1912–1913 Balkan Wars; Ottoman loss of most remaining European territories, up to 400,000 Muslim refugees or expellees entering the shrinking Empire. CUP takes power by a coup, establishes single-party rule, and starts politics of revenge, including expulsion of Rûm and preparation of a new war against Greece. Bilateral peace treaties include a voluntary Bulgarian–Turkish population exchange; a Greek–Turkish exchange is envisaged.

1914 Based on the 1878 Berlin Treaty, international reform negotiations result in the February 1914 Reform Agreement for seven eastern provinces (i.e. the eastern half of Asia Minor). The CUP obstructs the implementation of this reform plan that gives non-Muslims, particularly Armenians, equal rights and political participation under international supervision. It speeds up the expulsion of Aegean Rûm (roughly 200,000 until June 1914).

July 1914 The main CUP leaders (notably Enver, Talaat) welcome the impending World War, seeking active participation at Germany's side from mid-July. They conclude the alliance of 2 August and wage an irregular war in the Caucasus, before official entrance in November. The CUP abolishes the capitulations, Lebanon's autonomy, and the Reform Agreement for the eastern provinces.

1915–1916 The failed Caucasus campaign in late 1914–early 1915 brings devastation to the eastern provinces, while the Entente starts attacking the Dardanelles. Genocide of the Armenians and, in parts of the eastern provinces, of other (Assyrian) Christians.

1917 Talaat Pasha, the informal head of the CUP since late 1912, is appointed grand vizier. Ottoman losses in the Arab parts of the empire increase. However, revolutions in the Russian Empire open the door for Ottoman reconquests and advances in the South Caucasus.

1918 Despite the triumphal Treaty of Brest-Litovsk – with German advances in Eastern Europe and Ottoman advances into the South Caucasus, nearly leading to Armenia's destruction – the war is also lost for Istanbul due to the Western front.

Fall 1918 Armistice of Mudros between the Entente and Istanbul (30 October). CUP leaders flee or go underground, while planning for continued struggle domestically and abroad, in a synergy of pan-Islamic and Turkist forces.

1919 Paris Peace Conference starts in January. First decisions lead to strong reactions by those frustrated. Reactions include the Fourth May (1919) Movement in China, Fascism in Italy, and the nascent Kemalist movement. Treaty of Paris-Versailles, headed by the Covenant of the League of Nations (28.06.1919). The US Senate rejects a US mandate over Armenia (01.06.1919) as well as the Treaty of Versailles including the Covenant (19.11.1919).

Greek occupation of Izmir with Allied backing (15.05.1919).

Based on intact army units in unoccupied Anatolia, former CUP general Mustafa Kemal Pasha (Atatürk) coordinates the Turkish-nationalist resistance against Western plans with Asia Minor (Amasya meeting, Erzurum and Sivas Congresses). He establishes his headquarters in Ankara at the end of 1919. Synergy with cells and leaders abroad, notably with Talaat Pasha in Berlin. First contacts with Bolsheviks.

1920 "National Pact" (Misak-ı Millî, early 1920): Turkish nationalist consensus on the goal of unitary Turkish-Muslim rule in Asia Minor plus a few neighboring regions.

"Grand National Assembly" inaugurated in Ankara (23.04.1920): a counter-government born in war against the Entente-dependant sultanate in Istanbul and against the Sèvres Treaty (10.08.1920).

From late June: Greek army proceeds to occupy Eastern Thrace and parts of Western Anatolia.

Ankara starts waging war in the name of Islam, the sultanate-caliphate, and the Turkish nation. It fights against League-supported claims by the Republic of Armenia, the sultan's troops, the French occupation in Cilicia (which protects returning Armenians), and the Greek army.

Late 1920: South Caucasus divided between invading Bolsheviks and invading Kemalists (Treaty of Alexandropol/ Gümrü, 02.12.1920).

1921 Meetings in Rome followed by London conference, on revisioning the Sèvres Treaty. The Turkish–Russian Treaty of Moscow recognizes the National Pact and institutionalizes critical support for Ankara (16.03.1921).

Ankara brutally suppresses claims for self-determination by Pontus Rûm (Pontus genocide) and Alevi Kurds. Main perpetrators: militia leader Topal Osman and General Nurettin Pasha.

July: Greek offensive toward Ankara. Kemal Pasha made commander-in-chief by the National Assembly in August, and honored as "Gazi" (hero of gaza/jihad) in September, after Greek setback at the battle of Sakarya.

French–Turkish Accord of Ankara (20.10.1921) followed by French withdrawal from Cilicia. Secret support of Ankara against Greece by Italy and France. Greek PM Eleftherios Venizelos, the architect of Greece's involvement in Asia Minor, loses the elections and goes into exile (November 1921).

1922 Near East conference by the Allies in Paris (March 1922).

Ankara's final offensive against Greek forces (August). Izmir's reconquest, destruction, and carnage (of Christians) by the Turkish army under Nurettin Pasha in September.

1919–1922: The Paris–Geneva Peace

The Paris Treaty System and Geneva's League of Nations

1919

28.06.1919 Treaty of Paris–Versailles with Germany; it is headed by the Covenant of the League of Nations like all subsequent Paris treaties, except the Lausanne Treaty.

Polish Minority Treaty (so-called Little Treaty of Versailles) signed the same day, the first of a series of minority treaties between a number of non-Western powers and the League, thus establishing the League's minority protection system.

10.09.1919 Treaty of Paris–St. Germain with Austria.

29.11.1919 Treaty of Paris–Neuilly with Bulgaria.

1920

10.01.1920 Geneva-based League of Nations founded by the Paris Peace Conference.

25.04.1920 San Remo Resolution by the Supreme Council (of the Great War victors), determining the mandates in the Ottoman Middle East.

04.06.1920 Treaty of Paris–Trianon with Hungary.

10.08.1920 Treaty of Paris–Sèvres with Ottoman Turkey's government in Istanbul.

Application for League membership by the Republic of Armenia rejected. No Western defense of Armenia against invading Kemalists and Bolsheviks despite calls by the Council of the League to intervene in fall 1920. Strong – verbal – support for Armenia by the League's Assembly from 1920 to 1922.

The Conference of Lausanne (1922–1923)

Diplomatic Steps towards Dismantling and Revising the Sèvres Treaty, 1920–1922

(for action on the ground, see also under the head "The Long Final Ottoman War Decade")

1920

Early September: Bolshevik Congress of the Peoples of the East in Baku. Ankara and Moscow are vocal in condemning the "imperialist" Paris treaties, particularly those of Versailles and Sèvres.

Fall 1920: South Caucasus divided between invading Bolsheviks and invading Kemalists. They thus thwart the Sèvres Treaty's stipulations for Eastern Anatolia and the South Caucasus, without facing action by the League (i.e. the powers backing the Paris–Geneva peace).

02.12.1920 The Treaty of Alexandropol/Gümrü between Ankara and the Republic of Armenia enforces new borders on Armenia, without parts of Eastern Anatolia ("Western Armenia").

1921

Rome meetings (January) followed by London conference (February) between Allied diplomats and representatives from the Istanbul government and the new Ankara counter-government.

16.03.1921 Treaty of Moscow between Bolsheviks and the Ankara government. It formalizes the Bolshevik–Kemalist cooperation in place since 1920. Nagorno-Karabakh incorporated to Azerbaijan by the Communist Party's Central Committee with Stalin (July 1921).

13.10.1921 Treaty of Kars confirms the National Pact boundaries in the Caucasus, as fixed by the Treaties of Moscow and Gümrü. Concluded by Soviet Georgian, Armenian, and Azerbaijani ministers in the presence of a Soviet Russian plenipotentiary.

20.10.1921 The French–Turkish Accord of Ankara amounts to France's factual resigning from the Sèvres Treaty, accepting the National Pact, agreeing with Ankara on the borders to mandatory Syria, and abandoning the returned Armenian survivors.

1922

22–25.03.1922 Allied conference in Paris on Near East issues.

11.10.1922 Armistice of Mudanya agreed between Ankara as well as Britain, France, Italy, and – three days later – Greece.

The Eve of the Conference (Fall 1922)

In early October, British diplomats start to suggest Lausanne as the place for a new Near East peace conference, rejecting the Turkish suggestion of Izmir.

26.10.1922 In the name of the World War victors, Britain invites these and the governments of Istanbul and Ankara to a Near East Peace Conference in Lausanne.

Select Chronology 303

The same day, Ismet Pasha (Inönü) is appointed foreign minister of the Ankara government.

31.10.1922 After the Fascist March on Rome, Mussolini is tasked with Italy's prime-ministry. He also assumes the foreign ministry. The same day, Fridtjof Nansen, League commissary for refugees, meets Hamid Bey, Ankara's representative in Istanbul, who is instructed "to negotiate on the basis of a total and enforced exchange of populations."

01.11.1922 Ankara abolishes the sultanate, thus making itself the only representative of Turkey for the Conference of Lausanne.

Fall of Lloyd George's cabinet, due to failed Middle East politics, and ensuing elections. Britain defers the opening of the Conference from 13 to 20 November.

From before mid-November, journalists, delegations and observers arrive in Lausanne.

18.11.1922 Preparatory talks in Paris between Poincaré and Curzon.

19.11.1922 Italy's PM and foreign minister Mussolini arrives at Territet where he meets with Poincaré and Curzon.

The First Half of the Conference

This first half addresses and by and large settles questions on borders, minorities, population exchange, and the Straits. It shelves the Armenian question and keeps silent on Turkey's Caucasian borders.

20.11.1922 Inaugural ceremony, Swiss president's conciliatory address and, out of program, Ismet Pasha's assertive nationalist speech.

21.11.1922 Plenary sessions on procedure. Curzon is made president; determines the Conference agenda.

22.11.1922 Negotiation starts with meetings of the Conference's First (territorial and military) Commission on questions regarding Thrace and the Aegean islands.

28.11.1922 Five ministers and a general executed in Athens, because considered mainly responsible for the "Asia Minor Catastrophe."

01.12.1922 Nansen's appearance and first discussion of population exchange.

04.12.1922 Discussion of the Straits. First appearance of the Bolshevik delegation and lofty speech by its chief Georgy Chicherin, People's Commissar for Foreign Affairs.

11.12.1922 Soirée organized by the Turkish-Sephardic Friendship Association in Geneva. Lobbying for Turkish positions.

12–14.12.1922 The First Commission discusses the question of minorities including controversial history. Particularly intense moments of the Conference. Afterwards, negotiations on minority rights and population exchange continue in a sub-commission where Rıza Nur, a pan-Turkish ultranationalist, represents the Ankara government.

Ismet promises Turkish adherence to the League right after the Conference. Curzon's anti-Soviet strategy thus succeeds regarding both the League and (on 4 December already) the Straits.

16.12.1922 Soirée by the Swiss Society of Friends of Turkey in Lausanne, presided by Swiss fascist Arthur Fonjallaz. Lobbying for Turkish positions and Swiss–Turkish industrial cooperation.

28.12.1922 Second meeting (after a first on 02.12.1922) of the Second Commission on the Régime of Foreigners, including questions of nationality, judicial system, and capitulations. The hawks in Ankara's delegation threaten rupture of the Conference and war.

06.01.1923 Nur and his team leave the sub-commission meeting on resettlement for Armenians, Assyrians and Bulgarians under protest. Diplomatic death of the "Armenian Home."

11.01.1923 French occupation of the Ruhr because of outstanding German reparation payments.

23.01.1923 The First Commission discusses the future of Mosul. Ismet Pasha labels the Kurds "Turanians" (from Turkish racial background) and pretends their democratic representation in Ankara.

30.01.1923 Convention Concerning the Exchange of Greek and Turkish Populations signed.

31.01.1923 Draft treaty presented by the Allies.

04.02.1923 "Day of drama." Ismet refuses to sign after presenting counter-demands. The main bones of contention are financial and economic. Final meeting in Curzon's hotel room. Departure of Curzon. Break of the Conference.

The Conference Interval (February–April 1923)

06.02.1923 Ultimatum against the Allies by the National Assembly in Ankara; demands that all big foreign warships leave the harbor of Izmir ("Izmir Incident"). Risk of war.

17.02.1923 Gazi Kemal at the opening of the economic congress in Izmir: The Lausanne Conference "absorbs the attention of us all."

08.03.1923 Turkish counter-proposals to the Allies draft treaty.

29.03.1923 High Treason Law of 1920 (Hiyanet-i Vataniye Kanunu) tightened.

01.04.1923 Kemal and his loyalists dissolve the restive National Assembly and prepare Turkey's first general elections in a climate of repression.

09.04.1923 Concession to the American Chester company approved in Ankara. This triggers Ismet's efforts in Lausanne, from late April, to speedily conclude a separate Turkish–American treaty, putting the Allies under zugzwang.

The Second Half of the Conference (Late April–July 1923)

The second half mainly addresses unsolved questions regarding reparations, the Capitulations, amnesty and return, the Ottoman public debt, Ottoman concessions to Western companies, and the Allies' evacuation of Istanbul.

23.04.1923 Conference reopened.

10.05.1923 Soviet delegate Vatslav Vorovsky assassinated by Maurice Conradi, a Swiss expat back from Russia. The trial in Lausanne turns into an indictment of Bolshevism.

May 1923 Insistent Turkish demands of Greek reparations (while refusing reparation for genocide and restitution for confiscated, stolen, or destroyed Christian property) nearly trigger a Greek military advance through Eastern Thrace toward Istanbul.

31.05.1923 Frustrated, the sub-commission dealing with amnesty issues states, "it could not usefully discuss the question whether certain persons who had left Turkey, in particular Armenians, should be entitled to return freely to their homeland under the general amnesty provisions." Ankara's delegation makes clear in further meetings, including the very last on 17 July, that the Turkish government alone would decide on returns (the issue of collective return being out of question since 6 January). Ankara confiscates the property of those prohibited from return.

28.06.1923 Unfree first general elections in Turkey.

17.07.1923 Last negotiation meetings of all three Commissions.

24.07.1923 Signing of the Treaty together with sixteen diplomatic instruments (conventions or agreements) annexed to the proper Treaty.

The Immediate Aftermath of the Conference

06.08.1923 Turkish–American treaty signed in Lausanne (never ratified by the US).

13.08.1923 Opening of the newly elected National Assembly. Fundamental speech by Gazi Kemal referring to Lausanne.

23.08.1923 The National Assembly in Ankara ratifies the Lausanne Treaty, republican Turkey's international "birth certificate."

29.10.1923 Republic of Turkey declared in Ankara; Ismet Pasha appointed its PM.

03.03.1924 Caliphate as well as the ministries for religious affairs and pious foundations abolished. All religious and communitarian institutions submitted to state control, including Sunni Islam, henceforth administered by the new Directorate of Religious Affairs. The Law on the Unification of Education completes state control of all aspects of education.

06.08.1924 Lausanne Treaty in force after ratification by Turkey, France, Italy, Japan, and Britain.

15.09.1925 Under pressure, the Jewish community in Turkey starts to renounce on the privileges in Lausanne Treaty Art. 42 (civil law autonomy), as do the Rûm and Armenian communities a little later.

17.02.1926 The National Assembly in Ankara adopts the translated, sharia-abolishing Swiss Civil Code that it considers the precondition of a secular and sovereign nation-state. As agreed in the Lausanne Treaty, European legal advisors accompany the legal reform process until 1931.

18.01.1927 US Senate rejects ratification of the August 1923 Treaty. However, several bilateral agreements equal the stipulations of the Lausanne Treat: a Treaty of Commerce and Navigation (1929), a Treaty of Establishment and Sojourn (1931), an extradition agreement (1934), and a claims settlement on Turkish violations of American persons and property 1914–22 (1934). This claims settlement discriminates against Armenian-American citizens who are excluded from remuneration.

15–20.10.1927 Gazi Kemal's speech (*Nutuk*) at the congress of the ruling single party (Republican People's Party, CHP). He refers multiple times to Lausanne as the diplomatic apogee of Turkish history. Published, the *Nutuk* becomes the bible of Turkey's Atatürk-centric national history.

The Lausanne Treaty's (Long) Aftermath

1926 For early Nazis and German nationalists in general, "contemporary Turkey, with its radical expulsion of the Greeks and its reckless Turkish nationalization of the country" is a role model, rubber-stamped by the

Lausanne Treaty (Carl Schmitt, 1926 preface to his *Die geistesgeschichtliche Lage des heutigen Parlamentarismus*).

1930 The coming about of the Ankara Convention, a Greek-Turkish treaty of friendship, benefits from personal efforts by Venizelos and Mustafa Kemal. It confirms the Lausanne borders and waives outstanding property claims. The new – transient – Turkish-Greek friendship facilitates the League-inspired Balkan Conferences (1930–3), Turkey's accession to the League of Nations (1932), and the Balkan Pact (1934) for common security among Balkan States.

1936 The Montreux Agreement revises regulations of the Lausanne Treaty and allows the Turkish remilitarization of the Straits.

1938 Ankara's desire to expand the "Lausanne borders" succeeds a first time with the incorporation of Iskenderun and Antakya in Northwestern Syria. The step is approved by mandatory France and the League of Nations.

1943–1945 The positive reception of the Lausanne population exchange explicitly impacts Allied planning of Eastern Europe after the Holocaust, genocide, and ethnic cleansing in the Second World War. This process of not questioning and stopping, but rather legalizing and accomplishing demographic engineering now concerns not a few millions, but many millions of people, notably ethnic Germans (Conferences of Yalta and Potsdam, 1945).

1949 Failed Lausanne Peace Conference between Israel, Arab neighbor states, the (Palestinian) Arab Higher Committee and refugee representatives; convened by the new United Nations Conciliation Commission for Palestine which includes experts active in the 1923 population exchange. Israeli PM and "father of the nation" David Ben Gurion adopts a "Kemalist stance" (comparable to Ankara at the 1922–3 Lausanne Conference): he considers the Arab-Palestinian refugees as potential enemies of Israel, taking victory in the preceding war as the real basis of Israel's foundation as a Jewish state.

1955 The state-sponsored pogrom against the Rûm in Istanbul leads to the exodus of this group exempted from the 1923 population exchange.

1976 Turkish invasion of Cyprus (on which Ankara had renounced in Lausanne) and establishment of a state in Northern Cyprus dependent on Ankara.

1995 Treaty of Dayton for ex-Yugoslavia. Though endorsing results of preceding ethnic cleansing, in contrast to the 1923 Treaty of Lausanne, it does not facilitate total ethnic "unmixing," but establishes federal states for different population groups. Nationalist leaders had sought radical "solutions" explicitly in the vein of 1923.

1998 Kurdish activist Erdal Aksu hijacks a Turkish Air Lines plane, wanting to redirect it to Lausanne to protest against the 1923 Lausanne Treaty, demanding Treaty revision in favor of the Kurds.

2005 On 24 July 2005, the Turkish ultranationalist Doğu Perinçek, a member of the Ankara- and Lefkoşa-supported "Talat Pasha Committee," gives a public speech in Lausanne that denies the Armenian Genocide.

2016 After a failed coup and under growingly arbitrary rule, Turkey starts occupying parts of Northern Syria and establishing Ankara-depending proto-state structures. At the same time, Ankara has built up a chain of military bases along the Iraqi-Turkish border, creating a Turkish-controlled zone in Northern Iraq. These steps amount to a forceful "Lausanne revisionism."

2017 Turkey's president Recep T. Erdogan publicly denounces the Treaty of Lausanne and puts into question Turkey's "Lausanne borders" with Iraq, Syria, and Greece, including maritime borders and rights to exploit natural resources.

2022 The Turkish president threatens to invade Greece (September).

Select Bibliography

Archives

Archives cantonales vaudoises, Lausanne (ACV, Cantonal Archive of Vaud).
Başbakanlık Cumhuriyet Arşivi, Ankara (BCA, Republican State Archives).
Başbakanlık Osmanlı Arşivi, Istanbul (BOA, Ottoman State Archives).
Bibliothèque Nubar, Paris (BNu, Armenian Library Nubar).
Bundesarchiv, Bern (BAr, Swiss Federal Archive). E21, E1004, E2001.
Centre des Archives diplomatiques du ministère des affaires étrangères (MAE), La Courneuve, Paris (French diplomatic archives).
Houghton Library, Harvard University, Joseph Clark Grew papers.
League of Nations Archive, Geneva (LNA, largely accessible on https://libraryresources.unog.ch/lontad).
Türk Tarih Kurumu (TTK, Ankara), *Lozan Türk Yurdu Cemiyeti'nin Muharrerat ve Zabt-ı Sabık Defteri*, Y 653.

Newspapers and Periodicals

Gazette de Lausanne (www.letempsarchives.ch).
Journal de Genève (www.letempsarchives.ch).
Neue Zürcher Zeitung (www.nzz.ch).
Turkey: Monthly Organ of the Turkish Congress at Lausanne. Printed by Giesser & Held, Lausanne.
Türk Yurdu, 1911–1931. Transcribed edition. Ankara: Tutibay, 1998–2001 (17 vols.).

Lausanne Conference Proceedings

Conférence de Lausanne sur les affaires du Proche-Orient (1922–1923): Recueil des actes de la conférence. Paris: Imprimerie Nationale, 1923 (CLA, 6 vols. in two series).
Lausanne Conference on Near Eastern Affairs (1922–1923): Records of Proceedings and Draft Terms of Peace. London: His Majesty's Stationery Office, 1923 (LCP, limited to the first half of the Conference, and without subcommission proceedings).
Lozan Barış Konferansı. Tutanaklar, Belgeler, transl. and ed. Seha L. Meray. Istanbul: YKY, 2001 (LKT, 8 vols., the most complete collection of Conference proceedings and documents).

Printed Primary Sources

Açık ve Gizli Oturumlarda Lozan Tartışmaları: TBMM'de Lozan Müzakereleri Tutanakları, ed. Taha Akyol and Sefa Kaplan. Istanbul: Dogan Kitap, 2014.
Aras, Tevfik R. *Lozanın izlerinde*. Istanbul: Akşam, 1935.
Atatürk, Kemal. *Gazi Mustafa Kemal Atatürk, Atatürk'ün Söylev ve Demeçleri* (3 vols.).Ankara: Atatürk Kültür Dil ve Tarih Yüksek Kurumu, 1997.
  Nutuk: Vesikalar. Ankara: Atatürk Kültür, Dil ve Tarih Kurumu, 1991.
British Foreign Office. *Further Correspondence Respecting Turkey, October to December 1922*, Confidential Print 12330, FO 424/255. London: Foreign Office, n.d. And analogous subsequent volumes.
Derso, Alois, and Emery Kelèn, *Guignol à Lausanne*. Lausanne: A. Marsens, 1923.
Documents diplomatiques français 1922. Brussels: Peter Lang, 2007. And analogous subsequent volumes.
Gökalp, Ziya. *Türkçülüğün esasları*, ed. Salim Çonoğlu. Istanbul: Ötüken, 2014 (1923).
Inan, Afet (=Ayşe Afetinan). *L'Anatolie, le pays de la "race" turque: recherches sur les caractères anthropologiques des populations de la Turquie, enquête sur 64.000 individus*. Preface by Eugène Pittard. Geneva, 1941.
League of Nations. *Protection of Linguistic, Racial or Religious Minorities by the League of Nations: Resolutions and Extracts*. Geneva: League of Nations, 1929.
Oran, Baskın. *Türk dış politikası. Vol. 1: Kurtuluş Savaşından Bugüne olgular, belgeler, yorumlar. 1919–1980*. Istanbul: Iletisim, 2019.
Recueil des Traités et des Engagements Internationaux enregistrés par le Secrétariat de la Société des Nations/Treaty Series: Publication of Treaties and International Engagements registered with the Secretariat of the League of Nations, vol. 28. Geneva: League of Nations, 1924.
Sadak, Necmeddin S. *Necmeddin Sadık (Sadak) Bey'in Lozan Mektupları*, ed. Mustafa Özyürek. Ankara: Gece, 2019.
Şimşir, Bilal (ed.). *Lozan Telgrafları*, vols. 1–2. Ankara: TTK, 1990 and 1994.
TBBM Gizli Celse Zabıtları, vols. 3–4. Ankara: Türkiye İş Bankası, 1985.
"Tripartite Agreement between the British Empire, France and Italy Respecting Anatolia," *American Journal of International Law*, 15 (April 1921), 153–159.
Varlık, M. Bülent, ed. *Umumî Müfettişler Toplantı Tutanakları*. Ankara: Dipnot, 2010.

Printed Diaries, Memoirs, and Insider Retrospectives or Perspectives

Aharonian, Avedis. *From Sardarabad to Sèvres and Lausanne: Political Diary*. Boston: Hairenik Press, 1943 (in Armenian).
Aralov, Semyon. *Bir Sovyet Diplomatının Anıları 1922–23*. Istanbul: Türkiye İş Bankası, 2010.
Bilsel, Cemil. "Medenî Kanun ve Lozan Muahedesi." In *Medenî Kanunun XV. Yıl Dönümü İçin*. Istanbul: Kenan Matbaası, 1944, 21–71.

Bovet, Ernest. *Die neue Ordnung.* Lausanne: Schweizerische Vereinigung für den Völkerbund, 1933.
Bozkurt, Mahmut E. "Türk Medenî Kanunu nasıl hazırlandı?" In *Medenî Kanunun XV. Yıl Dönümü İçin.* Istanbul: Kenan Matbaası, 1944, 7–20.
Cavid Bey, Mehmed. *Meşrutiyet Rûznamesi*, vol. 4. Ankara: TTK, 2015.
Şiar'ın Defteri. Istanbul: Iletisim, 1995.
Gentizon, Paul. *Mustapha Kemal ou l'Orient an marche.* Paris: Bossard, 1929.
Grew, Joseph C. *Turbulent Era: A Diplomatic Record of Forty Years 1904–1945.* Boston: Houghton Mifflin, 1952 (2 vols.).
Inönü, Ismet. *İsmet İnönü'nün hatıraları: Büyük zaferden sonra Mudanya Mütarekesi ve Lozan Antlaşması.* Istanbul: Yenigün, 1998.
Kerr, Stanley E. *The Lions of Marash: Personal Experiences with American Near East Relief, 1919–1922.* New York: SUNY, 1973.
Khatissian, Alexandre. *Eclosion et développement de la République arménienne.* Athens: Editions Arméniennes, 1989.
Kraft-Bonnard, Antony. *L'Arménie à la Conférence de Lausanne.* Alençon: Foi et vie, 1923.
Mehmed Cavid Bey, see Cavid Bey.
Nicolson, Harold G. *Curzon: The Last Phase, 1919–1925: A Study in Post-War Diplomacy.* London: Constable, 1934.
Nur, Rıza. *Hayat ve Hatıratım*, ed. Abdurrahman Dilipak. Istanbul: İşaret, 1992 (3 vols).
Oeri, Albert, et al. *Zehn Jahre Völkerbund.* Glarus: Glarner Nachrichten, 1930.
Rappard, William E. *The Geneva Experiment.* Oxford: Oxford University Press, 1931.
Rıza, Ahmed. *La faillite morale de la politique occidentale en Orient.* Ankara: Ministry of Culture, 1990 (1922).
Ryan, Andrew. *The Last of the Dragomans.* London: Geoffrey Bles, 1952.
Sauser-Hall, Georges. *La réception des droits européens en Turquie*, Geneva: Faculté de Droit de l'Université de Genève, 1938.
Sforza, Carlo. *L'Italia dal 1914 al 1944: Quale io la vidi.* Verona: Arnoldo Mondari, 1946.
Tröbst, Hans. *Soldatenblut: Vom Baltikum zu Kemal Pascha.* Leipzig: Koehler, 1925.

Unpublished Works and Notebooks

Carelos, Markos. The 1923 Lausanne Peace in Greek Political Thought: The Cases of Georgios Streit and Emmanouil Emmanouilidis. University of Zurich: Ph.D. thesis, 2022.
Carpenter, Kaley M. A Worldly Errand: James L. Barton's American Mission to the Near East. Princeton: Theological Ph.D. dissertation, 2009.
Demirci, Sevtap. The Lausanne Conference: The Evolution of Turkish and British Strategies, 1922-1923. London School of Economics and Political Science: Ph.D. Thesis, 1997.
Gennai, Andrea. La Question d'Orient: La gestion multilatérale de la Dette Publique Ottomane. University of Geneva: M.A. thesis, 2015.

Montebello, Caroline. *Eugène Pittard, un anthropologue genevois en Turquie nationaliste (1910–1950): Idéologie d'exclusion, corruption intellectuelle et logiques sociales*. Paris: Ecole des Hautes Etudes en Sciences Sociales, master thesis, 2016.

Nur, Rıza. *Ermeni Tarihi*, Ottoman manuscript, 508 pages. Staatsbibliothek zu Berlin, Ms. Orient Quart 1394, written in the 1910s and 1920s.

Straumann, Lukas. *L'humanitaire mis en scene: La cinématographie de CICR des années 1920*, internal CICR study. Geneva: Le Comité international de la Croix-Rouge, 2000.

Secondary Literature

Albrecht-Carrié, René. *France, Europe and the Two World Wars*. Geneva: Droz, 1969.

Al-Rasheed, Madawi, and Marat Shterin, eds. *Demystifying the Caliphate: Historical Memory and Contemorary Contexts*. London: Hurst, 2013.

Ambrosius, Lloyd E. "Wilsonian Diplomacy and Armenia: the limits of power and ideology." In Jay Winter (ed.), *America and the Armenian Genocide of 1915*. Cambridge: Cambridge University Press, 2003, 113–145.

Anderson, Matthew S. *The Eastern Question, 1774–1923*. New York: St. Martin's Press, 1966.

Ardıç, Nurullah, *Islam and the Politics of Secularism: The Caliphate and Middle Eastern Modernization in the Early 20th Century*. London: Routledge, 2012.

Baer, Marc. *Sultanic Saviors and Tolerant Turks: Writing Ottoman Jewish History, Denying the Armenian Genocide*. Bloomington: Indiana University Press, 2020.

Bali, Rıfat. *Musa'nın Evlatları. Cumhuriyet'in Yurttaşları*. Istanbul, İletişim, 2001.

Banken, Roland. *Die Verträge von Sèvres 1920 und Lausanne 1923: Eine völkerrechtliche Untersuchung zur Beendigung des Ersten Weltkrieges und zur Auflösung der sogenannten "Orientalischen Frage"*. Berlin: LIT-Verlag, 2014.

Bauer, Yehuda. *Rethinking the Holocaust*. New Haven, CT: Yale University Press, 2002.

Bein, Amit. *Kemalist Turkey and the Middle East: International Relations in the Interwar* Period. Cambridge: Cambridge University Press, 2017.

Bozarslan, Hamit. *Histoire de la Turquie: De l'Empire à nos jours*. Paris: Tallandier, 2013.

L'anti-démocratie au XXIe siècle: Iran, Russie, Turquie. Paris: CNRS éditions, 2021.

Nikos Christofis, ed. *Erdoğan's "New" Turkey: Attempted Coup d'état and the Acceleration of Political Crisis*. London: Routledge, 2020.

Conlin, Jonathan, "An Oily Entente: France, Britain, and the Mosul Question, 1916–1925." *Diplomacy & Statecraft*, 31:2 (2020), 246–249.

Dadrian, Vahakn, and Taner Akçam. *Judgment at Istanbul: The Armenian Genocide Trials*. New York: Berghahn, 2011.

Davis, Juliet. "The New World and the 'New Turks': The American-Turkish Claims Commission and Armenian-Americans' Contested Citizenship in the Interwar Period." *Journal of Genocide Research*, 19:3 (2017), 299–317.

Davison, Roderic H. "Middle East Nationalism: Lausanne Thirty Years After." *Middle East Journal*, 7:3 (1953), 324–348.
"Turkish Diplomacy from Mudros to Lausanne." In Roderic H. (ed.), *Essays in Ottoman and Turkish History 1774–1923*. Austin: University of Texas Press, 1990, 206–242.
Demirel, Ahmet. *Birinci Meclis'te Muhalefet: İkinci Grup*. Istanbul: Iletisim, 1994.
DeNovo, John A. "A Railroad for Turkey: The Chester Project, 1908–1913." *The Business History Review* 33:3 (Autumn 1959), 300–329.
Dockrill, M. L., and J. D. Goold. Peace Without Promise: Britain and the Peace Conferences,1919-23. Hamden, Conn.: Archon,1981.
Ekmekcioglu, Lerna. "Republic of Paradox: The League of Nations Minority Protection Regime and the New Turkey's Step-Citizens." *International Journal of Middle East Studies*, 46:4 (2014), 657–679.
Fromkin, David, *A Peace to End All Peace: The Fall of the Ottoman Empire and the Creation of the Modern Middle East*. New York: Holt, 2009 (1989).
Georgelin, Hervé. *La fin de Smyrne, du cosmopolitisme aux nationalisms*. Paris: CNRS, 2005.
Gerwarth, Robert. *The Vanquished: Why the First World War Failed to End*. New York: Farrar, Straus and Giroux, 2016.
Göçek, Fatma M. *The Transformation of Turkey: Redefining State and Society from the Ottoman Empire to the Modern Era*. London: I.B. Tauris, 2011.
Grabill, Joseph L. *The Protestant Diplomacy and the Near East: Missionary Influence on American Policy, 1810–1927*. Minneapolis, University of Minnesota Press, 1971.
Guieu, Jean-Michel, and Stanislas Jeannesson, eds. *La Société des nations. Une expérience de l'internationalisme*. Special issue of *Monde(s)*, 19 (2021).
Halévy, Elie. *L'ère des tyrannies: Etudes sur le socialism et la guerre*. Paris: Gallimard, 1938.
Harootunian, Harry. *The Unspoken as Heritage: The Armenian Genocide and Its Unaccounted Lives*. Durham, NC: Duke University Press, 2019.
Harris, George S. *Atatürk's Diplomats*. Istanbul: ISIS, 2010.
Hassan, Mona. *Longing for the Lost Caliphate: A Transregional History*. Princeton, NJ: Princeton University Press, 2016.
Hirschon, Renée, ed. *Crossing the Aegean: An Appraisal of the 1923 Compulsory Population Exchange Between Greece and Turkey*. New York: Berghahn, 2008.
Hofmann, Reto. *The Fascist Effect: Japan and Italy, 1915–1952* (Ithaca, NY: Cornell University Press, 2015.
Hovannisian, Richard G. *Between Crescent and Sickle: Partition and Sovietization. Vol. 4: The Republic of Armenia*. Berkeley: University of California Press, 1996.
Ihrig, Stefan. *Atatürk in the Nazi Imagination*. Cambridge, MA: Harvard University Press, 2014.
Jeffery, Keith, and Alan Sharp. "Lord Curzon and Secret Intelligence." In Christopher Andrew and Jeremy Noakes (eds.), *Intelligence and International Relations*. Exeter: Exeter University Press, 103–126.
Kaiga, Sakiko. *Britain and the Intellectual Origins of the League of Nations, 1914-1919*. Cambridge: Cambridge University Press, 2021.

Kayış, Yasin. "Lozan Antlaşması'nın Karikatürlere Yansıması." In İsmail Şahin and Ersin Müezzinoğlu (eds.), *Atatürk Türk dış politikası II*. Istanbul: ideal, 2018, 391–436.

Kaynar, Erdal. *L'héroïsme de la vie moderne: Ahmed Rıza (1858–1930) en son temps*. Paris: Peeters, 2021.

Kévonian, Dzovinar. *Réfugiés et diplomatie humanitaire: les acteurs européens et la scène proche-orientale pendant l'entre-deux-guerres*. Paris: Publications de la Sorbonne, 2004.

La danse du pendule: les juristes et l'internationalisation des droits de l'Homme, 1920-1939. Paris: Editions de la Sorbonne, 2021.

"Usages du droit et espaces de pouvoir transnationaux: la pratique pétitionnaire de la section des minorités de la Société des nations face aux rescapés d'un crime de masse, 1920–1939," *Monde(s)* 19 (2021), 73–95.

Kieser, Hans-Lukas. *Der verpasste Friede. Mission, Ethnie und Staat in den Ostprovinzen der Türkei*. Zürich: Chronos, 2021 [2000].

Talaat Pasha: Father of Modern Turkey, Architect of Genocide. Princeton, NJ: Princeton University Press, 2018.

Leonhard, Jörn. *Der überforderte Frieden: Versailles und die Welt 1918–1923*. Munich: C.H. Beck, 2018.

Liebisch-Gümüş, Carolin. *Verflochtene Nationsbildung: Die Neue Türkei und der Völkerbund 1918–38*. Munich: De Gruyter Oldenbourg, 2020.

Mandelstam, André N. *La Société des Nations et les puissances devant le problème arménien*. Paris: A. Pedone, 1926.

Mango, Andrew. *Atatürk*. London: John Murray, 1999.

Mazower, Mark. *Dark Continent: Europe's Twentieth Century*. London: Penguin, 1999.

No Enchanted Palace: The End of Empire and the Ideological Origins of the United Nations. Princeton, NJ: Princeton University Press, 2009.

Mısıroğlu, Kadir. *Lozan: Zafer mi, hezimet mi?* Istanbul: Sebil, 1992 (3 vols.).

Moyn, Samuel. *The Origins of the Other*. Ithaca, NY: Cornell University Press, 2005.

Naimark, Norman M. *Fires of Hatred: Ethnic Cleansing in Twentieth-Century Europe*. Cambridge, MA, Harvard University Press, 2001.

Oran, Baskın, *Türkiye'de azınlıklar: kavramlar, teori, Lozan, iç mevzuat, içtihat, uygulama*. Istanbul: İlestişim, 2004.

Othman, Ali. "The Kurds and the Lausanne Peace Negotiations, 1922–1922." *Middle Eastern Studies*, 33:3 (1997), 521–534.

Özsu, Umut. *Formalizing Displacement: International Law and Population Transfers*. New York: Oxford University Press, 2015.

Payk, Marcus M. *Frieden durch Recht: Der Aufstieg des modernen Völkerrechts und der Friedensschluss nach dem Ersten Weltkrieg*. Berlin: Gruyter, 2018.

Pedersen, Susan. *The Guardians: The League of Nations and the Crisis of Empire*. Oxford: Oxford University Press, 2017.

Pekesen, Berna. "The exodus of Armenians from the Sanjak of Alexandretta in the 1930s." In H. L. Kieser (ed.), *Turkey beyond Nationalism*. London: I.B. Tauris, 2006, 57–66.

Phillips Cohen, Julia. "A Model *Millet*? Ottoman Jewish Citizenship at the End of Empire." In Abigail Green and Simon Levis-Sullam (eds.), *Jews, Liberalism, Antisemitism: A Global History*. London: Palgrave, 2020, 209–231.

Plagemann, Gottfried. "Die Einführung des ZGB im Jahre 1926: Das neue ZGB als Bedingung eines sökularen und souveränen Nationalstaats." In H. Kieser, A. Meier, and W. Stoffel (eds.), *Revolution islamischen Rechts: Das Schweizerische ZGB in der Türkei*. Zürich: Chronos, 2008, 21–34.

Rappard, William E. *The Crisis of Democracy*. Chicago, IL: The University of Chicago Press, 1938.

Scheuermann, Martin. *Minderheitenschutz contra Konfliktverhütung?* Marburg: Herder-Institut, 2000.

Segesser, Daniel M. "Die historischen Wurzel des Begriffs 'Verbrechen gegen die Menschlichkeit'." *Jahrbuch der Juristischen Zeitgeschichte*, 8 (2006–7), 75–101.

Sjöberg, Erik. *Internationalism and the New Turkey: American Peace Education in the Kemalist Republic, 1923–1933*. Cham: Springer, 2022.

Stamatopoulos, Dimitris. *Byzantium after the Nation: The Problem of Continuity in Balkan Historiographies*. Budapest: Central European University Press, 2022.

Steiner, Zara. *The Lights that Failed: European International History 1919–1933*. Oxford: Oxford University Press, 2007.

Szurek, Emmanuel. "Auto-da-fe in Istanbul: Nationalist Turkey's first denialist crisis (1935)." In Seyhan Bayraktar, Hans-Lukas Kieser, and Khatchig Mouradian (eds.), *After the Ottomans: Genocide's Long Shadow and Armenian Resilience*. London: I.B. Tauris, in press.

Teitelbaum, Joshua. *The Rise and Fall of the Hashimite Kingdom of Arabia*. New York: New York University Press, 2001.

Toynbee, Arnold J. *The Western Question in Greece and Turkey: A Study in the Contact of Civilisations*. London: Constable, 1922.

Tunçay, Mete. *Türkiye'de sol akımlar 1908–1925*. Istanbul: Iletisim, 2009.

Tusan, Michelle. *The British Empire and the Armenian Genocide: Humanitarianism and Imperial Politics from Gladstone to Churchill*. London: I.B. Tauris, 2019.

Walters, F. P. *A History of the League of Nations*. London: Oxford University Press, 1952.

Weber, Thomas. *Becoming Hitler: The Making of a Nazi*. Oxford: Oxford University Press, 2017.

Winter, Jay. *Dreams of Peace and Freedom in the Twentieth Century*. New Haven, CT: Yale University Press, 2006.

The Day the Great War Ended, 24 July 1923: The Civilianization of War. Oxford: Oxford University Press, 2022.

Yerasimos, Stefanos. *Türk-Sovyet İlişkileri: Ekim Devrimden Milli Mücadeleye*. Istanbul: Boyut, 2000.

Yıldırım, Onur. *Diplomacy and Displacement. Reconsidering the Turco-Greek Exchange of Populations*. New York: Routledge, 2012.

Index

Abalıoğlu, Yusuf Nadi, 187
Abandoned Property, 99, 157, 210, 212
Abdulhamid II, 11, 50, 71, 112, 151, 234, 298
Abdulmecid II, caliph, 268
Abu Bakr al Baghdadi, 270
Açıkalın, Cevat, 158, 290
Adana, 40, 69, 70, 103, 298
Adorno, Theodor, 43
Aegean, 48, 264
Aegean coast, 95
Afetinan, Ayşe, 114
Afghanistan, 269
   treaty with, 106
Africans, 133
Ağaoğlu, Ahmed, 68, 186
Ağralı, Fuat, 290
Aharonian, Avedis, 105, 159, 161, 162
Ahmed Rıza, 102, 117–118
Aintab, 103
Akşam, 119, 141, 227, 296
Aleppo, 125
Alevis, 62, 141, 155
   Kurdish Alevis, 8, 13, 26, 61, 76, 87, 156, 240, 261, 300
Alexander the Great, 41, 70
Alexandropol, 89
Ali Cenani, 236
Ali Said. *See* Talaat, Mehmed (Pasha/Bey)
Ali Suavi, 114
Ali Şükrü, 61, 227, 230
al-Nuri mosque, 270
Al-Qaeda, 265
al-Rasheed, Madawi, 271
American College for Girls, 254, 292
American missionaries, 7, 62, 101, 214
   American Board of Commissioners for Foreign Missions, 214
   secular millenarism, 7
Amin al-Husayni, 270
amnesty
   and return, 202, 211, 243

Declaration on general amnesty, 210, 211
Anatolia, 74, 81
   human geography before genocide, 94
   plural Anatolia, 94
   plural society, 226
   synonymous with Asia Minor, 4
   Turkification, 13, 68, 149, 156, 251, 256
   Turkish national home, 94
   war over, 1, 16, 26, 33, 39, 54, 70
   zones of influence, 94
Anatolia Agency, 164
Anderson, Matthew S., 25, 27
Anglo-French contest, 27
Anglo-French Iraqi Petroleum Company, 221
Ankara Accord, 103, 105
Ankara Convention with Greece, 246, 248
Ankara government, 1, 7, 8, 21, 37, 57, 76, 87, 101, 107, 113, 122
   First Group, 90
   legal successor of Istanbul, 174
   Second Group, 90, 201, 227, 231
   weapons sent to, 104
Antakya, 248
   incorporation of, 263
anti-Armenianism, 90, 270
   and anti-Semitism, 250, 266
anticommunism, 206
antidemocracy, 5, 6, 23, 29, 79, 223, 233, 234, 248, 263, 272, 273–285
   cooperation of autocracies, 265
Apaydın, Zekai, 61, 173, 245, 290, 293
apocalypse, 82
appeasement, 25, 34, 48, 110, 225, 274, 277, 278
   primacy of, 244
Arab Spring, 265
Arabian peninsula, 25, 31, 269
Arabs, 11, 15, 64, 70, 80, 189
Aralov, Semyon, 19, 98, 140
Ararat, 65
Aras, Tevfik Rüştü, 225, 247, 249, 250

Index

Aras, Tevfik Rüştü, 246
arbitral commissions, 99
Ardahan, 89
Armenia, 6, 21, 33, 38, 41, 87, 88, 89, 101, 105, 299
　division of, 97, 179
　Turkish–Armenian frontier, 96, 169
　viable Armenia, 102
Armenian Catholicos of Sis, 104
Armenian Genocide, 7, 26, 29, 43, 47, 48, 157, 158, 178, 213, 243, 248, 249, 269, 271, 287, 308
Armenian home, 121, 141, 158–169, 190, 215, 252
　abandonment of, 193
Armenian Question, 39, 41, 90, 167, 169, 186, 190, 221, 254, 303
Armenian Revolutionary Aspirations and Movements, The, 64
Armenian Revolutionary Federation, 53, 71, 178
Armenians, 11, 15, 28, 37, 43, 45, 49, 62, 67, 68, 74, 75, 76, 107, 112, 154, 155, 188, 189, 209, 214, 244, 275
　concentration camps in Syria, 260
　return of survivors, 101, 160, 179, 210
　surviving in Dersim, 244
　united delegation, 161, 164
Armenians in History and the Armenian Question, The, 254
Armistice
　of Mudanya, 109, 140, 293, 302
　of Mudros, 77, 181, 299
Arslan, Shakib, 49, 269
Artvin, 89
Aryanism, 12, 42
Asia Minor. *See* Anatolia
Asians, 133
Assyrians, 15, 37, 74, 76, 163, 243, 244, 275, 304
　Assyro-Chaldeans, 154, 158, 163
Atabinen, Reşit Saffet, 48, 56, 61, 112, 116, 119, 135, 153, 174, 185, 189, 219, 249, 253, 290, 292
Atatürk, 2, 8, 12, 13, 28, 40, 43, 45, 50, 55, 58, 61, 65, 69–70, 76, 77, 78, 79, 83, 90, 91, 97, 98, 100, 105, 106, 108, 112, 114, 125, 134, 140, 170, 185, 200, 216, 224–264, 269, 282, 287, 290, 294, 296
　Adana speech, 185
　multiday speech. *See Nutuk*
　opening speech of the economic congress in Izmir, 229
　speech at the reopening of the Assembly, 224

Atatürk's Revolution. *See* Turkish Revolution
Atay, Falih Rıfkı, 108, 236, 239, 249, 296
Athens, 136, 248
Atlantic Charter, 281
Aubert, Théodore, 205
Australians, 133
Austria, 37, 298
autocracy. *See* dictatorship
Azerbaijan, 87, 89

Baha Said, 187, 223, 253
Bahaeddin Şakir, 173, 178
Baku, 89
　Bolshevik Congress of the Peoples of the East, 32, 301
Balfour Declaration, 162
Balkan conferences, 247
Balkan Pact, 246
Balkan Wars, 72, 96
　First Balkan War, 52
Balkans, 40, 112
Baltic Sea, 88
Barrère, Camille, 190, 195
Barton, James, 214–216, 218, 220
Başak, Seniyettin, 290
Basra, 227
Bauman, Zygmunt, 160
Bayar, Celal, 236, 293
Bayatlı, Yahya Kemal, 290, 295
Baydur, Hüseyin Ragıp, 295
Baykut, Abdülkadir Câmi, 102
Bayur, Yusuf Hikmet, 187, 290, 293
Belge, Burhan Asaf, 249
Belger, Nihat Reşat, 166, 174, 295
Benjamin, Walter, 280
Berlin, 74, 77, 82, 103, 172, 178
Berlin Treaty, 91, 187
Bern, 268
Beşikçi, Ismail, 29
Beyatlı, Yahya Kemal, 119, 224
Bismarck, Chancellor, 27
Bitlis, 95
Bıyıklıoğlu, Mehmet Tevfik, 187, 253, 290, 294
Black Sea, 92, 101, 145, 147, 201
Bolsheviks, 31, 33, 54, 77, 80, 86, 89, 91, 92, 97, 152, 205, 300
　national Bolsheviks, 78
　support for Ankara, 1, 11, 51, 78, 82
Bolshevism, 6, 43, 166, 244
Bompard, Madame, 196
Bompard, Maurice, 183, 195, 197, 198
Bosnia, 298
Bosporus, 68

Bovet, Ernest, 83, 278
Bozarslan, Hamit, 71
Bozcaada. *See* Tenedos
Bozkurt, Mahmut Esat, 75, 113, 115, 193, 229, 238, 240, 261
Brest-Litovsk
    Conference of, 77
    Treaty. *See* Treaty of Brest-Litovsk
Bristol, Mark, 98, 142, 192, 216, 220
Britain, 8, 11, 15, 31, 35, 86, 95, 102, 112, 236, 243
Bulgaria, 15, 140, 144, 298
    "Bulgaria in the East," 87
Bulgarians, 154, 158
Byzantines, 64, 70

Cairo, 56, 59
Cairo Conference, 110
Çakmak, Fevzi, 83
Calcutta, 62
caliphate, 48, 71, 120, 146, 227, 264–271, 306
    abolition of, 17, 217, 239, 253, 265
    Caliphate Congress, 270
    nostalgia, 271
    restoration, 58, 269, 270
    separation from sultanate, 226
Camerlynck, Gustave, 137
Canaanites, 286
Çankaya, 236, 282
Canonica, Pietro, 83
Capital Tax, 242
capitalism, 206
Capitulations, 26, 113, 123, 126, 145, 157, 193, 202, 237, 252, 299
Casino Montbenon, 141
Caucasus, 31, 37, 48, 52, 87, 92, 97, 147, 168, 251, 264
    Caucasus campaign by Ankara, 89
    CUP's Caucasus campaign, 87
    South Caucasus, 30, 33, 51, 87, 89, 179
Cavid Bey, 11, 50, 102, 105, 112, 118, 119, 121, 125, 126, 159, 161, 170–179, 198, 206, 223, 228, 232–237, 249, 292, 294
    Ankara trial, 234
    April 1923 meetings, 233
    judicial assassination, 171, 236
    Cemal Azmi, 178
    and Ismet Pasha, 175
    and Rıza Nur, 176
Cemal Pasha, 73
Chamberlain, Austin, 277
Chamberlain, Neville, 277
Chanak Crisis, 109

Château d'Ouchy, 138, 145, 149, 158, 189
Chester
    company, 305
    concession, 201
    project, 216
Chester, Colby M., 220
Chicherin, Georgy, 133, 145, 146, 303
Child, Richard W., 128, 130
China, 2, 81, 82
    1911, 297
    Fourth May (1919) Movement, 299
Churchill, Winston, 110
Cilicia, 31, 94, 103, 104
Cilician kingdom, 67
Çilli, Ahmet Muhtar, 290, 294
Civil Code, 113, 223, 283
    introduction of Swiss, 217
civil liberties, 11, 15, 35, 84, 132, 246, 281
civilizationism, 12, 16, 110, 188, 191, 226
    without democracy, 276
Cold War, 101
Comintern, 6, 78, 79, 81
Commissions
    First Commission on Territorial and Military Questions, 144
    Second Commission on the Regime of Foreigners, 145
    Sub-Commission on Minorities, 152, 158
    Sub-Commission on the Exchange of Populations, 150
    Third Commission, 172, 207
    Third Commission on Economic and Financial Questions, 145
Committee of Union and Progress. *See* CUP
common good, 1, 85, 276, 279, 282–288
communions in crime, 284
comprador bourgeoisie, 92
concessions, 202, 207
    pre–Great War, 201
Conferences of Yalta and Potsdam, 307
Conradi, Maurice, 205
Constantine I, King, 106, 127
Convention Concerning the Exchange of Greek and Turkish Populations, 156, 190
Corfu, 135
    Italian occupation, 38
covenant
    between humans and God, 285
Covenant of the League of Nations, 6, 14, 32, 37, 75, 84, 110, 281
    Covenant Article 11, 136
craniology, 40

Crete, 298
crimes against humanity, 53, 118, 193, 284
　international court for, 99
Criss, Nur Bilge, 264
Critique of Violence, 280
Crusaders, 67
Cuno, Wilhelm, 194
CUP, 50, 71–78, 80, 101, 108, 113, 126, 141, 144, 149, 151, 163, 170, 171, 177, 178, 236, 279, 298
　and Armenians, 64
　central committee, 71, 73
　ex-CUP cadres in Lausanne, 289
　facing international prosecution, 75
　party-state, 50, 52, 56, 71, 72, 75, 80, 110, 132, 185, 189, 228, 238, 248, 277, 298
　revival, 232
Curzon, 121, 124, 127, 128, 137, 143, 162, 166, 190, 195, 196, 197, 202, 272
　and İnönü, 152
　lofty words, 156
Curzons, 129, 134
Cyprus, 248, 264

Damascus, 267
Dardanelles, 147, 299
Dashnaksutiun. *See* Armenian Revolutionary Federation
de-Armenization, 211
　policy of de-Armenization cum dispossession, 212
Debt Administration, 173, 175
　Rûm and Armenian employees, 176
Decalogue, 286
Declaration on general amnesty, 211
Declaration Relating to the Administration of Justice and a Convention respecting Conditions of Residence and Business and Jurisdiction, 204
Defense of (Muslim) Rights Associations, 294
Defense of National [Muslim] Rights in Anatolia and Rumelia, 228
delegations
　Ankara's, 112
　Armenian delegation, 18, 49, 53
　British delegation, 124
　Greek delegation, 127, 150
　Soviet delegation, 37, 133, 145
　Turkish delegation, 12, 16, 39, 42, 119, 124, 133, 152, 153, 155, 167, 289
　instructions to, 141
demilitarization, 147
democracy, 11, 17, 22, 35, 47, 129, 132, 168, 201, 214, 238
　disabled by exclusion of alterity, 250
　full-fledged, 281
　perverted, 238
　rhetoric of, 216, 217, 218
Democratic Party, 293
democratic social contract, 15, 23, 30, 51, 227, 246, 259, 271, 280–285
　antipode of national pacts, 288
　fundament of peace, 275
　rejection of, 97
demographic engineering, 25, 47, 74
denialism, 116, 163, 176, 249, 283, 292
Der Völkische Beobachter, 249
Dersim, 244, 261
　resettlement of Dersimis, 261
Dersim genocide, 8, 13, 26, 29, 87, 156, 223, 259–262, 295
Derso, Alois, 139
Derviş Mehmet, 245
Deutsche Bank, 174
Devereux, Robert, 238
diaspora
　Islamic, 76
　Turkish, 74, 133
dictatorship
　allegedly benign, 13, 185, 239, 244
Directorate of Religious Affairs, 306
　substitute for Sheykhulislamate and Ministry of Sharia and Islamic Foundations, 239
dispossession, 38, 117, 125, 157, 164, 169, 202, 210
　restitution, 75, 99, 158, 179, 252
Diyarbekir, 158
Dodecanese, 129, 145
dönme, 113, 170
Dr Reşat. *See* Belger
draft treaty, 195, 196, 199, 200, 202
Drummond, Eric, 93
Dumlupınar
　battle of, 141, 255

Eastern Europe, 6, 14, 47, 82, 148, 265, 282, 307
Eastern Question, 2, 25, 298
Edirne, 204
　recovery of, 255
ego-nation, 229
Egypt, 12, 47, 124
Enver Pasha, 43, 73, 77, 82, 87, 299
equality of races, 86
Erasmus of Rotterdam, 3
Erdogan, Recep T., 39, 248, 274, 308
Ertegün, Mehmet Münir, 43, 48, 77, 119, 158, 187, 249, 250, 290, 294

320 Index

Erzberger, Matthias, 194
Erzerum, 95
eschatology, 215
Esenbel, Mehmed Atıf, 290, 292
Etatism, 246
Etchmiadzin, 62
Ethiopia, 132
  Italian invasion, 262
Eurasianism, 55
European Union, 265, 274
evlad-ı fatihan, 80
exploitation, 130, 284, 285. *See also* imperial bias

Faisal, King, 31, 80
Fascism, 6, 13, 28, 38, 231, 273
fascisms, 8, 29, 31, 34, 280, 283
  definition, 277
  proto-fascism, 54, 231
fascisms, Fascism, 127–137
February Revolution 1917, 54
Fevzi Çakmak, 228
Feyzi Pirinççizâde, 236, 295
Fonjallaz, Arthur, 132, 134, 231, 304
forced conversions, 99
Foreign Office, 122
Forty Days of Musa Dagh, The, 43, 44, 165, 247, 249
fossil dependency, 21, 23, 137, 221, 285
Fourteen Points, 80, 93, 97
Foyers Turcs. *See* Turkish Home Associations
France, 15, 31, 35, 86, 95, 102, 106, 112, 202, 228
Franklin-Bouillon, Henry, 103–105, 123
Franz Werfel. *See also Forty Days of Musa Dagh*
Fribourg, 113
Frunze, Mikhail, 83, 97

Gallipoli, 74, 144
  defense of, 255
Garroni, Eugenio C., 129, 142, 153, 198
Gazi Kemal. *See* Atatürk
Gazi, or warrior of Islam, 106, 186
general elections, 222, 230–231, 252
Geneva, 23, 35, 62, 80, 270
Genoa Conference, 109, 124, 133
genocide, 4, 12, 13, 24, 35, 38, 178, 185, 284, 299
  1948 UN Convention on, 101
  and justice, 178
  commands, 286
  current international terminology and legal practice, 260

genocide denial. *See* denialism
Gentizon, Paul, 230
George, Lloyd, 102, 106, 110, 128, 132, 142, 161
Georgia, 87, 89, 133
Germany, 13, 15, 21, 27, 34, 37, 47, 77, 79, 82, 101, 109, 111, 123, 129, 194, 241
  Wilhelmine, 52, 74
global conscience, 85
global economic crisis, 206
Göbbels, Joseph, 249
Gökalp, Ziya, 50, 52, 59, 61, 69, 73, 81, 92, 186, 238, 251, 292
Gökçeada. *See* Imbros
Golden Rule, 286
Gospel narrative, 287
Graham, Ronald W., 124, 268
Grand National Assembly. *See* Ankara government
Greater Europe, 50
Greater Syria, 80
Greco-Turkish war, 98
Greece, 15, 38, 55, 88, 93, 94, 95, 96, 102, 112, 126, 143, 144, 202, 298
  National Schism, 93, 106
  refugees. *See* refugees
  Second Hellenic Republic, 127
  September 1922 Revolution, 127
  Trial of the Six, 127
Greeks, 43, 97
Grew, Joseph
  and Ismet İnönü, 217
  US ambassador in Ankara, 220
Grew, Joseph C., 20, 23, 48, 123, 128, 130, 141, 159, 160, 199, 204, 211, 216, 218, 220, 282, 283
  and Ismet İnönü, 201, 216
Guignol à Lausanne, 139
Gulf of Aden, 88
Gümrü. *See* Alexandropol
Günter, Franz, 173

Haab, Rudolf, 137
Hagia Sophia, 265
Hague Convention for the Pacific Settlement of International Disputes, 298
Haim, Nahum, 134, 174
Hâkimiyet-i Milliye, 295, 296
Halajian, Bedros, 161
Halévy, Elie, 3
Halli, Reşat, 260
Hamid (Bey). *See* Hasancan
Harun Aliçe, 113, 115
Hasan al-Banna, 270

Index

Hasancan, Hamit, 147, 154, 173, 175, 303
Hashemites, 31
Hatay, 248. *See also* Antakya
  pretended place of ancient proto-Turkish Hittites, 264
Hebrew Bible, 286
Hejaz Railway, 267, 294
Hemingway, Ernest, 24
Herbert, Aubrey, 111
Herzegovina, 298
High Treason Law of 1920, 230
history doctrine
  Atatürk's and Ankara's, 251
  Kemalist, 253
History of the Armenians, 188, 262
History of the Turkish Revolution, 262
  History of the Turks, 262
history-writing, 184–192
  Turanian master narrative, 185
Hitler Putsch, 195
Hitler, Adolf, 8, 42, 44, 136, 213, 277
Hittites, 66, 68
Hollywood
  planned film of *The Forty Days of Musa Dagh*, 250
Holocaust, 28, 29, 41, 43, 46, 278
Hotel Beau Rivage, 196, 199
Hotel Lausanne Palace, 127, 197, 199
Hughes, Charles E., 219
human dignity, 285
human rights, 281
humanitarianism, 214
Hungary, 1, 14, 37
hunger crises, 76, 82
Hussein bin Ali, 31, 269
Hussein, Saddam, 26
hyperinflation, 109, 123, 194

Ibn Saud, 11, 31, 33, 269
Ihrig, Stefan, 136
Imbros, 144
imperial bias, 16, 33, 80, 94, 242, 276
  in Kemalism, 261
  and racial bias, 96
imperialism, 72
India, 47, 124, 140, 269
  Muslims of, 79, 106
India Office, 124
İnhan, Zühtü, 290
İnönü
  battle of, 107, 141
İnönü, İsmet, 45, 48, 55, 83, 112, 125, 133, 139, 151, 158, 163, 172, 173, 192, 198, 203, 211, 237, 241, 245, 247, 249, 290
  and the Armenians, 158–165
  declaration on 17 July 1923, 211, 243, 305
  and Rauf Orbay, 224
  prime-minister, 267
  speech at the inaugural ceremony on 20 November 1922, 139, 143
  speech on 12 December 1922, 153, 186
  speech on Mosul's history, 186
Inspectorate General, 262
Institutes of the Turkish Revolution, 254
International Anticommunist Entente, 206
internationalism, 6, 36, 38, 80, 214, 280, 281
  Protestant, 35, 101
Iran, 47, 251
Iranians, 70
Iraq, 25, 26, 30, 95, 96, 196, 221, 236, 251, 264, 270
İş Bankası, 293
Iskenderun, 68, 227
  incorporation of, 263
Islam
  deemphasizing, 217
Islamic State, 26, 265, 270
Islamism, 25, 26, 86
  pan-Islamism, 71, 74, 123
  Turkish, 40
islands, 125, 144, 227, 248
  demilitarization, 145
Ismail Canbolad, 236
Ismet Pasha. *See* İnönü
Israel, 266
  ancient, 286
Israel–Palestine, 265
Istanbul
  a free city, 101
  evacuation of, 202
  internationalised, 124
Istanbul government, 76, 92, 97
Istanbul Law Faculty, 294, 295
Istanbul trials, 100, 103
Italy, 5, 13, 15, 21, 34, 38, 75, 95, 102, 106, 111, 112, 145, 202, 228, 236, 241
  Ankara ahead of Fascist Italy, 236
  March on Rome, 129, 136
Izmir, 75, 88, 95, 96, 102, 105, 107, 117, 122, 149, 157, 236, 252
  assassination plot against Gazi Kemal, 234
  carnage of, 39, 108, 141
  Greek occupation of, 75, 124
  Izmir Incident, 228
  recovery, 255

Japan, 15, 21, 34, 112, 230
Jesus, 286

Index

Jews, 44, 62–63, 133, 154
  model minority, 188
jihadism, 32, 186, 217, 256, 269, 300
  anti-Western, 80
  domestic, 107
judicial nationalism, 192

Kajaznuni, Hovhannes, 53
Kara Kemal, 236
Karabekir, Kâzım, 89
Karacan, Ali Naci, 296
Karagatch, 204
Kara-Schemsi. *See* Atabinen
Kars, 89, 102
Kavala, Osman, 279
Kaya, Şükrü, 108, 158, 224, 236, 245, 260, 262, 267, 268, 294
Kemal Pasha. *See* Atatürk
Kemalism, 244, 251
  calendar of national memorial days, 254
  dictatorship, 200
  party-state, 38
  reforms/revolution, 13, 16, 239
Kemalists, 25, 29, 31, 33, 71, 79, 86, 91, 105, 155
Kennan, Georges, 28
Kennedy, John F., 132
Khatissian, Alexandre, 53, 104, 159, 162, 165, 166
Khilafat Movement, 79
Kingdom of Serbs, Croats, and Slovenes, 112, 144
Kissinger, Henry, 28
Kıran, Süleyman Saib, 293
Kısakürek, Necip Fazıl, 270
Kızılelma, 52, 114
Koçgiri, 108, 141
Koçgiri-Dersim uprising, 260
Köprülü, Mehmet F., 69, 186
Krafft-Bonnard, Antony, 159
Kunduh, Bekir Sami, 103, 105
Kuomintang, 81
Kurdish question, 39, 48
Kurdish state, 95
Kurdistan, 6, 88, 202, 252
Kurds, 11, 13, 15, 26, 28, 45, 62, 66, 155, 189, 244, 265, 275
  killed in the Interwar period, 240
  Kurdish uprising of Sheykh Said, 234, 260

labor battalions, 74
Lake of Urmiah, 158
Lausanne
  choice of, 122
  city, 118
  Turkish Congress, 75, 91, 115
Lausanne Conference
  between Israel, Arab neighbor states, the (Palestinian) Arab Higher Committee and refugee representatives (1949), 307
  interval (1923), 40, 61, 233, 304
  school of Turkish diplomacy, 289
Lausanne elite, in Turkey, 289
Lausanne Treaty
  Articles 12–15, 248
  Article 28, 204, 225
  Article 39, 241
  Article 40, 242
  Article 42, 194, 240
  Article 44, 240
  deal and pact between ageing imperialists and new strongmen, 225, 244, 264, 273
  discussion of the draft treaty in Ankara's National Assembly, 227
  draft treaty, 228
  legal advisors, 193
  Lozan myths, 266
  minorities' renouncement on rights, 241
  Protocol relating to the Evacuation of the Turkish territory occupied by the British, French, and Italian Forces, 224
  ratification, 224, 306
  revisionism, 39, 68, 265, 271
Lausanne University, 135
Lausanne: Victory or Defeat?, 271
Lausanne Palace hotel, 134
League of Nations, 3, 6, 11, 14, 17, 21, 23, 24, 26, 31, 32, 33, 34, 36, 75, 81, 83, 86, 99, 101, 124, 129, 136, 147, 150, 152, 162, 163, 167, 191, 196, 213, 214, 263, 273, 276, 280, 282, 296
  archive, 243
  Assembly, 86, 162
  Associations for, 35, 83, 87, 281, 282
  International Union of, 84
  Council of, 86, 95
  Covenant. *See* Covenant of the League of Nations
  impacting on Balkan conferences, 247
  International Union of Societies for the League of Nations, 278
  Mandates Section, 86
  Minorities Section, 86
  Minority Commission, 243
  minority protection system, 213, 242
  Permanent Court of Arbitration, 93
  petitions to, 86, 243

Index

plebiscites, x, 88, 95, 183
Swiss Society for the League of Nations, 278
Turkey and, 152
Turkish membership, 246
Union of Societies for permanent Commission of Minorities, 278
Lebanon, 11, 25
legal advisors, 241, 306
Lemkin, Raphael, 284
Lenin, Vladimir, 32, 54, 77, 97
speech against League of Nations, 81
Les Minorités Nationales, 278
Liberal Party, 56
liberalism
condoning its negation, 280
liberals, 54, 85, 91, 107, 215
Ottoman, 74, 76
Libya, 5, 113, 129, 132, 264
Italian invasion, 298
Liebisch-Gümüş, Caroline, 94
Locarno Treaties, 247
London Conference, 105, 116, 161, 192
Loti, Pierre, 61
lynching, 284

mahdism, 245
Malta exiles, 106, 295
mandates, 12, 21, 31, 34, 37, 88, 124, 137
A Mandates, 32
American mandate, 101
American mandate for Anatolia, 86
American mandate for Armenia, 75, 85
French mandate over Syria, 31, 80
US refusal of, 94
Mandelstam, André, 28, 118, 211
Mango, Andrew, 234
Marash, 103, 141
Mardin, 104
Mdivani, Polikarp, 145
Mecca, 31
Medina, 267
sacred objects removed from, 267
Mehmed Cavid. *See* Cavid Bey
Mehmed the Conqueror, 188
Menemen riot, 245
Merzifon, 62
Mesopotamia, 35, 38, 88, 96, 107, 110
Metaxas, Ioannis, 247
Meyer, Karl, 165
Middle East
exploitable, 272
Military Medical School, 56, 291, 295

millenarism, 215. *See also* American missionaries
post-millenarism, 215
pre-millenarism, 215
millet, 154
Millioud, Maurice, 135
minorities, 151–158
Ottoman tolerance, 187
protection of, 14, 26, 93, 155, 187, 240. *See also* League of Nations
restricted definition, 155, 156, 193
Mısıroğlu, Kadir, 68, 270
Montagna, Giulio Cesare, 130, 136, 150, 154, 159, 195, 199, 204
Montbenon Casino, 137
Montreux, 127
Montreux Convention, 145, 264
remilitarization of the Straits, 263
moral benefits, 167, 169
moral settlement of wrongs, 221
Moscow, 33, 57, 77, 92, 97
Moscow Treaty, 103, 146
Mosul, 48, 68, 123, 125, 158, 163, 179–184, 195, 197, 201, 227, 236, 263, 278
Mudanya. *See* Armistice
Mülkiye, 291, 293, 295
Munich, 44
Munich Agreement, 277
Muslim Brotherhood, 270
Mussolini, Benito, 12, 28, 38, 103, 127–133, 142, 262, 303
Mustafa Kemal. *See* Atatürk
Mustafa Suphi, 228
myth
of the nation's innocence, 107

Nansen, Fridtjof, 98, 127, 147–151, 303
National Assembly in Ankara. *See* Ankara government
national economy, 74
Turkified economy, 229
National Pact, 76, 89, 92, 120, 146, 201, 227, 246, 267, 300
territory, 154
National Pact of Labor, 229
nationhood
civic-territorial versus racial and religious, 242
denaturalization, 243
NATO, 8, 13, 46, 222, 240, 244, 293
appeasement of antidemocracy, 279
Naville, Edouard, 164, 165
Nazism, 6, 8, 28, 33, 42, 43, 45, 136, 223, 231, 244, 249, 262, 273, 280, 281

324 Index

Nazım, Doctor, 173, 236
Near East
 notion, 3
Near East Relief, 214
neo-Ottomanism, 39, 46, 274
New Turkey, 186, 193, 210, 216, 229, 231, 273
 rhetoric of, 5, 13, 21, 52, 115, 141, 161, 164, 165
Nicholson, 199
Nicolson, Harold, 94, 97, 129, 145, 152, 196
Niebuhr, Reinhold, 28
Noradounghian, Gabriel, 53, 159, 161, 164, 167
nostalgia
 imperial, 274
 in post-Ottoman Turkey, 265
Notebook for Şiar, 171, 175, 233
Noubar, Boghos, 53, 161
Nureddin Pasha, 108, 300
Nuremberg Charter, 284
Nursi, Said, 245, 270
Nutuk, 40, 67, 223, 230, 238, 251–253, 306
 ego-narrative, 252

occidentalism, 239
October Revolution, 32, 81, 162
oil. *See* fossil dependency
Okyar, Fethi, 245
Open Door policy, 207, 216
opposition party
 experiment with, 245
Orbay, Hüseyin Rauf, 125, 163, 224
Orient Express, 200
Orthodox Turks, 188
otherizing, 288
Ottoman constitution, 71, 72
 1876, 298
Ottoman Debt, 100, 145, 172–176, 202, 206, 263, 305
 Administration, 125, 126, 172, 206
 currency of the interest payments, 206
 Distributed Public Debt of the Former Ottoman Empire, 206
Ottoman diaspora, 111, 170
Ottoman Empire, 5, 37
 eastern provinces, 107
 imperial bankruptcy, 172
 liquidation, 7
 Military Academy, 140
 Ottoman Islamic Army, 89
Ottoman spring, 71
Ottomanism, 39
Ouchy Treaty, 145
Özkan, Mustafa Şeref, 290, 295

pacifism, 85, 147
pact of silence, 285
Pakistan, 269
Palais de Rumine, 208
Palestine, 11, 25
Pangalos, 130
pan-Islamism, 124. *See* Islamism
pan-Turkism. *See* Turkism
Paris, 56, 62, 103
Paris Peace Conference, 75, 76, 299
Paris treaty system, 2, 14, 26, 31, 32, 33, 37, 82, 85, 301. *See also* treaty
Paris-Geneva peace project, 3, 5, 12, 31, 33, 34, 59, 66, 79, 80, 81, 87, 89, 91, 92, 99, 109, 133, 155, 272, 276
 asymmetry in, 93
 dismantled, 237
 synergies against, 77
Pasdermadjian, Garo, 162
past
 attempts to come to terms with, 30
 buried in Lausanne, 244
 claiming grandeur, 58, 259
 envisioning a Turanian past, 65
 erased, 118, 238
 forgetting the past, 51, 164, 178, 191, 220
 framing at Lausanne, 153, 190
 repression of, 26, 55
patriarchate, ecumenical
 removal of, 267
Paul, of Tarsus, 287
peace, notion of, 14, 25, 30, 49, 225, 272, 280, 285
Pektaş, Hüseyin, 254, 290, 292
Pellé, Maurice, 203, 206, 210
Persia, 12, 15, 82
 1906, 297
Persians, 64, 189
Petit-Lancy
 Turkish congress in, 112
Petros, Agha, 158, 163
Pittard, Eugène, 114, 134
Plastiras, Nikolaos, 127
pogroms, 284
Poincaré, Raymond, 108, 120, 123, 128, 162, 195, 272
Poland, 32, 33, 82, 213
Pontic State, 98
Pontus, 108
Pontus genocide, 69, 141, 300
pope, 54
population exchange, 17, 26, 30, 38, 47, 121, 147–156, 190
 Bulgarian–Turkish, 299

Greek–Turkish, 299
nonobligatory exchanges in the Balkans, 148
Population Exchange Commission, 249
post-genocidal Turkey, 213
press
  CUP, 74
  Swiss, 19
  Turkish, 71
Prince Sabahaddin, 56, 57
prisoners, 82, 98, 149, 192, 204
Progressive Republican Party, 294
Protestant utopias, 214. *See also* millenarism
Protocol relating to certain Concessions granted in the Ottoman Empire, 207
proto-fascism, 91, 133, 137, 188
public history, 37, 169
  and public memory, 179
public opinion, 85

Radek, Karl, 77–79, 81, 82
Radio Yerevan, 41
Ragaz, Leonhard, 84
Rakowski, Christian, 145
rape, 60, 61
Rathenau, Walther, 77, 194
realpolitik, 7, 8, 17, 23, 36, 37, 85, 110, 279, 280
Red Army, 32, 87
  Red Guards, 205
Red Cross, 16, 280
referendum, 116, 144, 183, 252, 263
Reform Agreement of 1914, 91, 118, 161, 191, 299
refugees, 212. *See also* Nansen
  Armenian and Kurdish, 101
  Armenians in Lebanon and Syria, 165
  in Greece, 127, 148, 247
  Muslim, 298
Renda, Mustafa Abdülhalik, 108, 236
reparations, 27, 68, 125, 126, 145, 202, 204
  German, 194
Republic of Armenia, 53, 94, 105, 163, 300
Republic of Turkey, 38, 46, 58, 121, 167, 184
  1924 constitution, 242
  justice system, 157, 236
  Law of Resettlement, 260, 262
  Law on the Unification of Education, 239, 306
  Law Revolution, 223, 241, 244
  proclamation of, 16, 135, 266
Republican People's Party, 229
Reşat. *See* Belger
Reşit Saffet. *See* Atabinen

revanchism, 72
revisionism. *See also* Lausanne Treaty
revolution
  right–left synergy, 92, 133
revolution from the right, 33
  counter-revolution, 72
revolutionism from the left and the right, 82
Rhodes, 129, 145
Riga, 44
Riyadh, 23
Rıza Nur, 15, 26, 42, 44, 48, 55–70, 108, 112, 121, 126, 154, 158–160, 167, 170, 185, 186, 196, 199, 210, 217, 223, 227, 233, 237, 249, 253, 260, 262, 269, 290, 291, 304
  and Cavid Bey, 172, 173, 174
  historical-political thought, 45
  History of the Armenians, 42, 59
  History of the Turks, 60
Robert College, 254, 292
Rochau, A.L. von, 27
Romania, 15, 112, 144
Romans, 64, 70
Rome, 124
Rome Conference, 102, 111, 118
Rome Statute of the International Criminal Court, 284
Roosevelt, Franklin, 216
Rosenberg, Alfred, 44
Rousseau, Jean-Jacques, 114
Royalists, 106
Ruhr
  another Ruhr question at Constantinople, 206
  occupation, 27, 79, 123, 194
Rûm, 28, 61, 68, 74, 76, 95, 97, 107, 148, 154, 156, 188, 190, 204, 210, 275
  expulsion of, 298
  in Istanbul, 150, 156, 248
  Pontus, 61
Rumbold, Horace, 48, 56, 139, 154, 157, 165, 210, 211
Russia, 36, 50, 78, 82, 92, 94, 112, 188
  1905, 297
  civil war, 32, 76, 81
Russian émigrés, 205
Ryan, Andrew, 160, 212, 267

Saadabed Pact, 246
Sadak, Necmettin Sadık, 45, 119, 121, 141, 142, 187, 263, 296
Said, Edward, 239
Saka, Hasan, 172, 173, 174, 291
Sakarya
  battle of, 107, 141

Salih Bey, 268
Saloniki, 40, 229
Saltıkgil, Veli, 290, 295
Samsun–Sivas railway, 207
San Remo, 103
  Resolution, 31, 86
Saraçoğlu, Şükrü, 75, 113
Sarıkamış, 89
Saudi Arabia, 12, 13, 221
Sauser-Hall, Georges, 241
scandal of the cross, 287
scapegoating, 261, 282, 283, 286
Schanzer, Carlo, 162
Scheubner-Richter, Erwin von, 44
Scheurer, Karl, 207
Schmitt, Carl, 43
Second Socialist International, 32, 298
Second World War, 13, 14, 47
secularism, 185, 186, 192
  Swiss Code of Obligations and Civil Code, 218
Seljuks, 67
separate French–Turkish peace, 195
separate Greek–Turkish peace, 204
separate Turkish-British peace, 196
separation of powers, 243
settler colonialism, 284
Sèvres Syndrome, 40, 266
Seyyid Rıza, 261
Sforza, Carlo, 102, 130
sharia, 17, 70, 192, 223, 266
Shkodër, 227
Shoah, 7, 213, 278, 280
Şiar, 171
Sinop, 57, 60
Sivas congress, 228
Skinner, Robert P., 250
slavery, 284
Smyrna. *See* Izmir
social Darwinism, 26, 33, 34, 42, 45, 47, 57, 63, 67, 97, 168
sovereignty, 80, 95, 175, 226, 237, 253, 285
  law as an expression of, 192
  law on the intangibility of national sovereignty, 230
  national, not legal, 241
  perverted, 234
Soviet Russia, 15, 109, 123, 133
Soviet Union, 33, 34, 48, 219
  collapse, 265
Spain, 21
Spalaikovitch, Miroslav, 190
Spartacus uprising, 77
Srebrenica massacre, 1995, 261
St. Petersburg, 54, 205

Stalin, Josef, 254, 281
Straits, 48, 123, 126, 140, 145, 196
  Convention, 147, 219
Streit, Georgios, 93
Stresemann, Gustav, 194
Suleiman the Magnificent, 70
sultanate
  abolition, 226, 266
sultanate-caliphate, 1, 5, 49, 71, 75, 76, 79, 107, 178, 300
  betrayed, 266
Sumerians, 66
Sun Yat-sen University, 81
Swiss Code of Obligations and Civil Code, 81
Swiss Federation of the Friends of the Armenians, 165
Swiss Society of Friends of Turkey, 134
Swiss Union in Istanbul, 268
Switzerland, 1, 3, 32, 35, 52, 72, 111, 114, 170, 205, 241, 268, 270, 282
Sykes-Picot Agreement, 32, 265
Sykes-Picot-Sazonov agreements, 53
Syria, 11, 25, 26, 30, 158, 240, 251, 270
  Greater Syria, 31
  Northern Syria, 264
Syrian Arab Congress, 80
Syrian mandate, 103
Syrian National Congress, 31
Syrians, 37

Taksim Square, 83
Talaat, Mehmed (Pasha/Bey), 50, 58, 64, 73, 77, 78, 82, 92, 100, 103, 108, 111, 113, 116, 117, 133, 134, 141, 158, 163, 170, 171, 174, 178, 194, 224, 226, 229, 232, 236, 248, 260, 293, 294, 299
  assassination, 111
  boulevard named after, 118
Taner, Tahir, 290, 295
Tanin, 173
Tehran, 23
Tenedos, 144
Tengirşek, Yusuf Kemal, 140
Territet, 127, 268
Tevfik Pasha, 105
Thessaloniki. *See* Saloniki
Thessaly, 65
Thrace, 68, 109, 125, 144, 156, 204, 227
Tigranes the Great, 67
Tigrel, Mehmet Zülfü, 290, 295
Topal Osman, 58, 61, 228, 300
totalitarianism, 231, 235, 246, 273

treaty
  Paris treaty system
    Treaty of Lausanne. *See* Lausanne Treaty
    Treaty of Neuilly, 144
    Treaty of Paris-Sèvres, 2
    Treaty of Sèvres, 12, 22, 26, 31, 32, 33, 55, 75, 86, 87, 88, 90, 92–101, 106, 144, 145, 148, 158, 161, 177, 193, 252
    Treaty of Trianon, 2, 14
    Treaty of Versailles, 2, 31, 75, 82, 109
  Treaty of Lausanne-Ouchy (1912), 298
  Treaty of Alexandropol, 89, 163, 186
  Treaty of Brest-Litovsk, 89, 299
  Treaty of Bucharest, 144
  Treaty of Kars, 89, 163
  Treaty of Lausanne-Ouchy (1912), 129
  Treaty of Moscow, 77, 82, 89, 90
  Treaty of Rapallo, 77, 109, 124
Trebizond, 95
Tribunals of Independence, 234, 235, 268
Tripartite Agreement Respecting Anatolia, 95
Tröbst, Hans, 43
Trotsky, Leon, 72, 77
Tunceli, 260. *See also* Dersim
Tunceli Law, 262
Turan, 65, 89
  between Europe and China, 65
  union of, 251
Turanian argument, 12, 26, 66, 68, 70, 253
Turanianism, 12, 45, 65, 185
  fiction of a Turanian or proto-Turkish past of Anatolia and Mesopotamia, 264
  Turanian, or proto-Turkish, indigenousness, 65, 69
Turanians, 41, 42, 45, 60, 251
Türk Yurdu, 223. *See* Turkish Home
Türkçülüğün Esasları, 251
Turkey: Monthly Organ of the Turkish Congress at Lausanne, 116
Türkgeldi, M. Emin Ali, 293
Turkification, 46, 254. *See also* Anatolia
  of language, names, institutions, 240
Turkish Congress in Lausanne
  Permanent Bureau, 134
Turkish counter-proposal, 202
Turkish History Thesis, 12, 17, 40, 68, 69, 119, 135, 186, 223, 251, 253, 255–259, 264, 292
Turkish Home, 89
Turkish Home associations, 74, 75, 112–116
Turkish nationalism, 251. *See also* Turkism
  coercion and indoctrination, 246
  exterminatory, 262
  nondemocratic Gökalpian, 264
Turkish Petroleum Company, 207
Turkish Revolution, 115, 155, 223, 238
  History of, 253
Turkish–American treaty, 201. *See also* USA–Turkey
Turkish–British friendship, 116
Turkish–Sephardic Friendship Association, 134
Turkism, 6, 43, 45, 58, 72, 81, 112, 239, 254, 298
  pan-Turkism, 38, 52
Turkistan, 251

Ukraine, 48, 82, 133
ultimatum
  by the National Assembly, February 1923, 228
ultranationalism, 12, 13, 16, 25, 26, 29, 34, 54, 72, 81, 104, 110, 127, 166, 167, 175, 218, 236, 276
ümmet, 75, 107, 269
Ünaydın, Ruşen Eşref, 290, 296
United Nations Organization, 47, 281
  Charter, 281
  Security Council, 281
University of Geneva, 114
University of Istanbul, 157
University of Lausanne, 131
University of the Toilers of the East, 81
Urartu, 66
Uras, Ahmet Esat, 159, 254
Urfa, 103
USA, 15, 62, 75, 85, 94, 201, 214–221
  Middle East diplomacy, 221
  Senate, 47, 75, 218, 219, 299, 306
USA–Turkey
  claims settlement on Turkish violations of American persons and property, 220, 306
  claims settlement on Turkish violations of American persons and property, 220, 306
  extradition agreement, 220, 306
  separate Lausanne Treaty, 221
  Treaty of Commerce and Navigation, 220, 306
  Treaty of Establishment and Sojourn, 220, 306
Uzer, Tahsin, 236

Van, 95, 102
  Lake of, 66
Venice, 62

Venizelists, 106
Venizelos, Eleftherios, 93, 106, 127, 142, 149, 189, 190, 205, 247, 248, 300
victimhood
  Armenian, 158, 165, 169, 221
  Muslim, 149
  Ottoman, 253
  Turkish, 141, 142, 177
violence
  in the name of the nation, 236
  political, 246
  polity-founding role of, 286
Völkerfrühling, 27
Vorovsky, Vatslav, 145, 205, 305
voting by foot, 240

Walters, Francis P., 28
war guilt, 93, 100
War Office, 108, 124
Warsaw, 32
Washington, 110
Washington, George, 216
Werfel, Franz, 43, 165, 247
White Armies, 205
Wilson, Woodrow, 11, 54, 67, 85, 93, 96, 143
world government, 85
world opinion, 85
world peace, 1, 3, 5, 146, 147, 272
world revolution, 32, 80, 81

Yalçın, Hüseyin Çahit, 173, 177, 187
Yazidis, 26, 66
Yerevan, 87, 105
Yiddishland, 6
Young Turk party state. *See* CUP party state
Young Turk Revolution, 11, 22, 71, 232, 255, 297, 298
  Feast of Liberty, 255
Young Turks, 25, 28, 32, 71, 231. *See also* CUP
Yugoslavia, 15, 144
  see Kingdom of Serbs, Croats, and Slovenes

Zekai. *See* Apaydın
Zimmerwald Socialist International, 54
Zionism. *See also* Balfour Declaration
  anti-Zionism, 80
Ziya Gökalp. *See* Gökalp
Zurich, 54

www.ingramcontent.com/pod-product-compliance
Ingram Content Group UK Ltd.
Pitfield, Milton Keynes, MK11 3LW, UK
UKHW031825020325
455765UK00012B/97